Reading African American Autobiography

Wisconsin Studies in Autobiography

WILLIAM L. ANDREWS
Series Editor

Reading African American Autobiography

Twenty-First-Century Contexts and Criticism

Edited by

ERIC D. LAMORE

The University of Wisconsin Press

The University of Wisconsin Press
1930 Monroe Street, 3rd Floor
Madison, Wisconsin 53711-2059
uwpress.wisc.edu

3 Henrietta Street, Covent Garden
London WC2E 8LU, United Kingdom
eurospanbookstore.com

Copyright © 2017
The Board of Regents of the University of Wisconsin System
All rights reserved. Except in the case of brief quotations embedded in critical articles and reviews, no part of this publication may be reproduced, stored in a retrieval system, transmitted in any format or by any means—digital, electronic, mechanical, photocopying, recording, or otherwise—or conveyed via the Internet or a website without written permission of the University of Wisconsin Press. Rights inquiries should be directed to rights@uwpress.wisc.edu.

Printed in the United States of America

This book may be available in a digital edition.

Library of Congress Cataloging-in-Publication Data

Names: Lamore, Eric D., editor.
Title: Reading African American autobiography: twenty-first-century contexts and criticism / edited by Eric D. Lamore.
Other titles: Wisconsin studies in autobiography.
Description: Madison, Wisconsin: The University of Wisconsin Press, [2017] |
Series: Wisconsin studies in autobiography | Includes bibliographical references and index.
Identifiers: LCCN 2016012950 | ISBN 9780299309800 (cloth: alk. paper)
Subjects: LCSH: Autobiography—African American authors—History and criticism.
| African Americans—Biography—History and criticism.
Classification: LCC PS366.A35 R43 2017 | DDC 810.9/4920009296073—dc23
LC record available at https://lccn.loc.gov/2016012950

For my grandparents:

BENSON and MILDRED LAMORE

DONALD and MARY JANE SUBLETTE

Contents

Acknowledgments ix

Introduction: *African American Autobiography in the "Age of Obama"* 3
ERIC D. LAMORE

"A Dying Man": *The Outlaw Body of Arthur, 1768* 19
LYNN A. CASMIER-PAZ

Early Black Men's Spiritual Autobiography: *Marriage and Violence* 41
JOYCELYN K. MOODY

Olaudah Equiano in the United States: *Abigail Mott's 1829 Abridged Edition of the* Interesting Narrative 66
ERIC D. LAMORE

The Visual Properties of Black Autobiography: *The Case of William J. Edwards* 89
ANTHONY S. FOY

Richard Wright's Environments: *Mediating Personhood through the South's Second Nature* 117
SUSAN SCOTT PARRISH

"A Space of Concentration": *The Autobiographical Comics of Richard "Grass" Green and Samuel R. Delany* 145
BRIAN CREMINS

Born into This Body: *Black Women's Use of Buddhism in Autobiographical Narratives* 174
TRACY CURTIS

From Blog to Books: *Angela Nissel, Authorship, and the Digital Public Sphere* 196
LINDA FURGERSON SELZER

Grafted Belongings: *Identification in Autobiographical Narratives of African American Transracial Adoptees* 216
MARINA FEDOSIK

Reading Signs of Crazy: *Pam Grier, a Black Feminist in Praxis* 232
KWAKIUTL L. DREHER

Contributors 259
Index 261

Acknowledgments

It is a pleasure to have the opportunity to thank a number of individuals who helped me in various ways while I worked on this book. I would like to extend a special thanks to William L. Andrews, editor of the Wisconsin Studies in Autobiography series, who offered valuable support during the multiple stages of this project. I greatly appreciate all the energy the University of Wisconsin Press editorial team, especially Amber Rose, Sheila McMahon, and Raphael Kadushin, invested in this book. This editorial team selected two teacher-scholars who closely examined the book proposal and offered commentary that tightened the argumentation in selected parts of the book. I also wish to thank the leaders of the Autobiography Society and the editors of *a/b: Auto/Biography Studies*, Ricia A. Chansky and Emily Hipchen, for allowing me to reprint several articles with revisions from my special issue of their journal devoted to the futures of African American life narrative.

As always, Ricia read over my writing and made insightful comments. Her commitment to the field of auto/biography studies continues to inspire. Finally, I am indebted to the teacher-scholars whose contributions appear in this book. Thank you for your dedication to studying and teaching African American lives and life narratives.

Reading African American Autobiography

Introduction

African American Autobiography in the "Age of Obama"

ERIC D. LAMORE

Reading African American Autobiography: Twenty-First-Century Contexts and Criticism responds to Robert B. Stepto's *A Home Elsewhere: Reading African American Classics in the Age of Obama*. In Stepto's book, which grew out of his 2009 W. E. B. Du Bois Lectures at Harvard University, he writes that his project addresses "how we read African American literature at the present moment, knowing, and actually being stunned by the fact, that an African American *writer* is our president" (3). To achieve this objective, Stepto, in the first part of his book, comparatively reads Frederick Douglass's *My Bondage and My Freedom*, W. E. B. Du Bois's *The Souls of Black Folk*, James Weldon Johnson's *The Autobiography of an Ex-Colored Man*, Zora Neale Hurston's *Their Eyes Were Watching God*, and Toni Morrison's *Song of Solomon* alongside Barack Obama's memoir, *Dreams from My Father: A Story of Race and Inheritance*. Stepto maintains that his merging of "classic" African American texts with Obama's *Dreams* "refreshes our readings and recollections of the whole of African American literature" (5). By establishing this provocative relationship between the past and the present, Stepto's book essentially announces that a new period in African American studies has arrived. However, Obama contributes to the oeuvre of African American literature with an autobiographical narrative. An important qualifier must therefore be added to Stepto's statement: the current president of the United States is not just an "African American *writer*" (3) but an African American *life writer*.[1] The fact that President Obama is an African American life writer provides one significant justification for revisiting the canon of African American life narrative in the twenty-first century.[2]

Reading African American Autobiography: Twenty-First-Century Contexts and Criticism takes stock of the current state of African American life narrative. This particular "age of Obama" assessment makes a number of arguments concerning how the field may continue to develop as scholars expand the range of critical approaches relevant to studying the multilayered texts in this canon. It is impossible for one book to offer a comprehensive examination of the entire canon of African American life narrative; nevertheless, these chapters, which I present chronologically based on the publication date of the earliest autobiographical text in the respective contributions, promote (to borrow the language of Michael A. Chaney) "new kinds of seeing" (9) within this textual field. Specifically, this twenty-first-century study of the African American life narrative canon seeks to accomplish the following critical work: to embrace newly recognized African American life writers from a wide range of historical periods, to widen the field's understanding of the myriad ways in which African Americans have engaged in examining the self, to analyze the more contemporary routes of dissemination that have been used to circulate autobiographical acts, to trouble the types of "texts" that have been traditionally housed in the canon of African American life narrative, to tease out new textual layers in African American life narratives that count as important, and to enlarge the already wide range of critical methods used by scholars.

The contributors to this book utilize a variety of twenty-first-century critical approaches in order to sidestep what Michael J. Drexler and Ed White have identified as the dangers of "privileging representative extremes over nuanced complications" (2) in studying and teaching African American literature. In their efforts to continue to expand the antebellum African American life narrative canon, some of the contributors evaluate neglected texts and lives from this period. In doing so, they extend Xiomara Santamarina's crucial point about recognizing "heterogeneous communities of Black writers and readers" (142) from the antebellum period. Furthermore, though some of the chapters comment on and draw connections to the slave narrative, this book avoids the privileging of antebellum life narratives related or written by enslaved or formerly enslaved persons.[3] Focusing only on antebellum slave narratives ultimately generates a limited understanding of African American lives and life narratives. Other contributors to this book recover overlooked African American life narratives published after the antebellum period. These readings continue to complicate the field's understanding of the types of African Americans who have chosen to engage in examining the self. Yet another productive outcome of this further canon expansion is the recognition that the term *writer* falls short of capturing the full range of ways in which African Americans have conducted these explorations of the self. Reading these largely overlooked texts from the antebellum and postbellum periods, then, expands the repertoire of critical tools that practitioners in the field have traditionally employed in reading African American life narratives as well as the types of texts that have been traditionally accepted as the most representative documentation of the lives and experiences of African Americans. Nevertheless, reading "classic" African American literature, as Stepto holds, is crucial in the twenty-first century. Therefore, some chapters analyze canonical African American life narratives, thereby demonstrating that approaches to reading "classic" African American life narratives are also subject to the ebb and flow of disciplinary tides.

This book begins with Lynn A. Casmier-Paz's "'A Dying Man': The Outlaw Body of Arthur, 1768," which focuses on the told-to, autobiographical confession of an enslaved twenty-one-year-old African American servant named Arthur, whose "last words" were printed on a widely circulated broadside in Worcester,

Massachusetts. While Casmier-Paz submits that Arthur's life narrative anticipates some of the well-known characteristics of the nineteenth-century slave narrative, she builds on Jeannine Marie DeLombard's proposal to "concentrate our attention on the black persona [and its] metamorphosis from civilly dead property to criminally liable *person*" (38; emphasis added). Starting from this premise, Casmier-Paz identifies the importance of the body and clothing in this understudied broadside to highlight certain shifts in the politics of slavery and abolition in this particular historical moment in Massachusetts. Though Arthur was ultimately executed, Casmier-Paz maintains that his told-to confession captures a unique moment in print, one in which this African American male attempts, as the author puts it, "to wrest control of his own body, agency, and visibility in order to assert his *manhood* within the contexts of colonial slavery."

While Casmier-Paz offers a reading of a largely overlooked antebellum text, Joycelyn K. Moody's chapter, "Early Black Men's Spiritual Autobiography: Marriage and Violence," illustrates how to work with a canonical antebellum text as a foundational point for comparative study. Drawing on Eve Kosofsky Sedgwick's term *homosociality*, Moody traces—in ways that parallel Stepto's careful linking of texts throughout the African American literary tradition—what she calls a "genealogy of pious African American men" found in a selected body of texts. Interestingly, Moody finds the roots of this genealogy in one of the most radical antebellum texts, David Walker's *Appeal to the Coloured Citizens of the World*. Even though the *Appeal* may be productively classified as a political manifesto rather than an autobiography, the value of Walker's text, Moody proposes, reaches beyond the work's popularity in the early nineteenth century and even in the reemergence of this seminal work in the 1970s Black Power Movement.[4] According to Moody, Walker's *Appeal* may be read as a work that offers a unique representation of black masculinity with special emphases placed on blackness equating maleness, resistance to white hegemony, distinct "places" for black men and women, and Christian heteronormativity. Moving from her discussion on Walker, Moody then navigates specific scenes in *The Life, History, and Unparalleled Sufferings of John Jea, the African Preacher, The Life of William J. Brown of Providence, R.I., With Personal Recollections of Incidents in Rhode Island,* and in some of Andrew P. Watson's interviews with African American Civil War veterans and finds that they mirror, in interesting ways, Walker's observations. In these texts, Moody locates the celebration of resistance to white hegemony and domination through conversion to Christianity, calculated violence, military service, and black homosocial communities. At the end of her chapter, Moody makes the crucial point that the relationship between masculinity, theology, and power still preoccupies and challenges the thinking of contemporary African Americans, including male preachers and feminist theologians.

Like Moody's contribution, my chapter, "Olaudah Equiano in the United States: Abigail Mott's 1829 Abridged Edition of the *Interesting Narrative*," offers a comparative reading that includes a life narrative from the canon of early black Atlantic literature. While Moody uses John Jea's narrative, my chapter focuses on different versions of Olaudah Equiano's best-selling *The Interesting Narrative of the Life of Olaudah Equiano, or Gustavus Vassa, the African. Written by Himself.* There is no doubt that Equiano's life and life writing have been rigorously studied. This important scholarly work has consistently positioned him as an Afro-British rather than an African American writer. Nonetheless, Equiano scholars have been hesitant to study the editions of his autobiography published in the United States mainly because they were altered by editors and book publishers in ways that the life writer did not necessarily endorse, have control over, profit from, or, in some cases, even see in his lifetime. Instead of dismissing the United States editions of the *Interesting Narrative*, however, I suggest that scholars should more productively read these versions of Equiano's autobiography as "fluid text[s]," that is, as ones that "exist in more than one version" (Bryant 1). Therefore, my chapter contributes the first sustained discussion of one particular manifestation of the *Interesting Narrative* as a fluid text, the 1829 *The Life and Adventures of Olaudah Equiano; or, Gustavus Vassa, the African. From an Account Written by Himself, Abridged by A. Mott. To Which Is Added Some Remarks on the Slave Trade*, which was published in New York by Samuel Wood and Sons thirty-two years after Equiano's death in London. In constructing this abridged edition, Mott edited Equiano's *Narrative* for students of African descent at the New York African Free School, a controversial educational institution created by the New York Manumission Society in 1787. My interpretation of Mott's abridged version begins to uncover a more complicated narrative of how different readers at different historical periods and in different countries engaged with different editions of Equiano's autobiography; it also begins to make a more legitimate case for Equiano's place in the canon of African American life narrative because of the various editions of his autobiography published in the United States. In this respect, then, we can see that the trope of the talking book has begun to give way to the history of the book.[5]

The status of another foundational component of African American life narratives—the engraved portrait—has also been recently interrogated. As early as James Olney's "'I Was Born': Slave Narratives, Their Status as Autobiography and as Literature," the "engraved portrait" (50) has been recognized as a fundamental part of African American life writing. In more recent years, Deborah Willis and Barbara Krauthamer's *Envisioning Emancipation: Black Americans and the End of Slavery* and Maurice O. Wallace and Shawn Michelle Smith's *Pictures and Progress: Early Photography and the Making of African American Identity*, among others, have added to Olney's comments on the "engraved portrait" by identifying a variety of technologies that African Americans have used to create visual texts for different rhetorical and political purposes. Even more recently, Joel Christian Gill's *Uncelebrated Narratives from Black History* has documented African American lives through the medium of graphic narrative. Despite this clear progress with understanding visual narratives, however, Anthony S. Foy claims, in his chapter, "The Visual Properties of Black Autobiography: The Case of William J. Edwards," that scholars have yet to examine the full cultural impact of the photograph in African American life narrative. Foy acknowledges that the frontispiece did not altogether disappear from African American autobiographies published after the Civil War; nevertheless, he specifically argues for the significance of photographs in postbellum African American life writing that do not portray strategically posed life writers. According to Foy, the photographs of buildings found in William J. Edwards's rarely studied 1918 uplift autobiography, *Twenty-Five Years in the Black Belt*, serve two purposes: they highlight "privacy as the prerogative of the uplifted New Negro" as well as reinforce "a black self that is itself more seeing than seen." Consequently, Foy concludes that Edwards's text and the photographs of buildings in it serve a type of "managerial function," one that ultimately reinforces Booker T. Washington's ideas on progress for early twentieth-century African Americans.

Whereas Foy interrogates the presence of photos in Edwards's neglected uplift autobiography, Susan Scott Parrish critiques a long-standing premise about a life writer who continues to occupy a secure place in the African American life narrative canon, Richard Wright. According to Parrish, in her chapter, "Richard Wright's Environments: Mediating Personhood through the South's Second Nature," Wright scholars have consistently insisted—and based their readings of his life writing on the premise—that this African American subscribed, without hesitation, to nineteenth-century sociological theories on the environment, particularly ones addressing the urban city and its pivotal role in conditioning humans. Parrish observes that Wright scholars typically point to his naturalistic writing, his subscription to the scholarship that emerged from the Chicago School of Sociology, and his move to the North from the South to conclude that the urban, and the theorizing of this space, significantly shaped the African American writer's view of the world. However, Parrish's chapter deliberately troubles Wright scholars' understanding of the term *environment* and offers a "challenge" to "the truism that it was the urban 'street' that gave Wright his critical edge." Parrish's ecocritical reading—or what she refers to as a "critical greening"—of some of Wright's life writing carries with it key ramifications. As she maintains, "by recovering the importance of the rural environment and its disturbances to Wright," her interdisciplinary work offers "a new reading of Wright's autobiographical work, including the highly canonical *Black Boy*." In other words, Parrish's chapter provides a new way to approach "classic" African American life writing in the twenty-first century.

Unlike Parrish, who moves away from the space of the urban in her chapter on Wright, Brian Cremins, in his chapter, "'A Space of Concentration': The Autobiographical Comics of Richard 'Grass' Green and Samuel R. Delany," pays particular attention to the representations of human contact in urban spaces in two African American autobiographical comics, Green's *Un-Fold Funnies*, which he produced in the early 1980s, and Delany's 1999 graphic novel, *Bread & Wine: An Erotic Tale of New York*, which documents his relationship with his partner Dennis Rickett. Cremins—in ways that align with Foy's chapter—makes a strong case for continuing to examine the full range of how the visual has contributed in shaping African American life narrative. According to Cremins, a complete understanding of the visual must include a more rigorous study of the rhetoric of graphic art found in African American autobiographical comics. Cremins argues that Green's and Delany's autobiographies "serve as records of contact" and communicate "the psychological and phenomenological density of casual, unexpected, but telling urban encounters." Cremins's focus on autobiographical comics ushers in a more sophisticated focus on the interplay between the verbal and visual in African American life narratives.

With its emphasis on African American autobiographical comics, Cremins's chapter also functions as an appropriate bridge to the final four chapters in the book, all of which explore African American life narratives published in the twenty-first century. In an important way, Green's and Delany's autobiographical comics call attention to the connection between popular culture and African American life narrative. This link defines some of the characteristics of twenty-first-century African American life narrative, as the final four chapters in the book address online lives, remediated lives, celebrity lives, and self-help culture, along with the expectations of contemporary African American readers who consume life narratives. The authors of these chapters assert that practitioners in the field are just beginning to understand twenty-first-century African American life narratives.[6] Twenty-first-century African American life narrative, they argue, matters for a number of reasons: it addresses the importance of religious traditions other than Judeo-Christianity; its nuances require that scholars acknowledge the role that digital technologies have played (and will continue to play) in autobiographical acts by African Americans; it makes clear that the search for "home" and "self" is by no means exclusive to the nineteenth-century slave narrative; and, finally, it validates that African American celebrity narratives offer interesting case studies on the expectations of contemporary African American readers.

The focus on twenty-first-century African American life narrative begins with Tracy Curtis's chapter, "Born into This Body: Black Women's Use of Buddhism in Autobiographical Narratives." Curtis insists that African American women have consistently engaged with Buddhism for both spiritual and political reasons. Unfortunately, Curtis claims, specialists who study African American life writing have failed to recognize the significance of Buddhism. Curtis stresses that life writing scholars' understanding of the genre of the spiritual autobiography, the earliest form of African American life narrative in the United States, needs to expand to include texts that incorporate non-Western or even hybrid religious traditions. The remainder of Curtis's chapter studies three texts published within the first five years of the twenty-first century: Angel Kyodo Williams's *Being Black: Zen and the Art of Living with Fearlessness and Grace* (2000), Jan Willis's *Dreaming Me: An African American Woman's Spiritual Journey* (2001), and Faith Adiele's *Meeting Faith: The Forest Journals of a Black Buddhist Nun* (2004). According to Curtis, the authors' unique perspectives on subjectivity, gender roles, and the relationship between the individual and the community figure prominently in these contemporary African American women's life narratives. Additionally, Curtis finds that these life narratives articulate how Buddhism can be relevant for twenty-first-century African Americans, even though parts of the texts expose the authors' anxieties about their readers' reception of this religious tradition and the implementation of principles taken from this religion into their lives.

The subscribing to non-Western religious traditions is not the only salient characteristic that begins to describe twenty-first-century African American life writers. These contemporary African American life writers have used new media—or a combination of old and new media—in exploring and documenting their selves. Linda Furgerson Selzer's chapter, "From Blog to Books: Angela Nissel, Authorship, and the Digital Public Sphere," synthesizes the relationship between Jürgen Habermas's conception of the public sphere, digital technologies, new media studies, and African American life narrative. Furgerson Selzer rightfully acknowledges that printed life narratives and activism in the mainstream public sphere have offered essential discourse on the self in African American history. Nevertheless, she argues that the surfacing of blogs, chat rooms, and social networking sites along with the digitizing of the book have created new ways to fashion the self in African American life narrative. In tackling this topic, Furgerson Selzer comments on the unique life writing history of the blogger, author, Hollywood screenwriter, producer, and entrepreneur Angela Nissel, as well as selected parts from her two books, *The Broke Diaries: The Completely True and Hilarious Misadventures of a Good Girl Gone Broke* (2001) and *Mixed: My Life in Black and White* (2006). Furgerson Selzer posits that Nissel's life may be read as one that mirrors the emergence of a new generation of African American life writers. Technologically savvy, these contemporary life writers effectively juggle both old and new media in exploring their multidimensional selves. This chapter also invites readers to consider how other contemporary African American life writers' use of digital platforms challenges the status of the printed book as the most important "text" for disseminating autobiographical acts. Subsequent developments in African American life narrative will be digitized.[7]

Marina Fedosik's chapter, "Grafted Belongings: Identification in Autobiographical Narratives of African American Transracial Adoptees," provides further insights into the autobiographical acts of cosmopolitan, twenty-first-century African American life writers. She uncovers the complexity of two twenty-first-century life narratives written by adult African Americans who were adopted by white parents: Jaiya John's *Black Baby White Hands: A View from the Crib* (2002) and Catherine E. McKinley's *The Book of Sarahs: A Family in Parts* (2002). According to Fedosik, an understanding of this vein of African American life narrative first requires contextualizing the history of adoption legislature and even resistance within the African American community to white parents adopting African American children. While these contexts need to inform any study of transracial adoptees, Fedosik clearly establishes that a close reading of these narratives ultimately yields the most engaging insights into this type of twenty-first-century life narrative. John's and McKinley's texts, Fedosik insists, overlap in several ways. For instance, both authors draw on elements from the adoption narrative, and their texts address topics such as maturing while living with a white family, locating and reuniting with birth parents, and attempting to understand their multidimensional selves. Yet Fedosik carefully argues that, while John attempts to locate an "authentic" self, the line between "self" and "other" remains even more blurred for McKinley. Ultimately, Fedosik posits, based on McKinley's experience, that the self of the transracial adoptee may be found in a variety of locations, including the private histories of the person's birth and adoptive families, the history of African Americans in the United States, and the transnational and transatlantic histories of individuals of African descent.

In the final chapter in the volume, "Reading Signs of Crazy: Pam Grier, a Black Feminist in Praxis," Kwakiutl L. Dreher interprets the celebrity narrative *Foxy: My Life in Three Acts* (2010). As Dreher notes, scholarly focus on Grier, up to this point, has largely concentrated on physicality in studying the legendary actress's body and its presence in several films from the 1970s. Dreher's chapter, however, navigates the ways in which Grier, in *Foxy*, writes about her commitment to black feminism, especially when signs of "crazy" surface in her relationships with Kareem Abdul Jabbar, Freddie Prinze Sr., and Richard Pryor. In these particular sections of her memoir, Dreher argues, Grier narrates how her relationships with these men bring about a conflict between patriarchy and her embrace of black feminism. According to Dreher, this conflict consistently alerts her to a need to read these signs of "crazy" in order to maintain her sense of self and her commitment to black feminism. Dreher concludes that, because *Foxy* invites the twenty-first-century African American reader to consider Grier's insights on her relationships with these men and to understand their problematic nature on different levels, her memoir also purposefully participates in and adds to contemporary self-help culture.

The contributors to *Reading African American Autobiography: Twenty-First-Century Contexts and Criticism* chart new disciplinary paths and establish the directions in which the field is moving at present. Based on their work presented here and other recently published studies of African American life writing, I maintain that an "age of Obama" assessment of African American life narrative has only begun. There are other avenues for us to pursue. According to the important scholarly work of Katherine Faull and Henry Louis Gates Jr., the archive will also play a significant role in shaping the future study of African American life narratives. Faull's "Self-Encounters: Two Eighteenth-Century Memoirs from Moravian Bethlehem," published in Drexler and White's volume, *Beyond Douglass: New Perspectives on Early African-American Literature*, instructs readers on how the archive will continue to shape the field. Faull narrates how she located two eighteenth-century autobiographical texts in German, the memoir of Andrew (or Ofodobendo Wooma) and the memoir of his wife, Magdalene Beulah Brockden, in the Moravian Archives in Bethlehem, Pennsylvania. According to Faull, "until recently the existence of these two documents were unrecorded by anyone outside the Moravian Archives" (22). "And until now," she continues, "they have not been discussed at all either in the exploration of cultural connections between Germany and Africa or in examinations of the interconnectedness of race, gender, and the autobiographical act" (22). Crucially, Faull's chapter demonstrates that discovering neglected life narratives in the archives is still possible. Furthermore, the memoirs of Andrew and Magdalene reinforce the significance of the multilingual, transnational, and transatlantic dimensions present in African American life narrative.[8]

Gates's recent work highlights, in a different way, how the future of African American life narrative will be found in the archives. While one can trace a consistent preoccupation with African American life writing in Gates's scholarly work, his books, *Finding Oprah's Roots: Finding Your Own* and *In Search of Our Roots: How 19 Extraordinary African Americans Reclaimed Their Past*, along with his PBS television series, *African American Lives*, explore how genealogical research and the mapping of an individual's genetic makeup provide contemporary African Americans with a productive space in which to locate their selves in the history of the slave trade, the institution of slavery in the United States, and with a simple swab of a Q-Tip, he compellingly claims, in Africa.[9] These important projects on the significance of genetics and genealogy in the twenty-first century illustrate that African Americans who choose to study their pasts will consistently come to see themselves as "global subjects" (Smith 567) with genetic and cultural ties to various peoples, instead of ones whose pasts and selves are confined within the geographical borders of the United States. Understandably, without the help of professional historians, genealogists, and archivists or the training that an individual like Gates has successfully completed, the intellectual work required to complete this ambitious undertaking may seem too overwhelming for the nonspecialist.[10] Nevertheless, the most striking part of Gates's recent work is that he purposefully demystifies—in his books and in his television series—the necessary steps involved in the process of beginning to trace one's roots. Gates outlines the concrete strategies an African American can employ when she or he commits to the arduous process of interviewing family members, locating archival documents relevant to one's past, deciphering these archival materials, and engaging with a past that reveals painful—yet rewarding—connections between the transatlantic slave trade, the institution of slavery, and her or his self.[11]

Given these unique components found in Gates's projects, African American life narrative scholars will need to acknowledge the fact that many of these searches for the self will not necessarily be aired on television or published in books available in the literary marketplace. Rather, these narratives about successfully (or unsuccessfully) locating one's past via Gates's advice and techniques will likely be more consistently disseminated and circulated via blogs, social networking sites, as well as through private conversations during holiday celebrations, family reunions, and other types of familial gatherings.[12] Consequently, African American life narrative scholars will be charged with the task of judging the overall success and implementation of Gates's push for research on the self not necessarily in reading books on the interplay of genealogy and genetics that are available for public consumption but through a mapping of all the channels currently available for disseminating African American autobiographical acts. Understanding the impact of Gates's project on recovering narratives in African American history and tracing the parameters of the self requires further theoretical reflection and the implementation of a unique methodology.

Sidonie Smith's 2011 Modern Language Association presidential address identifies another relevant future direction for studying African American life narratives. In particular, Smith's commentary on the scholarship of Julie Rak and Gillian Whitlock may be used productively to read this body of life writing in a different way. Rak's and Whitlock's intellectual work, as Smith notes, highlights how "life writing is caught up in the circuits of production, circulation, and reception" (567).[13] Building on Smith's call to investigate the production, circulation, and reception of life narration, I propose that, rather than taking for granted the textual stability of African American life narrative, scholars put to use John Bryant's aforementioned concept of the "fluid" text.

In his book *The Fluid Text: A Theory of Revision and Editing for Book and Screen*, Bryant writes that "a literary work evolves through various stages of revision in [the writing] process from the earliest creative moments of mental transcription (when writers make up words in the mind and transfer them on the page) to moments of publication and on to moments of adaptation in other media" (3). While Bryant concedes the point that readers generate different and competing interpretations of any single text, he argues that many scholars, especially ones not working in the field of textual scholarship, have resisted "the thought that single literary works are themselves multiform, that they exist in various and varied physical states, each capable of yielding its own set of interpretations" (2). Beyond their refusal to acknowledge the fluidity of the text, Bryant also points out that when readers do discover different versions of a given text, they often consider them as "either anomalous corruptions with no real critical relevance or at best simply 'other' texts to be treated separately" (2).

Another reason for dismissing the fluid text, Bryant states, may be found in the stance that insists that scholars working in the field of textual scholarship are the only ones responsible for studying different versions of a single text in order to establish an "authoritative" or "definitive" edition for use (3). To remedy these disciplinary problems, Bryant stresses that, rather than viewing the literary text as either "definitive," "singular," or even "stable," scholars need to embrace the premise that "literary works invariably exist in more than one version, either in early manuscript forms, subsequent print editions, or even adaptations in other media with or without the author's consent" (1).[14] Textual fluidity, Bryant continues, occurs in other cases when the text "changes in other ways through censorings, bowdlerizations, translations, adaptations, and even scholarly editions" (3).[15] Interestingly enough, Bryant's comments on the fluid text parallel contemporary autobiography theorists' suggestion

Introduction

that there is no unified self. Multiplicity, therefore, comprises our contemporary understanding of both self and text.[16] Bryant's work remains fixed on the Melvillean text, yet his ideas need to be applied to and modified for exploring the dynamics of textual fluidity found in African American life narratives. To judge from Bryant's preliminary remarks cited here, we can turn to his challenge to "try to find a text that is *not* fluid, one that has *not* changed materially, and in significant ways, over the years for some reason or another" (3–4) and conclude that it is one that stands as a legitimate call for scholars working with African American life narratives to pursue.

This particular "age of Obama" assessment of the African American life narrative canon proves that interdisciplinary and comparative inquiry infuses new interpretive life into the field; that is, the contributors to this book put into practice the diverse critical methods required in reading the full range of African American life narratives in the "age of Obama." Additionally, the studies presented here confirm, on a number of levels, that the rethinking of commonly held assumptions and critical perspectives remains an essential disciplinary initiative. As the second term of Obama's presidency comes to a conclusion, one point is certain: the canon of African American life narrative and the methods by which scholars read these explorations of the self have never been more diverse and more necessary.

NOTES

Parts of this chapter were published as "The Futures of African American Life Writing," *a/b: Auto/Biography Studies* 27.1 (2012): 1–18. © 2012 The Autobiography Society. Reprinted by permission.

1. The terms *life writing* and *life narrative* are used throughout the book to examine different types of autobiographical acts by African Americans and individuals of African descent, such as Olaudah Equiano and John Jea, who were born in Africa, according to their narratives, and whose lives intersected, on different levels, with what eventually became the United States. While the term *auto/biography* has been used to encompass the significance of both autobiography and biography in the field of autobiography studies, Sidonie Smith and Julia Watson note that the terms *life writing* and *life narrative* are "more inclusive of the heterogeneous nature of self-referential practices" (4). They define *life writing* as "a general term for writing that takes a life, one's own or another's, as its subject. Such writing can be biographical, novelistic, historical, or explicitly self-referential and therefore autobiographical" (4). Furthermore, they state that *life narrative* functions "as a general term for acts of self-presentation of all kinds and in diverse media that take the producer's life as their subject, whether written, performative, visual, filmic, or digital" (4). Given that the autobiographical acts of African Americans have become increasingly heterogeneous in nature, perhaps it is time to move away from the term *African American autobiography* and use instead *African American life narrative*.

2. For a prediction on the rhetoric of Obama's postpresidency life writing, see Remnick.

3. In ways mirroring Drexler and White's call to move "beyond Douglass," scholars have rigorously reassessed antebellum African American life narrative. Frances Smith Foster and Kim D. Green, for instance, offer a new narrative on the origins of African American

literature before the Civil War based on "ports" and pulpits" in their contribution to Gene Andrew Jarrett's *A Companion to African American Literature*, but they make the essential point that a number of seminal works published during the 1970s and 1980s "promoted the personal narratives by enslaved and formerly enslaved writers as the *ur*-genre, and the archetypal movement of African American literature to be from slave South to free North" (49–50). Recent investigations have called attention to a much wider range of African American life narratives than the type of familiar text identified by Foster and Green. For instance, Foster ("Narrative" 723–24), Ala Alryyes, Patrick E. Horn, and Katherine Faull, whose work I discuss in more detail later in this chapter, have published on the multilingual nature of life narratives documenting the lives of individuals of African descent that consistently straddle various parts of the Atlantic world. However, what are the additional critical avenues when an "English plus other languages" (Sollors 3) focus is applied to African American life narratives? Additionally, Santamarina's push toward moving beyond "race" and slavery captures another critique of the types of texts that have been traditionally studied from the antebellum period. William L. Andrews has also repeatedly encouraged scholars to move beyond the antebellum period altogether in his outlining of the shortcomings in the field's understanding of post–Civil War African American life narratives. Specifically, Andrews has insisted that the privileging of antebellum life narratives has obstructed an ability to appreciate the canon of postwar life narratives on its own terms ("African-American" and "Toward"). More crucially, measuring post–Civil War slave narratives by the characteristics found in antebellum slave narratives, Andrews holds, further prohibits recognizing identifiable patterns of revision in the representations of the self throughout the history of African American life narrative. Consult as well his introduction to *Slave Narratives after Slavery* for additional arguments on the importance of post–Civil War African American life narratives.

4. Even though parts of the *Appeal* are based on Walker's experiences, the ideas of this early nineteenth-century African American literary text arise largely from the author's engagement with print and oral sources. For more information on Walker's use of sources in his *Appeal*, refer to the introduction in Peter P. Hinks's edition of the *Appeal* as well as his single-author book.

5. On the lack of dialogue between scholars working in the fields of African American studies and book history, Leon Jackson makes the following points: "The nontalking book has been supplemented by the nontalking book historian. The result is that while we know a great deal about the talking book as *trope*, we know very little about the production, dissemination, or consumption of the books that deployed that trope, and still less of the books that were begged, borrowed, stolen, owned, or encountered by the authors who wrote them" (252).

6. Texts such as Common's *One Day It'll All Make Sense*, Serena Williams's *On the Line*, Lisa Leslie's *Don't Let the Lipstick Fool You*, John Lewis's *March: Book One* and *March: Book Two*, Robin Roberts's *Everybody's Got Something*, Rick James's *Glow: The Autobiography of Rick James*, Nina Simone's *I Put a Spell on You: The Autobiography of Nina Simone*, and Louis Gosset Jr.'s *An Actor and a Gentleman*, among others, underscore that celebrity lives make up an important part of twenty-first-century African American life narrative.

7. Consult Anna Poletti and Julie Rak's *Identity Technologies: Constructing the Self Online* for further elucidation on studying lives online.

8. As Faull writes, "Magdalene's memoir exists in both English and German. . . . Andrew's memoir was written in German. All manuscript sources for this article are written

in German script. Special training is required to read these manuscripts—even for native German speakers. A two-week script seminar is held every summer at the Moravian Archives in Bethlehem, Pennsylvania, for those who wish to acquire that skill" (49–50n1). See also Crystal J. Lucky's edition of *A Mysterious Life and Calling*, the autobiography of Charlotte Levy Riley, for a recently published text from the African American life narrative archive.

9. Gates has continued his work on genealogy and genetics in his television series/DVD/book, *Faces of America*. For an interesting merging of life narrative and genetic studies, see Linda Strausbaugh, Joshua Suhl, Craig O'Connor, and Heather Nelson.

10. Of course, websites such as ancestry.com will play a role in these searches for the self.

11. See Regina A. Mason's afterword to her and Andrews's edition of the *Life of William Grimes, the Runaway Slave, Brought Down to the Present Time. Written by Himself* for an autobiographical essay that narrates her experiences with archival work and genealogy. One of the impressive results of Mason's persistent archival and genealogical work is captured in the following sentence: "Undeniably, William Grimes—author of the first fugitive slave narrative published in America—was my great-great-great-grandfather" (134).

12. For instance, some African Americans (and individuals of African descent elsewhere in the world) have posted their reactions to the results of their DNA tests on digital platforms such as YouTube. These particular YouTube posts are digital, autobiographical confessions. While these web users may not necessarily deliberately reference Gates's book in their posts, these virtual texts provide just one example of how African Americans have used digital platforms both to understand their selves in new ways and to disseminate information on their selves.

13. For Smith, Rak's work on the editions of Marjane Satrapi's *Persepolis* published in France and the United States along with Whitlock's work on post-9/11 narratives from Middle Eastern nations and Afghanistan shed light on the significance of the production, consumption, and reception of life writing. Both of these studies document the unstable nature of life narrative.

14. Consult Bryant's articles in *Textual Cultures* ("Witness") and *PMLA* ("Rewriting") along with his online archive devoted to Herman Melville's *Typee* (*Herman*) for a more nuanced understanding of his proposal. According to Bryant, a significant part of his project requires that editors rethink the ways that critical editions have typically referenced any changes to a given text in different editions. Rather than burying these changes in an appendix or refusing to acknowledge textual fluidity in any way, Bryant argues, editors must develop more productive ways for readers to gain access to the fluidity of a given text. The challenge of capturing adequately the fluid African American life narrative in critical editions counts as another future in this field. For an application of Bryant's theory to African American life narrative, see John Ernest (125–28). For texts merging textual scholarship and African American studies, consult George Hutchinson and John K. Young's *Publishing Blackness: Textual Constructions of Race since 1850* as well as Young's *Black Writers, White Publishers: Marketplace Politics in Twentieth-Century African American Literature*. This type of scholarship needs to include attention to pre-1850 texts.

15. Celeste-Marie Bernier, Ivy G. Wilson, Peter P. Hinks ("Editor's"), and Anna Brickhouse have contributed scholarly work on some of the manifestations of the African American fluid text. See also Christopher Mulvey's Clotel *by William Wells Brown: An Electronic Scholarly Edition*.

16. Autobiography scholars will likely hear echoes of Philippe Lejeune's "Genetic Studies of Life Writing" in Bryant's prose. In this article, Lejeune posits that "the purpose of textual genetics is to understand why and how someone created something, whether that thing is a text, a painting, a symphony, or a film. . . . What makes textual genetics unique is its diachronic aspect: it is a study of the history of a composition" (162).

WORKS CITED

Alryyes, Ala, ed. *A Muslim American Slave: The Life of Omar ibn Said*. Madison: U of Wisconsin P, 2011.

Andrews, William L. "African-American Autobiography Criticism: Retrospect and Prospect." *American Autobiography: Retrospect and Prospect*. Ed. Paul John Eakin. Madison: U of Wisconsin P, 1991. 195–215.

———. "Introduction." *Slave Narratives after Slavery*. Ed. William Andrews. New York: Oxford UP, 2011. vii–xxxii.

———. "Toward a Poetics of Afro-American Autobiography." *Afro-American Literary Studies in the 1990s*. Ed. Houston A. Baker Jr. and Patricia Redmond. Chicago: U of Chicago P, 1989. 78–104.

Bernier, Celeste-Marie. "A Comparative Exploration of Narrative Ambiguities in Frederick Douglass's Two Versions of *The Heroic Slave* (1853, 1863?)." *Slavery and Abolition: A Journal of Slave and Post-Slave Studies* 22.2 (2001): 69–86.

Brickhouse, Anna. "The French Caribbeanization of Phillis Wheatley: A Poetics of Anti-colonialism." *Transatlantic Literary Studies: A Reader*. Ed. Susan Manning and Andrew Taylor. Baltimore: Johns Hopkins UP, 2007. 207–12.

Bryant, John. *The Fluid Text: A Theory of Revision and Editing for Book and Screen*. Ann Arbor: U of Michigan P, 2002.

———. *Herman Melville's* Typee: *A Fluid-Text Edition*. U of Virginia P, 2006.

———. "Rewriting *Moby-Dick*: Politics, Textual Identity, and the Revision Narrative." *PMLA* 125.4 (2010): 1043–60.

———. "Witness and Access: The Uses of the Fluid Text." *Textual Cultures: Texts, Contexts, Interpretation* 2.1 (2007): 16–42.

Chaney, Michael A. *Fugitive Vision: Slave Image and Black Identity in Antebellum Narrative*. Bloomington: Indiana UP, 2008.

Common, with Adam Bradley. *One Day It'll All Make Sense: A Memoir*. New York: Atria Books, 2011.

DeLombard, Jeannine Marie. *In the Shadow of the Gallows: Race, Crime, and American Civic Identity*. Philadelphia: U of Pennsylvania P, 2012.

Drexler, Michael J., and Ed White. "Canon Loading." *Beyond Douglass: New Perspectives on Early African-American Literature*. Ed. Michael J. Drexler and Ed White. Lewisburg, PA: Bucknell UP, 2008. 1–19.

Ernest, John. *Chaotic Justice: Rethinking African American Literary History*. Chapel Hill: U of North Carolina P, 2009.

Faull, Katherine. "Self-Encounters: Two Eighteenth-Century Memoirs from Moravian Bethlehem." *Beyond Douglass: New Perspectives on Early African-American Literature*. Ed. Michael J. Drexler and Ed White. Lewisburg, PA: Bucknell UP, 2008. 21–53.

Foster, Frances Smith. "A Narrative of the Interesting Origins and (Somewhat) Surprising Developments of African-American Print Culture." *American Literary History* 17.4 (2005): 714–40.

Foster, Frances Smith, and Kim D. Green. "Ports of Call, Pulpits of Consultation: Rethinking the Origins of African American Literature." *A Companion to African American Literature*. Ed. Gene Andrew Jarrett. Malden, MA: Blackwell, 2010. 45–58.

Gates, Henry Louis, Jr., co-executive producer. *African American Lives*. Written by Henry Louis Gates Jr. PBS, 2006.

———. *African American Lives 2*. Written by Henry Louis Gates Jr. PBS, 2008.

———. *Finding Oprah's Roots: Finding Your Own*. New York: Crown, 2007.

———. *In Search of Our Roots: How 19 Extraordinary African Americans Reclaimed Their Past*. New York: Crown, 2009.

Gill, Joel Christian. *Uncelebrated Narratives from Black History*. Strange Fruit 1. Golden, CO: Fulcrum, 2014.

Gosset, Louis, Jr., and Phyllis Karas. *An Actor and a Gentleman*. Hoboken, NJ: John Wiley and Sons, 2010.

Hinks, Peter P. "Editor's Note: The Three Editions of the *Appeal*." David Walker's Appeal to the Coloured Citizens of the World. Ed. Peter P. Hinks. University Park: Pennsylvania State UP, 2000. xlv–li.

———. Introduction. *David Walker's* Appeal to the Coloured Citizens of the World. Ed. Peter P. Hinks. University Park: Pennsylvania State UP, 2000. xi–xliv.

———. *To Awaken My Afflicted Brethren: David Walker and the Problem of Antebellum Slave Resistance*. University Park: Pennsylvania State UP, 1997.

Horn, Patrick E. "Coercions, Conversions, Subversions: The Nineteenth-Century Slave Narratives of Omar ibn Said, Mahommah Gardo Baquaqua, and Nicholas Said." *a/b: Auto/Biography Studies* 27.1 (2012): 45–66.

Hutchinson, George, and John K. Young, eds. *Publishing Blackness: Textual Constructions of Race since 1850*. Ann Arbor: U of Michigan P, 2013.

Jackson, Leon. "The Talking Book and the Talking Book Historian: African American Cultures of Print—The State of the Discipline." *Book History* 13 (2010): 251–308.

James, Rick, with David Rita. *Glow: The Autobiography of Rick James*. New York: Atria Books, 2014.

Lejeune, Philippe. "Genetic Studies of Life Writing." *a/b: Auto/Biography Studies* 25.2 (2010): 162–71.

Leslie, Lisa, with Larry Burnett. *Don't Let the Lipstick Fool You*. New York: Kensington, 2008.

Lewis, John, Andrew Aydin, and Nate Powell. *March: Book One*. Marietta, GA: Top Shelf Productions, 2013.

Lewis, John, Andrew Aydin, Nate Powell, and Chris Ross. *March: Book Two*. Marietta, GA: Top Shelf Productions, 2015.

Mason, Regina E. Afterword. *Life of William Grimes, the Runaway Slave*. Ed. William L. Andrews and Regina E. Mason. New York: Oxford UP, 2008. 119–38.

Mulvey, Christopher, ed. Clotel *by William Wells Brown: An Electronic Scholarly Edition*. U of Virginia P.

Olney, James. "'I Was Born': Slave Narratives, Their Status as Autobiography and as Literature." *Callaloo* 20 (1984): 46–73.

Poletti, Anna, and Julie Rak, eds. *Identity Technologies: Constructing the Self Online*. Madison: U of Wisconsin P, 2014.

Remnick, David. "Charleston and the Age of Obama." *New Yorker* 19 June 2015: n. pag.

Riley, Charlotte S. *A Mysterious Life and Calling: From Slavery to Ministry in South Carolina*. Ed. Crystal J. Lucky. Madison: U of Wisconsin P, 2016.

Roberts, Robin, with Veronica Chambers. *Everybody's Got Something*. New York: Grand Central, 2014.

Santamarina, Xiomara. "Antebellum African-American Texts beyond Slavery and Race." *Beyond Douglass: New Perspectives on Early African-American Literature*. Ed. Michael J. Drexler and Ed White. Lewisburg, PA: Bucknell UP, 2008. 141–53.

Simone, Nina, with Stephen Cleary. *I Put a Spell on You: The Autobiography of Nina Simone*. New York: Da Capo Press, 1993.

Smith, Sidonie. "Presidential Address 2011: Narrating Lives and Contemporary Imaginaries." *PMLA* 126.3 (2011): 564–74.

Smith, Sidonie, and Julia Watson. *Reading Autobiography: A Guide for Interpreting Life Narratives*. 2nd ed. Minneapolis: U of Minnesota P, 2010.

Sollors, Werner. Introduction. *Multilingual America: Transnationalism, Ethnicity, and the Languages of American Literature*. Ed. Werner Sollors. New York: New York UP, 1998. 1–13.

Stepto, Robert B. *A Home Elsewhere: Reading African American Classics in the Age of Obama*. Cambridge, MA: Harvard UP, 2011.

Strausbaugh, Linda, Joshua Suhl, Craig O'Connor, and Heather Nelson. "The Genomics Perspective on Venture Smith: Genetics, Ancestry, and the Meaning of Family." *Venture Smith and the Business of Slavery and Freedom*. Ed. James Brewer Stewart. Amherst: U of Massachusetts P, 2010. 207–30.

Walker, David. *David Walker's Appeal to the Coloured Citizens of the World*. Ed. Peter P. Hinks. University Park: Pennsylvania State UP, 2000.

Wallace, Maurice O., and Shawn Michelle Smith, eds. *Pictures and Progress: Early Photography and the Making of African American Identity*. Durham, NC: Duke UP, 2012.

Williams, Serena, with Daniel Paisner. *On the Line*. New York: Grand Central, 2009.

Willis, Deborah, and Barbara Krauthamer. *Envisioning Emancipation: Black Americans and the End of Slavery*. Philadelphia: Temple UP, 2013.

Wilson, Ivy G. "Periodicals, Print Culture, and African American Poetry." *A Companion to African American Literature*. Ed. Gene Andrew Jarrett. Malden, MA: Blackwell, 2010. 133–48.

Young, John K. *Black Writers, White Publishers: Marketplace Politics in Twentieth-Century African American Literature*. Jackson: UP of Mississippi, 2006.

"A Dying Man"

The Outlaw Body of Arthur, 1768

LYNN A. CASMIER-PAZ

For readers familiar with antebellum African American slave narratives, the confessional life narrative of a condemned criminal, Arthur, opens with a remarkably similar introduction when the narrator begins, "I was born" (Arthur 2).[1] However, the life narrative of Arthur, "a Negro of about 21 years of age," who was hanged "for a RAPE" in Worcester, Massachusetts, differs from this lengthier confessional life narrative when it appeared in a shorter, earlier form (1768) that was printed and sold as a broadside consisting of one page with four columns.[2] Although Arthur's narrative, like other gallows literature about black criminals, presages the antebellum slave narratives in important ways, his life story stands apart from other criminal confessions as a distinctive text that articulates both the limits and the possibilities of life writing in the contexts of chattel slavery in America's colonial era. In order to understand Arthur's story, this study embraces Jeannine Marie DeLombard's invitation for critics and other readers to "[redirect] temporarily our gaze ... away from the piety, industry, and activism" of antebellum slave narratives and focus instead on crime and punishment in African American literary history so that we may "concentrate our attention on the black persona [and its] metamorphosis from civilly dead property to criminally liable *person*" (38; emphasis added). Although this chapter accepts the historical and political distinctions between "human being" and "person" in DeLombard's seminal study, *In the Shadow of the Gallows: Race, Crime, and American Civic Identity* (2012), the "redirected gaze" of this chapter will read another set of signposts in Arthur's 1768 criminal confession. Within the contexts of theories of the body, identity, race, and criminality, this chapter examines Arthur's story in order to understand one man's desperate efforts to wrest control of his own body, agency, and visibility to assert his *manhood* in the milieu of colonial slavery.

    Arthur's life writing stands as one of the roughly sixty condemned black criminal confessions that form part of the gallows literature tradition that flourished during the American colonial era.[3] Michel Foucault, in his *Discipline and Punish: The Birth of the Prison* (1995), writes that these "last words of a condemned man" are what "the law requires [in order to] authenticate in some sense the tortures he had undergone" and to further "consecrate his own punishment by proclaiming the blackness of his crimes" (66). "Justice," Foucault further asserts, "required these apocrypha in order to be grounded in truth" (66). DeLombard agrees with Foucault's interpretation of early life narrative texts by condemned criminals; at the same time, she aligns herself with African American literary theorists and historians when she argues that the confessional narratives of colonial America's condemned *black* criminals anticipate, in different ways, later slave narratives.[4] Within the larger body of gallows literature, which was published in conjunction with execution-day rituals, the criminals' confessions form "the biographical portions of this crime literature [which] was gradually superseded by more politicized forms of personal narrative" (DeLombard 5) by formerly enslaved men and women in the nineteenth century. Furthermore, gallows literature from this period consistently comments on *criminals of African descent*, who appear in approximately one-third of the well over 160 works published from 1674 to 1800 (DeLombard 17, 18).

Arthur's life writing provides useful historical details about the people, places, and events of the prerevolutionary colonial era, yet DeLombard's study offers the first sustained analysis of the text. Scholars in African American studies have referenced the text only in passing, which DeLombard speculates can be explained by the vexed and complex status of the text in relationship to the generic categories of "autobiography" versus "biography."[5] In sum, readers of Arthur's text cannot definitively *prove* that Arthur himself penned the confessional testimony that bears his name, and whose narrative elements DeLombard claims "differ little in content and style from the confessions attributed to white malefactors" and black criminals alike in the eighteenth-century Atlantic world (95). This chapter argues for understanding Arthur's story as a "life narrative," whose first-person narrator indicates that his story may not be read as a "biography," even if the impossibility of verifying the identity of the author means whoever wrote the story could have been someone else.[6] This chapter also distinguishes significant elements found in Arthur's life narrative from those of the "white malefactors" and other black confessions, which reveal the relationship of colonial masculinity to the black body.

Despite DeLombard's observation concerning a "high body count" of criminals who are "Negro," or "black," she claims that the gallows literature has "surprisingly little to say about 'the body' per se," since "colonial and early national crime literature devoted very little space to the violence inflicted upon the bodies of either the victim or the condemned" (19). Whereas DeLombard's analysis explains that a "lack of attention to the corporeal is doubtless due to the fact that historically the gallows tradition concerned itself with souls, in contradistinction to bodies," this chapter contends that Arthur's story may be read as an *exception* that illustrates important elements of the life narrative as gallows literature (19). That is, Arthur's text certainly offers commentary on "'the body' per se," as the following analysis seeks to establish. In fact, in his confessional catalog of criminality, Arthur's thefts and transgressions reveal an *obsessive attention* to his own body—its needs and desires—and his repeated arrests and punishments (along with his unique ability to avoid them) bring to the forefront of his narrative a story about physical abuse and bodily torture.

Insofar as Foucault's theory of biopolitics "stands for the biological threshold of modernity," Arthur's body presents an important literary and historical index of the eighteenth century's revolutionary "transformation of sovereign power into biopower [which] leads to a shift from a political-military discourse into a racist-biological one" (Lemke, Casper, and Moore 40). Arthur's body emerges just before America's revolution began to serve as an important landscape—a first battleground, if you will—on which an important political-historical transformation plays out *at the same time*. As Thomas Lemke, Monica J. Casper, and Lisa Jean Moore understand from Foucault's *Discipline and Punish* (1995), "the body is directly involved in a political field; power relations have an immediate hold upon it; they invest it, mark it, train it, torture it, force it to carry out tasks [and] to perform signs" (25). As such, this political body becomes "caught up in a system of subjection [and is] . . . a useful force *only if it is both a productive body and a subjected body*" (26; emphasis added). Arthur's criminal activity *unmoors* his fugitive body, which is neither productive nor (de)subjected as a slave body. Thus the biopolitics of colonial American slavery cannot hold him; the power-knowledge paradigm of slavery's subjection becomes the power-knowledge of an outlaw body. As Arthur moves from slavery to freedom and out into the community of free men, he seeks the performance of his own masculinity and humanity outside the margins of an emergent, mainstream discourse of resistance to sovereignty that will soon develop its own discourse of revolution against the tyranny of Great Britain's king.

The "challenge to royal power," which Lemke, Casper, and Moore's reading of Foucault identifies as "emerging in the Puritan rebellion of prerevolutionary England," will soon see the emergence of a new "expression of race," but it was not yet linked to its devastating biological signification. The disposition of Arthur's fugitive, gratified body has not yet been marked with the racism "of permanent purification [and] social normalization" that will "facilitate a dynamic relation between the life of one person and the death of another" (Lemke, Casper, and Moore 42). Arthur will die; Arthur *must* die, according to colonial law and to the generic conventions of the gallows confessional life writing. But before he does, Arthur's body performs the radical, revolutionary, and desperate freedom of an individual who resists the "sovereign power" that subjects his body and therefore produces the knowledge of slavery, and which denies to him the possession of *himself* and the gratification of his bodily needs and desires. This reading of Arthur's body can therefore interpret the ways in which he attempts to empower and subject himself outside the political field of chattel slavery through the power-knowledge of sartorial self-fashioning and masculine heterosexuality.

Like the other gallows confessional life writing, Arthur's one-page broadside recalls his life of reprobate, criminal degeneracy that, in turn, explains and justifies the narrator's immanent and public execution. The dynamics of Arthur's narrative mark it as distinctive within the larger body of criminal confessions, since he describes, in remarkable detail, the criminal exploits of a young man who was born into slavery—but who refused to surrender his body to the invisible, ontological death sentence that circumscribed the lives of the enslaved people of his time.

As a final act before his execution, Arthur's confession describes a short life of desperate ambition and desire for personal freedom. According to Daniel E. Williams, Arthur's dictated chronicle of his criminal life contains a "progressive series of transgressions" that "exhibit his corrupt tendencies" ("'Gratification'" 197). The narrative, Williams further writes, "dramatize[s] a return to the dominant order" in his execution; moreover, Williams provocatively concludes that Arthur becomes "the first black rapist in American literature" who "set the foundation for what would later become an unfortunate stereotype—the immoral, hypersexual black wildly pursuing women to satisfy his prodigal lusts" (200). Despite Williams's interesting argument, it is not my intention here to argue whether Arthur functions as an origin for a racist stereotype. Rather, the character who emerges from his autobiographical narrative should be understood as far more complicated and interesting than any stereotype could contain. Arthur's often wisecracking confession details his reckless, desperate disregard for prohibitions and legal constraints regarding personal property and the class hierarchies in colonial Massachusetts. Contextual analysis of the specific decisions Arthur makes—the decision to run away, the places where he finds shelter, his relationships, the specific items he steals, and the ways in which he takes control of his own body—enables the emergence of a first-person narrator who refuses to be reduced to a racist stereotype.

Arthur runs away from multiple masters; steals clothing, fabric, shoes, and horses; breaks out of jail more than once; sails to the West Indies; fornicates (his preferred partner is a neighborhood "Squaw"); drinks to excess; and suffers the final condemnation after he has "ravished a local widow," who afterward pleads for his life (Arthur 3). His life ends with the ontologically ironic affirmation of his own execution. In dictating his life's story as a condemned man's confession, Arthur offers an exegesis of the ways in which the complementary economies of chattel slavery and rule of law interpellate the invisibility of enslaved black bodies—and how those bodies refuse to disappear into their use value and instead assert their visibility, humanity, agency, and sentience as outlaws.

Arthur's declaration "I was born at Taunton, January 14, 1747," parallels the aforementioned "I was born," which begins multiple texts of the antebellum slave narrative genre. James Olney's analysis of the antebellum slave narrative argues that the common "I was born" phrase figures as a critical part in any interpretation of these life narratives to the extent that he even uses this phrase in the title of his seminal study. Olney contrasts the formerly enslaved antebellum narrator's *purpose* for (relating or) writing his story with that of Benjamin Franklin's *Autobiography* to conclude: "While any reader was free to doubt the motives of Franklin's memoir, no one could doubt his existence. . . . With the ex-slave, however, it was his existence and his identity, not his reasons for writing, that were called into question: if the former could be established the latter would be obvious and the same from one narrative to another" (155). Whereas Olney's analysis classifies the antebellum-era "I was born" phrase as an "existential claim" (the narrator *exists*), I propose that "I was born" actually submits an *ontological* claim that reaffirms Arthur's *gendered humanity*, which the subtitle identifies as the story of a "Negro man of about 21 years of age" (Arthur 2). The ontological importance of this claim becomes clear when the narrative explains that Arthur was born into "the house of Richard Godfrey, Esq.," with his "Mother being his slave" (Arthur 2). Since his mother was an enslaved woman, Arthur himself was born into slavery. The title itself confirms Arthur's status as an enslaved person, since the term *Negro*, in colonial America, "denoted, specifically, an enslaved African" (Monaghan 241). The incidents of the narrative confirm his enslaved status when he is repeatedly bought, sold, beaten, and traded.

Arthur's "many notorious crimes" begin immediately as apparent concern to seize control of, and gratify, his body: its freedom of movement, needs, and appetites. He steals clothing, liquor, food, horses, and heterosexual gratification. Although Arthur's confession precedes the final destruction of his body—and the release of his penitent, eternal soul to everlasting glory—the care, control, and power of his body illustrate both a distinctive agency and the indices of critical concern for colonial America.

As Kathleen Brown has argued, "the bodies of enslaved men—or, more precisely, the social persons rooted in those bodies—were more crucial to the meanings and experience [of those bodies] than was the case for other men" in colonial America (173). Without property or wealth, the value of men lay in the labor that could be extracted from their bodies: "The propertyless free laborer made his way in the world by virtue of his strength and his wits, but at least he owned his labor. His bound [i.e., enslaved] counterparts were not so lucky; although their only value might be calculated in reference to their bodies, even this most personal resource was owned by another" (Brown 173). An important strategy that enslaved men used to resist the ownership of their bodies was to "steal themselves," or run away, which denied the principle that their bodies belonged to someone other than themselves (173). Even more relevant to Arthur's story, Brown argues, "the enslaved man also claimed possession of his own body . . . by expressing personhood through clothing, speech, dance, song, eating, lovemaking, and fighting. For men in slavery, then, the body was the most important resource for expressing manhood" (173). The objectives for Arthur's short life certainly include the successful effort to "[claim] possession of his own body" and assert his manhood.

The narrative details the efforts of one enslaved man to garner for himself a gendered subjectivity in a time when the complex and contradictory meanings of manhood and masculinity were shaping the founding and development of early America. Where historians have shown that early American manhood equated the establishment of a household, a successful calling or career, and "self-control over one's masculine comportment" (Brown 173), during Arthur's short, fugitive life, he achieved none of these important requirements. Rather, theories and histories of early American manhood show the limits of *the enslaved man's* possibility to become what Crèvecoeur called "the new man" of America (69).[7] When he finally faces his own execution, Arthur has no home, no career, and no family; he has only his own body, which is no small accomplishment given his circumstances.

Arthur's first decision regarding the status of his own body involves his decision to escape from "the Displeasure of [his] Mistress" when, at the age of fourteen, he runs away from his master for the first time, and his "notorious crimes" begin apace when he immediately runs to the town of Sandwich, where he lives for two months in an avowed state of "Drunkenness and fornication" (Arthur 2). Once he frees his young body from the bonds of forced labor and abuse, he wishes to evade recapture and indulge in self-gratification, thereby satisfying his body's pubescent needs. Arthur claims possession of his own body and immediately indulges his body's pleasures and positions himself as "a Negro young man" who has little concern for colonial standards of decency and propriety.

The needs and pleasures of his body consume all of Arthur's youthful energy and attention in the earliest months of his frantic, evasive movements throughout eastern Massachusetts. However, given his ability to dress himself in a manner that he believes is appropriate, his bodily needs also include the more pragmatic. To these ends, Arthur's first criminal act occurs when he "steals a shirt," but he repeats this act multiple times in the narrative, as he steals clothing whenever and wherever the possibility affords itself. The items Arthur chooses to steal explain how he both violates important laws of the eighteenth-century American colonies and sees himself in relationship to the strict hierarchy and class distinctions of his times. Arthur's status as a slave in colonial Massachusetts means that the kinds of fabric and articles of clothing with which he dresses his body are strictly controlled and limited by law.

Historians of clothing, fashion, and adornment find that clothing, or "sumptuary laws" of colonial America, strictly controlled what colonists—and the citizens of the empire nations that ruled them—could and could not wear. As clothing archaeologist Diana DiPaolo Loren and other theorists have found, "clothing and adornment are a means of communication: a visual statement about status, prestige, gender, society, politics, and religion. Clothing faces both inward and outward, a notion historian Terence Turner evoked when he coined the term, 'social skin'" (Loren 8). Arthur's desire to groom himself and adorn his "social skin" with stolen clothing remains constant in his narrative outlining his short, furtive life of frequent movement and bodily pleasures.

Arthur steals "trowsers" (twice), a jacket, shoes (twice), shirts (three times), and a pair of stockings (socks). At one point, the jacket he steals is distinctive enough that later, when he "got drunk . . . and [wore] the Jacket, [he] was detected" (Arthur 2). The stolen jacket is recognized, and he is captured, "whip'ed with fifteen Stripes, and committed to Gaol" (Arthur 2). He later escapes, however, by "breaking the Lock" (Arthur 2). Colonial sumptuary laws offer insight into Arthur's repeated thefts of clothing. Historians define sumptuary laws as "imperial mandates about how certain individuals were to clothe and adorn themselves with respect to gender, ethnicity, and status. Sumptuary laws also reinforced the fashion tastes of certain groups. . . . What people wore and how they wore it were always concerns of those in power" (Loren 23). The jacket he steals marks his fugitive, outlaw status; it does not properly belong to him, and it is likely that he not only violated laws about theft but also failed to observe the strict rules about class and clothing.

Arthur's criminal behavior reveals an important concern to clothe his body in a manner he finds appropriate to the way in which he views himself, not by how society views him. His urgent desire to offer a "visual statement" that "faces inward and outward" and the effects of this representation in regard to status and power parallel other defiant acts involving clothing in colonial America, a point that explains why sumptuary laws identified clothing as critical to the maintenance of the fragile, unstable power structure. As Loren explains: "Colonial authorities in North America passed sumptuary laws because people commonly used clothing in ways that blurred the rigid social and political boundaries elites hoped to reinforce. Sumptuary laws were intended to restrict lavish dress in order to curb extravagance, protect fortunes, and visually mark the distinctions between levels of society" (25). Arthur clothes his body in ways that *undermine the invisibility of the slave* and assert the visibility of a fugitive. Whereas he repeatedly steals the raiment of colonial manhood ("trowsers," stockings, and new shoes), the hierarchy of colonial America reads his clothing as *transgressive*. Rather than serving as desirable, legible signs of his manhood, the illicit clothing instead marks Arthur with the signs of a criminal, and within the clothing, the authorities read the more salient and crucial sign of his "Negro" flesh, which communicates his status as a fugitive.

As Loren explains, in Arthur's eighteenth-century colonial America, many different types of bodies and "many interpretations of bodies were coming together in a transitional world of cultural contact, conquest, [and] adaptation. . . . The measurement and classification of difference was intimately tied to the body and bodily presentation" (87). Arthur's multiple thefts of clothing reveal the importance of his "bodily presentation" to himself and further enable us to see how clothing, as a discursive practice, enables him to "construct and reconstruct" (Loren 93) himself in a larger, colonial social landscape. Clothing his body in the manner of colonial manhood, he believes, will enable him to construct an identity that rejects the pure use value of the slave body.

Arthur indulges the drunken, fornicating pleasures of his body and adorns it as one who clearly interprets his own body as that of a man. In his urgent desire to escape the invisibility of a slave, he becomes visible, but not as a man; rather, authoritative whites see him as a criminal fugitive. According to his text, Arthur prefers the position of a fugitive, criminal subject since he refuses every opportunity to surrender his body to the invisibility of slavery and chooses instead the visible body of a fugitive whom authoritative whites whip, jail, and ultimately execute.

Yet in between his three whippings, five arrests, and four escapes, Arthur indulges his appetites for new clothing, stolen rum, and women. That he is eventually condemned and executed for "a RAPE [*sic*] upon the body of the widow, Mrs. Deborah Metcalf," figures as an equally important element of his narrative, since the incidents of the narrative clearly reveal that not *rape* but rather *consensual heterosexual relations* drive his body's needs.

Arthur's fugitive exploits from town to town include criminal activity, but they also reveal a man whose desire for women knows no limits or appreciation for appropriate conduct. The narrative states that a teenaged Arthur "goes to Town with some Negroes" and becomes drunk, only to then go into a "house where were several Women only to whom [he] offered indecencies," the punishment for which was a whipping of "thirty-nine stripes" (Arthur 2). An incurable ignorance about proper behavior accompanies his insatiable desire to be with women. In no less than five visits to "a young Squaw" with whom he "commenced an acquaintance" as a teenager, Arthur finds a helpful companion and partner.

The "young Squaw" of Arthur's narrative makes repeated appearances throughout the story, but she is initially his coconspirator in a remarkably creative strategy of evasion. When authorities return Arthur to a new master after another escape, he then steals money from his master's son. To avoid punishment for the theft, "some other Negroes" "advis[e] [him] to run away, to avoid being taken up" (Arthur 2). To this end, the "Squaw" devises an elaborate plan: "By Advice of my Companion (who like the rest of her Sex, was of a very fruitful Invention) I had recourse to the following Expedient: I dressed in the Habit of a Squaw, and made of my own Cloaths a Pappouse; in this manner we proceeded to Hadley [Massachusetts] undiscover'd where I was introduced by my Companion, to an Indian Family, where I tarried only one Night" (Arthur 2). This scene instructs readers that clothing's ability to "blur the rigid social and political boundaries" in colonial America also applies to the realm of gender. The young woman's "fruitful Invention" perfectly aligns with Arthur's ontological sleight of hand. He accedes to her plan and wears the clothing of an Indian woman. The strategy succeeds in a way that parallels Arthur's escape: he will change the subject if the subject he becomes is not a slave.

Arthur wears the clothing of an Indian woman because he believes in clothing's discursive power, as evidenced by the multiple criminal acts he performs to secure specific articles of clothing for himself. Arthur moves frantically in the liminal spaces between the invisible/visible and the man/slave. He understands the nuances of a life "between" the binary options, so he agrees, without hesitation or doubts about the outcome, to a strategy that asks him to shift the locus of his subject-position from man to woman. Interestingly, in a way, this "between" space allows Arthur to distinguish himself from "the Negroes" with whom he often travels, and from whom he often seeks advice and guidance. Despite the promise of shifting gender roles, the day after his night clad as a "Squaw" with the "Indian Family," an individual who becomes his new master captures Arthur; this time his new master carries him "to

Middleton with a drove of Horses," then sells him "to a Dutch gentleman, whose Name [Arthur has] since forgot" (Arthur 2). Arthur does not stay even one day with this new master before he escapes again, so readers may excuse this memory lapse.

Arthur's multiple escapes from bondage repeatedly remove him from the invisibility of slavery and out toward a world of women where he adorns himself in newly stolen clothing and performs his manhood as he repeats his earlier, inappropriate, awkward, and consequential "offer of indecencies." Insofar as he searches for women's companionship and intimacy, Arthur usually offers lewd advances instead. Arthur escapes and searches for the same bodily gratifications every time: he looks for his "Squaw" companion—or else, *she seeks him*—or he and "some Negroes" attend "husking" parties, where colonial men and women perform what one critic from the era has called "vile lewdness" and "indecent frolics" (Dow 18).

The women he desires rarely turn him away. Arthur describes an occasion when "some Negroes" introduced him to a woman after a husking party: "On the same Night, [they] introduced me to a white Woman. . . . And as our Behavior was such, as we have both Reason to be ashamed of, I shall for her sake pass it over in Silence" (Arthur 2). Up to this point in his text, Arthur has shown no "shame" about his own criminal behavior, or the "Indecencies" he has offered to a woman in the past. Yet, "for her sake," he deliberately chooses to omit the details of his "Behavior" with a "white Woman." Repeated overnight visits to his "Squaw," where he freely indulges his masculine body's sexual needs, have no accompanying "shame"— neither for his behavior, nor for the Indian woman's sake. Arthur even describes his experiences "drinking and whoring with the Squaws" (Arthur 3); he offers no commentary on being ashamed of participating. Importantly, Arthur's shame occurs only when he performs his masculine identity by indulging his body's sexual desires with the body of a married white woman. Clearly his shame may be understood as a posture of obeisance before the unseen presence of a more powerful masculinity, whose identity Arthur reveals in the sentence that follows: "On the next Day I went to Boston, [and] was pursued by her Husband" (Arthur 2). Arthur narrates an incident where his masculine, heterosexual agency cowers in shame before a husband, and he must withdraw behind the veil of decency. However, Arthur quickly recovers his urgent search for women to gratify his body's needs because within twenty-four hours after he evades the husband, Arthur attends yet another husking party.

The aforementioned husband has not given up his pursuit, however, so Arthur must keep running. And since he has "a natural Aversion to walking," he steals "a Horse, Saddle, and Bridle and proceed[s] to Easton" to visit his parents (Arthur 3). Arthur's sardonic "aversion to walking" indicates an ironic reversal of the social order and rejection of his class status: he may be of the lowest class, but he certainly does not view himself so low that he will escape on foot when a horse appears within his grasp. On his stolen horse, Arthur "visits [his] parents," who advise him to return to his master. Arthur promises them that he will; however, he reassures his reader that he made that promise "without either Thoughts or Inclination" (Arthur 3) of fulfilling it. Instead, he returns to "the Squaws [and] spent [his] time in a manner which may be easily guessed" (Arthur 3).

In his return to the "Squaw" and her Indian community, Arthur finds a safe haven where he "tarrie[s] for six weeks" without detection or harassment in the "praying town" of "Southsea, an Indian village in Sandwich" (Arthur 3). The Indian praying towns, which colonial religious authorities formed in order to contain multiple bands of Massachusetts Natives after they had been decimated by war and disease, function as safe havens for Arthur throughout his fugitive escapes and wanderings. His relationship with the "Squaw" and the welcome he finds within the Native communities reveal the close kinship of African Americans with Native peoples during the colonial era, for both ethnic groups experienced the tragedies and hardships of prejudice and discrimination. "Indians had no place in colonial society," according to Julius H. Rubin (83). By the mid-eighteenth century, the Native populations of Massachusetts "once powerful and numerous . . . no longer existed as autonomous bands who occupied extensive homelands" (Rubin 83) after their mass conversion to Christianity and containment within the praying towns, like those where Arthur often finds shelter, food, and sex.

Arthur's relationship with these Indian communities and his apparent affection for his "Squaw" should not be read as unusual given the context of colonial Massachusetts, however. The Native population's outcast status as racial others, combined with declining numbers of marriageable Native men, who left to pursue seafaring and transient labor, and who suffered frightful mortality rates as English allies in colonial wars, resulted in the growing intermarriage of Native women with African American men (Rubin 83).

It is after this particular six-week visit to the "Squaw" that Arthur finds himself "almost naked" for reasons that he does not explain. Perhaps his "Time in drinking and fornicating" has resulted in a critical memory lapse, and he forgets where he left his clothing. In any event, Arthur finds himself without any clothing at all. In light of his previously obsessive concern regarding the procurement of clothing, his sudden nakedness brings about an extreme crisis of personal dignity and identity. As Kate Soper describes it, "human dignity and autonomy are intimately bound up with the wearing of clothes. . . . To take away a person's clothing is to snatch away the clutched straw of human dignity" (21). The "straw of human dignity" that Soper understands as clothing becomes far more than a mere "straw" for Arthur's defiant manhood. Clothing, according to his narrative, creates for him the outward sign of a humanity that repeated arrests and slavery seek to erase.

Arthur emerges from the Indian village without the necessary outward signs of identity, wearing only the skin that colonial Massachusetts designates as the flesh of a slave. So he immediately performs his perfected expertise of theft and begins his new wardrobe with a trip to the nearby town of Falmouth, where he enters a "Shoemaker's Shop and from thence [he] stole a pair of Shoes" (Arthur 3). This commentary on theft functions as a single instance in which he specifically mentions his theft

"A Dying Man"

as a matter of absolute necessity. He does not, however, steal shoes from the Indian village. Arthur reserves his crimes for the white people of Massachusetts, from whom he steals clothing with which to adorn his body and enable him to perform a manhood that becomes realized through intimate relations with women.

Arthur's persistent search for heterosexual relations links him in perhaps the only way with those heterosexual white men who consistently pursue him. Historians read the correspondence between seventeenth- and eighteenth-century slave holders to find that enslaved men often requested women for themselves, and "white slaveholders recognized a common manhood [that is] rooted in their [slaves'] 'need'" for women (Brown 180). Despite the daily suffering of slavery, enslaved men sought sexual relationships that might affirm their essential humanity (Brown 180). In Arthur's search for intimacy, he repeatedly finds the same "Squaw," and on one occasion he experiences an unmentionable night with a "White woman." However, Arthur's narrative provides no mention of a free or enslaved black woman as desirable.

Certainly relations with an enslaved black woman would involve fewer risks since, for both enslaved and free black men, sex with white women was mostly a perilous enterprise (Nagel 109). Yet Arthur's desires are as fugitive and lawless as the behavior that they produce. Like other fugitive formerly enslaved men of his time, as seen in runaway slave advertisements, stolen garments are part of Arthur's renegade behavior that becomes for him a gesture of "sartorial self-assertion, . . . a bold refutation of the drab garb that was an Atlantic slave's allotment" (Brown 181). Moreover, the political and historical contexts for Arthur's inordinate concern about his clothing, his "social skin," occurs during a critical moment in colonial society's *political deployment* of clothing and fabric in its resistance against British rule.

In the years preceding the American Revolution, fabric and clothing manufacture were highly politicized elements of colonial life. At the same time that Arthur was repeatedly stealing clothing—"and some Callicoe" fabric—from Boston-area tailors and merchants, colonial citizens were strategically using local clothing manufacture and "homespun" domestic fabric as a means to resist taxation and dependence on imported fabric and clothing. Therefore, the turn toward locally made clothing— spun from locally harvested raw materials—registered their own independent American identity.

Taking their cue from a homegrown, Puritan ethos of simplicity and self-dependence, mid-eighteenth-century colonial patriots publicly urged colonists to resist their recently unabated imitation of British elegance in fashion and the increasing taxes that were levied by the Crown on those sumptuary trappings. Outspoken ideologues like Benjamin Franklin criticized luxurious fashion created with imported and heavily taxed fabrics (such as the imported and desirable "Callicoe" Arthur mentions in his narrative) and encouraged the embrace of "homespun," coarse clothing, and more simplified dress.[8]

When Arthur raids colonial merchants to adorn himself with stolen, ready-made clothing, he insinuates himself into a political movement against the British

Empire's influence and taxation. Since Arthur does not *pay for* the clothing, his actions undermine the nascent and emerging relationship between capitalism, domestic manufacturing, British taxation, and colonial industrialization. Politically significant, the clothing he steals (and his refusal to pay for it) undermines both the required deployment of capital in exchange for goods and—possibly, more important—the colonial patriot's emphasis on homemade clothing as a political message of resistance.

Mid-eighteenth-century commentators like Franklin urged patriotic colonists to dress in unrefined and locally produced clothing as a way to renounce British fashion, arrogance, and taxation. The wearing of coarse, local fabrics and simplified dress was a way to promote investment in localized, semi-industrialized reproduction (Zakim 11). Whereas clothing emerged as a strategy for political resistance, Arthur's theft of clothing served a similar function: he steals and wears illicit clothing as an act of resistance to the colonial culture that wishes to enslave him. In this way, Arthur's clothing may be understood as important to his sense of liberty against the tyranny of slavery as the colonists' emphasis on homespun was in relation to their resistance against the tyranny of the British Crown.

In order to contextualize further the importance of clothing for Arthur, Monica L. Miller's analysis of the colonial "black dandy" reveals how this character represents the intersections of race, slavery, and sartorial deportment in colonial America. According to Miller, dress and fashion help to shape, on practical and symbolic levels, a colonial slave's sense of individuality and liberty (5). Interestingly, Arthur's ironic wit and obsessive sartorial concerns as well as his outrageous behavior and illicit desires all point to "the dandy's signature method: a pointed redeployment of clothing, gesture, and wit" (Miller 5). Here Arthur symbolizes the colonial Massachusetts "black dandy," a figure who "embodies the construction and deconstruction of . . . identity relative to negotiations of race, sexuality, and class" (5). Furthermore, Miller argues that the dandies of Western culture are "best known not only as snappy dressers" but "also [as] beings whose self-presentation identifies them as outrageous. . . . Dandyism functions as a symptom of changing social, political, cultural, and economic conditions [which are] descriptive of radical changes in social, economic, and political hierarchies that result in new expressions" (8). In the instance of black dandyism during the era of colonial slavery, however, Miller finds that "dandyism becomes above all a lesson in interrogating identity (of the self, race, nation) and analyzing representations of identity. . . . Black dandyism becomes a strategy of survival and transcendence" (8).

European and (white) colonial dandies of the eighteenth century distinguish themselves as flamboyant characters through highly stylized and flamboyant dress, notable exploits, and often androgynous deportment that manifest an unmistakable element of style and charisma when the privileges of wealth and social status might be absent (Miller 9). The European and colonial dandy, Miller concludes, "is a kind of embodied, animated sign system that deconstructs given and normative categories of identity (elite, white, masculine, heterosexual, patriotic) and re-performs them in a manner more in keeping with his often avant garde visions of society and self" (10). Black dandies—especially the dandified enslaved black man—appear in the runaway slave ads that describe the extravagant clothing, outrageous conduct, and gender-ambiguous behavior of runaway slaves.[9]

Scholars, however, should understand the deportment of the black dandy as more complicated than a "re-performance" of European dress and style. The *performances* of flamboyant sartorial style within the equally performative elements of racialization determine that Arthur, as a colonial black dandy, "exploits the 'ambivalence' inherent in [his] performance, exposing race as a 'device' of cultural resistance" (Miller 15). For the black dandy, the stolen costumed performance of manhood serves as a "weapon of the weak," an "everyday resistance" to power, oppression, racism, and the dehumanization of slavery during the colonial era (Miller 15).

In order to perform a dandified identity—with its required fashionable dress— and slip outside the raiment of bondage, he will necessarily utilize the dandy's characteristic "mimicry," which will, for the black dandy, produce a "slippage between repetition and difference" that will become for him the location and accrual of power in colonial Massachusetts. Arthur mimics an illicit style that does not belong to his enslaved station, but in the site of slippage, or "the space between the body and its materiality," he will access and apprehend the cultural meanings of colonial manhood (Miller 14). The performance of black dandyism by a fugitive enslaved man, however, has serious consequences, since "black dandyism has a tortured relationship to consumption in that the procurement of clothing [and] accessories that enable the performance comes literally at a high cost" (Miller 17).[10] The "high cost" of Arthur's dandyism does not include the cost of clothing or accessories since he steals them; rather, the cost, in Arthur's case, is paid by his life.

Arthur's criminal appropriation of clothing parallels the actions of other enslaved men during the colonial period in America because slaves were routinely responsible for making or buying their own clothes. Additionally, those who desired more than the poorest fabrics (purchased with what little money they could earn away from forced labor for masters and mistresses) would often steal them. Advertisements for runaway slaves record multiple instances of clothing theft and often identify the runaway by his or her love for fashion. The enslaved peoples of the colonial era stole clothing not only because it was relatively easy (and very portable) but also because clothing allowed them to move more easily about as free persons within the community; clothing gave enslaved people a sense of freedom for their own self-expression to "display the difference between purported essence, self-worth, and aspiration" (Miller 92).

Arthur steals himself, and he steals clothing that will express his own idea of manhood—the outlaw man whose subject position stands in direct opposition to institutions that legislate and mandate his invisibility. In addition to clothing, criminal behavior, and illicit sexual experiences, Arthur steals for himself the subject position of a *man*, and not a "chattel." Accordingly, he further performs the subject position of colonial man in his use of both physical violence and resistant language directed against those who would see him as otherwise.

Arthur's violent performance occurs after he proposes lewd "Indecencies" to a white woman, and "Mr. Williams, Esq. and Mr. Smith" apprehend him and commit him to jail. The next day, Arthur is "tried before the same Mr. Williams, and whip'd thirty-nine Stripes *for abusing him, uttering three profane Oaths, and threatening to fire Mr. Smith's House*" (Arthur 2; emphasis added). In colonial America, individuals understood "profane Oaths" as likely very serious—if not damning—behavior and fire as the worst of all disasters that could befall a person's home. Arthur's threat to "fire Mr. Smith's house," therefore, likely horrified everyone within earshot.

Four years before Arthur's arrest and enraged threats, and after Boston had already suffered three days of small fires, the city experienced "its worst conflagration of the entire colonial period," which consumed a large part of the city's central section: 174 houses and tenements (roughly 10 percent of all the city's dwellings) and 175 warehouses, shops, and other commercial buildings had burned to the ground (Archer, Loc. 337). The following year, Faneuil Hall, the site of the town meeting, disappeared in flames; then Harvard Hall, which contained the college's library, telescopes, and other "valuable treasures," caught fire and was destroyed (Archer, Loc. 337). Given this important historical context, Arthur rages against his captors' abuse in the strongest terms; he uses language and issues threats that ensure their immediate fear. His narrative describes his recent visits to Boston, so he certainly understands how recently traumatized the entire region has become due to the tragic loss of property—but no lives—that fire has caused in the nearby city of Boston (Archer, Loc. 337). Arthur deploys the weapons he has at hand—serious threats—which secure both severe punishment and his own visibility as a man.

Arthur further performs his full measure of manhood in an altercation with a would-be captor, whom he meets with physical violence. The "injured husband" of the white woman with whom Arthur experienced a night of "Behavior . . . to be ashamed of" pursues Arthur all the way from Waltham to Boston (a distance of about ten miles), where the two "came to Blows, and, coming off Conqueror, [he left] for Cambridge" (Arthur 2). Arthur's violent resistance to capture leaves him the victor who walks away unscathed to resume his freedom somewhere else, where more troubles—and opportunities to perform his manhood—wait for him. Yet with the visibility of his fugitive body—against the invisibility of a slave—comes the potential of violent abuse of his body with repeated lashes, when he is not a "Conqueror" at all. But Arthur manages to evade this possible subjection. As my recounting of his narrative reveals above, white men beat Arthur multiple times; however, he does not always receive his punishment. For instance, when he is sentenced to "receive fifteen Stripes" for unmentioned crimes later in his text, his master comes to his aid. Arthur never receives the whipping white people wish to inflict on him; rather, as he states, his "Master was so good natur'd, or rather silly, as to pay the [fine] and let

[him] go with impunity" (Arthur 2). His body momentarily escapes a criminal's/slave's suffering. After his penultimate arrest, when he is sentenced to "receiving twenty Stripes," he again escapes punishment. He explains, "This time I again got off unpunished because I was unwell" (Arthur 3). In this instance, Arthur's master arrives *yet again* to retrieve him and take him back home. Arthur escapes the ontological death of slavery, he escapes from jail, and he further evades corporal punishment twice. With the constantly reassuring touchstone of an Indian woman's companionship and strategic assistance, Arthur finally ends his escapades with a fatal error in judgment at the home of a local widow.

After his ill health enables him to avoid a beating, his master takes him home, where he spends "not three Weeks" before "another Negro of [his] Master's told [him] that the young Squaw, so often mentioned, was desirous of seeing [him]," so Arthur "stole some Rum from [his] Master, got pretty handsomely drunk, took one of his Horses, and made the best of [his] way to her usual Place of Abode" (Arthur 3). In his drunken stupor, he finds the "Squaw" not home. Arthur explains, "The Devil put it into my Head to pay a Visit to the Widow Deborah Metcalfe, whom I, in a most inhumane manner, ravished: The Particulars of which are so notorious, that it is needless for me here to relate them" (Arthur 3).

Arthur gives no details of this crime; however, the details about what happens afterward are so unusual that historians and literary scholars have mentioned them in multiple lines of inquiry. As Arthur tells it, the widow did not want Arthur arrested, since it was certain he would suffer what would likely be the fatal consequences of his crime. The following day, "the unhappy Woman came and acquainted [Arthur's] Master" of the crime. His master immediately tied Arthur, "to prevent [him] running away," and then "told her (if she was desirous of prosecuting [Arthur]) to get a Warrant as soon as possible" (Arthur 3). Mrs. Deborah Metcalfe then chooses a curious course of action. Arthur says she was "unwilling to have [him] hanged," so she "proposed taking the Matter up for a Proper Consideration, provided [his] Master would send [him] out of the Country; to which he agreed" (Arthur 3). One historian has characterized Metcalfe's unusual decision as "one of the few known cases where a white victim purposefully avoided prosecution of a black rapist" (Block 191). Certainly there were critically important "Considerations" about which Mrs. Metcalfe would need to ruminate when she imagined how she would testify that she was sexually assaulted by "a Negro" in colonial Massachusetts.

Mrs. Metcalfe would make her charge of rape within the social and legal contexts of colonial America, whose inherited language from British common law provided the basic definition of rape. The boundaries between rape and consensual sexual relations were blurred. Seventeenth-century colonial law followed British common law regarding the definition of rape as "*unlawful and carnal Knowledge of a Woman by Force or against her Will*" (qtd. in Block 29). Historians of colonial law explain that the difference between "force" and "against her will" were very distinct, and more importantly, "force alone did not mean rape; force could be an acceptable part of a sexual encounter, and a woman's will had to stand up to some force" (Block 29).

As Mrs. Metcalfe took time to ruminate about how—or whether—she would file "a Warrant" to have Arthur arrested for the rape he had committed, she probably considered her vulnerable social status as a widow (i.e., one whose virtue was unprotected by a husband) and the double standard that held women culpable for sexual immorality.[11] Since there was apparently no witness to the sexual attack, Mrs. Metcalfe would likely be unable to *prove* that the attack was an act of force and violence, in which case the eighteenth-century courts were more likely to dismiss the case; this outcome would have a decidedly deleterious effect on her moral standing in the community. Even if a colonial woman could prove that sexual intercourse did occur, a judge or jury could conclude that the intercourse had *not been* forced. The perpetrator would be exonerated, whereupon the surrounding community would conclude that she must have consented, and the woman would be judged sexually immoral (Block 38). Whether she ever filed a warrant for his arrest remains unclear: Mrs. Metcalfe informed his master, and Arthur immediately surrendered to his fate. Although Arthur's life narrative confesses that he had "ravished" Mrs. Metcalfe, the final judgment regarding the severity of his attack occurs in the subtitle of the narrative, which describes the criminal act as a "RAPE upon the body of Mrs. Deborah Metcalfe," which underscores the reason for his execution.

Arthur's repeated thefts, incarcerations, and escapes and his drunkenness and "lewd fornications" do not bring about the death sentence. If he were a white man, even the charge of rape would not necessarily mean he should die. The litany of criminal acts that Arthur's testimony recounts—had they been the acts of a white man—would be understood as the behavior of one who is not in control of *his passions*. Sharon Block explains that "the publications and writings on rapists in the Revolutionary era repeatedly linked uncontrolled passions to rape, . . . and [white] men who petitioned the court for leniency against a charge of rape often explained that rape occurred when the passions of man are let loose" (36). In colonial America, uncontrolled "passions" could be used to exonerate a rapist, since eighteenth-century white petitioners "all used passions to illustrate the naturalness of rape" (Block 36). Perhaps Mrs. Metcalfe hesitated in submitting a warrant for Arthur's arrest because she considered the possibility of such a claim in public court: if Arthur could, like a white man, successfully defend his crime as one of "uncontrolled passion," then Metcalfe's virtue would be tarnished for the rest of her life.

Whatever defense Arthur offered against his accusers—and it is not clear if Mrs. Metcalfe ever charged Arthur with rape in a court of law—his text states that he is sentenced to die for this specific crime. Arthur's death sentence for the criminal act of rape—without any petition for "leniency" pursuant to the claim of "uncontrolled passions"—aligns with historical data that indicate black men were more frequently convicted of rape than of other crimes; moreover, between the years

1700 and 1776 in the American colonies, "nearly two thirds of all sexual assaults prosecuted against black men ended with a death sentence" (Block 193).

But it would be months after the crime before white authorities actually arrest Arthur. In the meantime, his master agrees to Mrs. Metcalfe's request to save Arthur by sending him out of the country, so he plans a trip to Albany, where he will secure the means for the accused's international travel. Arthur never makes the trip because he escapes from his master and steals the horse of the man who holds a warrant for his arrest on other charges (Arthur 3). Arthur immediately steals more objects of bodily needs and deportment: "Flour, a Comb, and a Razor," a goose, a kettle to boil it in, "Cyder Brandy," another pair of shoes; then in another town he steals some "Bread, Meat," and more rum (Arthur 3). In his final criminal act, Arthur and two escapee accomplices ("the celebrated FRASIER, and a young lad, who was confined for stealing") each steal "a Shirt, and one pair of stockings . . . some butter . . . some Chocolate and Rum [and] a Brass Kettle" (Arthur 3). Arthur's narrative tells about one lavishly excessive, illicit, criminal indulgence after another: ready-made clothing, sex with Indian women and another man's wife, alcohol intoxication, wild "husking" parties with loose women, and finally, consumption of butter and chocolate.

After his friends abandon him, Arthur enters an establishment where his notoriety and criminal infamy precede him: they "knew" him on sight. They "immediately secured" him and brought him to jail, where, "on the 17th of September following, [he] was tried and found guilty" (Arthur 3). After "a Year's consideration," on "the 24th of Sept. last," white authorities sentence Arthur "to be hanged," which he "must confess is but too just a Reward" (Arthur 3) for years of lawlessness, during which he lived with more unrestricted personal freedom and luxury than most white colonists in eighteenth-century America.

In order to understand fully the significance of Arthur's story, we must return to claims that readers should interpret Arthur's story as one about a black outlaw who is "beyond all control," whose actions therefore "set the foundation for an unfortunate stereotype," and whose execution will "dramatize a return to the dominant order" (Williams, "'Gratification'" 200). Certainly no scholar can dismiss the claim that Arthur's "notorious" criminal exploits created a local crisis in the "dominant order" of Boston in the mid-eighteenth century. Certainly, white authorities treat Arthur, as the slave of a local lawyer, Richard Godfrey, Esq., with an unusual degree of legislative forgiveness when his master appears repeatedly to save his life and protect him from punishments. Yet, apparently, Arthur positions himself in ways that repeated arrests and brutal punishments inflicted on his body (he is whipped on no less than three different occasions) become the price he consistently pays in order to move freely in search of experiences that successfully enforce upon others his own self-perception as a *man*. And historical texts explain that the local authorities have more serious political and social problems with which to concern themselves since the years during which Arthur's crime spree occurs; these critical years correspond with the fate of the British colonists in their nascent but rising revolt against the Crown of England.

In his outlaw behavior, Arthur attracts to his body the fatal attention of those colonial enforcers of the social order, whose final execution will deploy the rope of extermination in order to strangle the youthful, exuberant life from a *man* whose execution proves he cannot be considered chattel; rather, he ends his life as a criminal *person*. However, does Arthur's execution merely "dramatize a return to the dominant order" of eighteenth-century Massachusetts (Williams, "'Gratification'" 200)? In his urgent and repeated insistence on visibility and on the fact of his final confession and execution as a person, this chapter concludes that the exploits of this "Negro man," who was executed in 1768, affected the "social order" of eighteenth-century Massachusetts.

Arthur does *not die* a slave; he does not die a "Negro," either. In the discursive, historical moment of his execution, Arthur's death does not perform the early modern, nascent racism where "the death of the [racialized] other is something that will make life in general healthier" (Lemke, Casper, and Moore 42). On the contrary, Arthur's death signals a final exclamation mark on the outlaw body of a *man* whose experiences emphatically—if also briefly—outline the limits and presage the *weaknesses* of a fragile social order in the moments before that order would make concrete a distinction between those who could live and those whose lives are necessarily forfeited. Arthur's dandyism performed an outrageously liberated, illicit, and defiant dance of self-empowered manhood. The Boston Massacre—another outrageous performance whose actors were revolutionary, transgressive colonists—occurred shortly thereafter, fewer than forty-five miles away on the city's streets.[12]

Arthur concludes his confessional narrative with a clear statement about the text's purpose in retelling his crimes. As the narrator says, "I earnestly desire that this Recital of my Crimes, and the ignominious Death to which my notorious Wickedness has bro't me, may prove a Warning to all Persons who shall become acquainted therewith" (Arthur 3). Similar to the condemned confessions that form the genre of gallows confessional narratives, the condemned criminal "consecrates his own punishments by proclaiming the blackness of his crimes" through the production of a catalog of his misdeeds as a confession (Foucault 66).

Although Foucault concludes that the broadside publication of condemned confessions enabled "the convicted criminal [to] become after his death a sort of saint," where the "criminal has been almost entirely transformed into a positive hero" (67), this claim does not necessarily describe the case of Arthur. Although he successfully evades a final return to slavery and escapes numerous times from the captivity of the jail to find comfort in the homes and beds of Indian women who help him, these events do not save him from the final attempted racialization of his body on the scaffold.

In the scaffold sermon that accompanies Arthur's execution, the minister Thaddeus Maccarty, "Pastor of the Church in Worcester," affirms that his audience and Arthur share an immortal soul when he concludes, "What a sad and sorrowful spectacle have we before us! One of our fellow-creatures, whose soul is as precious as ours, to be made an example of public justice this day!" (25). However, the title of the sermon undermines any common "humanity" between Arthur and the onlookers who hear the sermon just before his execution, since they are all reminded that the condemned is a "Negro of about 21 Years old." Arthur's story denies that "Negro"—slave, captive site of sovereign power manifest in the subjection and control of a racialized (inferior) body—names the body, which stands upon the scaffold that autumn day in the city of Worcester, Massachusetts.

The last page of the published sermon includes Arthur's formal speech that "was deliver'd at the Place of Execution, in the Name and at the Desire of the Criminal," which begins, "I, *Arthur*" and offers a last glimpse of how the condemned criminal sees himself. Accordingly, Arthur sees himself as one who has "provoked God—fallen into the hands of civil justice, and must now die before the time" (qtd. in Maccarty 28). In Arthur's final speech, he "hopes for mercy from God" and reminds his audience that the whirlwind escapades of the past seven years should be understood not as those of "a Negro" but rather as the vivified, raucously defiant outlaw acts of "a dying *man*" (qtd. in Maccarty 28; emphasis added).

NOTES

1. The American literary genre known as "slave narratives" is a body of autobiographical, first-person narratives that critics Charles T. Davis and Henry Louis Gates Jr. define as those related or written by ex-slaves before 1865 (xii). The most important narratives are included in a collection edited by William L. Andrews and Gates.

2. All idiosyncrasies of spelling, capitalization, punctuation, and phrasing of the original 1768 manuscript, "Arthur," are reprinted in the direct quotes found in this chapter.

3. See the work of Ronald A. Bosco, Daniel A. Cohen, and the anthology of criminal narratives edited by Daniel E. Williams, *Pillars of Salt: An Anthology of Early American Criminal Narratives*.

4. DeLombard cites multiple critics of African American literature, who all agree that the eighteenth-century autobiographical confession of a condemned black criminal functions as an "obvious literary ancestor to the slave narrative [that] served primarily to throw into relief its progeny's 'rhetorical achievements'" (14). For more about the relationship between slaves' criminal confessions and slave narratives, see William L. Andrews (*To Tell*) and Frances Smith Foster.

5. African American literary scholars have not offered a sustained analysis or interpretation of Arthur's *Life, and Dying Speech*. Foster, Andrews (*To Tell* 41), and Block, in her study *Rape and Sexual Power*, mention the life narrative in their respective texts.

6. In regard to the distinction between "autobiography" and "biography," this chapter uses "life writing" and "life narrative" to prioritize the function of first-person memory. Since the incidents and memories are relayed in the first person and attributed to Arthur himself, we may conclude that the narrative is Arthur's life writing, irrespective of whoever inscribed

and published the dictated narrative. As Sidonie Smith and Julia Watson explain, a "biographer almost invariably writes about the object of his or her study in the third person, while the life narrator usually employs the first person. . . . For life narrators, personal memories are the primary archival source" (7).

7. On the formation of early American masculinities, consult the work of Thomas A. Foster, Mark E. Kann, and John G. McCurdy.

8. Franklin's 1722 essay "Pride of Apparel," for instance, bemoaned the imitation of luxurious fabrics and British style, which he believed had "overtaken the colonies . . . ever since [the colonists] parted with [their] Homespun Cloaths for Fourteen Penny Stuffs" (qtd. in Zakim 17). Franklin's political exhortation veils a more class-conscious judgment that fashionable clothing blurred the lines of social distinction where "the natural hierarchy was obfuscated by people dressing beyond their rank" (Zakim 17).

9. On runaway slave advertisements and the clothing of the enslaved, see Helen Bradley Foster's *"New Raiments of Self"* (15–16).

10. In her analysis of the "mimicry" that attends black dandyism, Miller cites Harry J. Elam Jr.'s essay "The Black Performer and the Performance of Blackness: *The Escape, or, A Leap to Freedom* by William Wells Brown and *No Place to Be Somebody* by Charles Gordone." Miller agrees with Elam's earlier essay "The Device of Race," which understands blackness as "always already 'performed,' [since] blackness [is] a dialectic between performer and audience. . . . Black people have had to be black for white or European audiences since their designation as black or African [or, Arthur's case, 'Negro'] replaced a sense of themselves as being from specific geographic regions and ethnic groups. . . . Black and blackness are themselves signs of diaspora, of a cosmopolitanism that African subjects did not choose but from which they necessarily reimagined themselves" (Elam, "Device" 4).

11. For further historical work on women's sexuality and the changing roles of women in colonial America, see also Bloch.

12. Whether the pre–Revolutionary War years in America—with the repeated conflicts, acts of vandalism, and resistance against the occupying forces of Great Britain—had any influence on (or, in fact, inspired) Arthur's actions, it is not possible to know. Certainly the officers of the court, who repeatedly imprisoned him, sentenced him to violent punishments, released him, then caught and imprisoned him again, were aware of—if not distracted by—the unfolding violence and other destabilizing events (e.g., the Stamp Act) in the area around Boston.

In the months before Arthur's execution in October—while he languished in the Worcester jail and contemplated whether his pleas for clemency would save his life—Boston, a city only forty miles away, erupted in mob violence: angry colonists assaulted British customs officials, dragged them through the streets, and later threw rocks and broke out the windows of their homes (McNeese and Jensen 33). By October 1—nine days before Arthur's execution—the Crown answered their violence with a show of force when roughly twelve hundred British officers and soldiers shocked the residents as they disembarked from the six ships of war, two armed schooners, and at least six other naval vessels that had sat menacing the harbor and its colonial residents since the ships' arrival earlier in September (Archer, Loc. 129). With drums beating, fifes playing, and flags streaming, they marched slowly through downtown Boston's streets to begin their hostile occupation of the colonies, which would not end until the first shots were fired to begin the American Revolution (Archer). It is, therefore, safe to maintain that the colonists of eastern Massachusetts would have likely *understood* Arthur—his desperate flight from forced servitude, evasion of authority, and retaliatory language—in ways unique to the region of Boston and its singular role in the American Revolutionary War's fight for freedom, which would follow soon after his death.

WORKS CITED

Andrews, William L. *To Tell a Free Story: The First Century of Afro-American Autobiography, 1760–1865*. Champaign: U of Illinois P, 1988.

Andrews, William L., and Henry Louis Gates Jr., eds. *Slave Narratives*. New York: Library of America, 2000.

Archer, Richard. *As If an Enemy's Country: The British Occupation of Boston and the Origins of the American Revolution*. New York: Oxford UP, 2010.

Arthur. *The Life, and Dying Speech of Arthur, a Negro Man; Who Was Executed at Worcester, October 20, 1768. For a Rape Committed on the Body of One Deborah Metcalfe*. Electronic ed. Broadside, 1 p. Boston [s.n.], 1768. *Documenting the American South*. 13 Jan. 2004.

Bloch, Ruth. "Changing Conceptions of Sexuality and Romance in Eighteenth-Century America." *William and Mary Quarterly* 60.1 (2003): 13–42.

Block, Sharon. *Rape and Sexual Power in Early America*. Chapel Hill: U of North Carolina P, 2006.

Bosco, Ronald A. "Early American Gallows Literature: An Annotated Checklist." *Resources for American Literary Study* 8 (1978): 81–107.

Brown, Kathleen. "'Strength of the Lion . . . Arms like Polished Iron': Embodying Black Masculinity in an Age of Slavery and Propertied Manhood." *New Men: Manliness in Early America*. Ed. Thomas A. Foster. New York: New York UP, 2011. 172–94.

Cohen, Daniel A. *Pillars of Salt, Monuments of Grace: New England Crime Literature and the Origins of American Popular Culture, 1674–1860*. New York: Oxford UP, 1993.

Davis, Charles T., and Henry Louis Gates Jr., eds. *The Slave's Narrative*. New York: Oxford UP, 1991.

Crèvecoeur, J. Hector St. John de. *Letters from an American Farmer and Sketches of Eighteenth-Century America*. Ed. Albert E. Stone. New York: Penguin, 1981.

DeLombard, Jeannine Marie. *In the Shadow of the Gallows: Race, Crime, and American Civic Identity*. Philadelphia: U of Pennsylvania P, 2012.

Dow, George Francis. *Everyday Life in the Massachusetts Bay Colony*. 1675. Project Gutenberg.

Elam, Harry J., Jr. "The Black Performer and the Performance of Blackness: *The Escape, or, A Leap to Freedom* by William Wells Brown and *No Place to Be Somebody* by Charles Gordone." *African American Performance and Theater History: A Critical Reader*. Ed. Harry J. Elam Jr. and David Krasner. New York: Oxford UP, 2001. 288–306.

———. "The Device of Race: An Introduction." *African American Performance and Theater History: A Critical Reader*. Ed. Harry J. Elam Jr. and David Krasner. New York: Oxford UP, 2001. 3–16.

Foster, Frances Smith. *Witnessing Slavery: The Development of Ante-Bellum Slave Narratives*. Westport, CT: Greenwood Press, 1979.

Foster, Helen Bradley. *"New Raiments of Self": African American Clothing in the Antebellum South*. Oxford: Bloomsbury Academic Press, 1997.

Foster, Thomas A. *Sex and the Eighteenth-Century Man: Massachusetts and the History of Sexuality in America*. Boston: Beacon Press, 2006.

Foucault, Michel. *Discipline and Punish: The Birth of the Prison*. Trans. Alan Sheridan. New York: Vintage, 1995.

Kann, Mark E. *A Republic of Men: The American Founding Fathers, Gendered, Language, and Patriarchal Politics*. New York: New York UP, 1998.

Lemke, Thomas, Monica J. Casper, and Lisa Jean Moore. *Biopolitics: An Advanced Introduction*. New York: New York UP, 2011.

Loren, Diana DiPaolo. *Archaeology of Clothing and Bodily Adornment in Colonial America*. Gainesville: UP of Florida, 2010.

Maccarty, Thaddeus. *Sermon Preached at Worcester, October the Twentieth, 1768. Being the Day of the Execution of ARTHUR, A Negro of about 21 Years Old, for a RAPE*. Boston: Printed and sold by Kneeland and Adams, 1768.

McCurdy, John G. *Citizen Bachelors: Manhood and the Creation of the United States*. Ithaca, NY: Cornell UP, 2009.

McNeese, Tim, and Richard Jensen. *Revolutionary America: 1764-1789*. New York: Chelsea House, 2010.

Miller, Monica L. *Slaves to Fashion: Black Dandyism and the Styling of Black Diasporic Identity*. Durham, NC: Duke UP, 2009.

Monaghan, E. Jennifer. *Learning to Read and Write in Colonial America*. Amherst: U of Massachusetts P, 2005.

Nagel, Joane. *Race, Ethnicity, and Sexuality: Intimate Intersections, Forbidden Frontiers*. New York: Oxford UP, 2003.

Olney, James. "'I Was Born': Slave Narratives, Their Status as Autobiography and as Literature." *The Slave's Narrative*. Ed. Charles T. Davis and Henry Louis Gates Jr. New York: Oxford UP, 1985. 148-74.

Rubin, Julius H. *Tears of Repentance: Christian Indian Identity and Community in Colonial Southern New England*. Lincoln: U of Nebraska P, 2013.

Smith, Sidonie, and Julia Watson. *Reading Autobiography: A Guide for Interpreting Life Narratives*. 2nd ed. Minneapolis: U of Minnesota P, 2010.

Soper, Kate. "Dress Needs: Reflections on the Clothed Body, Selfhood, and Consumption." *Body Dressing*. Ed. Joanne Entwistle and Elizabeth Wilson. Oxford: Bloomsbury Academic Press, 2001. 13-32.

Turner, Terence. "The Social Skin." *Reading the Social Body*. Ed. C. B. Burroughs and J. Ehrenreich. Iowa City: U of Iowa P, 1980. 15-39.

Williams, Daniel E. "'The Gratification of That Corrupt and Lawless Passion': Character Types and Themes in Early New England Rape Narratives." *A Mixed Race: Ethnicity in Early America*. Ed. Frank Shuffleton. New York: Oxford UP, 1993. 194-221.

———, ed. *Pillars of Salt: An Anthology of Early American Criminal Narratives*. Madison, WI: Madison House, 1993.

Zakim, Michael. *Ready-Made Democracy: A History of Men's Dress in the American Republic, 1760-1860*. Chicago: U of Chicago P, 2003.

Early Black Men's Spiritual Autobiography
Marriage and Violence

JOYCELYN K. MOODY

> They (the whites) know well, if we are men. . . . They know, I say, if we are men, and see them treating us in the manner they do, that there can be nothing in our hearts but death alone, for them. . . . When we see them murdering our dear mothers and wives, because we cannot help ourselves[,] . . . they are afraid that we, being men, and not brutes, will retaliate, and woe will be to them.
>
> DAVID WALKER,
> *David Walker's* Appeal to the Coloured Citizens of the World

> Transformative strategies of black liberation linked to a liberatory vision of black manhood and masculinity reflect a critically oppositional view of black men's racial oppression and the power we possess to oppress women precisely because we are men.
>
> GARY L. LEMONS,
> "To Be Black, Male, and 'Feminist': Making Womanist Space for Black Men"

Written by one of the most influential men of nineteenth-century black America, David Walker's 1829 *Appeal to the Coloured Citizens of the World* is best known for its jeremiadic arguments against chattel slavery.[1] This text advocates armed resistance to forced bondage by free(d) and enslaved blacks and eschatologically warns whites that the Christian God they worship will punish them unless they end slavery immediately. The *Appeal* so forcefully calls black men in particular to fight against slavery that it legendarily (if not factually) inspired Denmark Vesey, Gabriel Prosser, and Nat Turner to mayhem, revolt, and murder across the South.[2] Now a canonical text, Walker's *Appeal* was one of the earliest and most powerful African American condemnations of white supremacy in the United States, in large part because the *Appeal* arouses black male homosocial desire by defining black masculinity both as armed force and armed protection of black women and children. Here I use *homosociality* as employed by Eve Kosofsky Sedgwick, who locates it on a continuum of "male friendships, mentorships, entitlement, and rivalry," as the conscious cultivation of "social bonds between persons of the same sex" (1). With its repeated rhetorical question, "Are we MEN?!," Walker's *Appeal* promotes a black masculine collective subjectivity of embodied dominance, separate gender spheres, and Christian heteronormativity. Significantly, the *Appeal* rhetorically equates blackness and maleness from the first words of article I; addressing "My beloved brethren," Walker furiously observes that "all the inhabitants of the earth (except however, the sons of Africa) are called *men*, and of course, are, and ought to be free. But we, (coloured people) and our children are *brutes!!*" (9). The *Appeal* remained popular along the Eastern Seaboard for most of the antebellum era. Not surprisingly, it garnered new attention with the 1970s black power and black arts movements, for its black masculinist values were directly in line with the masculinist nationalism of that period. So Walker's place in the canon of African American heroes has been secure since the institutionalization of black studies.

However, because Walker's galvanizing and pious *Appeal* as manifesto for (black) masculinity theologizes heteronormativity, it warrants scholarly reconsideration. Because of the *Appeal*'s influence on later black men's writings, we should also reread the spiritual autobiographies of nineteenth-century black men who, knowingly or not, endorse Walker's gynophobic Christianized heteronormativity. This chapter examines the intersection of religious devotion, heterosexuality, and embodied discipline portrayed in the life writings of John Jea, William J. Brown, and Civil War veterans interviewed by Fisk University graduate student Andrew Polk Watson.[3] The gender codes of these texts assert that men and women *should* occupy separate social spaces—literally and figuratively speaking—and that men are *naturally* more intelligent than women. Such thinking forms the basis of conventional Western Christianity, and it treats as aberrant and unnatural all "deviations" from its code of normalcy. As Stuart Hall instructs, the "hardness" of a conventional black masculinity can be claimed "only at the expense of the vulnerability of Black women and the feminization of gay Black men. . . . Dominant ethnicities are always underpinned by a particular sexual economy, a particular figured masculinity, a particular class identity" (262). I argue that the black masculinity depicted in the selected spiritual autobiographies posits a phallocentric Christianity at once transgressive and oppressive even as the authors challenge and revise stereotypes of black men as innately violent and brutal.

Black Male Homosocial Conditioning

In attending to a black Christian masculinity imperiled by sexism, I focus on black male converts to Christianity. Among these converts, preachers in particular have consistently set social and political standards for black people. Typically the most educated or charismatic leaders, black preachers often stand in for divine authority.

Black Christians generally believe that those endowed with a divine call to preach Christianity exhibit exceptional wisdom, prudence, compassion, and mercy—characteristics, along with male gender, attributed to the Christian Holy Trinity.[4] Although caricatures of black (male) preachers have populated black vernacular culture since the slavery era, black preachers have traditionally embodied a black *male* civic and religious leadership—one that many black feminist scholars have exposed as sexist and hegemonic.[5] Thus black male preachers have generally authorized conformity to heteronormativity, either to preserve patriarchal power for themselves as a select group or to promote black respectability that would be otherwise threatened by whites' disrespect for black deviance. As Jacqueline Grant observes, "black church precepts imply that (1) either Black women have no place in the enterprise [of black theology], or (2) Black men are capable of speaking for us [Black women]" (422). Grant posits that when black male ministers insist that only men possess the power to "master" professional theology, they establish a false dualism that has rendered black women "invisible in theology" (422, 423). Like white male preachers, black Christian men have advanced a masculinity that upholds a convenient standard they claim emanates from Scripture: women cannot and should not preach.

Following Hazel V. Carby's reminder in *Race Men* that "ideologies of masculinity always exist in a dialectical relation to other ideologies" (2), we can trace a genealogy of pious African American men, the forefathers of such contemporary preachers as Jeremiah Wright and T. D. Jakes. This genealogy would enable a comparison of the conceptualizations and performances of maleness by black Christian men across African American history. The nineteenth-century spiritual autobiographies of John Jea and William J. Brown, two black men of very different backgrounds, also enable analysis of the intersection of military service with Christian piety. Significantly, Jea was jailed for refusing to serve as a soldier, and though Brown was never a soldier himself, he worked zealously with other black men in Rhode Island to secure black men's right to serve in the Union army during the Civil War. Further, Brown extols military service for its expression of national identity and fidelity, patriotism, discipline, self-sacrifice or nation before self, and the like. Significantly, however, *The Life, History, and Unparalleled Sufferings of John Jea, the African Preacher* and *The Life of William J. Brown of Providence, R. I., With Personal Recollections of Incidents in Rhode Island* distinguish between military service and brutal violence; they studiously reject notions of (black) masculinity based on violence in any form, for any reason.[6] Generally, Jea and Brown typify nineteenth-century black men who espouse and pursue hegemonic masculinity but for whom the endorsement of heteronormativity did not yield the shares of (white) patriarchal power they sought.[7] When it came to displays of physical aggression, both Jea and Brown practiced what Christian ethicist Gay L. Byron calls a "hermeneutic of resistance" to heteropatriarchal paradigms (113). However, like virtually all men of their day, the preachers seem never to have questioned a gendered, Scripture-based hierarchy that placed men over women.

I argue here that the spiritual autobiographies by Jea and Brown and selected conversion narratives in Watson's research delineate a continuum of black men's regard for military discipline and Christian ethics to challenge the stereotype of the black brute by reifying male domination over women. Informing my reading is the theology of James S. Tinney, which advances the concept of *mutuality* to replace black Christians' cultivation of respectability.[8] Tinney defines mutuality as sacred praxis, as a form of Christian love that "places emphasis in actions rather than sentiments, and . . . includes the element of reciprocal relations" (74)—in sum, the Gospels' Golden Rule. He also argues that mutuality can both cultivate black collective power and invalidate white patriarchal heteronormativity. Tinney contends that "love or mutuality is possible only between equals. Otherwise, love becomes mere sentimentality or beneficence that causes the powerful to feel good when they do something that pacifies the powerless, who are seen as 'unfortunates'" (74). That is, the achievement of mutuality would transform not only black Christian practices but, more, it would subvert (black) masculinist condescension toward African American women by recognizing the latter as independent and formidable potential allies in the struggle for human and civil rights. Thus, as defined by Tinney, mutuality transcends problematic constructions of American black masculinity that rely on the subordination of black women.

As research by Christopher Looby, Robert Reid-Pharr, Aliyyah Abdur-Rahman, and others has illuminated, within the United States heteronormativity not only collapses sex into race but reads race—specifically blackness—as determinative of sex. More precisely, within heteronormativity, black is a female sign. Unveiling these truths, moreover, exposes white male fear and envy of mythic, hypersexualized African maleness. African American men have subverted white supremacy's stereotypes of black men as alternately Buck (the embodiment of excessive, aberrant sexuality) and Sambo (an emasculated, servile figure). Conversely, black masculinity's own envy of white power is manifested in appropriations of patriarchal dominance that include compulsory heteronormativity, psychosexual sadism, and surveillance of black women's sociopolitical activism.

Slavery scholarship has documented the great brutality with which slave traders handled African bodies. Ironically, that violence exposes the white lie of innate African barbarism promulgated by these same slavers. While the triangular slave trade was still active, Thomas Jefferson's *Notes on the State of Virginia* insisted that Africans were "not of the human family" but instead descendants of "tribes of *Monkeys* or *Orang-Outangs*" (qtd. in Walker 12). Not surprisingly, enslaved blacks engaged in violent self-defense against physical and textual debasement.[9] Walker prophesied that the highest Christian authority would instigate generational violent resistance: "Will he [the Lord] not cause the very children of the oppressed to rise up against them [their oppressors], and oftentimes put them to death?" (6). Physical force, ranging from violence to discipline, forms a central trope in representations of nineteenth-century black masculinity, including, as the 1831 *Confessions of Nat Turner* suggests, in accounts of black (male) Christian conversion.[10] Patriarchy not only authorizes men to commit violence but also makes force and virility essential to manhood; by imitating white patriarchy, then, black men have placed physical power at the center of codes of black masculinity. In his *Appeal*, Walker calls expressly for black male homosocial alliance in masculinist protection of women (as we see in the first epigraph to this chapter [63–64]).

Invoking such "American" phenomena as the Constitution, the Declaration of Independence, and the Revolutionary War, Walker's *Appeal* repeatedly tropes militarism and the "God of armies." Inspiring Walker, Prince Hall had repeatedly petitioned for black men's right to enlist in the Continental Army at Bunker Hill (Wallace, *Constructing* 55). Indeed, black men sought military participation as a means of pursuing civil and human rights for Africans in colonial British America before and after Hall. The Massachusetts Committee of Safety denied every one of Hall's petitions because, as both Maurice O. Wallace and Christopher Looby have cogently argued, white men did not want to pay black men for service, they did not want to believe that black men were capable of feelings of loyalty to the nation, and they did not trust that black men would not use their military weapons against whites to redress slavery.[11] In 1784 the Grand Lodge of England finally granted Hall a charter for Provisional African Lodge No. 1; Hall "served as inaugural master of the African Masonic Lodge No. 459 in Boston" (later renamed the Prince Hall Grand Lodge), as noted by Richard S. Newman (141). Hall's creation of the quasi-religious and ritualistic black Masons illustrates black men's eagerness to challenge whites' claim that blacks had no capacity for either piety or patriotism. During his lifetime, Hall was both a lay Methodist preacher and three times a husband (Newman 141); in other words, Hall's foundational contributions to early black New England community-building were shaped in large part by Christian marriage and leadership, and he drew on black masculinist interpretations of those institutions to campaign for mutual aid and racial justice for African Americans of his day. Such was the legacy he left to Jea and Brown.

John Jea: "I Was Willing to Suffer Any Thing, Rather Than Fight"

The material lives of Jea and Brown were marked by vast differences—of class and caste, education, geography, and so on—but, studied together, perhaps they reveal what we can learn or simply whether we can extrapolate anything about early African American male Christians before and after abolition. To be sure, the themes of physical strength, gender differences, and black heteronormativity aggregate in their respective narratives of Christian ministry, and thus they form ironic complements to each other and ironic antecedents to later black men's spiritual autobiographies. According to *The Life, History, and Unparalleled Sufferings of John Jea, the African Preacher,*

Compiled and Written by Himself, Jea was born around 1773 and spent his childhood enslaved in New York. As an adult at the end of the eighteenth century, Jea traveled throughout the United States, the West Indies, and Europe as an itinerant preacher facing every shade of Christian denomination; Brown served intermittently as a local Baptist preacher among antebellum blacks throughout his adulthood.

Notably, an amanuensis might well have inscribed Jea's narrative, though it deploys what Henry Louis Gates Jr. names "the trope of the talking book" (158).[12] The early sections of the autobiography narrate an account of divinely bestowed literacy: the narrator one day discovers that he can read. He is gifted with a very limited literacy, for it turns out that the New Testament Gospel of John is the only book he can read. Nevertheless, the marvelous gift buttresses his appeal for manumission when he testifies before magistrates, who pronounce him "free from his master, and at liberty to leave him" (33). (This legal decision would have violated colonial New York law, however.) The only indication that he pursues and attains greater literacy is his international ministry, which takes him among Europeans who contest and test his biblical knowledge. That he can meet the challenge suggests he has mastered the Bible since leaving bondage. However, in the concluding pages of *The Life*, the narrator discloses his reliance on an interlocutor: "My dear reader, I would now inform you, that I have stated this in the best manner I am able, for I cannot write, therefore it is not quite so correct as if I had been able to have written it myself; . . . nor would I allow alterations to be made by the person whom I employed to print this Narrative" (95). Self-authored or not, Jea's narrative argues for a black masculinist pursuit of heteronormativity.

The respective narrators of Jea's and Brown's autobiographies deploy strategic violence before conversion to Christianity at around age fifteen—Frederick Douglass's age when he fought Covey for his "manhood" and also the age at which records show most enslaved men physically lashed out against bondage.[13] Notably, Brown (who was born free) turned fifteen in 1829, the year that Walker's *Appeal* was first published. Looking back, Jea and Brown insist that they engaged in acts of violence only when provoked. Put another way: each man's autobiography exhaustively documents cruelties wrought on black bodies by white men. Although both recall experiences of racialized violence that they might have textually represented using jeremiadic rhetoric—experiences that they could have credibly transformed into eschatological events of millennialistic significance à la Walker's *Appeal*—both authors chose a more passive, covert rhetoric of spiritual autobiography. For his part, Jea condemns the family that bound him as comprised of so many religious hypocrites and reports that when they beat him "in a most dreadful manner," his "rage and malice . . . was so very great that [he] would have destroyed them all, had it been in [his] power" (94).[14] Jea states that along with brutal whippings, his experience of slavery consisted of malnutrition, starvation, and compulsory religious instruction. He so resented the latter that during his adolescence, he obsessively planned the murder of his owners' minister.

Eventually, Jea succumbs to the power of sacred discourse, and his religious zeal becomes fervent enough to rouse his masters' ire and his family's derision. He is beaten more than ever, and other slaves "ridiculed [him] and said [he] was mad" (14). Rather than kill the minister, "whom once [he] had so much despised," the narrator explains, he went "and enquired of him, what [he] must do to be saved; begging of him to read and pray for [him]" (14). Ultimately, as William L. Andrews contends, Jea's *Life* is more conversion narrative than antislavery argument (*To Tell* 48), for it recounts Jea's Christian conversion and establishes his authority as a preacher from age seventeen. *The Life* depicts Jea as a fierce opponent of mortal sin, once he converts through a conventional spiritual dark night of the soul. Conversion functions as a trope for resistance to slavery; that is, for the preacher Jea, sin binds as forcefully as chattel slavery, and it demeans all: sinners and their prey, slaveholders and those they enslave. Indeed, Jea abhors slavery as a sin that deleteriously affects slaveholders—many of whom, Jea grieves, blasphemously proclaim themselves God before slaves—no less than it abjectly withholds salvation from slaves.

The Life thematizes spiritual control over sin, including corporeal violence against others, in an extended episode featuring Jea's first wife, Elizabeth, an enslaved woman of indigenous ancestry, or, as he phrases it, "of the Indian colour" (44). Notably, just as his autobiography ends without mention of his three later wives or their children, Jea provides no details of his relationship with Elizabeth before their marriage, instead describing their union abruptly:

> After being at Boston three years and a half, I returned to New York, to see my mother, sisters, brothers, and friends, and after arriving there, I thought it necessary to enter into the state of matrimony, and we lived very comfortably together about two years, being of one heart and one mind, both of us belonging to the Methodist society in New York. . . . To add to our comfort the Lord was pleased to give us a daughter. (44)[15]

Although he does not detail the courtship preceding it, Jea describes his marriage as one of "felicity"—at least until his

> wife's mistress had been trying to persuade her not to be so religious, for she would make herself melancholy to be so much at the house of the God, and she did not like it; she told her she thought it was no harm to sing songs, and to do as the rest of the people of the world did. . . . From this it appeared that her mistress did not understand the things which were of God, although she was a professor of religion. (44)

By this time, Jea has already begun preaching, and in his "determin[ation] to live by the grace of God, to live and die for God" (45), he warns Elizabeth of the mistress's perfidy. Apparently driven insane by the conditions of slavery, however, Elizabeth yields to pressures applied by her owner, for she murders both her pregnant mother and her daughter by John Jea. Elizabeth is summarily indicted and executed for infanticide. The narrator nearly collapses with grief:

> This, my dear reader, you must think, was a fiery trial for me to endure; it almost cast me down to the ground, and to make shipwreck of faith and a good conscience: indeed, my state of mind was such, that it caused me to go to a river, several times, in order to make away with myself; thus the old lion would have devoured me; but, thanks be to God, he gave me grace to withstand the temptations of the Devil at last. (47)

The episode illustrates Jea's religious devotion, his condemnation of his wife's murderous violence, and his conceptualization and renunciation of suicide as violence. More than a condemnation of female gender, the protracted passage demonstrates Jea's ardent opposition to violence as propelled by Satan ("the old lion") to demonic temptation. By proclaiming that Elizabeth's tragedy ensued from her rejection of godliness, Jea implies that his own control over others correlates to his self-control. Or perhaps the inverse: he insinuates that his capacity to lead as a minister depends on textual demonstrations of his self-control, especially control over violent impulses such as those that drove him to plot the murder of his owners' minister. Without the rhetorical display of command over the respect of others, Jea risks not only readers' faith but also their recognition of him as a leader disciplined by heteronormative manhood.[16]

As a widower, Jea expands his itinerant ministry and travels with another black man. Together, they form homosocial bonds with other (black) ministers; *The Life* depicts an intimate and supportive black male community. While the spare spiritual narrative (only ninety-five pages in the first edition) never names Jea's closest compeer, it does describe some of their travels together. Those details are significantly more numerous than those *The Life* offers about Jea's subsequent, presumably less dramatic marriages after Elizabeth's death and about the several children he fathered. In other words, black male homosociality predominates in Jea's narrative over his relationships with women and children. Ironically, in its exposé of religious hypocrisy among white ministers in the United States and Europe, the autobiography further pays more attention to men's bonds with one another, even across race, than with their marital partners, implying a greater intimacy among men than between men and women. At one point, while preaching in Paris, he is arrested as an American, an identity he vehemently rejects because, for him, slaveholding "Americans" are "the tyrants of this world" (89).[17] Jea's imprisonment means that he and his wife remain separated from one another for five years, and yet the spiritual autobiography more thoroughly documents his anger toward his capturers than the cost of his incarceration to his marriage or his spouse. Narratives of masculinity, then, seem to require rhetorical displays of men's virility and triumph. Among Western men, black and white, the Golden Rule—which requires what Tinney names mutuality and love across difference—is no match for self-rule and/or military rule.

Significantly, in the narrative episode that reconstructs his arrest and subsequent imprisonment in France, Jea repudiates violent acts at least four times, even in the name of national defense:

> As soon as we [Jea and others detained as Americans] arrived at Brest we were sent on board of a French corvette, under American colors, to go and fight against the English, but twenty, out of near two hundred that were sent on board, would not enlist under the banner of the tyrants of this world; for *far be it from me ever to fight against Old England, unless it be with the sword of the gospel*, under the captain of our salvation, Jesus Christ. Those of us who would not fight against the English, were sent on board of a French man of war, that they should punish us . . . but [they] sent us to Morlaix, about thirty miles from Brest, where they put us in prison, and kept us upon bread and water for a fortnight, then all the rest consented to go back on board of the corvette . . . for we were to be sent back loaded with chains, and under joint arms. I was the only one that stood out; and I told them *I was determined not to fight against any one and that I would rather suffer any thing than do it*. They said they would send me back to Cambria, and they would keep me upon bread and water, until the wars were over. *I said I was willing to suffer any thing, rather than fight*. They then took me before the council and the head minister of the Americans, to examine me. . . . I told them they might send me on board of the vessel, if they liked; but if they did I was determined not to do any work, for *I would rather suffer any thing than fight or kill any one*. (89–90; emphasis added)

This passage elucidates Jea's sense of the interconnections of religious devotion, manly conviction, and embodied discipline; for him, the only moral military service is Christian piety under the leadership of "the captain of our salvation, Jesus Christ." Choosing jail—and estrangement from his spouse—over soldiering, Jea actively resists heteropatriarchal paradigms that require violence and dishonor.

William J. Brown: "I Had Had Frequent Skirmishes on the Street"

Though published more than forty years apart and bearing strikingly opposed dispositions, the respective spiritual narratives of John Jea and William J. Brown convey that the subjects exhibited divergent ways of serving God. Whereas *The Life, History, and Unparalleled Sufferings of John Jea* forms a straight-laced and staid admonition, *The Life of William J. Brown of Providence, R. I.* punishes with an adroit, dry wit the venomously racist environment in which the author lived virtually all his life. The episodic *Life of William J. Brown* details the autobiographer's spiritual and secular educations. This Brown, of African and indigenous ancestry, was born into the first generation of free blacks among the prominent Brown brothers' slaves on November 10, 1814, in Providence, Rhode Island.[18] His African grandfather, Cudje, had been born among the slave-trading Browns' chattel property in 1746 in Providence; Cudje's father, the narrator tells us, had been born in Africa. Published in 1883, Brown's autobiography proudly relates this black patrilineage, in part because the men's survival documents progeny and endurance against the odds: "The estimated population of Providence in 1821, according to the [first Providence] directory, was 15,000, including about 1,400 colored persons" (Cady 89n2). As a boy in the 1820s, Brown attended a school taught by a "Miss Eliza B. Gano, daughter of Dr. Gano, a Baptist minister, afterwards Mrs. Joseph Rogers" (24). Brown's childhood education would also include lessons in race relations, for Providence was the site of two race riots: in October 1824 in the Addison Hollow (or "Hardscrabble") neighborhood and in "Snowtown" in September 1831, within a month after the revolt led by Nat Turner in Virginia.

In contrast to *The Life, History, and Unparalleled Sufferings of John Jea, the African Preacher*, *The Life of William J. Brown of Providence, R. I.* is more hybrid than conventional spiritual autobiography. Nonetheless, *The Life of William J. Brown* reports its author's conversion to Christianity during "protracted meetings" (83) at a Free Will Baptist Church in Providence in the spring of 1835 (78–83). With a precision echoed in the conversion narratives collected by Watson in the early 1930s, Brown writes, "[I] was on Prospect Street between Lloyd and Jenckes Streets, when he [the Lord] spoke peace to my soul and my burden left me" (83). He would be licensed by Baptists to preach in 1855, a generation after Jea disappears from historical records.

Citing his 1855 ordination as minister only in passing, Brown more meticulously inscribes in *The Life* a number of secular episodes that establish his black male homosociality; these scenes demonstrate his deliberate cultivation of relationships with other local men of color from boyhood. For example, there is a hilarious, straight-faced account of young Billy and his "comrade boys" raiding Dorr's fruit orchard with anguishing consequences (28–30), despite their pact of solidarity. Inspired by a traveling military band, "twelve of the best boys [they] could find," a group that included Brown, vainly but solemnly contrive to raise money to buy instruments for a band of their own (30). Led by Brown, the adolescents' pledges of collective identity and mutual aid extend to their adulthood: "A vote was then passed that the boys who joined our company should use no bad language and keep no bad company, also, to keep to ourselves from the company of boys whose characters were not good, and if any of our members were in trouble to do what we possible [*sic*] could to get them out" (30). On June 17, 1828, Brown's associates elected him president of the Young Men's Union Funds Society, the formality of which is illustrated through their constitution (one complete with a preamble) and the appointment of officers (46). In 1844 Brown and his colleagues established the Young Men's Union Friend Society. Soon afterward, both the Young Men's Friendly Assistant Society and the

Seaman's Friend Society were incorporated. Brown's *Life* further documents the organization of other black fraternal societies in Providence, in many of which Brown was directly involved, including the Mutual Relief, the Young Men's Morning Star, and the Temperance Society Investment. These benevolent societies would provide extensive leadership opportunities for black men and even yield governance positions through local "Negro Elections." In later years, Brown and his black male associates would agitate for the formation of African American troops in the Civil War. (Like other northern and southern sociopolitical descendants of black militiaman Prince Hall, they struggled so that, between 1861 and 1865, more than 180,000 black men fought in the Civil War, though not always with weapons.)

The black men's collectives that Brown led and joined exemplify that black organizations were active across the nineteenth century. As Theda Skocpol, Ariane Liazos, and Marshall Ganz write, "between the early 1800s and the mid-twentieth century, dozens of African American fraternal federations emerged and flourished" (3–4). Representing "many occupations and walks of life," the membership stressed "community under God and shared citizenship" (4) as they engaged in diverse social, civic, and political activities. Insisting on the universalism of their values, they nonetheless advocated black separatism over the loss of dignity and self-respect ensuing from acquiescence to white racism. Though church-based, many federations promoted armed self-defense against white tyranny.

Conversely, from Hall forward, white resistance to black infantry was based primarily on the fear that armed and organized black men would retaliate against racism and white supremacist governments.[19] That paranoia would have little basis in reality, for notwithstanding numerous slave revolts, early nineteenth-century black fraternal organizations balanced agendas of (mostly nonviolent) resistance to oppression with progressive social change for black people. To demonstrate that both individual African Americans and social networks of blacks were prepared to defend themselves against racialized violence, Brown casts his narrator as a man with a far-reaching reputation for physical resistance to white racist maltreatment. Moreover, he complicates this figure by adding to it qualities of both Christian piety and rakish flirtation. One poignant episode in *The Life of William J. Brown* foregrounds resistant black male homosociality formed for the protection of black women. With characteristic understatement and humorous bravado, Brown describes how he and another black man drove off two strange white men who taunted the gallant Brown and "two ladies" he was escorting after church one Sunday: "Who they were I do not know, but [I] think they must have been fellows who had heard of me, and as I had had frequent skirmishes on the street they wanted to test my religion. It was a common thing for colored people to be disturbed on the street, especially on the Sabbath" (73). Elsewhere, Brown reveals his masculinist sense of duty to black womanhood through a willingness to defend his future wife: "[I] wished Mr. Anthony to see that I was escorting her so that if he used such language to her again I would show myself interested in her behalf, for I considered it an honor to defend the ladies in any respectable case" (90). In this way, Brown implies that Christian devotion requires him not to forego violence but, ironically, to exert it, as if self-protection against white brutality, and the corporeal protection of other blacks, especially women, are not merely divinely sanctioned acts but in fact divinely ordained ones.

Published just two years before Brown died on February 19, 1885, *The Life of William J. Brown* indicates the centrality of marriage to notions of manliness and manhood for ambitious free black men in Rhode Island for most of the nineteenth century. Jea's earlier narrative had suggested the pragmatic importance of the business of marriage to black masculinity through the narrator's unsentimental pronouncement that a visit among family had led him to deem "it necessary to enter into the state of matrimony" (44). In contrast, even devoting a whole chapter to his life as a gallant, Brown proclaims himself both more romantic and more rascal: "I was remarkably fond of being in the society of ladies" (89). Still, he consciously pursues a good wife, as an implement vital to a young black man's social and political pursuits in early nineteenth-century Providence. For more than two years, he waits on "Miss Slain" (whom he would eventually marry), thinking at one point to "break off the easiest way [he] could" because he concludes he cannot afford a family (89). His catalog of his own shortcomings—"I could not boast of beauty, and was near-sighted" (90)—is shorter than the list of qualities he claims to bring: good employment prospects, a good education that "excelled that of [his] associates at this time," and a good character; he assesses his future wife's suitability in this way: "I considered her every way qualified, so far as domestic affairs were concerned . . . and every one spoke well of her character. Her temper was mild, and there were but few who could equal her in looks, besides she enjoyed the best of health, having a carriage and appearance well calculated to sustain it" (90–91). Ideally, Brown's wife would not necessarily work outside the home, for while he "made it a practice to call [on his sweetheart] twice a week," he does not propose marriage to her as soon as he desired: "The reason I did not want to make a wife of her then was because I was not able to support her, having no permanent business that would warrant me a living" (89). Describing the shift in his financial fortunes and thus in his marital hopes, however, Brown waxes almost as pragmatic as Jea before him: "I decided to settle down at home; my business was good, everything seemed to warrant my success in supporting a family" (91). Notably, the racist grip of white Providence's economic control proved Brown's perceptions of an improved financial landscape for blacks fantastical. According to *The Life*, before his marriage, white businessmen had often misread Brown as an easy mark to cheat him of his wages. The autobiographer repeatedly insists on his extraordinary math skills, documenting one after another of the narrator's courageous confrontations with swindler employers about unpaid wages. Then hard times in 1844 drove Brown to join his wife as a custodian for the Boston & Providence railroad depot—where they were *both* shortchanged. While he could expose and protest the inadequate pay, Brown lacked the political clout (read: white power) to compel this employer to pay in full.

Significantly, as the autobiography unfolds, Brown insinuates that fiscal victimization as a married man does not provoke him to physical force. Like Jea's narrator before him, Brown's narrator performs a black masculinity based on a *deliberate rejection* of acts of aggression, actively abdicating violent dominance (especially against white men) as inconsistent with Christian virtue.[20] By specifying their disavowal of aggression as a personal religious decision, they protect their investments in hegemonic masculinity. Neither preacher will go so far in reforming conventional black masculinity as to reject its mandate for Christianized heterosexual marriage.[21] For them, marriage and heteronormativity putatively, reflexively signify each other, and both are by definition central to hegemonic masculinity. In nineteenth-century America, marriage endowed economic, social, cultural, and, of course, sexual(izing) certifications—for free blacks before the Civil War, and for freed blacks afterward.[22] As spiritual autobiographers, Jea and Brown inscribe marriage as an institution between a man and his carefully selected female spouse, and they thereby uphold and reinvigorate conventional Christianity. This theology regards black men's marital "protection" of black women as a *gendered* duty,[23] and since U.S. law and custom did not sanction marriage between two enslaved persons before Emancipation, Jea and Brown represent early black Americans who regarded "'marriage rites [as] signs of liberation and entitlement to both democracy and desire'" (Ann duCille qtd. in Diana 187). Speaking in 1846 in Moorfields, England, Frederick Douglass demanded: "What is to be thought of a nation boasting of . . . its Christianity, boasting of its love of justice and purity, and yet having within its own borders three million persons denied by law the right of marriage?" (qtd. in Waters 383).[24] A year earlier, writing between Jea and Brown, Douglass had reproduced the certificate licensing his marriage to Anna in the *Narrative of the Life of Frederick Douglass, an American Slave*: proof positive of the autobiographer's transformation from slave to man, and, as Maurice O. Wallace has observed, to "*proper* man more exactly" ("'I AM'" 136).

From Slave to Soldier during the Civil War

Contemplating "the Anxious Construction of Black American Manhood," in his essay "'I AM A MAN!,'" Wallace contends that "the Civil War is singular in its importance, for it represents nothing short of the *discursive genesis of black manhood in the US imaginary* since . . . the association of 'black' and 'man' could hardly create a meaningful syntagmatic pairing before emancipation" (139). The claim is indisputably supported by Civil War service remembrances included in *God Struck Me Dead*, a collection of religious conversion narratives transcribed by Fisk University student Andrew Polk Watson for his 1932 master's thesis in sociology. Among the converts Watson interviewed were black soldiers. As amanuensis for these formerly enslaved Christian veterans, Watson inscribed and reified heteronormative notions of military service during the Civil War. One (unnamed) former soldier remembers the feelings of manhood that joining the army aroused in him; rather than resist or revise them, his description parallels hegemonic notions of manhood. Under the title "Times Got Worse after the War," the narrator reports:

> I ran off from my master when I was about fifteen years old and joined the army. I was in the field shucking corn on the Murfreesboro Pike. All at once I heard a band playing. Everybody in the field broke and ran. Not a man was left on the place. We all went and joined the army. . . . We told [the captain] who our master was, and that we had come to join the army. . . . I was sent to Tullahoma for training. This was the biggest thing that ever happened in my life. *I felt like a man, with a uniform on and a gun in my hand.* (Johnson 105; emphasis added)

The veteran narrator reveals that he is drawn into military life by multiple forces, each illustrating black male homosocial desire. First, he perceives joining the troops as an opportunity to leave slavery's involuntary and unpaid labor. Also, similar to William J. Brown's call to manhood by a military band, military music and a desire to participate in ending slavery seduce this man into service. Furthermore, he cites manliness as a source of personal empowerment as he brandishes his weaponry. In other words, reflecting on his voluntary enlistment in the war effort, the formerly enslaved speaker names manhood as a feeling evoked by the putatively empowering effects of wearing a uniform (an aesthetic symbol of homosocial affiliation with a respected group) and holding a gun (a means to repel danger as well as to threaten it, to protect the self and to disable or destroy another). Whereas Douglass's famous revisionary chiasmus names one-on-one fisticuffs with the slaver Covey as the means by which he transitioned from slave to man, Watson's subject attributes his maturation into collective black manhood as emanating from the society of other fugitive men: "*Not a man was left on the place*" (105; emphasis added). In sum, a community, an *army* of righteously indignant black men arouses his sense of self-determination.

This same veteran-convert's memories of Ku Klux Klan persecution of black Civil War soldiers highlight the intersection of racialized violence, institutional military, and religious devotion. His memories specify the Klan's attacks on black men who had dared violate the racialized social order by taking up arms against white men and by pursuing independent collective and individual civil rights for African Americans. The narrator reports: "After the war . . . [the] K.K.K. were raising the devil on every hand. They were especially hard on us soldiers. Once a bunch of them caught me" (107). The Klan's assault drives him to deny "that [he] had ever been a soldier" (107). He recalls, "One of them stuck a pistol to my nose and asked me what church I belonged to. I said, 'None.' They told me I had better pray and made me get down on my knees. They had caught and killed a lot of Negroes that they found out to be old soldiers" (107). Violently yoking church worship and Christian prayer with white supremacy and military dishonor, these Klansmen illustrate postbellum white southerners' attempt to extirpate black men and the major institutions of black masculinity. Significantly, the narrator portrays Klan corporeal terrorism as leveled against individual, isolated black men—too cowardly, he implies, to confront a collective of black men who have already faced and survived armed warfare. He suggests that the KKK feared that the homosociality ardently developed by black men who had committed themselves in the Civil War would have easily overpowered disparate groups of Klansmen.

Charlie, the narrator of one of the longest narratives in *God Struck Me Dead*, titled "The Slave Who Joined the Yanks," also joins the Civil War army as a young fugitive slave. Near the end of Charlie's narrative, Watson gives an indirect account of Charlie's Sunday morning religious conversion to Christianity. By this narrative point, he has traversed in readers' imaginations through a series of familiar types of secular black masculinity: rebellious albeit fearful slave, devoted brother, brave soldier, philanderer, and drunkard. In fact, Charlie boasts local acclaim as a boxer: "All the bad fellows around Nashville stood back when I came around. I was a great boxer" (Johnson 41). Moreover, he states that even on the Saturday night before the Sunday dawn of his religious conversion, "I was given up to be the best boxer around, and I laid them cold as fast as they came at me" (45). The first boxers in the United States were enslaved men just like Charlie, according to *Africana: The Encyclopedia of the African and African American Experience*; (involuntary) participation in a boxing exhibition could yield manumission ("Boxing" 600). So, even the prestandardized versions of the sport required staunch discipline as "an elaborate set of regulations and traditions designed to channel violence into craft, aggression into honor" (Denby 2).[25] Watson records the narrator's account of a boxing match between himself and "Bad Frank," who "was much bigger and taller than [he] was, and stronger too, and was known to be a bad man" (Johnson 41). Charlie brags that he triumphed over Frank because he "was a scientific boxer . . . [who] sorter [*sic*] crouched like a tiger, leaped right under his arms, and landed two blows on his chin before he could say scat. He fell clear across the room" (42). Frank's fall enables Charlie to give "a wild whoop . . . and run nearly six miles" before stopping (42). As an elderly man some forty years later, he obliquely apologizes for both the aggressions and the transgressions of his youth. In spite of its erratic chronology, his story of bondage conveys an unbroken chain of beatings, discipline, resistance, antagonism, and power struggles.

Charlie recalls a recalcitrant and battered childhood: "I used to be awfully high-tempered even when I was a boy. My [owners] kept my back sore from whipping because I fought so much. . . . Every time [their children] crossed me I jumped them. I just couldn't help it" (Johnson 24). This assertion proclaims that his lifelong tendency toward violent behavior is natural and irrepressible. However, in the same breath, Charlie suggests an alternative motivation for his incorrigibility: learned retaliation against violent punishment and provocation more than instinctive habit. At the outset of his narrative, then, he willfully resists domination from any quarter; disrespected himself, he harbors no respect for age or gender boundaries, nor will he heed social codes that prohibit violence against white women and children. Once, for example, his mistress slaps him; he recalls, "I saw stars. As soon as I got back to myself I swung at her, and if she hadn't been so quick I would have almost killed her, for I hit her with my fist and with all the force I had" (24–25). Another time he fights with a slaveholder's son: "He was getting the best of me, so I up and bit him on the jaw. I tried to pull a plug out of him" (25). Charlie thus disavows an ability to win every fight; he confesses his wildly desperate efforts to overpower an opponent. His violent behavior implies that enslaved persons already enraged by bondage were driven to utter irrationality by the physical domination slavers held over them.

Ironically, although fear is a trait one might expect black masculinity to reject (or at least disparage), Charlie acknowledges his many fears. Regarding contemporary African American men, Patricia Hill Collins has suggested that "virtually all . . . representations of black masculinity pivot on questions of weakness, whether it is a weakness associated with an inability to control violent impulses, sexual urges, or their black female heterosexual partners or a weakness attributed to men . . . relegate[d] . . . to inferior social spaces" (75). To be sure, fear forms a recurring refrain in Charlie's story: "It nearly scared me to death" (Johnson 32) and "I got scared and jumped behind a tree" (33); then "I ran nearly all night, scared to death" (35); and "I hollered, 'O Lord, save me, save me!'" (36)—and so on. Charlie also divulges a dread of soldiers: "I was scared of the Yankees and especially the cavalry, for I had seen troops of horses go by and they looked so awful and sounded like thunder" and "Mars' Bill had always told me that the Yankees were mean and would kill all the Negroes they could get their hands on" (31). Notably, while this entire conversion narrative is cast in the first-person singular, Watson emphasizes Charlie's chronic panic through a distinct repetition of the pronoun "I." This rhetorical move contrasts sharply with the narrative perspective of the more confident plural/collective subjectivity deployed when Watson represents Charlie's experiences with other black men, as when the narrator asserts: "The Yankees didn't see us, so I ate my bread and meat in peace. When we got through we went on our way. We met an old slave man way late that day" (Johnson 33). In other words, Watson marks the ameliorative comfort of black male homosociality in this otherwise fearful black soldier. By this point, Charlie's only brother has returned from the war to entice him to join, too, so they can stay together (31). Joining the army with his brother initiates Charlie's transition from anxious adolescent to self-confident adult; through the distinctively black male homosocial experience of deserting slavery and fighting white men en masse with other, now-fugitive black men in a collective effort, the violent, blustery youth becomes an intrepid soldier.[26]

"The Slave Who Joined the Yanks" illustrates several significant ways in which Charlie's military experience changes him. One transformation is his religious conversion, but the formulaic details of Christian conversion that characterize traditional spiritual autobiographies do not appear here. Instead, Watson structures

Charlie's narrative so that his conversion marks the channeling of his violent resistance to slavery into the discipline of military service. Together, the conversion and the service lend structure and control to Charlie's life experiences. As the title states, Charlie lends his aggression to the "Yanks" against white southerners and the peculiar institution that has bound him. The narrator suggests that military service *motivates* his religious conversion, which he regards as gendered male; that is, for him, Christian devotion signals his evolution specifically into manhood such that the disciplining of his aggression through soldiering effects his transformation from slave to man.

Through Watson, Charlie reports that a chance postbellum meeting with his former master provided him with an opportunity to extend manly Christian clemency. Charlie's story features a classic confrontation with a former master during Reconstruction. Recurrent in many postbellum slave narratives is a scene of *recognition* in which former slave and former slaveholder meet in the aftermath of war, often unexpectedly, and perceive anew the terms of their antebellum relationship. Such scenes are generally surprising for their element of forgiveness. Charlie's report, however, is consistent with the changes in his comportment that his narrative traces as he matures. In other words, after having spent his youth shielding his more frightened self with violence, after having fought in the Civil War and having "felt the power of God and tasted his love," Charlie proclaims himself "a man among men," a man who can pity his former master: "I love you as though you never hit me a lick, for the God I serve is a God of love, and I can't go to his kingdom with hate in my heart" (Johnson 40). This assertion comes in the middle of a lengthy passage in which Charlie alternately signifies on and proselytizes to his now decrepit "old master." Thus in 1932, through Charlie's spiritual narrative, Watson defines a complex postbellum black masculinity of violent defiance, Afro-Christian compassion, and soldierly dignity.

In a fascinating rhetorical shift, perhaps mimetically reflecting an errant chronology in Charlie's original storytelling, Watson implies his own code of black masculinity by *following* this vivid, moving memory of Christian forgiveness with more backstory of Charlie's "younger days" as "a hellcat." Charlie recalls, "I used to drink a lot of whiskey," and often, "I felt my manhood and wanted to carouse a little" (Johnson 41). Oddly, Watson so organizes the narrative that Charlie has already identified himself to his old master as "a man [who] has been killed dead and made alive in Christ Jesus" (40) when he interjects Charlie's tale of the portentous juke-joint brawl with Bad Frank just hours before the former's religious conversion. Such assertions remind readers of Charlie's violent past, and, moreover, they imply the role of heteronormativity in black men's religious conversions. Charlie describes himself as a man who drifts from one affair, one tryst, to another until he ultimately marries "S," to whom he apparently was still married at the time Watson interviewed him for the Fisk master's thesis. Details of Charlie's casual heterosexist romantic relations and his marriage form a sidebar that precedes the disclosure of his fistfights on the morning of his conversion: thus as amanuensis, Watson projects and protects notions of heteronormative black masculinity by insinuating "natural" intersections between virile men, casual sex, and random violence.

Furthermore, Watson uses Charlie's narrative to outline intersections of black manhood, Christian piety, and physical strength. The narrative portrayal of Charlie's sexual subjugation of poor black women suggests a disturbing, black masculinist desire to mimic white patriarchal masculinity's subordination of all women across U.S. history. Wallace's provocative essay on black masculinity titularly subverts the familiar slogan "I am a man!" to meditate on "Latent Doubt, Public Protest, and the Anxious Construction of Black American Manhood." Wallace suggests that black men before and after David Walker equated blackness with maleness and equated both with hegemonic masculinity that defined women as weak and dependent.[27] As Walker's plea resounded along the East Coast in 1829, it inspired blacks to armed resistance to slavery by insisting that blacks are "MEN!—and not *brutes*" (qtd. in Wallace, "'I AM'" 135)—an assertion that collapses race and gender. Further, Walker proclaims that God, "being a just and holy Being[,] will at one day appear fully in behalf of the oppressed, and arrest the progress of the avaricious oppressors" (Walker 5) *as long as* black men live up to the divine mandate to honor their God with balanced acts of physical force and spiritual zeal. One hundred years later, Watson's Civil War veteran informant, Charlie, constructs black masculinity almost identically. That is, cultural histories of masculinity uniformly—and as far as I can tell, *un-ironically*—suggest that across U.S. history, black men have repudiated the myth that Africans were subhuman brutes by advocating progressive race reform through "manly" force. This equation yields a chilling tautology: nineteenth-century African American men demanded of one another—in print and in deed—physical aggression to refute white myths about black bestiality. And it is further ironic that, as Phillip Brian Harper makes clear, in terms of hegemonic masculinity, "the 'feminine' still strongly connot[es] degradation even [today]" (ix). For "in many ways," as Gary L. Lemons observes, "being black and male in feminist alliance means being an 'invisible (wo)man'—not a woman but neither a man in traditional phallocentric terms" ("To Be Black" 103).

Conclusion: Toward Liberation through Mutuality

As devout forefathers, Jea and Brown modeled for later African American men a black Christian masculinity based on sacred pacifism. Readers of their spiritual narratives find in them early rejections of physical force and brute strength—but they do not also find rejections of the phallocentricism that posits men's superiority to women, nor, more importantly, can they locate rejections of the prevailing patriarchal claim that men have a natural and sacred responsibility to rule and protect women. In short, the nineteenth-century spiritual autobiographies by Jea and

Brown inscribe an enduring license for black sexist supremacy, one that inspired Tinney to theologize in the late twentieth century an African American sociopolitical commitment, a love, rooted in mutuality—in its simplest redaction, the Golden Rule. Contemplating *women*'s roles in black (masculinist) theology, Grant concludes that "Black men must ask themselves a difficult question. How can a white society characterized by Black enslavement, colonialism, and imperialism provide the normative conception of women for Black society? . . . How can a Black minister preach in a way that advocates St. Paul's dictum concerning women while ignoring or repudiating his dictum concerning slaves?" (423). Grant adds that many "Black women are enraged as they listen to 'liberated' Black men speak about the 'place of women' in words and phrases similar to those of the very white oppressors they condemn" (423). She calls for a black masculinity that repositions women from fragile dependents to fully able peers. For Grant, as for Byron and other black feminist scholars of religion, a *progressive* black Christian masculinity that destabilizes oppression and revises existing power structures, that advocates pacific love and social justice—the ostensible aims of black liberatory theology—remains elusive.[28] One might argue, however, that it has emerged somewhat in the single, polemical figure of the black bishop Carlton Pearson. Once well known (and well heeled), Pearson now exemplifies some of the repercussions suffered by those who antagonize a virulent U.S.-based Christianity. For preaching a Protestantism without hell, in 2002, Pearson was summarily excommunicated as a heretic, and within weeks, his megachurch congregation dwindled from thousands of believers to a few hundred eccentrics.[29] If Christianity depends on firm and fearful belief in Satan and hell, perhaps we cannot expect a progressive black masculinity to emerge from those who yet brook no deviation from an orthodox creed.[30]

Looking back in search of (secular) womanist forefathers, Lemons finds Frederick Douglass and W. E. B. Du Bois to be leaders among nineteenth-century profeminist black male champions of women's unqualified liberation.[31] Lemons is not alone among contemporary black men striving to revise harmful conceptualizations of black masculinity. The "Mission Statement of Black Men for the Eradication of Sexism" declares one fraternal federation's recognition that "patriarchal notions of manhood, which we have internalized from our oppressors, demand that our existence as men be defined by our sexual ability and our ability to produce economically and dominate others" (201). Thus, these Morehouse College students pledge to "reject relationships based on domination and the violence against women and prostitution they [i.e., such relationships] create" (200). Perhaps most hopefully, Rudolph P. Byrd outlines an inspired new "Mode of Black Masculinity" in a meditation on the black folk figure of High John the Conqueror. Byrd effectively recasts Alice Walker's pioneering essay-definition of *womanist* to offer High John as an archetype of revolutionary black masculine power. Byrd's High John is deeply spiritual, for his "various acts of resistance are reflected in his most exemplary values and attributes: motherwit, the power of laughter and song, self-assertion, self-examination, self-knowledge, a belief that life is process grounded in the fertile field of improvisation, hope, and, most importantly, love" (7). In revising High John for the twenty-first century, Byrd recalls the folk figure from the historical settings in which Jea and Brown lived; he asserts that he "conceived the tradition of John as a mode of masculinity designed to address the historical and contemporary conditions of men of African descent" (10). Together with black feminist scholars and theologians ranging from Grant and Byron to Tinney and Lemons, Byrd reminds us that critical inquiry into early black religious and spiritual masculinity can prove both recuperative and celebratory. Such inquiry will broaden the repertoire of diverse and progressive black masculinities, and it will honor African American Christian men whose spiritual autobiographies have long illuminated a path toward greater liberation.

NOTES

An earlier version of this chapter was published as "'I Hadn't Joined Church Yet, and I Wasn't Scared of Anybody': Violence and Homosociality in Early Black Men's Christian Narratives," *a/b: Auto/Biography Studies* 27.1 (2012): 153–82. © 2012 The Autobiography Society. Reprinted by permission.

1. For more on the African American literary jeremiad, see Howard-Pitney and Moses.

2. According to Hinks, the notion that the *Appeal* motivated Turner's revolt in 1831 remains "mere speculation" (xli).

3. Watson's unpublished ninety-seven-page thesis is catalogued at Fisk University as "Primitive Religion among Negroes in Tennessee" (1932). I quote from Watson's interviews as they appear in Clifton H. Johnson's *God Struck Me Dead*.

4. Black cultural, vernacular, and sacred expressivities all include numerous representations of deviant (male) ministers. The figure of the malevolent black preacher in film, for example, extends back to the satirical villain in Oscar Micheaux's *Body and Soul* (1925). Before that, in the 1919 novel (and later film) *The Homesteader*, Micheaux parodied black preachers through a corrupt urban minister he named Rev. N. Justin McCarthy. See Butters, Carby, Sherrard-Johnson, and Weisenfeld.

5. Grant's essay is just one of many texts by black feminist ethicists, black feminist theologians, black feminist scholars, black civil rights veterans, and others who have critiqued rampant sexism and patriarchal domination in both everything subsumed under monolithic notions of the black church and the mid-twentieth-century civil rights movement.

6. See also Loeb for a discussion of African American autobiography by Vietnam War veterans, including one woman, Phillipa Schuyler. Loeb observes the centrality of Christianity to these war memoirs. For a more complete discussion of Brown, see Moody.

7. Following Bailey, I am interested in ways that Afro-Protestantism developed into a faith system that privileges male gender over female. See Andrews ("Politics") for a brief discussion of the "idea that the servant of God would be fully engaged in racial uplift" (115). See Smith for the distinction between a liberation theology tradition epitomized in the twentieth century by Martin Luther King Jr. and a prosperity gospel tradition epitomized by T. D. Jakes.

8. Giggie reports on post-Reconstruction black male preachers' double bind: to help blacks pursue an elusive and white-defined respectability (while lining their own pockets) or to practice black separatism from white power structures and consequently remain poor, wretched, and dependent.

9. Hinks reports that when individuals and groups of enslaved people resisted the violence of slavery by running away or staging revolts, whites retaliated by beheading them (xviii). Significantly, white responses to the slave revolt led by Denmark Vesey included the founding of the Citadel military academy in South Carolina. See Hamilton.

10. Early nineteenth-century black autobiography documents both enslaved men's and enslaved women's violent resistance to slavery. Such antebellum legal cases include those of Celia Newsom in Missouri and Margaret Garner in Kentucky. The defendants' alleged violent acts were complexly narrated in white media before Harriet Jacobs's *Incidents in the Life of a Slave Girl* (1861) depicted enslaved women as victims rather than perpetrators of violence, even in self-defense. Enslaved women's acts of violence and their victimhood further signify the equation of black racial identity with a single gender category and (thus) transgressive sexuality. See also Jacobs and McLaurin.

11. See Wallace, "'I AM A MAN!'" and *Constructing the Black Masculine*; see also Looby.

12. See also Saillant (214).

13. Across disciplines, several scholars have noted the rise in black masculinist aggression at puberty. See Franklin and Schweninger.

14. Jea writes that he came to "look upon them [the white family who enslaved him] as devils" (94). See also Ferguson on the figure of the devil in antebellum slave narratives.

15. Saillant writes: "Vital records in Portsmouth, England, list his 1816 marriage to Jemima Davis, who would have been his fourth wife, and the 1817 baptism of their child Hephzabah, who was born after the publication of his *Life*" (213).

16. For more on Jea's leadership, see Pierce (114).

17. Controversy surrounds Jea's birthplace. Saillant and others have challenged *The Life*'s designation of Africa as Jea's continent of origin, locating it instead in New York. Alternatively, we can read Jea's *Life* as signaling that, regardless of his particular birthplace, his progenitors indisputably were forced into slavery through the Middle Passage. Moreover, in rejecting an American nationality for the narrative representation of the experience in France, Jea condemns slavery.

18. Brown's *Life* describes a period he spent hospitalized in Boston for blindness, but otherwise he seems to have spent his life in Providence. Although Brown's autobiography suggests that he attached importance to his Native American maternal ancestry, the text privileges a black male subjectivity.

19. See Looby for an analysis of white patriarchal paranoia.

20. My reading, then, contradicts Richards's interpretation, which argues that Jea's narrative and George White's text "depict the careers of ambitious young Black men following the only profession open to African Americans of talent, that of the minister. Whites [*sic*] and Jea's memoirs depict such youthful Black ministers negotiating opportunity and obstacles as they enter pastoral careers where they may achieve social power" (74–75).

21. McBride and other twenty-first-century black gay scholars critique marriage as exclusionary within the predominantly Christian United States (Preface 5).

22. One fascinating episode in Brown's *Life* details a morality test that the narrator gives

his fiancée when a would-be patron offers him the opportunity to study formally for the ministry. The fiancée passes, but the effect is that Brown compromises his own religious devotion, and the couple marries and suffers financial insecurity for several years (84–88).

23. Lemons reads W. E. B. Du Bois as saying that marriage is one of the three obstructions to black women's self-actualization ("'When'" 77).

24. Thanks to Patrick J. Barry for identifying this point in a personal conversation as the "Reception Speech," by Frederick Douglass, at the Finsbury Chapel (May 12, 1846); Barry adds that the speech is excerpted in *My Bondage and My Freedom* (Douglass 302–3).

25. See Bederman (17) for shifts in attitudes toward boxing and prizefighting as a coarse working-class activity to a respectable middle-class sign of masculinity.

26. See also the representation of individual and collective fear as a motivation for young black men's wild behavior in McCall's late twentieth-century autobiography.

27. On the difficulty that black men faced in achieving fin-de-siècle whites' notions of manhood, Bailey diverges from Wallace and others who argue that eighteenth-century black men theorized acts of physical force (especially as resistance to racism) as integral to manhood. See Bailey (39).

28. See Mutua (Introduction) on progressive black masculinities.

29. Pearson has written and spoken about his excommunication in diverse media, including in his 2009 book.

30. See also McBride: "Any understanding of black oppression that makes it possible, and worse permissible, to endorse at any level sexism, elitism or heterosexism is a vision of black culture that is finally not politically consummate with liberation" ("Can" 367). Also, McBride's *Why I Hate Abercrombie & Fitch* cites the book of Ephesians immediately after the dedication page (vii). At least one reviewer characterizes this collection of essays as "a *black gay Christian man*'s journey into academe" (Polk 310; emphasis added).

31. See Lemons, "'When and Where [We] Enter.'" In this essay, Lemons also specifies limits to the antifeminism articulated by Douglass and Du Bois, outlining expansions needed in their nineteenth- and twentieth-century advocacy of women's rights.

WORKS CITED

Abdur-Rahman, Aliyyah. "'The Strangest Freaks of Despotism': Queer Sexuality in Antebellum African Slave Narratives." *African American Review* 40.2 (2006): 223–37.

Andrews, William L. "The Politics of African-American Ministerial Autobiography from Reconstruction to the 1920s." *African-American Christianity: Essays in History*. Ed. Paul E. Johnson. Berkeley: U of California P, 1994. 111–33.

———. *To Tell a Free Story: The First Century of Afro-American Autobiography, 1760–1865*. Urbana: U of Illinois P, 1986.

Bailey, Julius H. *Around the Family Altar: Domesticity in the African Methodist Episcopal Church, 1865–1900*. Gainesville: UP of Florida, 2005.

Bederman, Gail. *Manliness and Civilization: A Cultural History of Gender and Race in the United States, 1880–1917*. Chicago: U of Chicago P, 1995.

Bobo, Jacqueline, Cynthia Hudley, and Claudine Michel, eds. *The Black Studies Reader*. New York: Routledge, 2004.

"Boxing." *Africana: The Encyclopedia of the African and African American Experience.* Ed. Kwame Anthony Appiah and Henry Louis Gates Jr. Vol. 1. 2nd ed. New York: Oxford UP, 2005. 600–601.

Brown, William J. *The Life of William J. Brown of Providence, R. I., With Personal Recollections of Incidents in Rhode Island.* 1883. Ed. Joanne Pope Melish. Durham: U of New Hampshire P, 2006.

Butters, Gerald R., Jr. "Portrayals of Black Masculinity in Oscar Micheaux's *The Homesteader.*" *Literature/Film Quarterly* 28.1 (2000): 54–59.

Byrd, Rudolph P. "The Tradition of John: A Mode of Black Masculinity." *Traps: African American Men on Gender and Sexuality.* Ed. Rudolph P. Byrd and Beverly Guy-Sheftall. Bloomington: Indiana UP, 2001. 1–24.

Byron, Gay L. "Images of Masculinity in the Pauline Epistles: Resources for Constructing Progressive Black Masculinities, or Not?" *Progressive Black Masculinities.* Ed. Athena D. Mutua. New York: Routledge, 2006. 101–20.

Cady, John H. *The Civic and Architectural Development of Providence, 1636–1950.* Providence, RI: Book Shop, 1957.

Carby, Hazel V. *Race Men.* Cambridge, MA: Harvard UP, 1998.

Collins, Patricia Hill. "A Telling Difference: Dominance, Strength, and Black Masculinities." *Progressive Black Masculinities.* Ed. Athena D. Mutua. New York: Routledge, 2006. 73–97.

Denby, David. "Hard Knocks: *X-Men Origins: Wolverine, Fighting, Tyson.*" Rev. of *X-Men Origins: Wolverine, Fighting, Tyson,* dir. by Gavin Hood, Dito Montiel, and James Tobeck. *New Yorker* 11 May 2009: 112–14.

Diana, Vanessa Holford. "Narrative Patterns of Resistance in Frances E. W. Harper's *Iola Leroy* and Pauline Hopkins' *Contending Forces.*" *Black Women's Intellectual Traditions: Speaking Their Minds.* Ed. Kristin Waters and Carol B. Conaway. Lebanon, NH: UP of New England, 2007. 173–91.

Douglass, Frederick. *My Bondage and My Freedom.* 1855. Ed. John David Smith. New York: Penguin, 2003.

Ferguson, Sally Ann H. "Christian Violence and the Slave Narrative." *American Literature* 68.2 (1996): 297–320.

Franklin, John Hope, and Loren Schweninger. "Profile of a Runaway Slave." *Slavery in America: A Reader and Guide.* Ed. Kenneth Morgan. Athens: U of Georgia P, 2005. 281–308.

Gates, Henry Louis, Jr. *The Signifying Monkey: A Theory of Afro-American Literary Criticism.* New York: Oxford UP, 1988.

Giggie, John M. "'Preachers and Peddlers of God': Ex-Slaves and the Selling of African-American Religion in the American South." *Commodifying Everything: Relationships of the Market.* Ed. Susan Strasser. New York: Routledge, 2003. 169–90.

Grant, Jacqueline. "Black Theology and the Black Woman." Bobo, Hudley, and Michel, *Black Studies Reader* 421–33.

Hall, Stuart. "What Is This 'Black' in Black Popular Culture?" Bobo, Hudley, and Michel, *Black Studies Reader* 255–63.

Hamilton, Kendra. "Breaking Down the Walls." *Black Issues in Higher Education* 21.15 (2004): 26–29.

Harper, Phillip Brian. *Are We Not Men? Masculine Anxiety and the Problem of African-American Identity.* New York: Oxford UP, 2006.

Hinks, Peter P. Introduction. *David Walker's* Appeal to the Coloured Citizens of the World. Ed. Peter P. Hinks. University Park: Pennsylvania State UP, 2000. xi–xli.

Howard-Pitney, David. *The Afro-American Jeremiad: Appeals for Justice in America*. Philadelphia: Temple UP, 1990.

Jacobs, Harriet A. *Incidents in the Life of a Slave Girl. Written by Herself*. 1861. Ed. Jean Fagan Yellin. Cambridge, MA: Harvard UP, 2000.

Jea, John. *The Life, History, and Unparalleled Sufferings of John Jea, the African Preacher. Compiled and Written by Himself*. Electronic ed. *Documenting the American South*. U of North Carolina at Chapel Hill, 2001.

Johnson, Clifton H., ed. *God Struck Me Dead: Voices of Ex-Slaves*. Cleveland: Pilgrim, 1993.

Lemons, Gary L. "To Be Black, Male, and 'Feminist': Making Womanist Space for Black Men." *The Womanist Reader*. Ed. Layli Phillips. New York: Routledge, 2006. 96–113.

———. "'When and Where [We] Enter': In Search of a Feminist Forefather—Reclaiming the Womanist Legacy of W. E. B. Du Bois." *Traps: African American Men on Gender and Sexuality*. Ed. Rudolph P. Byrd and Beverly Guy-Sheftall. Bloomington: Indiana UP, 2001. 71–89.

Loeb, Jeffrey. "The African American Autobiography of the Vietnam War." *Arms and the Self: War, the Military, and Autobiographical Writing*. Ed. Alex Vernon. Kent, OH: Kent State UP, 2005. 218–35.

Looby, Christopher. "'As Thoroughly Black as the Most Faithful Philanthropist Could Desire': Erotics of Race in Higginson's *Army Life in a Black Regiment*." *Race and the Subject of Masculinities*. Ed. Harry Stecopoulos and Michael Uebel. Durham, NC: Duke UP, 1997. 71–115.

McBride, Dwight A. "Can the Queen Speak? Racial Essentialism, Sexuality, and the Problem of Authority." *Callaloo* 21.2 (1998): 363–79.

———. Preface. *Why I Hate Abercrombie & Fitch: Essays on Race and Sexuality*. New York: New York UP, 2004. 1–15.

McCall, Nathan. *Makes Me Wanna Holler: A Young Black Man in America*. New York: Random House, 1994.

McLaurin, Melton Alonza. *Celia, a Slave*. Athens: U of Georgia P, 1991.

"Mission Statement of Black Men for the Eradication of Sexism, Morehouse College." *Traps: African American Men on Gender and Sexuality*. Ed. Rudolph P. Byrd and Beverly Guy-Sheftall. Bloomington: Indiana UP, 2001. 200–204.

Moody, Joycelyn K. "The Truth of Slave Narratives: Slavery's Traces in Postmemory Narratives of Postemancipation Life." *The Oxford Handbook of the African American Slave Narrative*. Ed. John Ernest. New York: Oxford UP, 2014. 415–32.

Moses, William J. *Black Messiahs and Uncle Toms: Social and Literary Manipulations of a Religious Myth*. University Park: Pennsylvania State UP, 1993.

Mutua, Athena D. Introduction: Mapping the Contours of Progressive Masculinities. *Progressive Black Masculinities*. Ed. Athena D. Mutua. New York: Routledge, 2006. xi–xxviii.

Newman, Richard S. "Prince Hall." *Encyclopedia of African American History, 1619–1895: From the Colonial Period to the Age of Frederick Douglass*. Ed. Paul Finkelman. Vol. 2. New York: Oxford UP, 2006. 141–42.

Pearson, Carlton. *God Is Not a Christian, nor a Jew, Muslim, Hindu: God Dwells with Us, in Us, around Us, as Us*. New York: Atria Books, 2009.

Pierce, Yolanda Nicole. *Hell without Fires: Slavery, Christianity, and the Antebellum Spiritual Narrative*. Gainesville: UP of Florida, 2005.

Polk, Khary. Rev. of *Why I Hate Abercrombie & Fitch: Essays on Race and Sexuality*, by Dwight A. McBride. *WSQ: The Sexual Body* 35.1–2 (2007): 310–14.

Reid-Pharr, Robert. *Once You Go Black: Choice, Desire, and the Black American Intellectual*. New York: New York UP, 2007.

Richards, Phillip M. "Anglo-American Continuities of Civic and Religious Thought in the Institutional World of Early Black Writing." *Beyond Douglass: New Perspectives on Early African-American Literature*. Ed. Michael J. Drexler and Ed White. Lewisburg, PA: Bucknell UP, 2008. 69–89.

Saillant, John. "John Jea." *Encyclopedia of African American History, 1619–1895: From the Colonial Period to the Age of Frederick Douglass*. Ed. Paul Finkelman. Vol. 2. New York: Oxford UP, 2006. 213–14.

Sedgwick, Eve Kosofsky. *Between Men: English Literature and Male Homosocial Desire*. New York: Columbia UP, 1997.

Sherrard-Johnson, Cherene. *Portraits of the New Negro Woman: Visual and Literary Culture in the Harlem Renaissance*. New Brunswick, NJ: Rutgers UP, 2007.

Skocpol, Theda, Ariane Liazos, and Marshall Ganz. *What a Mighty Power We Can Be: African American Fraternal Groups and the Struggle for Racial Equality*. Princeton, NJ: Princeton UP, 2006.

Smith, Vern E. "Where Do We Go From Here?" *Crisis* 113.4 (2006): 31–35.

Tinney, James S. "Why a Black Gay Church?" *In the Life: A Black Gay Anthology*. Ed. Joseph Beam. Boston: Alyson, 1986. 70–86.

Walker, David. *David Walker's Appeal to the Coloured Citizens of the World*. Ed. Peter P. Hinks. University Park: Pennsylvania State UP, 2000.

Wallace, Maurice O. *Constructing the Black Masculine: Identity and Ideality in African American Men's Literature and Culture, 1775–1995*. Durham, NC: Duke UP, 2002.

———. "'I AM A MAN!': Latent Doubt, Public Protest, and the Anxious Construction of Black Manhood." *Ideology, Identity, and Assumptions*. Ed. Howard Dodson and Colin Palmer. East Lansing: Michigan State UP, 2007. 133–78. Schomburg Studies in the Black Experience.

Waters, Kristin. "Some Core Themes of Nineteenth-Century Black Feminism." *Black Women's Intellectual Traditions: Speaking Their Minds*. Ed. Kristin Waters and Carol B. Conaway. Lebanon, NH: UP of New England, 2007. 367–92.

Weisenfeld, Judith. *Hollywood Be Thy Name: African American Religion in American Film, 1929–1949*. Berkeley: U of California P, 2007.

Olaudah Equiano in the United States

Abigail Mott's 1829 Abridged Edition of the Interesting Narrative

ERIC D. LAMORE

> There are many questions about Equiano which have not been satisfactorily answered.
>
> S. E. OGUDE,
> "Introduction to the New Edition [of *Equiano's Travels*]"

The Interesting Narrative of the Life of Olaudah Equiano, or Gustavus Vassa, the African. Written by Himself, a text first published in London in 1789, remains a frequently read and debated eighteenth-century autobiography.[1] Equiano's life narrative is one of the most sophisticated literary texts from the eighteenth-century Atlantic world. Historians of slavery, the eighteenth-century Atlantic world, and abolitionist movements as well as scholars of United States, British, African, and Caribbean literatures continue to study and teach the *Interesting Narrative* because this autobiography provides the most detailed firsthand account of African cultural customs and the dynamics of the eighteenth-century transatlantic slave trade written by an individual of African descent in the English language. Given the inestimable cultural value of this life narrative, thousands of students from around the world read all of or portions from the *Interesting Narrative* each academic year in history, literature, and social science courses.[2]

Biographers, literary critics, and historians have benefited immensely from utilizing Paul Gilroy's influential thinking on the black Atlantic in positioning Equiano—along with other writers from the early black Atlantic—not as a product of a single nation but as part of a larger, interconnected Atlantic world. While critics have studied Equiano's and his autobiography's relationship to Great Britain and Africa in some detail, the writer's and his text's connections to the North American colonies have not received adequate attention beyond the heated debate on whether he was born in the Carolinas. In other words, Equiano's relationship to the United States is more complicated than the identity debate that has mostly dominated criticism on this autobiographer for the last twenty years. Curiously enough, like Equiano's life, the full-length and abridged editions of the *Interesting Narrative* published in the late eighteenth- and nineteenth-century United States emerge from the same components of black Atlantic culture that Gilroy has identified as "movement, transformation, and relocation" (xi). Even though the full-length and abridged editions of Equiano's life narrative published in the United States during his lifetime and after his death provide evidence of the full extent of the transatlantic and transnational life of the *Interesting Narrative*, many scholars have been hesitant to follow him and his book across the Atlantic to this country.

Most Equiano scholars have chosen not to study the U.S. editions of the *Interesting Narrative* because they were altered by editors and book publishers in ways that the life writer did not endorse, have control over, economically profit from, or, in some cases, even see in his lifetime. However, in several authorized editions of his highly popular autobiography, Equiano acknowledges his awareness of the publication of three unauthorized editions of his life narrative in the early Atlantic world. He writes, "Soon after I returned to London, where I found persons of note from Holland and Germany, who requested me to go there; and I was glad to hear that an edition of my *Narrative* had been printed in both places, also in New York" (Equiano, *Interesting Narrative and Other* 235). In this sentence, Equiano articulates his view of the unauthorized editions of the *Interesting Narrative* published in Holland, Germany, and New York. While Equiano's perspective may, in part, signify his desire to note the international appeal of the narrative, the point allows the autobiographer to market the unauthorized editions of his narrative. Even though Equiano knew that he would not benefit financially from the sales of these editions, the life writer states that he was "glad" to find that publishers in different places in the Atlantic world were circulating editions of his autobiography and that individuals from different countries were reading these editions of his book, even if they were unauthorized. For Equiano, in this case, the further circulation of his anti–slave trade arguments throughout various parts of the early Atlantic world trumped the acquisition of money from book sales. Equiano did not revise this passage in the fifth thorough ninth editions of his autobiography, which indicates that he consistently endorsed the publishing and reading of these unauthorized editions. But this sentence sheds light on important matters of textuality beyond just another way that Equiano manages to market his text. Crucially, Equiano's view of the unauthorized editions of the *Interesting Narrative* indicates that his view of textuality (that is, his take on what constitutes a legitimate autobiographical text) runs counter to twentieth- and twenty-first-century scholars' consistent privileging of one kind of text, the authorized editions of his autobiography. Equiano scholars have offered valuable insights on these authorized editions, yet it is crucial at this juncture to begin understanding the publishing and reception histories of the unauthorized, posthumous, and abridged editions of his autobiography.

This chapter offers the first sustained analysis of one posthumous edition of the *Interesting Narrative* published in the United States, the little-known and seldom referenced 1829 *The Life and Adventures of Olaudah Equiano; or, Gustavus Vassa, the African. From an Account Written by Himself, Abridged by A. Mott. To Which Is Added Some Remarks on the Slave Trade*, which was published in New York by Samuel Wood and Sons thirty-two years after Equiano's death in London. This thirty-six-page abridged edition of Equiano's *Narrative* was deliberately constructed to be read by students of African descent at the New York African Free School, a controversial educational institution created by the New York Manumission Society in 1787. Even though Abigail Field Mott's 1829 abridged text has occupied a place in reference sources widely available to those interested in African, Caribbean, and African American studies, scholars have yet to contribute an in-depth study on this text.[3] In fact, until now, remarks have been made largely in passing on the existence of Mott's 1829 abridged edition; in rare cases, critics offer limited commentary on the abridged edition.[4] This investigation maintains that Mott's abridged edition adds new depth to the phenomenon of Equiano.[5] Studying this abridged edition as one instance of the *Interesting Narrative* as a "fluid text" (Bryant 1) yields an additional benefit: it moves conversations beyond the disputed birthplace of Equiano and explores new critical territory. Furthermore, Mott's 1829 abridged edition aids in beginning to assemble the narrative concerning when, how, and why this life writer and his autobiography became part of the United States and African American autobiographical traditions. Mott's abridged edition, therefore, marks one of the entry points of this narrative into the canons of U.S. and African American literatures.

Historians and literary critics know relatively little about Abigail Mott other than the facts that she was related (through marriage) to Lucretia Mott, the famous nineteenth-century women's rights activist and abolitionist. Additionally, the historical archive contains more texts edited by A. Mott than ones written by her.[6] Perhaps this point offers one explanation of why scholars have mentioned Abigail Mott only in passing in books and articles on Frederick Douglass and nineteenth-century antislavery activities and educational reform. According to Robert K. Wallace, for instance, the June 12, 1845, issue of *The Liberator* names A. Mott as an individual who could be contacted for copies of Douglass's *Narrative* (26). Douglass occasionally visited Mott and her sister, Lydia, because they housed his daughter, Rosetta, from 1845 to 1848 while she attended school in Albany, New York.[7] The Mott sisters subscribed to the *North Star* (McFeely 152), and A. Mott occasionally corresponded with Douglass (Douglass 114n1). On at least one occasion, Douglass published A. Mott's correspondence to him in the *North Star* ("Calendar" 579). Historians have also noted that the Mott sisters allowed escaped slaves, abolitionists, and women's rights advocates to stay in their Albany home, which served as a men's clothing shop (Sterling 159; Gurko 114; Jeffrey 179). Given this limited information on Abigail Mott, scholars attempting to reconstruct the life of this editor face a biographical dilemma: how to piece together the life of an individual when she or he does not have access to an autobiography, a diary, or numerous letters written by this historical figure? Interestingly, the abolitionist's editing of life writing by and about individuals of African descent may be the most productive way to gather additional information on Mott.

Unfortunately, at this point it is difficult to judge exactly how the New York African Free School students responded to Mott's abridged edition because no known historical records provide direct access to these reactions. Nonetheless, Mott's editing of Equiano's *Interesting Narrative* raises at least two key questions.[8] First, what exactly did Mott keep from Equiano's eighteenth-century life narrative in her abridged edition? And how can we best explain Mott's editorial decision-making in relation to the curriculum in the New York African Free School in the 1820s? By exploring these questions, this chapter provides biographers, historians, literary critics, and students of Equiano with a better understanding of the circulation and consumption of the *Interesting Narrative* in the United States. In sum, this chapter explores some of the ways in which Mott's abridged edition reinforced elements in the Free School's curriculum. Many of the Free School's students, it should be noted, were the children of formerly enslaved persons.[9]

Mott's 1829 abridged edition is the end product forged from a chain of textual mutations, one that reveals the unstable nature of the *Interesting Narrative*. The abridged edition grew from two other full-length editions of the *Interesting Narrative*—the authorized second London edition (1789) and the unauthorized New York edition published by William Durell (1791). According to both Paul Edwards and Vincent Carretta, Durell used the second London edition of the *Interesting Narrative* for the printing of his 1791 edition (Edwards, Introduction [*Life*] ix; Carretta, "Note" xxxi). To create this "First American Edition" of the *Interesting Narrative*, as the title page indicates, Durell made significant changes to the second London edition. First, the New York publisher eliminated the frontispiece from the second London edition and replaced it with another visual text created by Cornelius Tiebout, a New York "copper plate engraver," as he is identified in the "List of Subscribers." Second, Durell's "List of Subscribers" does not include any names found in the subscriber list that appeared in the second London edition; instead, his "List of Subscribers" names readers from Connecticut, New Jersey, New York, Massachusetts, Pennsylvania, and Antigua. Third, unlike the title page from the second London edition, which indicates that the text was "Printed and sold for the Author," the New York edition's title page reads, "Printed and Sold By W. Durell, at his Book-Store and Printing-Office," thereby altogether eliminating Equiano's presence in the distribution process. Durell also did not print Equiano's petition to the members of the British Parliament in his edition. These nonauthorial changes reveal that Durell attempted, in the first parts of the book, to minimize Equiano's connection to Great Britain and his status as an Afro-British subject in the New York edition published for readers mostly in the United States.

Durell's "List of Subscribers" provides additional information on the textual chain leading to Mott's abridged edition. According to the list, the primary readers of this edition were artisans, including bakers, grocers, cabinetmakers, carpenters, tailors, tanners, and masons, who likely read Equiano's text to learn about geography, traveling, sailing, and survival (Ito 90). However, the "List of Subscribers" in the New York edition identifies four individuals whom Mott knew: Melancton Smith and John Murray, who were, at one point, both members of the Board of Trustees of the New York African Free School; Cornelius Davis, a teacher at this educational institution (Ito 87); and Robert Mott, Abigail's brother-in-law (Green 372). Smith's, Murray's, and Davis's names on the "List of Subscribers" are meaningful because Mott establishes, in the preface to her abridged edition, her connection to the New York African Free School. She writes:

> Having, for several years, been one of the Committee to visit the Female Department of the African Free School in New York; and having also been occasionally at that for boys, I have observed that the tickets given to the pupils, as rewards for attention to their studies, have a very favourable tendency. A specific value being given to those tickets, they become a sort of currency in the schools, and are received by the teachers in payment for toys and other articles which are provided as premiums for the scholars. Similar observation induces me to believe that there is scarcely any thing which can be given to a child as a premium for good behaviour which has a better tendency than a book. This belief prompted me to attempt an abridgement of the *Memoirs of Gustavus Vassa, the African*; which, as they contain many interesting circumstances, may not be thought unsuitable for distribution in those schools.
>
> Whether or not the design of these extracts meet the approbation of the Trustees of the African Schools, I think it will be an interesting little work for children of any class, and I have therefore placed it in the hand of the publisher. (Preface 4)

These prefatory remarks allow African American life narrative scholars to classify Mott's abridged edition as a children's and adolescents' literature version of the *Interesting Narrative*, which is appropriate because Charles C. Andrews identifies, in his 1830 *History of the New-York African Free-Schools*, students from this educational institution as ranging from seven to fifteen years of age (44, 118); these students would have different reading abilities of course, but their ages straddle the categories of child and adolescent.[10] This language from Mott's preface also establishes that she edited her abridged edition for readers of African descent in the United States, though she does acknowledge that the book "will be an interesting little work for children of any class" (4). This point does not apply to Durell's 1791 edition, nor does it offer an adequate description of Isaac Knapp's 1837 edition. Therefore, Mott's abridged edition occupies a central place in assembling an understanding of when, how, and why Equiano and his autobiography became part of the U.S. and African American autobiographical traditions.[11]

Additionally, the preface reveals that Mott had firsthand knowledge of the Free School and its students because she visited both the female and the male students at this educational institution on a number of occasions. Therefore, it is safe to conclude that Mott knew the three aforementioned individuals whose names appear on the "List of Subscribers" in Durell's edition who were also associated with the Free School: Smith, Murray, and Davis. Given the presence of Smith's, Murray's, and Davis's names on the "List of Subscribers" from the New York edition as well as Mott's numerous visits to the Free School, she very likely used Durell's edition to assemble her abridged text.[12] Mott, moreover, adds that she hoped her abridged edition of Equiano's *Interesting Narrative* would be available in the Free School's Library after it was purchased through the ticket system. As Mott states, the teachers at the Free School rewarded well-behaved students with tickets that "become a sort of currency for toys and other articles" (4), including, as the editor hoped, her abridged edition. In his *History*, Andrews notes that the "school tickets" had a "nominal value," but students in a particular class could use them "in purchasing books for the Library" (82).

Mott's understanding of this group of students at the New York African Free School certainly convinced her that Equiano's text was a relevant one for them. More specifically, her knowledge of the student body at the Free School very likely prompted her to place special emphasis on Equiano's reflections on his own youth and adolescence found in his *Interesting Narrative* to connect the autobiographer's life with the Free School's students' lives. In other words, for the most part Equiano's commentary on the different ages and developmental periods of his life in the opening chapters of his book conveniently aligned with the ages and developmental periods of the majority of students at the New York African Free School. Though their lives differed on cultural and geographical levels, this purposeful linking of their ages and developmental periods worked to minimize these gaps. Not surprisingly, then, Mott's abridged edition remains faithful to the chronology found in Equiano's autobiography, which begins with the life writer's reflections on his childhood and youth in Africa. This part of the *Interesting Narrative* contains several layers that likely appealed to the students at the Free School—including travel, danger, distant locations, and moral lessons—but it is also well suited to initiate the revisionary process known as autoadaptation (Lamore, "Futures" 14).[13]

Chapters 1, 2, and 3 from the authorized editions of the *Interesting Narrative* reveal why Equiano's autobiography lends itself extremely well to children's and adolescent literature autoadaptations. In these chapters, Equiano strategically describes life in his Eboe nation for the eighteenth-century reader. According to Equiano, his Eboe culture encompasses laws, a social hierarchy, a monotheistic worldview, a distinct celebration marking the new year, an impressive work ethic, important familial relationships, cleanliness, circumcision, a clear moral code, poets, and musical instruments, among other characteristics. All these features humanize the Eboe nation, Africans, and Africa, yet Equiano touches on them to form a cultural bridge between the Eboes and his eighteenth-century readers; that is, he presents his Eboe nation in familiar ways for these readers to see the clear links—as opposed to the culturally constructed divisions—between African and European cultures. More importantly, Equiano, as a mature adult writer reflecting on his youth in his Eboe nation years after he claims he lived there, structures the "narrating I" in this part of his text as if he were an eleven-year-old child, who, at that point in his life, experienced a relatively sheltered and peaceful life among his people. Equiano's construction of the "narrating I" as an eleven-year-old in this part of his text attempts to elicit sympathy from the eighteenth-century reader after Africans capture and enslave him and begin transporting him to the west coast of Africa. The fracturing of Equiano's innocence, furthermore, allows the author to instruct the eighteenth-century reader about the infrastructure of the transatlantic slave trade and the horrors an enslaved person encountered during the Middle Passage. Such a reading has become commonplace in Equiano studies.

Yet the dynamics of this part of the *Interesting Narrative* change with Mott's editing of these opening chapters for readers in a different country and in a different century, that is, for the nineteenth-century students of African descent at the Free School in New York. Tapping into this section of the autobiography enables Mott to minimize, in her abridged edition, the historical gap between the original publication date of the narrative along with the cultural gap between the young Equiano and the young student-readers at the Free School. In the fifth paragraph of Mott's abridged edition, for instance, the following language appears: "My parents had one daughter and a number of sons, of which I was the youngest. As I generally attended my mother, she took great pains in forming my mind and training me to exercise" (Equiano, *Life* 6). This passage from Equiano's autobiography establishes a cultural bridge, one that encourages the Free School student to familiarize and even identify with the innocent, eleven-year-old Equiano based on his narration of youth, which alludes to spending time with his mother, engaging in play, and interacting with his siblings. Encountering this part of Equiano's text would have allowed the Free School students to acquire a more comprehensive understanding of their selves in relation to other individuals of African descent and to the larger dynamics of the slave trade and institution of slavery beyond the confines of New York and the United States. Furthermore, the Free School students' engagement with Equiano's calculated description of life in Africa would have offered them a liberating commentary on their selves and their past, even though the legitimacy of these autobiographical descriptions have been seriously questioned by several twentieth- and twenty-first-century critics. Portions of the abridged edition may be understood as comprising a "story of freedom," to borrow (and modify slightly) the title of one of Shane White's books, for the Free School students of African descent in nineteenth-century New York.

Though Mott almost certainly consulted Durell's edition for her abridged one, she altered several parts from his 1791 New York edition, thus continuing this particular chain of textual mutations. Mott, for instance, eliminated Durell's "List of Subscribers." Of course, Durell's subscribers were not Mott's audience for her abridged edition. However, this editorial decision was likely motivated by the fact that a multipage subscriber list, like the one that appears in the unauthorized New York edition, would have overwhelmed the student readers at the Free School and occupied an unnecessary amount of space in a text designed for children and adolescent readers. Additionally, Mott chose not to reproduce Tiebout's frontispiece from Durell's edition; instead, she included a frontispiece created by another artist from the United States. The signature under the frontispiece in Mott's abridged edition reads "A.A.," indicating that the New York artist, Alexander Anderson, created this visual representation of Equiano along with other illustrations found in the abridged edition.[14] Harry B. Weiss notes that Alexander Anderson "made many wood engravings for the juvenile library of Samuel Wood" (759), the publisher of Mott's abridged edition.[15] Anderson's rendering of Equiano aligns with several visual components found in the frontispieces from the second London edition and Durell's edition: the author sits confidently, wears the clothes of a gentleman, locks eyes with his reader, and holds a Bible turned to Acts. The language under the frontispiece, however, only reads, "Gustavus Vassa," thus eliminating the life writer's African name, "Olaudah Equiano," and the designation "the African," which appear under the visual representation of the author in Durell's edition. Although the name Olaudah Equiano does appear in the full title of Mott's abridged edition, this elimination of both "Olaudah Equiano" and "the African" indicates another departure from Durell's edition.[16]

Nevertheless, perhaps the most striking alteration found in the abridged edition is the number of pages Mott eliminated from Durell's edition. James Green provides a rare albeit brief description of Mott's text:

> In 1829 Mott published a slightly fuller section from the narrative as a separate 36-page pamphlet, about the same size and price as the English "Negro's Friend" version, but a totally different text. Mott may have felt that the best way to reuse this text to promote abolition was to boil it down to a penny pamphlet, removing all the dated material, the English references, the travels and adventures, and the not very Quakerish religious speculation. (372)

Green's comments first identify the total number of pages in Mott's edition as thirty-six; however, language taken from the *Interesting Narrative* in the abridged edition runs from page 5 through the top of page 25. These page numbers need to be qualified because the abridged edition contains four pages of images created by Anderson (pages 7, 11, 16, 22). Specific page numbers from the abridged edition appear under all of these images. This interplay between the image and page number sometimes requires the Free School's students to make connections between the image and the language on the opposite page, whereas, in other cases, the connection between the image and the page number invites the students to turn back or forward in the text to establish connections between the verbal and the visual.[17] This interplay between the visual and the verbal would have honed the Free School students' reading skills.

Nonetheless, by taking into consideration these four pages that only display Anderson's images, Equiano's prose fills approximately sixteen and a quarter pages of Mott's text; in other words, Mott's abridged edition preserves less than 6 percent of the language from Durell's edition.

Pages 25 to 36 from the abridged edition continue the departure from Durell's edition, for they do not contain any language from the *Interesting Narrative*. Instead, Samuel Wood and Sons, who published "many thousands of children's books" (Weiss 755), added content to Mott's abridged edition. After the final sentence from the *Interesting Narrative* and Mott's "Note," Wood and Sons inserted the following language:

> The publishers have thought proper to enlarge this small work by adding the following Remarks upon the Slave Trade: not with a view to excite the indignation of any, but to give the young and the uninformed a correct idea of what the poor inhabitants of Africa suffer; for which their oppressors can give no better excuse, than that they are "guilty of a skin not coloured like their own." (Equiano, *Life* 25)

Following this observation, the Woods added "Remarks on the Slave Trade," an illustration of a slave ship, titled "Plan of a Slave Ship's lower deck, with Negroes in proportion of not quite one to a ton," which mirrors the widely circulated representations of the *Brookes*, "A Subject for Conversation and Reflection at the Tea-Table," which contains the British poet William Cowper's "The Negro's Complaint" and parts from his "The Task." Cowper's poetry is then followed by two visual representations created by Anderson of a white master overseeing his slaves and the poems "The Negro Boy" and "The Negro's Prayer." While "The Negro's Prayer" was "penned by a Black man, a slave in the lower part of Virginia" (Equiano, *Life* 36), according to Wood and Son, the content for "The Negro Boy" was inspired by "an African Prince on arriving in England, being asked what he had given for his watch, answered, 'What I never will again: I gave a fine Boy for it'" (Equiano, *Life* 35).

The Woods' intervention places the abridged edition of Equiano's text in a wider field of transatlantic and transnational discourse on the slave trade and institution of slavery. Whereas several of Mott's revisions either minimize or altogether eliminate Equiano's association with Great Britain, most of the textual material added by Wood and Sons reestablishes a connection between the abridged edition of the *Interesting Narrative* and British culture. In other words, it would be too sweeping to claim that all references and connections to Great Britain are eliminated in Mott's edition. The Woods' participation in shaping the abridged edition, nonetheless, results in an edition of the *Interesting Narrative* that moves further away from Durell's edition. Mott's abridged edition can be referred to as a "collaborative autobiography," that is, as Sidonie Smith and Julia Watson state, "the production of an autobiographical text by more than one person" (264).[18] In the 1829 abridged edition, Mott, the Woods, and Anderson contributed parts to the text that they thought were important for the African American student-readers at the Free School. Compared to Durell's edition, then, Mott's abridged edition contains a wider range of textual collaboration.

A cursory glance at the full title of Mott's abridged edition reveals additional departures from Durell's edition. Green employs, in the second sentence found in the above quotation, the word *may* to offer the possibility that Mott trimmed Equiano's adventures (among other elements) to promote abolitionism in nineteenth-century New York. While Green should be applauded for acknowledging the abridged edition in his important essay, his point on the alleged lack of adventures in Mott's text does not hold up.[19] As noted earlier, the full title of Mott's text is *The Life and Adventures of Olaudah Equiano; or, Gustavus Vassa, the African. From an Account Written by Himself, Abridged by A. Mott. To Which Is Added Some Remarks on the Slave Trade*. The language in this title starts to uncover the shakiness of Green's proposal that Mott may have "remove[d]" "the travels and adventures" from her abridged text. Contrary to Green's point, Mott's title actually indicates that she wished to emphasize the presence of adventures (in the plural sense, as the title indicates) to draw the Free School students into her abridged edition.

In fact, several portions of the abridged edition reflect Mott's editorial choice to keep Equiano's adventures in her text. Mott includes Equiano's extensive travels as an enslaved person throughout the Atlantic world, as well as his postslavery adventures in Italy, Turkey, the Archipelago Islands, Portugal, the West Indies, and the North Pole, his travel to Spain, his participation in Dr. Irving's plantation scheme in Central America, and his involvement with the Sierra Leone resettlement project. Contrary to Green's point, Mott's abridged edition ensures that the Free School students read an autobiographical account not stripped of but rather filled with Equiano's numerous travels and adventures. Mott's retaining of Equiano's transatlantic travel—while both an enslaved and a free person—reinforces the Free School curriculum's goal of "alert[ing] [the students] to a world larger than the neighborhood or city they inhabited" (Peterson 187); likewise, Mott's text would have provided the students with "a broader cosmopolitan outlook" (Peterson 187–88) through experiencing the autobiographer's many travels and adventures on the printed page.

Mott very likely utilized Equiano's travels and adventures to reinforce another part of the Free School's curriculum: the teaching of "practical knowledge" (Peterson 187). In one part of his *History*, Andrews includes a letter from three individuals—Alderman Seymour, Mr. St. John, and Mr. Cowdry—who visited the Free School in May 1824. According to the testimonies of the letter writers given at a New York City Common Council meeting, the students at the Free School displayed knowledge of "Spelling, Reading, Writing, Arithmetic, Grammar, Geography, and Elocution, and of Needlework in addition to these, on the part of the females" (qtd. in Andrews 36). Accounts of visitors observing and interacting with the Free School's students were routinely printed in nineteenth-century New York newspapers in hopes of securing additional funding for the educational institution. Seymour's, St. John's, and Cowdry's observations highlight the emphasis placed on the students' acquisition of practical skills at the Free School.

Many parts of Mott's abridged edition call attention to the benefits of obtaining an education and practical knowledge. Like the authorized editions of Equiano's autobiography, Mott's abridged edition focuses on the autobiographer's learning through his maritime adventures and other relevant educational experiences obtained on land. These scenes—in both the authorized editions and the abridged edition—not only underscore Equiano's development as an adolescent but also that his increased knowledge largely results from his interaction with whites on either ships or land, mostly through his position as Michael Henry Pascal's slave. The account of Equiano's learning in Mott's abridged edition documents, for the Free School's students, the adolescent Equiano's acquisition of practical knowledge aligning with increased exposure to and comfort around white peoples. In this way, Mott's text frames Equiano's representations of his adolescent years as a type of developmental blueprint for the Free School students. Similar to the adolescent Equiano found in the authorized editions of the *Interesting Narrative*, the adolescent students at the Free School were being instructed mostly by whites on the significance and benefits of practical knowledge.[20] Therefore, this emphasis in Mott's text on the adolescent period of Equiano's life stresses the benefits of reading, writing, arithmetic, geography, and ship navigation; it also consistently highlights the positive consequences resulting from the author's intellectual curiosity, his drive for additional education, and the benefits of learning practical knowledge largely from white persons.

Curiously, too, some parts of the adolescent portions included in the abridged edition report the problems that Equiano encountered when he visited the West Indies and what would later became the United States. Like the language in the authorized editions of *Interesting Narrative*, the abridged edition discloses that Equiano, in 1763, was robbed by two sailors who stole "about eight guineas," which he "had collected by doing small jobs on board the ships of war" (*Life* 14). Moreover, Equiano comments, in both the authorized and the abridged editions, on being beaten up by a "master" and "a very rough white man with him" (*Life* 15–16) when he attempted to sell goods in Georgia. However, following these negative remarks, Equiano, after he has acquired his freedom and matured into an adult in both the authorized and abridged editions, offers positive commentary on his second-to-last trip to the United States. During this trip to Philadelphia, he notes, he visited a free school in this city. He writes that "it rejoiced my heart when one of those people [a Quaker in Philadelphia] took me to the Free School where I saw the children of my colour instructed, and their minds cultivated to fit them for usefulness" (*Life* 24). Here Mott's abridged edition makes use of Equiano's commentary on his penultimate trip to the United States to form an additional link between the autobiographer and the student readers enrolled at the Free School. Equiano, in the passage from Mott's edition quoted above, applauds the Free School in Philadelphia because it not only taught "children of [his] colour," but, as he comments, this institution, through its pedagogical methods, educated students for "usefulness." If Equiano's life has been presented to the Free School students as a type of developmental blueprint, then the autobiographer's praise of the Free School in Philadelphia translates into an endorsement for the Free School in New York. It is as if the adult Equiano's endorsement of the Free School in Philadelphia erases the difficulties he faced in the colonies in earlier periods of his life.

Strikingly, Andrews, in one part of his *History*, uses the exact same language as Equiano in his commentary on the Philadelphia Free School. In an early part of his *History*, Andrews outlines the founding of the New York Manumission Society and quotes from an act passed on February 19, 1808. This act states that the Manumission Society "has established a free school in the city of New York, for the education of the children of such persons as have been liberated from bondage, that they may hereafter become useful members of the community" (qtd. in Andrews 11). Like Equiano's commentary on the Free School in Philadelphia found in the authorized and abridged editions, Andrews's language underscores that the pedagogical methods at the New York African Free School attempted to ensure that the children of formerly enslaved persons in nineteenth-century New York became "useful members" of that city. Because the abridged edition—like the authorized editions—traces Equiano's youth, adolescence, and adult years, the autobiographical text provides the Free School readers with a blueprint on how to mature, interact with whites, seek education, and become "useful" in nineteenth-century New York society after successfully completing their education at the institution.

The politics at the New York African Free School regarding how individuals of African descent could become "useful" members of society, however, shifted in the 1820s. Therefore, the publication date of Mott's abridged edition corresponds with an important change in the politics at the school and in the New York Manumission Society. By the mid-1820s, some members of the New York Manumission Society—including Andrews—began supporting the American Colonization Society's "programs for sending free blacks to Africa" (Harris 134). These same members, Leslie M. Harris observes, created the New York City Colonization Society in 1817 and played key parts in establishing the New York State Colonization Society in 1829 (134), the same year Mott's abridged edition appeared in print. As Harris adds, the "African Free Schools began to train blacks for emigration to Liberia" (134). Equiano's commentary on the Sierra Leone resettlement project, an initiative orchestrated by the British government in the mid-1780s to help the black poor and "lascars" who struggled to find adequate food, housing, and employment in England, may have been altered by Mott in her abridged edition to offer an endorsement for black New Yorkers' emigration to Africa.[21] Equiano, who learned about the project when he returned to London in August 1786, writes in the ninth edition of his autobiography, "I was very agreeably surprised to find, that the benevolence of government adopted the plan of some philanthropic individuals, to send the Africans from hence to their native quarter, and that some vessels were then engaged to carry them to Sierra Leona; an act which redounded to the honour of all concerned in its promotion, and filled me with prayers and much rejoicing" (Equiano, Interesting Narrative *and Other* 226).

At this point in his authorized life narrative, Equiano outlines what he sees as the potential in the resettlement project. However, following his appointment as "Commissary on the part of the Government," a position that charged him with handling supplies and serving the British government in interactions with African authorities (Carretta, in Equiano, Interesting Narrative *and Other* 299n638), he notes, in the ninth edition, that the white authorities associated with the resettlement project dismissed him after he exposed the mismanagement of goods (Equiano, Interesting Narrative *and Other* 228). Therefore, instead of going back to Africa, Equiano watched the ships sail to Sierra Leone from a port in Plymouth: "Thus provided, *they* proceeded on *their* voyage; and at last, worn out by treatment, perhaps, not the most mild, and wasted by sickness, brought on by want of medicine, clothes, bedding, etc. *they* reached Sierra Leona just at the commencement of the rains" (Equiano, Interesting Narrative *and Other* 228–29; emphasis added). Here Equiano clearly distances himself from the participants in the resettlement project through his use of "they" and "their." He nevertheless adds that the "expedition . . . was humane and politic in its design, nor was its failure owing to government; every thing was done on their part; but there was evidently sufficient mismanagement attending the conduct and execution of it to defeat its success" (Equiano, Interesting Narrative *and Other* 229). The autobiographer writes that theory and practice did not coincide in this particular case.[22]

In Mott's abridged edition, Equiano's reflections on the resettlement project appear in the third-to-last paragraph in this text. Mott apparently used Equiano's writing on the resettlement project to support the New York Manumission Society's resettlement politics. At first, Mott's abridged edition remains loyal to Equiano's observations on the resettlement project found in the authorized editions as well as Durell's edition. That is, the language found in this particular part from these editions indicates that Equiano heard about the initiative after returning to London in 1786 and mentions the autobiographer's concern that the transatlantic slave trade could undermine the resettlement project. This consistency in documenting Equiano's life in the abridged edition, however, ends with a sentence describing Equiano's recollection of the moment members of the resettlement project sailed for Sierra Leone: "After much difficulty and delay, *we* set sail with 426 persons on board, and reached *our* destination port in June, just as the rainy season commenced. Having been closely confined for several months *we* were unprepared for such a season, and many of them died. Thus was the benevolent intention frustrated for that time, and *I* returned to England" (Equiano, *Life* 24; emphasis added). The revision from "they" and "their," as seen in the authorized ninth edition, to "we," "our," and "I," as seen in the abridged edition, places Equiano in a radically different position in relation to the resettlement project: instead of a detached observer in his authorized autobiography who praises the potential of the project yet publicly denounces the corruption within the initiative, the life writer, according to Mott's abridged text, becomes an active participant and actually revisits the continent that he was forcibly removed from as a young child, as his narrative claims. According to all twentieth- and twenty-first-century accounts, Equiano never returned to Africa.

How should we make sense of this revision, one that reveals the presence of what we may refer to as the "edited I," a term that signifies instances in which an agent other than the life writer has manipulated the text in some way, without permission or acknowledgment? Pinpointing the exact agent or agents responsible for this instance of textual fluidity is difficult. Nevertheless, the language from Mott's abridged edition parallels the commentary found in her aforementioned *Biographical Sketches* devoted to Equiano and his participation in the Sierra Leone resettlement project, including his alleged travel back to Africa. Mott's texts documenting Equiano's travel to Africa with the Sierra Leone resettlement project are consistent. Another interesting point regarding the resettlement project in Mott's edited texts is that the language in Durell's edition of the *Interesting Narrative* remains faithful to the authorized editions and states that Equiano did not sail with the resettlement project. This part from Durell's edition reads, "Thus provided, they proceeded on their voyage; and at last, worn out by treatment, perhaps not the most mild, and wasted by sickness, brought on by want of medicine, cloaths [sic], bedding, &c. they reached Sierra Leona just at the commencement of the rains" (Equiano, *Interesting Narrative of the Life* 180). According to Durell's edition, Equiano draws a clear line between himself and the individuals who sailed to Sierra Leone.

The language in Mott's abridged edition documenting Equiano's commentary on the resettlement project reveals yet another departure from Durell's New York edition. The editorial consistency found in both Mott's abridged edition and the part devoted to Equiano in her *Biographical Sketches* suggests that she likely manipulated Equiano's language regarding his sailing with the resettlement project. Perhaps Mott altered this language in her abridged edition for the sake of increasing the probability that the Free School readers would understand the autobiography as a whole. In other words, by beginning her abridged edition in Africa and inserting Equiano's travel back to Africa near the end of her text, Mott may have purposefully constructed a largely circular narrative that provided the student readers with an understandable narrative arc. Another possible explanation may be that this revision ensures that Equiano's traveling back to Africa aligns with the title of Mott's abridged edition, which promises to showcase the adventures of the life writer. Nor should readers discount the possibility that Mott's respective publishers—Mahlon Day for *Biographical Sketches* and Samuel Wood and Sons for the abridged edition—may have been the agents who altered the language in Equiano's text. That is, perhaps the consistency of the alterations in Mott's texts derives from the fact that the Woods simply printed what Day had published three years earlier.

The fluidity of the resettlement project scene in Mott's abridged edition also requires readers to consider the political implications of this revision, which invites readers to explore connections to the American Colonization Society, an organization active in New York in the 1820s; the New York City Colonization Society; and the New York State Colonization Society. Given Andrews's position at the Free School and Harris's aforementioned points on the school's endorsement of resettlement in the 1820s, readers of Mott's text face a crucial interpretive question: whether she manipulates Equiano's language to encourage the student readers of African descent at the Free School to put their knowledge of navigation to use and abandon the United States, travel across the Atlantic, and attempt a resettlement project in Africa when they become adults. Of course, this change in Equiano's involvement with the resettlement project would not encourage the students to relocate to Sierra Leone. Such a location was not pertinent to nineteenth-century resettlement plans in New York at the time. The language in Mott's abridged edition noting that the Sierra Leone resettlement project was "frustrated for that time" (Equiano, *Life* 25) suggests that a door had been opened by the British in the late eighteenth century for a future and allegedly more successful resettlement project. This language highlighting the problems in the Sierra Leone project may very well endorse the resettlement project more familiar to the Free School and its students, namely, the American Colonization Society's effort to send black New Yorkers to Liberia. "Usefulness," in this case, may very well include expatriation and finding a "home" elsewhere. Further critical work on Mott's abridged edition will need to investigate Mott's relationship with the aforementioned colonization societies.[23]

Interpretations of what appears to be a politically charged revision likewise must attend to the ethical implications that accompany this nonauthorial alteration, especially considering the fact that Mott's abridged edition appeared in print in New York thirty-two years after Equiano's death in London. Though Equiano approved of the publishing and reading of unauthorized editions of his autobiography in Holland, Germany, and New York, contemporary readers may find this example of textual mutation as blurring what G. Thomas Couser has identified as the "not always clear lines between making, taking, and faking the life of another person in print" (36).[24] At this point, Mott's abridged edition—one manifestation of the *Interesting Narrative* as a fluid text—appears to embrace what may be viewed as conflicting rhetorical and political agendas, including liberation and empowerment but also subordination and expatriation. Beginning to explore this manifestation of the *Interesting Narrative* as a fluid text, however, can happen only when scholars relinquish the position that the nine authorized editions of Equiano's narrative are the only ones worthy of study, and that the Afro-British Equiano is the only acceptable version of this eighteenth-century autobiographer. As a product of transatlantic and transnational print networks, Mott's abridged edition productively challenges both of these positions in its situating of Equiano's autobiography as a text designed to be read by African American students, and as one that is part of the African American life narrative canon. This chapter provides one example of the intellectual benefits of moving beyond the nine authorized editions of the *Interesting Narrative* that were printed during Equiano's lifetime. Mott's abridged edition starts to open up opportunities to construct more-thorough publishing and reception histories of the unauthorized and posthumous editions of this seminal autobiography published in various parts of the eighteenth- and nineteenth-century Atlantic world.

The debate on the authenticity of Equiano's African origins has privileged certain archival documents arguing whether the life writer was born in Africa or the Carolinas. Until now, however, the presence of "Gustavus Vassa" (or variations thereof) on a baptismal certificate and a ship log has overshadowed other archival texts that provide new ways to understand Equiano's relationship to the United States beyond his place of birth. Even though Mott's text offers readers an abridged edition of the *Interesting Narrative* published thirty-two years after Equiano's death, brevity does not always equate with simplicity. Nor does Mott's editing of Equiano's eighteenth-century life narrative undermine the text's place in the canon of eighteenth-century British literature. Rather than diminishing the spirit of the best-selling editions of the *Interesting Narrative* published during Equiano's lifetime, Mott's abridged edition begins to uncover a more complicated—and interesting—narrative on how different readers at different historical periods and in different countries engaged different editions of the autobiography. In fact, Mott's trimming of the eighteenth-century life narrative into a pedagogical document for the Free School students adds new life to—instead of deflating—Equiano's autobiography.

NOTES

I am grateful to Paul J. Ericson, director of academic programs, and the staff at the American Antiquarian Society for providing me with a copy of Mott's abridged edition. I also wish to thank Ricia A. Chansky and Vincent Carretta for commenting on drafts of this chapter and Kevin S. Carroll for assisting in the acquisition of research materials.

1. Throughout this chapter, I refer to the writer of the *Interesting Narrative* as Olaudah Equiano, though he used and embraced the name Gustavus Vassa, one given to him by his master, Michael Henry Pascal, throughout the majority of his life. For more information on this topic, see Lovejoy ("Olaudah").

2. On the teaching of Equiano in a variety of twenty-first-century classrooms, see my *Teaching Olaudah Equiano's* Narrative: *Pedagogical Strategies and New Perspectives*.

3. References to Mott's abridged edition are found in the *National Union Catalog*, Dorothy B. Porter's "Early American Negro Writings: A Bibliographical Study," Janheinz Jahn's *A Bibliography of Neo-African Literature from Africa, America, and the Caribbean*, and Janheinz Jahn and Claus Peter Dressler's *Bibliography of Creative African Writing* (Potkay and Burr 163).

4. Vernon Loggins, in *The Negro Author: His Development in America to 1900*, notes that the poem "The Negro's Prayer" was "appended by A. Mott to his [*sic*] abridged edition of *The Life and Adventures of Olaudah Equiano, or Gustavus Vassa* (1829)" (30). Sidney Kaplan and Emma

Nogrady Kaplan include an image of the title page from Mott's edition in their book, *The Black Presence in the Era of the American Revolution* (219), and they point out that "in 1829 an illustrated juvenile edition of the *Narrative* with antislavery poems by the English poet William Cowper was published in New York, edited by Abigail Mott, a white abolitionist, for use as a text in the African Free Schools" (215–16n). Henry Louis Gates Jr. observes, in the introduction to his coedited book with William L. Andrews, *Pioneers of the Black Atlantic: Five Slave Narratives from the Enlightenment, 1772–1815*, that "by 1837, another eight editions [of *The Interesting Narrative*] had appeared, including an abridgment in 1829" (19n7). Robert J. Allison, in his introductory essay to his Bedford/St. Martin's edition of the *Interesting Narrative*, states that "in 1829, American abolitionist Abigail Field Mott published a short illustrated edition to give as a prize to black pupils in New York's Free African School" (32). Like Allison, Werner Sollors, in his introduction to the Norton Critical Edition of the *Interesting Narrative*, writes that "[Equiano's] memory was kept alive by American abolitionists; the last two editions published in the nineteenth century appeared in the United States, in 1829 and 1837, respectively" (xxviii). James Green lists the 1829 abridged edition as part of the publishing history of the *Interesting Narrative* (374n2) and writes three sentences on Mott's edition (372). James Walvin draws on Green's brief opinions of the abridged edition in the final chapter of his biography of Equiano. See his notes 12, 13, and 14 (194), all of which cite pages from Green's essay.

5. For commentary on the usage of the word *depth* in Equiano studies, see Hollis.

6. In 1825 Mahlon Day published A. Mott's *Observations on the Importance of Female Education, and Maternal Instruction, with Their Beneficial Influence on Society*, a text that she wrote.

7. During most of this period, Douglass lectured in Great Britain, Ireland, and Scotland, where he also networked with abolitionists and sold copies of his *Narrative* that differed from the 1845 Boston edition. This transatlantic voyage also protected the fugitive slave from being recaptured by his owners. On what they refer to as Douglass's "liberating sojourn," see Rice and Crawford.

8. One of Equiano's biographers maintains that "to make any impact in America," Equiano "had to be stripped of many of his defining experiences and qualities" (Walvin 190).

9. Peterson clarifies that "some boys [at the Free School] had close ties to slavery," while others "enjoyed origins with deeper roots in freedom" (184). Two key legislative acts contributed to differentiating the status of black New Yorkers. As Shane White writes, "Under the terms of the [1799] act, all children born to slave women after July 4, 1799, were to be free, but males were to remain in a form of indentured servitude until they reached the age of twenty-eight, and females were to be so bound until they were twenty-five. Those who were still slaves on July 4, 1799, were abandoned to their fate; not until 1817 would the legislature finally agree to free such persons and even then that was not to occur for another decade, until July 4, 1827" (13). Hence, White names the pace at which abolition occurred in New York as "glacial" (13). In a similar vein, Patrick Rael has referred to the "long death of slavery" in New York. Rael states that "in New York the process took particularly long, proceeding incrementally from 1777, when New York lawmakers first began proposing abolition measures, to 1827, when the state passed its last major piece of antislavery legislation" (114).

10. Karen Kennerly's *The Slave Who Bought His Freedom: Equiano's Story* (1971) and Ann Cameron's *The Kidnapped Prince: The Life of Olaudah Equiano* (1995) provide further insights on how the *Interesting Narrative* has been edited for young student readers in the United States.

11. It is crucial to observe here that portions from Equiano's *Interesting Narrative* appear in Mott's 1826 *Biographical Sketches and Interesting Anecdotes of Persons of Colour* (55–64). Like the abridged edition, *Biographical Sketches* was edited for students at the Free School.

12. Mott's note on p. 25 of the abridged edition provides another relevant point relating to Durell's edition. In this note, she admits consulting "a work that has lately come into [her] hands" (25), which refers to Henri Grégoire's *An Enquiry concerning the Intellectual and Moral Faculties, and Literature of Negroes; Followed with an Account of the Life and Works of Fifteen Negroes and Mulattoes, Distinguished in Science, Literature, and the Arts* (Brooklyn, 1810; translated by David Bailie Warden). It would have been impossible for Mott to construct her abridged edition based on Grégoire's *Enquiry* because his text did not include any language written by Equiano. On the other hand, Durell's edition is comprised of language written by Equiano.

13. This term—with its purposeful play on the Greek word for "self," *autos*, and the adaptation of this self—identifies the fluidity of an autobiographical text that remains somewhat true to the original autobiography but still emerges as a new version of the same autobiography because of editorial intervention (Lamore, "Futures" 14). In this type of autobiographical text, the author does not necessarily adapt herself or himself, as Equiano did repeatedly in the revisions he made to the nine authorized editions of his autobiography that appeared during his lifetime; rather, an agent other than the author—Mott, in this case—adapts a particular life narrative for specific rhetorical and political purposes. This term embraces John Bryant's stance on the inevitability of textual fluidity. As Bryant notes, "literary works invariably exist in more than one version, either in early manuscript forms, subsequent print editions, or even adaptations in other media with or without the author's consent" (1).

14. Jane R. Pomeroy refers to Anderson as "the first skilled relief engraver in America" ("New" 322), and he was known to individuals in the United States during the late nineteenth century as "the Father of American Wood Engraving," according to the language on his tombstone in Brooklyn's Green-Wood Cemetery ("New" 322). A number of the illustrations from Mott's abridged edition appear in "Alexander Anderson's Scrapbooks," a part of the New York Public Library's Digital Collections ("Alexander"). This digital archive showcases several pieces that reveal Anderson's engagement with the representation of enslaved peoples. I wish to thank Joycelyn K. Moody for drawing my attention to this digital archive. The frontispiece from Mott's abridged edition offers a different visual representation of Equiano compared to the ones found in the 1789 London, 1791 New York, and 1837 Boston editions. For a preliminary discussion of the different frontispieces found in the editions of the *Interesting Narrative* published in Great Britain and the United States, consult p. 247 from Srinivas Aravamudan's chapter, "Equiano and the Politics of Literacy," in his *Tropicopolitans: Colonialism and Agency, 1688–1804*. A comprehensive visual analysis of the frontispieces in the editions of the *Interesting Narrative* published in Great Britain and the United States remains to be completed.

15. The history of the Woods' publishing house solidifies this connection: several of their children's books were "illustrated with copper-plate engravings, both plain and handcolored, and a little later with wood-engravings by Dr. Alexander Anderson, . . . whose earliest work is found in these little books" (Wood 7).

16. Curiously, Mott's abridged edition of the *Interesting Narrative* more frequently refers to the author as Gustavus Vassa, the name given to him by his master, Michael Henry Pascal, instead of Olaudah Equiano. This observation relates to Paul E. Lovejoy's recent argument that contemporary scholars should not refer to the author of the *Interesting Narrative* as Olaudah

Equiano; instead, Lovejoy maintains that critics use the name Gustavus Vassa because the author referred to himself by this name for most of his life and, at one point, reacted strongly when individuals referred to him as Olaudah Equiano in "personal settings" (166). As Lovejoy states, "On at least one occasion, the man himself appears to have protested passionately at the use of his birth name" (166). The language under Anderson's frontispiece indicates that one posthumous U.S. edition of the *Interesting Narrative* used the name given to the autobiographer by Pascal instead of the name given to the writer by his parents in Africa.

17. For more information on Anderson's connections with several nineteenth-century book publishers in New York (including the publisher of Mott's abridged edition, Samuel Wood and Sons), consult Pomeroy (*Alexander*, "Alexander," and "New"). This scholar consistently draws on Anderson's life writing, specifically his diary and letters, in her work on this U.S. artist.

18. Up to this point, many Equiano scholars have submitted that, if the life writer was not born in Africa, then he most likely constructed the African origins section in his autobiography from oral narratives spoken to him by individuals of African descent who did experience life as free persons in Africa, as enslaved persons in Africa, as survivors of the Middle Passage, and as enslaved peoples in various parts of the Atlantic world. In other words, Equiano certainly read about Africa, but he likely utilized his extensive travel throughout the Atlantic world by internalizing the oral narratives he heard from displaced Africans about their experiences in Africa and the Americas. He then likely transformed these narratives from the realm of the oral to the printed page when he later wrote the first section of his autobiography. In this regard, even the authorized editions of the *Interesting Narrative* may be considered collaborative autobiographies; that is, the authorized editions not only map the life of Equiano, but these texts also contain interesting narratives about displaced Africans in the Atlantic world collected and written down by the author named Olaudah Equiano or Gustavus Vassa. If readers of the *Interesting Narrative* are willing to recognize the collaborative nature imbedded in the authorized editions of Equiano's text, then they should also acknowledge that a different yet equally meaningful type of collaboration exists in the unauthorized, posthumous, and abridged editions of the autobiography published in the United States.

19. To his credit, Green does remark, in his third sentence on Mott's abridged edition, that "she transformed the book [the *Interesting Narrative*] into a perfect exemplar of the slave narrative as the genre was then evolving" (372). Mott does not print Equiano's certificate of manumission in her abridged edition, but her edition of the *Interesting Narrative* adheres to the typical trajectory of a slave narrative, which traces an enslaved (or formerly enslaved) person's path to freedom, or, in Equiano's case, from freedom to enslavement to freedom.

20. Peterson posits that the Free School's founders' "view of the role of free black people was constrained by a genteel racism" (189). She adds that "the trustees promised to produce 'men of distinction,' but the school trained its graduates for places that were hardly distinguished. Boys were taught to be mechanics and artisans, and in the African Free School for girls, the female students learned skills such as sewing and knitting. An employment service sought to place the graduates in trades by means of indenture" (190).

21. According to Carretta, "The black loyalists arriving from America at the end of the Revolution joined the thousands of blacks already resident in England. Estimates of the total number of blacks in England in the last quarter of the eighteenth century range between five and twenty thousand" (*Equiano* 216). See Carretta (*Equiano* 202–35) for a discussion of the

economic and social conditions that led to the eventual creation of the resettlement project. Christopher Fyfe succinctly describes these conditions: "During the war the British offered slaves freedom if they left their American masters. Many ran away and joined the British army and navy. After the war some of them came to London, where they were free. But, though free, they were unemployed and had to beg in the streets" (22).

22. Equiano's positive endorsement of the spirit of the resettlement project can also be seen in the language from his will. Equiano decided that if both of his children, Ann Marie and Johanna Vassa, predeceased him, he chose to "give[,] devise[,] and bequeath" the "whole" of his "Estate" "to the Treasurer and Directors of the Sierra Leona Company for the Use and Benefit of the School established by the said Company at Sierra Leona" ("Will" 373). The resettlement project Equiano names here is not the same one he was involved with in 1787. Consult Edwards ("Descriptive") for additional information on Equiano's will.

23. Perhaps this tampering with Equiano's comments on the Sierra Leone resettlement project found in Mott's *Biographical Sketches* and her abridged version and its possible connection to colonization societies contributed to the quarrel that permanently divided Douglass and Mott sometime around 1850, the source of which "remains unknown" (Douglass 114n1), according to the editors of *The Frederick Douglass Papers*.

24. On the ethics of life writing, see also Eakin.

WORKS CITED

"Alexander Anderson's Scrapbooks." *The New York Public Library Digital Collections*.

Allison, Robert J. Introduction. The Interesting Narrative of the Life of Olaudah Equiano, Written by Himself *with Related Documents*. Ed. Robert J. Allison. 2nd ed. Boston: Bedford/St. Martin's, 2007. 7–35.

Andrews, Charles C. *The History of the New-York African Free-Schools, from Their Establishment in 1787, to the Present Time; Embracing a Period of More Than Forty Years; Also a Brief Account of the Successful Labors, of the New-York Manumission Society: With an Appendix*. New York: Mahlon Day, 1830.

Aravamudan, Srinivas. *Tropicopolitans: Colonialism and Agency, 1688–1804*. Durham, NC: Duke UP, 1999.

Bryant, John. *The Fluid Text: A Theory of Revision and Editing for Book and Screen*. Ann Arbor: U of Michigan P, 2002.

"Calendar of Correspondence Not Printed." *The Frederick Douglass Papers. Series Three: Correspondence*. Vol. 1: 1842–1852. Ed. John R. McKivigan. New Haven, CT: Yale UP, 2009. 559–601.

Cameron, Ann. *The Kidnapped Prince: The Life of Olaudah Equiano*. New York: Yearling, 1995.

Carretta, Vincent. *Equiano, the African: Biography of a Self-Made Man*. New York: Penguin, 2006.

———. "Note on the Text." The Interesting Narrative *and Other Writings*. Ed. Vincent Carretta. Rev. ed. New York: Penguin, 2003. xxxi–xxxii.

Couser, G. Thomas. *Vulnerable Subjects: Ethics and Life Writing*. Ithaca, NY: Cornell UP, 2004.

Douglass, Frederick. "Frederick Douglass to Abigail Mott." *The Frederick Douglass Papers. Series Three: Correspondence*. Vol. 1: 1842–1852. Ed. John R. McKivigan. New Haven, CT: Yale UP, 2009. 111–15.

Eakin, Paul John, ed. *The Ethics of Life Writing*. Ithaca, NY: Cornell UP, 2004.

Edwards, Paul. "A Descriptive List of Manuscripts in the Cambridgeshire Record Office Relating to the Will of Gustavus Vassa (Olaudah Equiano)." *Research in African Literatures* 20.3 (1989): 473–80.

———. Introduction. *Equiano's Travels*. Ed. Paul Edwards. 2nd ed. Oxford: Heinemann, 1996. xv–xxvii.

———. Introduction. *The Life of Olaudah Equiano, or, Gustavus Vassa the African*. Vol. 1. Ed. Paul Edwards. London: Dawsons, 1969. v–lxxii.

Equiano, Olaudah. The Interesting Narrative *and Other Writings*. Ed. Vincent Carretta. Rev. ed. New York: Penguin, 2003.

———. *The Interesting Narrative of the Life of Olaudah Equiano, or Gustavus Vassa, the African. Written by Himself*. New York: W. Durell, 1791.

———. *The Life and Adventures of Olaudah Equiano; or, Gustavus Vassa, the African. From an Account Written by Himself, Abridged by A. Mott. To Which Is Added Some Remarks on the Slave Trade*. Ed. Abigail Mott. New York: Samuel Wood and Sons, 1829.

———. "The Will and Codicil of Gustavus Vassa [Olaudah Equiano]." The Interesting Narrative *and Other Writings*. Ed. Vincent Carretta. Rev. ed. New York: Penguin, 2003. 373–75.

Fyfe, Christopher. *A Short History of Sierra Leone*. London: Longman, 1979.

Gates, Henry Louis, Jr. Introduction. *Pioneers of the Black Atlantic: Five Slave Narratives from the Enlightenment, 1772–1815*. Ed. Henry Louis Gates Jr. and William L. Andrews. Washington, DC: Civitas, 1998. 1–29.

Gilroy, Paul. *The Black Atlantic: Modernity and Double Consciousness*. Cambridge, MA: Harvard UP, 1993.

Green, James. "The Publishing History of Olaudah Equiano's *Interesting Narrative*." *Slavery and Abolition: A Journal of Comparative Studies* 16.3 (1995): 362–75.

Grégoire, Henri. *An Enquiry concerning the Intellectual and Moral Faculties, and Literatures of Negroes*. Trans. D. B. Warden. Brooklyn, NY: Thomas Kirk, 1810.

Gurko, Miriam. *The Ladies of Seneca Falls: The Birth of the Woman's Rights Movement*. New York: Schocken Books, 1976.

Harris, Leslie M. *In the Shadow of Slavery: African Americans in New York City, 1626–1863*. Chicago: U of Chicago P, 2003.

Hollis, Jessica L. "Flat Equiano: A Transatlantic Approach to Teaching *The Interesting Narrative*." *Teaching Olaudah Equiano's* Narrative: *Pedagogical Strategies and New Perspectives*. Ed. Eric D. Lamore. Knoxville: U of Tennessee P, 2012. 69–94.

Ito, Akiyo. "Olaudah Equiano and the New York Artisans: The First American Edition of *The Interesting Narrative of the Life of Olaudah Equiano, or Gustavus Vassa, the African*." *Early American Literature* 32.1 (1997): 82–101.

Jeffrey, Julie Roy. *The Great Silent Army of Abolitionism: Ordinary Women in the Antislavery Movement*. Chapel Hill: U of North Carolina P, 1998.

Kaplan, Sidney, and Emma Nogrady Kaplan. *The Black Presence in the Era of the American Revolution*. Rev. ed. Amherst: U of Massachusetts P, 1989.

Kennerly, Karen. *The Slave Who Bought His Freedom: Equiano's Story*. New York: E. P. Dutton, 1971.

Lamore, Eric D. "The Futures of African American Life Writing." *a/b: Auto/Biography Studies* 27.1 (2012): 1–18.

———, ed. *Teaching Olaudah Equiano's* Narrative: *Pedagogical Strategies and New Perspectives.* Knoxville: U of Tennessee P, 2012.

Loggins, Vernon. *The Negro Author: His Development in America to 1900.* 1931. Port Washington, NY: Kennikat, 1964.

Lovejoy, Paul E. "Olaudah Equiano or Gustavus Vassa—What's in a Name?" *Atlantic Studies* 9.2 (2012): 165–84.

McFeely, William S. *Frederick Douglass.* New York: Norton, 1991.

Mott, Abigail, ed. *Biographical Sketches and Interesting Anecdotes of Persons of Colour.* New York: Mahlon Day, 1826.

———. *Observations on the Importance of Female Education, and Maternal Instruction, with Their Beneficial Influence on Society.* New York: Mahlon Day, 1825.

———. Preface. *The Life and Adventures of Olaudah Equiano; or, Gustavus Vasa, the African. From an Account Written by Himself, Abridged by A. Mott. To Which Is Added Some Remarks on the Slave Trade.* Ed. Abigail Mott. New York: Samuel Wood and Sons, 1829. 4.

Ogude, S. E. Introduction [to the New Edition]. *Equiano's Travels.* Ed. Paul Edwards. 2nd ed. Oxford: Heinemann, 1996. vii–xiv.

Peterson, Carla L. "Black Life in Freedom: Creating an Elite Culture." *Slavery in New York.* Ed. Ira Berlin and Leslie M. Harris. New York: New Press, 2005. 181–214.

Pomeroy, Jane R. *Alexander Anderson (1775–1870): Wood Engraver and Illustrator; An Annotated Bibliography.* 3 vols. New Castle, DE: Oak Knoll; Worcester, MA: American Antiquarian Society with the New York Public Library, 2005.

———. "Alexander Anderson's Life and Engravings before 1800, with a Checklist of Publications Drawn from His Diary." *Proceedings of the American Antiquarian Society* 100.1 (1990): 137–230.

———. "A New Bibliography of the Work of Wood Engraver and Illustrator Alexander Anderson." *Proceedings of the American Antiquarian Society* 115.2 (2005): 317–40.

Potkay, Adam, and Sandra Burr. "Bibliographical Note [on Olaudah Equiano's *Interesting Narrative*]." *Black Atlantic Writers of the Eighteenth Century: Living the Exodus in England and the Americas.* Ed. Adam Potkay and Sandra Burr. Boston: Bedford/St. Martin's, 1995. 162–64.

Rael, Patrick. "The Long Death of Slavery." *Slavery in New York.* Ed. Ira Berlin and Leslie M. Harris. New York: New Press, 2005. 113–46.

Rice, Alan J., and Martin Crawford, eds. *Liberating Sojourn: Frederick Douglass and Transatlantic Reform.* Athens: U of Georgia P, 1999.

Smith, Sidonie, and Julia Watson. *Reading Autobiography: A Guide for Interpreting Life Narratives.* 2nd ed. Minneapolis: U of Minnesota P, 2010.

Sollors, Werner. Introduction. *The Interesting Narrative of the Life of Olaudah Equiano, or Gustavus Vassa, the African*[.] *Written by Himself.* Ed. Werner Sollors. New York: Norton, 2001. ix–xxxi.

Sterling, Dorothy. *Ahead of Her Time: Abby Kelley and the Politics of Antislavery.* New York: Norton, 1991.

Wallace, Robert K. *Douglass and Melville: Anchored Together in Neighborly Style.* New Bedford, MA: Spinner, 2005.

Walvin, James. *An African's Life: The Life and Times of Olaudah Equiano, 1745–1797.* New York: Continuum, 1998.

Weiss, Harry B. "Samuel Wood and Sons, Early New York Publishers of Children's Books." *Bulletin of the New York Public Library* 46.9 (1942): 755–71.

White, Shane. *Stories of Freedom in Black New York*. Cambridge, MA: Harvard UP, 2002.

Wood, William C. *One Hundred Years of Publishing [1804–1904]: A Brief Historical Account of the House of William Wood and Company*. New York: William Wood, 1904.

The Visual Properties of Black Autobiography
The Case of William J. Edwards

ANTHONY S. FOY

With its tidy set of halftones, the 1918 autobiography of William J. Edwards, *Twenty-Five Years in the Black Belt*, exemplifies a significant convergence between technology and ideology in the development of African American autobiography as the age of Jim Crow first congealed. On the one hand, black autobiographers harnessed new images to their narratives as the technology to illustrate books with photographs became fully mechanized by the late 1880s; on the other, racial uplift ideologies, concerned as they were with the race's image, arose within the black public sphere to dominate black autobiographical production by the end of the nineteenth century. It should hardly be surprising, then, that photographic illustrations would become a key feature of African American autobiography at the dawn of the twentieth century. Notwithstanding the intense debates that ideologies of racial uplift fueled—over accommodation and protest, over separation and integration, over education, economics, and politics—they all shared a key assumption about racial representation, insisting on a "direct relationship between the self and the race, between the part and the whole" (Gates 140).

Accordingly, the logic of these ideologies held that the public display of propriety among some black figures would spur political, social, and material gains for many others, if not for all. Thus construing the relationship between the individual and the collective in synecdochic terms, racial uplift ideologies wedded their cultural politics to the accredited figure of the respectable New Negro, who expressed a devotion to the bourgeois protocols of selfhood by publicly embracing and embodying the virtues of self-help, service, education, industry, thrift, piety, chastity, temperance, cleanliness, the patriarchal family, and racial solidarity.[1] As a result, the adherents of racial uplift challenged prevalent antiblack images with their own emblematic selves; if the indecent exploits of disreputable black people presumably confirmed essentialist myths of racial inferiority, then the demonstrated accomplishments of cultivated New Negroes like William Edwards presumably contradicted them.[2]

While ideologies of racial uplift appealed broadly to black people across class lines, they also provided the core vocabulary with which an emergent black middle class began to represent itself, and thereby reproduce itself, as a coherent formation. Because these ideologies stressed the political role of the synecdochic black self, their devotees embraced autobiography—the quintessential form of literary self-presentation—as an ideal instrument for reproducing the doctrines of the black middle class. Rather than simply prove the race's ability to create literature, autobiography in the age of Jim Crow could also demonstrate the race's ability to produce the properly bourgeois subject. Dominated by black educators, religious leaders, reformers, public servants, and professionals, postslavery autobiography did not simply vindicate the race. Instead, it emerged to become a cultural practice suited to the ideological expression of a specific formation within black America, a formation that often perpetuated stark distinctions between itself and the black working class. Autobiography thus evolved as a discrete practice for transfiguring the black image according to the various aims of this aspirational formation. Devotees of racial uplift certainly offered up their first-person narratives as both racial publicity and protest, and these life writers were determined to prove to their white readers that black people (or at least some of them) could satisfy a range of moral qualifications for citizenship. However, these autobiographers did not simply pander to a white audience. They also addressed black readers according to the specific interests of the managerial formation from which they issued. As a result, they sought to model their moral qualifications for a black working class presumed to be in need of elevation; they sought to demonstrate their own adherence to these qualifications in order to induce consent for their collective authority to lead the race; and they sought to coalesce a "better class" of African Americans through a narrative enactment of belonging that, in effect, suppressed disreputable subjectivities at this historical moment in the development of black autobiography.

Uplift ideologies rooted in the "cultural politics of racial synecdoche" (Foy, "Joe" 317) would place a premium on the visual image to "reconstruct" the meaning of blackness in the coeval contest over the production of racial knowledge in the United States (Gates 140–43; Ross, "New Negro" 266–73). As a feature of black autobiography, this strategic recourse to visual paratexts had had a much longer history, since authors' portraits often supplemented black narratives in order to document the body associated with the text. James Olney has identified the "engraved portrait, signed by the narrator" as one of the central conventions of the slave narrative, arguing that "the portrait and the signature (which one might well find in other nineteenth-century autobiographical documents but with very different motivation) . . . are intended to attest to the real existence of the narrator" (152, 155). Consistent with this tradition, Jim Crow–era autobiographers would continue to rely on portraiture, especially the author's frontispiece, to picture the uplifted black self with a direct appeal to the senses, conjoining the black body with its narrative. This interrelation of uplift narrative and visual paratexts thus offered compelling proof of the race's progress and promise. Still, the photograph, more widely available through such new methods of mass reproduction as the halftone process, would provide these uplift autobiographers with a distinctive visual form for contesting racial meaning through the illustrations in their books.

By the end of the nineteenth century, the halftone process had emerged to become the dominant method of photomechanical reproduction. By placing a lined screen or grid between a negative and a sensitized plate, "the halftone process ... translated the continuous tones of photography into a pattern of black and white dots, which could be engraved into metal or transferred to a lithographic stone or plate" (Lupton 57). In contrast to the earlier, labor-intensive hand engraving by which illustrations had been produced for publication, the halftone process allowed for both the mechanization of image production and the effective tonal reproduction of photographs in print (Benton 153). Because the halftone process produced a printing block that could be combined with type on a single page, it "increased, geometrically, the mass of pictorial matter presented to the public" (N. Harris 305) through popular newspapers and magazines. Thus this technology made the mass publication of photographs more practical, efficient, and inexpensive, leading to a relative profusion of photographical illustration in the African American autobiographies of the early twentieth century. Notwithstanding the historical significance of visual paratexts to antebellum slave narratives, for example, the halftone represented a distinct visual form that initiated "the modern world of visual reproduction" (N. Harris 307). As African American autobiographers came to illustrate their Jim Crow–era narratives with new pictures of themselves, their families, and their lives, their halftones formally marked such illustrated texts as fully modern; moreover, their halftones allowed the conceptual image of the race to assume more concrete forms in print. Such halftones provided black authors with an apparent fidelity— and persuasive force—that had been unavailable in earlier forms of illustration, since "the photographic image asserted itself as a primary fact: proof of the existence of a subject[,] an unshakeable witness bound to its subject by physical laws of chemistry and optics. The invention of the half-tone block further enabled the transference of these qualities directly ... without the intervention of the interpreting engraver" (Tagg 195). As a result, autobiography, an ostensibly referential form of narrative representation that overshadowed the novel among black cultural producers until 1925 (Andrews, "Forgotten Voices" 21), began to incorporate the photograph, an ostensibly referential form of visual representation newly available to black authors.

With its brief story of Edwards's rise from being an impoverished orphan in Alabama to becoming a graduate of Tuskegee Institute, with its survey of black life in the Black Belt both before and after the establishment of his own Snow Hill Institute, and with its assortment of photographs displaying both portraits and properties to illustrate his narrative, *Twenty-Five Years in the Black Belt* is a conventional uplift autobiography. Nonetheless, Edwards's book instantiates a wider challenge to readers and critics of African American autobiography: Given the visual field within which black people presented their personal narratives at the turn of the twentieth century, what, then, is the *autobiographical* function of such photographic illustrations that do not directly render the emblematic black autobiographers themselves? How do photographs *other than* authors' portraits—especially pictures of homes, schools, and places—serve as visual expressions of the black subject that do not merely document a life but alternately complement and complicate the narrative work of autobiography? As paratexts that occasion what I term a "black ideography"—arising as it does from the complex interaction among autobiographical practices, ideological discourses, and visual images—how do such illustrations constitute expressions of the black subject, challenging readers to see these narratives in relation to their full array of photographs?

While *Twenty-Five Years in the Black Belt* motivates these broad questions about the paratextual impress of photographic illustrations in black autobiography, the ideographic dimensions of Edwards's narrative also challenge his readers to reexamine the imperatives of racial publicity in the production of African American culture. In fact, Edwards's recourse to illustrations of transformed buildings effectively displaces the black male self; rather than simply rely upon the visual reconstruction of the black body as a synecdochic idol, *Twenty-Five Years in the Black Belt* also contrasts old cabins and new cottages as an alternative strategy of representation that figures racial progress in terms of the private, inaccessible interiors of improved homes. Consequently, the images of homes that Edwards harnesses autobiographically in his book suggest "a longing to abscond from the neurotically uncanny experience of social spectragraphia by a retreat away from the public sphere where the gaze tyrannizes" (Wallace, *Constructing* 123). The irony of this retreat, of course, is that Edwards asserts a racial privacy through a mechanism—the halftone, with its deceptive promise of objective, unmediated visuality—so closely associated with the mass media of the public sphere.[3] As a visual form, the halftone is "essentially public, ephemeral, and part of the everyday" (Beegan 14), but Edwards mobilizes it to signify that which does not appear, as we shall see. In this respect, Edwards's ideography claims a racial privacy that strains the uplift conventions of racial publicity, demonstrating that not all black ideographic practices are bound to the desiderata of racial publicity; even *within* forms of racial publicity, such as the uplift autobiographies of the early Jim Crow era, the interaction of visual and narrative modes of address might effect paradoxical moments when such autobiographers strategically withhold embodied racial meanings rather than counter them publicly. Ultimately, this discrete tension between private and public has its roots in a remarkable legacy involving "circumstances in which the sense-making capacity of vision, the significance of vision, is monopolized from a hostile perspective" (Barrett 215). Beyond the proximate significance of such illustrations in the narratives of Edwards and other black autobiographers, the visual production of race in the Jim Crow era would largely depend on an enduring historical problem—namely, the dilemma of black visibility, which burdened black people with lives suspended in the visual field between forces of surveillance, spectacle, and speculation.

The Dilemma of Black Visibility

The surveillance of slaveholders, overseers, and patrollers; the spectacles of the auction block, the abolitionist platform, and the minstrel stage; the racial speculation of scholars, scientists, and statisticians—throughout the long nineteenth century, such complementary visual practices of surveillance, spectacle, and speculation eventuated the dilemma of black visibility in the United States. According to Michel Foucault's influential *Discipline and Punish*, the disciplinary regime of visuality—a defining feature of modernity—would supersede the spectacle of exemplary violence in the exercise of power. Thus, "thanks to the techniques of surveillance, the 'physics' of power, the hold over the body, operate according to the laws of optics and mechanics, according to a whole play of spaces, lines, screens, beams, degrees and without recourse, in principle at least, to excess, force or violence" (Foucault 177). However, the fundamental role of New World slavery in the advent of modernity meant that "the public spectacle of torture, and the private discipline of the Panopticon, are fused in the private worlds of violence which characterised plantation societies" (Wood 230). In the context of racialized ways of seeing (and being seen), often enforced with brutal violence, surveillance would not supplant spectacle during the nineteenth century so much as converge with it. As Robyn Wiegman has argued, "the shift from the socially inscribed mark of visibility attending spectacle to the self-incorporated vision of the panoptic relation coalesced in the United States, not in successive stages but as intertwined technologies that worked simultaneously to stage the hierarchical relations of race" (39). In fact, the spectacles of public torture with which enslavers sought to control the enslaved would outlast the peculiar institution itself in the form of racial lynching, and these spectacles would in turn merge with the disciplinary possibilities of photography during the Jim Crow era (Goldsby 218–79; Raiford, *Imprisoned* 36–40; Wiegman 39).

The imbrication, rather than succession, of spectacle and surveillance would characterize the slaveholders' regime of control, wherein the consequences of black visibility could be dire. Consider just a few of the dogged strategies of surveillance and control that characterized antebellum slavery: circumscribing the assembly and movement of black people; authorizing militias, patrols, and, indeed, "any one having a white face" (Douglass, *Narrative* 340–41) to regulate and enforce such limits; prohibiting manumissions and expelling freed people; and devising equipment to prevent slaves from absconding, like the "iron horns" represented graphically in Moses Roper's 1838 narrative (497).[4] To be sure, these antebellum strategies of control were not strictly visual, but they contributed nonetheless to what it meant, both conceptually and materially, for black people to be seen within a visual field structured by racial power. Furthermore, these controls affected all black people, slaves and nonslaves alike, and they would stretch even further out of the South as slaveholders expanded their collective power to apprehend runaways, most notably with the Fugitive Slave Act of 1850.

While surveillance captures the force of the gaze to operate as a mechanism of social control, largely by inducing the modern subject's self-regulation, the production of racial knowledge through speculative practices—the computations of slave traders, the wonderment of audiences watching blackness performed on both abolitionist and minstrel stages, the observations of naturalists, and the calculations of statisticians—would also determine the stakes of black visibility across the long nineteenth century. In this respect, what I term "speculation" complements the forces of spectacle and surveillance by encompassing the racial gazes that operated across a range of sites motivated in part by the desire to understand the nature of difference, the meaning of race, and the value of blackness—that is, sites that contributed to the production of racial knowledge. To be clear, I proffer the concept of speculation here not to dismiss the racial gazes characterizing the laboratory, the auction block, and the stage as simply false and distorted. Rather, speculation recognizes how such gazes produced an array of racial meanings against which black autobiographers would mobilize both word and image: if the treatises of race science grasped the black body as an object of nature to be studied and scrutinized, then black autobiographers insisted that they would be the producers of knowledge about themselves; if the auction block constituted the site of dispossession, then black autobiography would be the instantiation of self-possession; if the minstrel stage established conventions of dehumanizing caricature, then black autobiography would recover the humanity of the black self.

Two naturalists who concerned themselves with the problem of racial difference, Thomas Jefferson and Louis Agassiz, exemplify a commitment to the observational tools with which race science sought to record, document, and classify the truths of blackness in the age of slavery. In "Query XIV" of his *Notes on the State of Virginia* (1787), Jefferson famously asserts the natural inferiority of black people, offering a variety of aesthetic, biological, sexual, cultural, and historical claims about blackness to justify slavery in the United States (264–69). Following these observations, Jefferson invokes the practices of scientific inquiry, registering the emergence of visuality itself, and not simply *logos*, as one crucial nexus between race, power, and knowledge.[5] First, Jefferson remarks that "though for a century and a half we have had under our eyes the races of black and of red men, they have never yet been viewed by us as subjects of natural history," thereby distinguishing between the gaze of surveillance that sought to control such populations and the gaze of scientific inquiry that sought to investigate them (Jefferson 270). Second, while he proposes, "as a suspicion only, that the blacks . . . are inferior to the whites in endowments both of body and mind" (270), he also calls for further scientific inquiry to verify essential racial differences through "many observations, even where the subject may be submitted to the Anatomical knife, to Optical glasses, to analysis by fire, or by solvents" (269).[6] For Jefferson, the scientific gaze—accompanied, perhaps, by the utilitarian violence of experimentation—becomes crucial to the future production of racial knowledge. Although Jefferson primarily *narrates* his own observations about the nature of racial differences in *Notes on the State of Virginia*, he nonetheless advocates for the scientific gaze as the means to understand the full significance of blackness.

By the mid-nineteenth century, Louis Agassiz, a Swiss-born naturalist and eventual founder of Harvard's Museum of Comparative Zoology, demonstrated his scientific gaze by capitalizing on newer visual technologies than Jefferson's "Optical glasses," commissioning a series of fifteen daguerreotypes of southern slaves to serve, presumably, as models of racial types. In 1850 Agassiz addressed a meeting of the American Association for the Advancement of Science in Charleston, South Carolina, where, as the featured speaker, "he sided with the Southern view of polygenesis and accepted the inferior status of blacks" (Wallis, "Black Bodies" 168). In the wake of this meeting, Agassiz toured a number of plantations with the assistance of a fellow scientist, Robert W. Gibbes, and chose seven slaves for a series of daguerreotypes—bust and full-length portraits, as well as side and rear views—that presented these stripped and immobile black bodies as types to be scrutinized ethnologically (Wallis, "Black Bodies" 170). The result, he hoped, would be photographic evidence proving his theory of polygenism, which, by denying the common origin of the races, complemented Jefferson's earlier observations in *Notes on the State of Virginia*. By appropriating the visual technology of daguerreotypy, these portraits transformed the camera into "an instrument of dissection, used to locate and capture difference," thereby adapting newer processes of image making to the imperatives of the scientific gaze (Collins 22–23).[7] Indeed, Agassiz's "slave daguerreotypes represent an early attempt not only to apply photography to anthropology, but also to form a coherent photographic archive" of distinct racial specimens (Wallis, "Black Bodies" 172).

As these two brief examples demonstrate, the gaze of nineteenth-century race science apprehends the black body as proof of deeply meaningful racial differences. In addition to these visual practices, the dilemma of black visibility also arose from the force of speculation to organize and stage black bodies at a number of other cultural (and often economic) sites. Despite their political incongruity, for example, the auction blocks of the South and the abolitionist platforms of the North served as sites upon which the values of black bodies fell and rose with the salience of their scars; likewise, the minstrel stages of blackface spectacle, which originated in the midst of slavery, emerged to justify the oppression of black people in the South, the North, and the West, and survived slavery well into the twentieth century.[8] This range of looking relations, constituted through practices of speculation, spectacle, and surveillance, thus produced the troublesome meanings that attended black visibility in a society grappling with the antebellum institution of racial slavery and its legacies. In this respect, the display of black bodies on auction blocks, abolitionist platforms, and minstrel stages certainly reinforced their objectification, and these sites resonated with one another in the symbolic production of racial signs.[9] As Michael D. Harris has argued, "blackness was both a danger and a fascination; it needed control, and yet it inspired voyeuristic consumption lasting nearly a century" (73). These dynamics of racial power thus meant that black people's visibility during slavery jeopardized their freedom; after emancipation, their visibility attenuated it.

Situated at the center of powerful gazes of speculation, surveillance, and spectacle, the black body would remain a primary site of contestation in the production of racial knowledge throughout the long nineteenth century. With the full mechanization of printing processes at the end of the nineteenth century, African American autobiographers were able to mobilize the newly available form of the halftone to address the dilemma of black visibility within their books. Insofar as this early proliferation of photographic illustration in black autobiographies engaged *this* dilemma, such books also attempted to narrate a free black self in relation to a racialized visual field, not simply in relation to a humanizing *logos* instantiated through elevating practices of writing. Furthermore, the mobilization of halftones in Jim Crow-era autobiography represents a strategic contribution to a "counterarchive" of blackness, thereby allowing black autobiographers to intervene in the visual field that denied African Americans personhood and to reconfigure racial publicity in the process.[10] Given the ongoing contest over racial knowledge both before and after emancipation, black autobiography at the end of the nineteenth century thus emerged as more than a creative literary form with which black people could display their mastery of language; it also served as a narrative form deploying the referential authority of self-narration to produce knowledge about the black subject. Armed with new mechanical means to republish photographs, black autobiographers thus relied on their illustrations to incorporate new, exact images of black life, such as portraits of themselves, pictures of their families and communities, symbols of their pasts, and images of their present circumstances. In turn, these illustrations complemented their narratives with indexical signs that carried their own formal authority for representing the truth of black lives. Ultimately, the dilemma of black visibility demanded a textual interaction between narrativity and visuality, and this interaction generated a black ideography, that complex form of self-presentation that arises from the symbiosis of autobiographical practices, ideological discourses, and visual images.

Because the self-referentiality of autobiography accords with the self-presentation of the portrait, the visual paratexts commanding the most attention from literary scholars have been those frontispiece portraits that introduce African American autobiographies, though most of this attention has been devoted to antebellum rather than Jim Crow-era narratives.[11] To the extent that the recent history of slavery haunts these postbellum narratives, such portraits connote a dramatic transformation of the freed black self. In this sense, the portraits instantiate a "visual chiasmus," magically "promising through affect what [the nation's] formal apparatus is not inclined to deliver" (Wallace, "'How'" 176).[12] If the pictorial aesthetic of the nineteenth century rarely welcomed blackness as a self-sufficient presence, then the photographic portraits of black autobiographers seek to address the lingering constraints on black citizenship by shaping the race's public image not simply as proof but also as promise. Furthermore, the frontispiece portrait of the black autobiographer authenticates the narrative's veracity by presenting "something material, the *embodied* subject, the unification (to recall the autobiographical pact [of Philippe Lejeune]) of author, name, *and* body" (Rugg 13). At the same time, these authors' portraits counter images of black degradation circulating widely during the nineteenth century. Thus the frontispiece portrait conjoins image, text, and name in a powerful constellation, one that simultaneously humanizes black autobiographers (through the expression of literacy augured by the text's title, for example), verifies their presence (through the named, and sometimes autographed, portrait), and establishes their dignity (through the conventional elements that constitute meaning in these portraits, such as posture, visage, clothing, accessories, setting, staging, and lighting). Incorporated into autobiography, such portraiture involves the burden of presenting oneself as a racial sign on behalf of black America; that is, such portraiture functions as a public act of self-fashioning contiguous with a synecdochic narrative equating black self-presentation with both racial recognition and collective aspiration.[13]

While black ideography often dictates that African Americans wed their narratives to images of the "reconstructed," refined black body, it also counters the hazards of visibility with images that displace the embodied subject of autobiography altogether. Indeed, even as they relied heavily on the authorial conventions of the frontispiece portrait, some Jim Crow–era autobiographies published after the advent of the halftone actually yoke their narratives of emblematic race-building to photographs of race buildings.[14] Consequently, a black ideography that offers up properties to signify the people betrays the tendency of such narratives to "treat the adaptation of individuals to institutions as the hallmark of a successful life" (Andrews, "Forgotten" 22).[15] In the remainder of this chapter, I focus on the chiastic halftones of property that appear in one such autobiography, Edwards's *Twenty-Five Years in the Black Belt* (1918), one of the Jim Crow–era texts associated with Booker T. Washington's Tuskegee Institute. Like Washington's own final *My Larger Education: Being Chapters from My Experience* (1911), Edwards's *Twenty-Five Years in the Black Belt* enacts a commitment to racial publicity that emphasizes propriety and property, displacing the body of the New Negro onto new schools and new homes.[16]

However, the strategies of visual chiasmus in Edwards's *Twenty-Five Years in the Black Belt* reveal even more clearly how such forms of self-presentation promote a managerial conception of racial uplift. To be sure, Edwards partly relies on portraiture, including the conventional frontispiece, to demonstrate his own respectability, refinement, and restraint, thereby mobilizing photographic evidence in the service of bourgeois antiracism. Nonetheless, I examine his additional illustrations of property here to argue that his recourse to images that do not picture his own body offer two alternative strategies for addressing the dilemma of black visibility: first, this displacement asserts privacy as the prerogative of the uplifted New Negro; second, it produces, in autobiographical terms, a black self that is itself more seeing than seen.

Such ideographic strategies thus converge to advance the managerial conception of racial uplift that was central to Tuskegee's institutional practices of self-presentation. As African Americans "turn[ed] increasingly inward in their efforts to preserve themselves" (Mitchell 13) in the fifty years after Reconstruction, the visual paratexts of uplift autobiography transfigure the bourgeois visibility of portraiture into a bourgeois visuality that surveys other black people to be managed and controlled by the race's representatives. Consequently, *Twenty-Five Years in the Black Belt* does not simply offer a counterimage of the black body to evince an interior self worthy of recognition. Rather, Edwards mobilizes other photographic subjects to signify his life without consistently presenting his own body to stand in for (or against, even) the overdetermined black body of American visual culture. These sorts of strategies underscore how the antiracist interventions of uplift autobiography were not limited to public struggles to reconstruct the race's image; they were also concerned with establishing, preserving, and protecting spaces of black privacy beyond the intrusive gaze of racial power.

The Ideographic Properties of William J. Edwards

While Washington did not live to endorse the publication of Edwards's autobiography, *Twenty-Five Years in the Black Belt* was firmly rooted in the hidden history of autobiographical and photographic practices that the Wizard had institutionalized at Tuskegee as he sought to consolidate his power as a black leader. Beginning in the early 1890s, Washington launched a series of annual conventions—the Tuskegee Negro Conference (1892) and the separate Women's Conference (1894) for the rural southern folk, and the National Negro Business League (1900) for the race's entrepreneurs and other businesspeople—that featured participants' narration of their personal experiences. As a specific, if limited, autobiographical practice, the spoken testimonial anchored each of these annual meetings and assumed ritual importance across all of them, establishing formal conventions for the collective narration of New Negro selves. Moreover, a number of the books that Washington produced between 1900 and 1915, particularly *The Story of My Life and Work* (1900), *Working with the Hands* (1904), and *The Negro in Business* (1907), actually interpolate these voices to varying degrees, giving such spoken narratives additional written forms that circulated beyond the black workers and entrepreneurs who had been their immediate listeners. In addition, another of Washington's publications, *Tuskegee and Its People* (1905), anthologized nearly twenty personal essays by students associated with the school to publicize Tuskegee's successes.

Beyond Washington's personal commitment to autobiography, his promotion of these interlocking practices—spoken, transcribed, and interpolated testimonials; personal narratives; and formal autobiographies by both himself and others associated with Tuskegee—institutionalized his conception of racial uplift as a process that necessarily effected autobiographical figures, black people for whom personal narrative and racial publicity converged. Furthermore, Washington did not present the substance of his own life as simply a Franklinian model for other black people to follow, nor did he encourage such testimonials simply to demonstrate, in synecdochic fashion, the race's progress; he also promoted such acts of personal narration, on both stage and page, as an institutional tactic for interpellating and transforming black subjects. Thus, this culture of autobiography coaxed those associated with Tuskegee to inhabit, through overdetermined ritual practices of self-presentation, those black subjectivities that conformed to Washington's conception of racial progress. During the same period, Washington's institutional commitment to autobiographical practices at Tuskegee was matched by a growing commitment to visual forms of representation.

As Michael Bieze has demonstrated, Tuskegee's emergence as a site of black visual culture originated in 1893—less than a year after the founding of the Tuskegee Negro Conference—when the school's catalog first included photographs and when "Washington's first nationally published image in the mainstream press appeared" (53). From that point forward, Washington increasingly relied on photography to promote himself and his school, and in time he "learned to place his image in a wide variety of formats from frontispieces in books, articles, broadsides, postcards, cabinet cards, and eventually Negro Business League buttons, Christmas cards, stereographs, and lantern slides" (Bieze 54). After 1900, Washington sought even greater control over both his own image and that of his institution by employing a corps of black photographers to serve his personal and institutional needs, such as Harry Shepherd, A. P. Bedou, and C. M. Battey, and by creating the position of official photographer at the school in 1909 (Bieze 69). For Washington, then, both visual and autobiographical practices of representation were fundamental to the growth of Tuskegee. Washington's efforts ensured that the school's uplifted New Negroes were not always, or solely, autobiographical figures of speech and script; they were also illustrative figures of portraits and pictures. Consistent with the ideographic melding of narrative and visual modes in black autobiography at the time, Washington thus promoted both autobiographical practices and visual production at the institutional level, largely because of the efficiency of these practices in demonstrating the conversion of the black self under his school's influence. At Tuskegee, then, the testimonial conventions fueling the school's narrative production found their analog in the "before-and-after" conventions of visual rhetoric. These differing modes of representation converged to produce, reproduce, regulate, and circulate depictions of black lives engaged in the hard struggle for racial progress.

Edwards's story of postslavery life would join other such synecdochic black lives to demonstrate the efficacy of Washington's institution, and long before he published *Twenty-Five Years in the Black Belt*, he had already practiced his conversion narrative according to Tuskegee's culture of autobiography. When Washington promoted his school in 1900 as a model for "educating and elevating about eight hundred thousand others of African descent in Cuba and Porto Rico" (Washington, "Signs" 472), he showcased Edwards's life story as an emblematic "sign of progress."[17] When Washington then published *Tuskegee and Its People* to commemorate the twenty-fifth anniversary of his school, Edwards added his own narrative to the nearly two dozen personal essays by former students attesting to the power of Tuskegee to transform their lives. In "Uplifting of the Submerged Masses," Edwards describes how Washington's institution inspired the orphaned young man to return to his native Snow Hill, Alabama, to survey this rural community, and to serve its needs. As a result of Edwards's little Tuskegee, Snow Hill's farmers were "rapidly passing from the renters' class to the owners' class," and the crude log cabin was "giving way to houses having three, four, and, in some places, six and seven rooms" (Edwards, "Uplifting" 244, 245). In time, Edwards would expand this earlier contribution to Washington's commemorative anthology to produce *Twenty-Five Years in the Black Belt*.

Published at the end of World War I, Edwards's book offers a chronological account of his life before presenting a series of topical chapters that acknowledge his supporters, trumpet his former students, and expound on his ideas about black education, systematic farming, and black patriotism in wartime. Most importantly, *Twenty-Five Years in the Black Belt* addresses itself to the intensifying migration of African Americans out of the rural South. In effect, his narrative seeks to resolve the problem that he poses clearly in his preface: despite the exploitative conditions that black tenant farmers face in the South, he asks, "How can we stop these people from leaving the country for the cities and other places of public works and again reclaim these waste fields?" (xv–xvi). The answer, Edwards insists, is that "these waste places can be reclaimed and the guttered hills made to blossom, only by giving the Negro a common education combined with religious, moral and industrial training and the opportunity to at least own his own home, if not the land he cultivates"; furthermore, "the remedy of these [southern] evils lies in the Negro himself" (xvi). Insofar as this preface frames the narrative to come, the story of Edwards's own life exemplifies the prospects for reclaiming the wasted places of the South.

Born in 1869, Edwards suffered throughout his childhood from the poverty, hunger, and sickness faced by many former slaves and their families in the postbellum South. According to his autobiography, the turning point in his life occurred in 1887, taking the form of a secular Washingtonian conversion that often marked narratives associated with Tuskegee's culture of autobiography. Without "suitable clothes" or shoes, Edwards was not allowed by his family to attend church, but he slipped out of his cabin one night to eavesdrop on a revival meeting nearby. It was here, barred from the church and standing in the shadows outside it, that he first heard of Booker T. Washington's school, "where . . . poor boys and girls could go without money and without price, and work for an education." He asserts, "From that night I decided to go to Tuskegee" (17). Eventually, he would get there, and under Washington's tutelage, he would return to Snow Hill prepared to start his own school. With this arc, Edwards's autobiography repays its generic debt to Tuskegee's culture of autobiography, and his narrative unfolds in Washingtonian fashion, grounding black progress in the emblematic conversion of the black self that had occurred in his own life. Transformed, Edwards viewed himself as being prepared to transform others, and *Twenty-Five Years in the Black Belt* melds word and image to demonstrate both his allegiances and his authority as a managerial New Negro.

Twenty-Five Years in the Black Belt incorporates nine illustrations offering a visual record of Edwards's life as the principal of Snow Hill. While Edwards narrates the story of his hard life as the history of the institution he founded in 1894, his illustrations present his life as a collection of people and buildings, all visual signs of racial progress associated with his school. The opening illustration is the frontispiece portrait of the photogenic author in his three-piece suit. The final illustration is a group portrait with Edwards surrounded by Snow Hill's thirty teachers, the sort of "careful arrangement that subordinates all individuals and actions to an overall design," demonstrating how such schools "produce order from the disorder of African American lives" (Wallis, "Dream" 12) in the Jim Crow South; moreover, this group portrait places Edwards at the center of a representative formation of uplifted black men and women for which he bears responsibility. While these illustrations frame Edwards's narrative visually, these are the only two in which he appears, and the author himself is absent from the book's seven intervening illustrations. Further situating the autobiographer within a black community of his sponsors and students, his illustrations include another group portrait of the school's five original trustees with "two of their wives" seated at the center, as well as four individual portraits of Snow Hill graduates arranged together on a single page. Edwards's frontispiece and the individual portraits of his former students allow them all to inhabit the formal conventions of middle-class portraiture—the plain background of the studio, the immaculate clothing, the slightly turned chest, the indirect gaze suggesting the sitter's interiority—and these conventions help to fashion these figures as efficient signs of the race's rise in the postslavery South.

Beyond his recourse to portraits of himself and others to demonstrate how they embody the race's rise, Edwards also includes illustrations of property that constitute the text's ideographic challenge. Besides a picture capturing an array of buildings on the school's campus, *Twenty-Five Years in the Black Belt* incorporates images of local homes, both older cabins representing the living conditions that once existed in the rural countryside as well as more recently constructed abodes presumably resulting from his school's influence. While these photographs of buildings are functional snapshots without the formal composition of similar images appearing in books like Washington's *My Larger Education*, they reflect the ideographic commitment to race buildings that Edwards shared with his mentor. However, these illustrations in *Twenty-Five Years in the Black Belt* offer meaningful variations on the "before-and-after" (or "old-and-new") conceits of Tuskegee's visual culture. First, Edwards's halftones of race buildings imply a historical contrast that depicts an inhabited, if residual, past while removing the black body from an improved present. Second, these illustrations manipulate perspective to create greater distance between Edwards's readers and the visual signs of progress that he offers them. Finally, Edwards's photographs of southern buildings reveal clearly the managerial assumptions of racial uplift, thus complicating further the role of racial publicity in the production of ideographic texts.

The four illustrations of race buildings in *Twenty-Five Years in the Black Belt* comprise two discrete pairs that effectively displace Edwards's personal transformation onto concrete structures that then augur collective transformation. The first of these dyads appears in "Appreciation," a later topical chapter in which Edwards acknowledges the support of both white and black allies for his work at Snow Hill, and it consists of halftones of two different homes juxtaposed on a single page (fig. 4.1). These contrasting images of an older cabin and a newer cottage certainly condense a narrative of Black Belt progress, but they also symbolize Edwards's own personal transformation. While the autobiographer uses this chapter to praise those philanthropists, trustees, officers, teachers, and friends who were "prominent in the building of the institution" (56), he honors just one man for helping him to build a self—the "immortal Booker T. Washington," who transformed his student with "the spirit and simplicity of the Master" (58).

In an otherwise impersonal chapter that primarily concerns itself with describing the qualities and contributions of others, this brief encomium to Washington marks a rare moment, the only place in the chapter where Edwards represents his own life in personal terms. Echoing his class motto at Tuskegee ("Deeds Not Words," which he repeats in quick succession at the end of his fourth chapter [24–25]), Edwards avows that Washington "changed my view of life. He changed me from the visionary to the substantial, from the shadow to the substance, from the artificial to the real, and from words to deeds" (58). This singular self-referential moment in "Appreciation" enunciates the logic of conversion that motivates much of *Twenty-Five Years in the Black Belt*. In turn, Edwards's personal conversion under Washington's influence suggests how we might see the autobiographical function of this chapter's two illustrations, which depict the residual and emergent symbols of Edwards's South. Published together on a single page, these two illustrations present the reader with a direct contrast between the impoverished cabin of the Black Belt and the improved cottage of a Snow Hill graduate. Still, while word and image in this chapter both contribute broadly to the autobiography's trope of conversion, the relationship between them turns nonetheless on the displacement of Edwards himself; the conversion of the black male self described in the narrative becomes a vision of two buildings that demonstrate the remaking of the Black Belt.

While their captions themselves do not explicitly contrast the two buildings they depict, the formal relationship of these two illustrations alone—with one photograph above the other—inevitably signifies the visual chiasmus that determines their meaning as viewers' eyes move from top to bottom. The photograph at the top of

Figure 4.1. "Typical Log Cabin in the Black Belt" (*top*) and "Home of a Snow Hill Graduate" (*bottom*). From Edwards, *Twenty-Five Years in the Black Belt* (facing 60). Courtesy Bryn Mawr College Library.

the page, titled "Typical Log Cabin in the Black Belt," shows two women at the threshold of a rough-hewn two-room log cabin. One of the women stands just inside one doorway, while the other stands just outside the structure and cradles a baby in her arms. Running across the image in the foreground, a rickety picket fence establishes a boundary that separates the log cabin's inhabitants from the photographer (and reader). Together, the two open doors and the picket fence produce a tension in this image between the hard boundary that sets these black women apart from the photographer (and reader) and the permeable boundary that makes the interior accessible from the outside. These visual cues suggest the vulnerability of these women to the photographer's intrusion.

In contrast, the picture at the bottom of the page, titled "Home of a Snow Hill Graduate," shows an unpretentious, single-story farmhouse with pitched roof, modern chimney, and modest porch; unlike the log cabin, this polished house also boasts glass panes in its windows, decisive signs of progress for Edwards.[18] Photographed at a greater remove than the log cabin, this neat home seems to rise from an expansive field of corn or sorghum, along with additional rows for another crop in the foreground, and if there are people posing with this home, they cannot be identified or even seen in this halftone. Judging from a series of posts running along the near side of this house, a fence evidently marks a boundary between the building and the photographer (and reader), though this unimposing fence contrasts sharply the stark barrier in the foreground of "Typical Log Cabin." Ultimately, the juxtaposition of these two images insists on a visual rhetoric of racial progress: insofar as the tidy cottage of the second image concretizes the transformation of the Black Belt, this distant house also appears to be solidly shut against the outside, with neither the typical bodies nor the open threshold of the regressive log cabin.

The contrast between these two pictures in "Appreciation" promotes Snow Hill's influence over those "young people [who] have bought farms and homes of their own, [who] have erected neat and comfortable cottages" (Edwards, *Twenty-Five* 51). More importantly, these contrasting illustrations of cabin and cottage attest to a series of transformations associated with Edwards's institution—from vernacular to modern, from "typical" to exceptional, from rough to smooth, from poor to propertied, from open to closed—that then substantiate the autobiography's operative trope of conversion. Insofar as this juxtaposition of these two images efficiently depicts racial uplift, this transformation effectively removes the black body from such progress at two levels. First, the regressive log cabin is presented to the reader with the black figures of the Black Belt who must be uplifted, whereas the modern cottage stands alone as a sign of progress, unaccompanied by any black bodies. Despite the conspicuous fence that keeps them apart from the viewer, the women who stand at the open thresholds of Edwards's "typical" log cabin are vulnerable to the scrutiny of the observer, whereas the graduate's home maintains a safe distance from the viewer, keeping *its* occupants out of sight. Second, this pair of illustrations figures the trope of conversion central to Edwards's narrative by displacing his own body, and this visual displacement is itself central to the conception of racial uplift he represents. With the collection of speeches in its later half, *Twenty-Five Years in the Black Belt* demonstrates Edwards's rise as a public authority speaking on behalf of the race, but the book's illustrations also suggest that racial uplift entails the refusal of publicity as the black self preserves an inaccessible interior.

Likewise, the second dyad of race buildings in *Twenty-Five Years in the Black Belt* consists of two photographs that also remove the uplifted black self from sight. These two images do not appear together in direct contrast, but their relationship to each other—the older subject precedes the newer one—forms a dyad representing progress across the narrative. As the first illustration to follow the author's frontispiece portrait, "Uncle Charles Lee and His Home in the Black Belt" (fig. 4.2) appears in the chapter recounting Edwards's return home from Tuskegee in 1893. Titled "Reconnoitering," this early chapter describes the young man's tour through the rural districts of Alabama to survey "the real condition of the people in this section" (29). Accompanied by "Uncle Jim," Edwards embarks on his journey one "bright beautiful morning" with a pastoral vision of a fecund land "truly clothed in His beauty and the fulness [*sic*] of His glory" (27). Nonetheless, this vision is quickly disrupted by two aged whipping posts, which cast shadows of the slave past over the landscape:

> But I had scarcely gone beyond the limits of the field when I came to a thick undergrowth of pines. Here we saw old pieces of timber and two posts. "This marks the old cotton-gin house," said Uncle Jim, my companion, and then his countenance grew sad; after a sigh, he said: "I have seen many a Negro whipped within an inch of his life at these posts. I have seen them whipped so badly that they had to be carried away in wagons. Many never did recover." (27)

Edwards does not comment on either Uncle Jim's remembrance or the posts themselves, but this interpolation of his companion's voice, evoking the eyewitness conventions of the slave narrative, tempers his initial optimism about the Black Belt. Moreover, this "uncle" figure is bound to the past as its living witness, and as Edwards recounts this trip, he establishes a clear distinction between the New Negroes he meets (Deacon Jones, Mr. Darrington) and the older "uncles" (Uncle Jim, Uncle Jake) who embody both the slave past and its contemporary legacy.

Thus, the halftone illustration of Uncle Charles Lee also presents the log cabin as an example of the unreconstructed black folk who represent the past's hold on the land. In this picture, an elderly black man poses in front of his one-room log cabin, a dilapidated structure with front door aslant and leaning dramatically to one side as though on the verge of collapse. Like his cabin, the aged Lee also requires support, leaning on both cane and walking stick. In the context of its chapter, this photograph becomes a surrogate for one of the sights that Edwards might have encountered during his reconnaissance in 1893. Although Lee himself is not one of

Figure 4.2. "Uncle Charles Lee and His Home in the Black Belt." From Edwards, *Twenty-Five Years in the Black Belt* (facing 32). Courtesy Bryn Mawr College Library.

the "uncles" that Edwards actually discusses in the chapter, he does ostensibly stand as evidence of the rural conditions that inspired the autobiographer to found his own school. Once again, the open threshold represents the permeable boundary between interior and exterior, suggesting in turn the availability of such rural black folk as Uncle Lee (and the black women of "the typical log cabin" who appear later in the book) to such gazes. Given the chapter's title, then, this illustration documents Edwards's own surveillance (however well meaning) of the rural folk, since the camera captures the conditions he faced while "reconnoitering" in Alabama's nearby country districts.

If Uncle Charles Lee's log cabin comprises the first half of a visual chiasmus, then the second half appears in the brief ninth chapter, titled "Results." In fact, the book's transition from the chronology of the earlier chapters to the commentary of the later chapters actually pivots on "Results," which encapsulates the successful growth of Edwards's thriving institution. Reaffirming Snow Hill's commitment to the "gospel of work" (51), Edwards notes, "From the [original] rented log cabin the school has grown until we have at present, to be exact, 1940 acres of land and twenty-four buildings, counting large and small" (50). The growth of the school itself from an outmoded log cabin to a substantial campus is central to Edwards's uplift narrative, but he also stresses that the school has "sent out into various parts of the South more than a thousand young men and women who are today leading useful and helpful lives" (51). Inspired by the example of the school's physical growth, Snow Hill's former students "have bought farms and homes of their own, have erected neat and comfortable cottages; have influenced their neighbors to buy land,

Figure 4.3. "A Newer Type of Home in the Black Belt." From Edwards, *Twenty-Five Years in the Black Belt* (facing 52). Courtesy Bryn Mawr College Library.

to build better homes, better churches and better school-houses" (51). In this chapter describing the products of his school, Edwards praises these "better men and better women" for their "social service," but he largely measures their success by the land they have bought and the homes they have built (51). Manifesting the school's spirit, these former students thus present their neighbors with improved homes that stand as powerful object lessons in black progress, representing concretely what racial uplift means. According to the narrative's formulation of success, then, the work of Snow Hill as an institution, like other schools modeled after Washington's Tuskegee, is not simply to refine black bodies, as Gates and Ross have argued; instead, the race's new buildings stand as emblems of its rise.

Thus, this pivotal chapter does not actually illustrate the "results" that Edwards has achieved at Snow Hill with, say, portraits of the school's graduates (though such portraits do appear elsewhere). Rather, its single illustration depicts, according to its caption, "A Newer Type of Home in the Black Belt," thereby presenting the racial building (and a home, specifically) rather than a refined racial body as the measure of institutional success (fig. 4.3). If this unattributed snapshot presumably offers tangible evidence of the influence of Snow Hill and other such schools on the Black Belt, then where is this "newer type of home"? Taken from the vantage of an overgrown hillside, adjacent to a country road, this photograph actually shows a number of houses, all of which appear in the distance. The most visible of these, a smaller, weathered clapboard building to the left, is hardly an improved home. The other three buildings are larger, and any one of these might be the "newer type of home" designated by the caption, but, curiously, all these homes remain hidden among trees and brush, barely visible beneath the peaks of their roofs. Insisting that this photograph displays the sort of home that evinces the upbuilding of a race, this caption asks readers and viewers to see beyond the surface of the image while, paradoxically, the illustration does not clearly show its apparent subject, rendering it inaccessible.

The sharp disjunction between caption and photograph in this illustration demonstrates a broader principle involving the imbrication of word and image, since the progressive deed remains hidden here without the specifying word. As Walter Benjamin has argued, "all photographic construction must remain bound in coincidences" without the textual direction of a caption (215). Indeed, all of Edwards's illustrations require their captions in order for the book's readers to glean those meanings that arise from "larger discursive conditions, invariably including those established by the system of verbal-written language" (83–84), according to Allen Sekula. "Photographic meaning is always a hybrid construction, the outcome of an interplay of iconic, graphic, and narrative conventions" (Sekula 84). As with other black autobiographies of the Jim Crow era, *Twenty-Five Years in the Black Belt* produces photographic meaning through its specific iteration of racial uplift discourses, and in this curious instance such meaning is distilled in a caption that heralds *not* the New Negro but the newer building, even though the reader and viewer may not see this structure. As a halftone presented within a pivotal chapter of autobiographical summation, "A Newer Type of Home in the Black Belt" thus presents Edwards's readers with two challenges: first, the photograph seems to contradict its caption, and by disguising rather than displaying "a newer type of home," it frustrates any attempt to apprehend this bounded, obscured house; second, the photograph seems to dodge its *autobiographical* purpose, since its relationship to Edwards himself is unclear.

The apparent discrepancy between the revealing textual caption and the concealing visual image in "A Newer Type of Home in the Black Belt" also distills one of the central tensions in Edwards's autobiography—namely, that between publicity and privacy in his narrative of racial uplift. The caption invokes the rhetoric of racial publicity since the improved home on display is meant to exemplify the race's potential, thus directing Edwards's readers to envision collective progress through this evocation of a transformed southern landscape in contrast to Uncle Charles Lee's collapsing home. At the same time, however, the photograph itself obscures the newer building, preserving its residential privacy by keeping its subject at an inscrutable distance. Moreover, the apparent contrast between old and new also removes the black body from a vision of racial progress. While *Twenty-Five Years in the Black Belt* relies on its halftones to demonstrate how institutions such as Snow Hill transform the Old Negro's log cabin, "A Newer Type of Home in the Black Belt" actually removes from view *all* signs of racial progress—the new cottage, the New Negro, and Edwards himself. Still, even as this paradoxical illustration evades the direct referentiality of an author's portrait, keeping Edwards himself unseen, it somehow serves the ends of autobiography, challenging readers and viewers to consider how it (and other such images) signify *him* in this generic context rather than merely document his life.

To be sure, the progressive race buildings that signify in chiastic relation to the inchoate structures of the past are not the sole visual emblems of a rising race in *Twenty-Five Years in the Black Belt*. The two portraits that frame *Twenty-Five Years in the Black Belt* stamp the narrative with Edwards's visage: his conventional frontispiece portrait situates him firmly within a tradition of bourgeois individualism, reinforced by the book form itself as the material instantiation of an accomplished subject; the final group portrait of the author among his Snow Hill teachers situates him within a specific configuration of New Negroes who embody the school's vision of racial uplift. Insofar as these portraits convey the prospects for racial uplift that are available to the postbellum autobiographer, the four illustrations in Edwards's book certainly resonate with his emphasis on conversion, since they conform to the efficient narrative and visual conventions—before-and-after, then-and-now, old-and-new—that characterized Tuskegee as a hub of black cultural production at the end of the long nineteenth century. However, by manipulating the viewer's relationship to their foci, Edwards's halftones of southern homes suggest just how the visual practices of such autobiographies hold the authorial body in abeyance between visibility and invisibility, a tense relation that becomes central to the constitution of the uplifted black self.

Consequently, the ideological work of Edwards's narrative leans heavily on visual paratexts that do not represent him directly. His two illustrations of improved homes, freighted as they are with the full aspirational weight of racial progress, draw the reader's eye to the exteriors of buildings rather than their domestic interiors. Much closer to the reader's view are the anonymous black women and elderly black men bound to their regressive, dreaded log cabins, and these illustrations produce a surveilling gaze that scrutinizes those "lost boys, lost girls, lost men and lost women" (51) that a school like Snow Hill Institute must save, according to its righteous mission. Edwards does not simply remove himself from view; he also structures such sights for others, according to an archival imperative that "constructs the knowledge it would seem only to register or make evident" (Smith 7). Insofar as this collation of paratexts mobilizes the rhetoric of visual chiasmus to produce the postslavery black subject, it also relies on the play of the seen and the unseen body. As a result, *Twenty-Five Years in the Black Belt* demonstrates a striking transition from the bourgeois *visibility* of the emblematic Race Man, which inheres in Edwards's frontispiece portrait, to an orchestration of the managerial *vision* of reformers and educators who seek to organize the black folk through discourses of racial uplift. Edwards's halftones of properties thus reveal how he, like Washington and other institutional Race Men among his contemporaries, deploys such halftones to produce ways of seeing through the author's ideographic production of meaning rather than simply ways of being seen as an emblematic black leader.

The dilemma of black visibility requires contemporary students of African American life narrative to look more closely at the full range of photographic images that autobiographers incorporated into their books at the close of the nineteenth century and beyond, especially since such images registered both the substance and the shadow of an expansive visual archive of race in the United States. For black autobiographers, the referential authority of the photograph resonated with forms of narrative self-presentation, and even when these authors did not themselves produce their halftones, they nonetheless curated such illustrations to function autobiographically. Thus, through ideographic practices that conjoin word and image in the service of black self-presentation, Edwards and his contemporaries proffer their postslavery autobiographies to intervene in the production of racial knowledge according to the cultural politics of synecdoche that once dominated the black public sphere. Still, if we focus strictly on the illustrations of embodied black subjects in these books—the authors' frontispiece portraits, for example—then we risk seeing only their publicness, as though these illustrations (and the autobiographies that contain them) are solely public expressions of dignity and respectability designed to counter the ineluctable abjection that obtains in racist representations of the black body on both stages and stakes during the long nineteenth century.

Appearing with increasing frequency as halftones in the Jim Crow–era publications of black autobiographers, those photographs that remove the author from view challenge us to consider how even *their* production of vision serves autobiographical, and not simply documentary, ends. Thus, Edwards's provocative example presents us with a particular strategic response to the dilemma of black visibility and requires us to qualify our conception of Jim Crow–era autobiography with an additional implication—namely, that the varied cultural practices of racial uplift have been as concerned with shielding the lives of black people from view as with redeeming them through public visibility. Seeking to display African American progress, Edwards's evidential illustrations add impressive buildings to his respectable body, thereby asking his readers and viewers to infer essences from exteriors. Even so, the managerial visuality practiced in *Twenty-Five Years in the Black Belt* also figures such progress in terms of the inaccessible interior, claiming an achieved privacy for the black male self.

NOTES

1. For more than two decades, the politics of racial uplift and, more broadly, the cultures of the black middle class have received extensive attention from scholars, though few of these studies address autobiography as such (that is, beyond its documentary utility). Aside from Gaines's influential study, my argument here about racial uplift has been shaped by the work of Moses, Gates, Carby, Reid-Pharr, McHenry, Mitchell, and Ross (*Manning*), as well as my own ("Joe Louis's" and "Matthew Henson").

2. In addition to such conventional terms as *African American* and *black*, with which I refer to people of African descent in the United States throughout this chapter, I will occasionally use other historically specific terms that deserve brief comment here. For Michele Mitchell, *Race Man* and *Race Woman* typically referred to "a self-made or high-achieving person who contributed to a local community and labored on behalf of the larger collective" (xix); for my purposes, these terms also designate members of a broad assortment of black people for whom *Race Woman* and *Race Man* connote an achieved identity of representative selfhood associated with the aims of racial uplift ideologies in the midst of Jim Crow. Likewise, *New Negro* refers, throughout this chapter, to those figures around the turn of the twentieth century who sought to transform the race's image through strategic practices of self-presentation; these New Negro autobiographers, then, emerged from "a well-scrubbed uniform body of self-sacrificing petit bourgeois rural teachers, family farmers, skilled laborers, and small-time entrepreneurs envisioned by Booker T. Washington's policies," as Marlon B. Ross has argued ("New Negro" 264).

3. I am indebted here to Kevin Everod Quashie's productive concept of "black quiet" (even as, admittedly, my own notion of "racial privacy" differs markedly, since it suggests withholding rather than expression). Cautioning against "a notion of [black] selfhood that is calibrated to the exterior world," Quashie argues that familiar tropes of doubling—double consciousness, masking, and signifying—figure black expressive practices solely in terms of publicity and resistance, thereby neglecting other forms wherein the inner lives of black people have also sought expression ("Trouble" 332). Quashie has extended this argument in *The Sovereignty of Quiet*.

4. On slavery's techniques of surveillance and control, see, for example, Camp, Hadden, and Jones.

5. According to Michelle Wright, the humanizing power of *logos* "came to represent man's inherent superiority to nature and, during the Enlightenment, achieved a status that overwhelmed all other modes of being: a thing could not exist if it could not be expressed or if it could not express itself through language" (56).

6. According to Harriet Washington, Jefferson used the slaves on his plantation to conduct his own experiments with smallpox vaccination (H. Washington 59–60). Examining the larger history of scientific and medical experimentation on black bodies throughout the nineteenth century, Washington also notes that "medical display was more than entertainment; it was also a dramatic argument for the alien inferiority of black bodies" (89).

7. Collins adds that "the work of the scientific laboratory was transferred to the photographer's studio, and the camera replaced the microscope" as a mechanism for constructing racial knowledge (23). For a critique of Agassiz's racial theory of polygenism, see Gould (62–82); on Agassiz's slave portraits, see Schneider, Trachtenberg (52–60), Wallis, "Black Bodies," and Young (26–54).

8. McBride draws similar connections between what he terms the "staging of slavery at the auction block" and the "staging of abolitionism, the carting out of black bodies onto the stage to bear witness to their authentic experiences of slavery" (4). All the same, this form of witnessing is overdetermined, as McBride stresses, because "the slave serves as a kind of fulfillment of the prophecy of abolitionist discourse. The slave is the 'real' body, the 'real' evidence, the 'real' fulfillment of what has been told before. Before the slave ever speaks, we know the slave" (5).

9. The auction block and the minstrel stage actually converge with the abolitionist platform, as when Frederick Douglass describes his early experiences with the abolitionists, who present his whip-scarred body as text (*"with my diploma written on my back!"* [*My Bondage* 365]) while prodding him to perform his racial role (with "a *little* of the plantation manner of speech" [*My Bondage* 367]) to reassure Yankee audiences of his authenticity.

10. According to Smith, the counterarchive consists of photographs that "work to dismantle and reconfigure the popular and scientific visual genealogies of African Americans that inform dominant turn-of-the-century viewing practices" (11).

11. William L. Andrews has long called upon scholars to examine both the postbellum slave narrative and "the large number of black autobiographies in the late nineteenth and early twentieth centuries that were written in [its] shadow" (Andrews, "Representation of Slavery" 63), and he continues to promote this effort with his recent anthology of postbellum slave narratives, *Slave Narratives after Slavery*; nonetheless, the antebellum slave narrative continues to command the attention of researchers. Likewise, scholarship on the interrelation of word and image in the antebellum slave narrative has outpaced work on the visual paratexts of black autobiography after emancipation. For examples of important work on frontispiece portraiture in antebellum slave narratives, see Olney, Casmier-Paz ("Footprints" and "Slave Narratives"), McCaskill, Foreman, Rohrbach, and Chaney.

12. According to Wallace, the "before-and-after" photographs of black men out of, then in, their Civil War uniforms were necessary to the legislative incorporation of black men as citizens following Emancipation; these photographs would also anticipate the industrial reconstruction of African Americans that Washington promoted at Tuskegee. Wallace has since revised this earlier essay as "Framing the Black Soldier."

13. While the portraits appearing in African American autobiography, especially during the Jim Crow era, constitute forms of racial publicity, portraiture is neither solely nor essentially public, of course. The private exchange of pictures between intimates is one obvious example, but the young activist Ida B. Wells offers another instance, since she would purchase portraits of herself and reflect on them in her diary. As Raiford notes, "More than merely attuned to the possibilities of photographic portraiture, Wells held clear standards and . . . actively sought out representations of herself that were aesthetically pleasing and of high quality" ("Ida B. Wells" 312–13). By producing a self-image for herself through both photography and diary, Wells would express a *private* desire through the quiet consumption of her own portraits.

14. Some examples of such black autobiographies wherein buildings figure significantly (though not exclusively) include Washington, *My Larger Education* (1911), Gaudet, *"He Leadeth Me"* (1913), Holtzclaw, *The Black Man's Burden* (1915), Ray, *Twice Sold, Twice Ransomed* (1926), and Hunter, *A Nickel and a Prayer* (1940).

15. Andrews adds that the "institutional man" of black autobiography rises "through the sublimation of his personal desires and ambitions in the work of an institution" ("Forgotten" 22). The centrality of institutions is a feature of Jim Crow–era autobiographies of racial uplift produced by *both* black women and black men.

16. In *My Larger Education*, Washington partly displaces his synecdochic narrative of racial progress onto the visual transformation of the race's buildings. See in particular the illustrations that contrast images of buildings on a single page, such as "A type of the unpretentious cabin which an Alabama Negro formerly occupied and the modern home in which he now lives"

(facing 124), "The 'Rising Star' Schoolhouse" (facing 146), and "'Little Texas' schoolhouse, Alabama" / "'Washington Model School,' Alabama" (facing 164) in *My Larger Education.*

17. Citing Joseph Citro, Cooper points out that "Edwards was one of only seven Tuskegee graduates repeatedly singled out and highly valued in school publications as an example of those who were spreading the Tuskegee message" (112).

18. Describing the Snow Hill countryside as it appeared when he started his school, Edwards writes, "The homes of the people consisted chiefly of one-room and two-room log cabins. There was not a single glass window to be found. I remember shortly after the founding of the school a Negro built a house and fitted it up with glass windows and people would go ten miles to see it" (49). Thus, not only are these glass windows the new signs of modernity that draw local onlookers, but their appearance coincides with the arrival of Edwards's school.

WORKS CITED

Andrews, William L. "Forgotten Voices of Afro-American Autobiography, 1865–1930." *a/b: Auto/Biography Studies* 2 (Fall 1986): 21–31.

———. "The Representation of Slavery and the Rise of Afro-American Literary Realism, 1865–1920." *Slavery and the Literary Imagination.* Ed. Deborah E. McDowell and Arnold Rampersad. Baltimore: Johns Hopkins UP, 1989. 62–80.

———, ed. *Slave Narratives after Slavery.* New York: Oxford UP, 2011.

Barrett, Lindon. *Blackness and Value: Seeing Double.* Cambridge: Cambridge UP, 1999.

Beegan, Gerry. *The Mass Image: A Social History of Photomechanical Reproduction in Victorian London.* Basingstoke, UK: Palgrave Macmillan, 2008.

Benjamin, Walter. "A Short History of Photography." *Classic Essays on Photography.* Ed. Alan Trachtenberg. New Haven, CT: Leete's Island Books, 1980. 199–216.

Benton, Megan. "Unruly Servants: Machines, Modernity, and the Printed Page." *History of the Book in America.* Vol. 4. *Print in Motion: The Expansion of Publishing and Reading in the United States, 1880–1940.* Ed. Carl F. Kaestle and Janice A. Radway. Chapel Hill: U of North Carolina P, 2009. 151–69.

Bieze, Michael. *Booker T. Washington and the Art of Self-Representation.* New York: Peter Lang, 2008.

Camp, Stephanie M. H. *Closer to Freedom: Enslaved Women and Everyday Resistance in the Plantation South.* Chapel Hill: U of North Carolina P, 2004.

Carby, Hazel V. "Policing the Black Woman's Body in an Urban Context." *Cultures in Babylon: Black Britain and African America.* London: Verso, 1999. 22–39.

Casmier-Paz, Lynn A. "Footprints of the Fugitive: Slave Narrative Discourse and the Trace of Autobiography." *Biography* 24.1 (Winter 2001): 216–25.

———. "Slave Narratives and the Rhetoric of Author Portraiture." *New Literary History* 34.1 (Winter 2003): 91–116.

Chaney, Michael A. *Fugitive Vision: Slave Image and Black Identity in Antebellum Narrative.* Bloomington: Indiana UP, 2008.

Collins, Lisa Gail. *The Art of History: African American Women Artists Engage the Past.* New Brunswick, NJ: Rutgers UP, 2002.

Cooper, Arnold. "Booker T. Washington and William J. Edwards of Snow Hill Institute, 1893–1915." *Alabama Review* 40.2 (April 1987): 111–32.

Douglass, Frederick. *My Bondage and My Freedom*. 1855. *Autobiographies*. Ed. Henry Louis Gates Jr. New York: Library of America, 1994. 103–452.

———. *Narrative of the Life of Frederick Douglass, an American Slave*. 1845. *Slave Narratives*. Ed. William L. Andrews and Henry Louis Gates Jr. New York: Library of America, 2000. 267–368.

Edwards, William J. *Twenty-Five Years in the Black Belt*. Boston: Cornhill, 1918.

———. "Uplifting of the Submerged Masses." Washington, *Tuskegee* 224–52.

Foreman, P. Gabrielle. "Who's Your Mama? 'White' Mulatta Genealogies, Early Photography, and Anti-Passing Narratives of Slavery and Freedom." *American Literary History* 14.3 (2002): 505–39.

Foucault, Michel. *Discipline and Punish: The Birth of the Prison*. Trans. Alan Sheridan. New York: Vintage, 1979.

Foy, Anthony S. "Joe Louis's Talking Fists: The Auto/Biopolitics of *My Life Story*." *American Literary History* 23.2 (2011): 311–36.

———. "Matthew Henson and the Antinomies of Racial Uplift." *a/b: Auto/Biography Studies* 27.1 (Summer 2012): 19–44.

Gaines, Kevin K. *Uplifting the Race: Black Leadership, Politics, and Culture in the Twentieth Century*. Chapel Hill: U of North Carolina P, 1996.

Gates, Henry Louis, Jr. "The Trope of a New Negro and the Reconstruction of the Image of the Black." *Representations* 24 (Autumn 1988): 129–55.

Gaudet, Frances Joseph. *"He Leadeth Me."* New Orleans: the author, 1913.

Goldsby, Jacqueline. *A Spectacular Secret: Lynching in American Life and Literature*. Chicago: U of Chicago P, 2006.

Gould, Stephen Jay. *The Mismeasure of Man*. Rev. and expanded ed. New York: W. W. Norton, 1996.

Hadden, Sally. *Slave Patrols: Law and Violence in Virginia and the Colonies*. Cambridge, MA: Harvard UP, 2001.

Harris, Michael D. *Colored Pictures: Race and Visual Representation*. Chapel Hill: U of North Carolina P, 2003.

Harris, Neil. *Cultural Excursions: Marketing Appetites and Cultural Tastes in Modern America*. Chicago: U of Chicago P, 1990.

Holtzclaw, William H. *The Black Man's Burden*. New York: Neale, 1915.

Hunter, Jane Edna. *A Nickel and a Prayer*. N.p.: Parthenon Press, 1940.

Jefferson, Thomas. *Notes on the State of Virginia*. *Writings*. Ed. Merrill D. Peterson. New York: Library of America, 1984. 123–325.

Jones, Norrece T. *Born a Child of Freedom yet a Slave: Mechanisms of Control and Strategies of Resistance in Antebellum South Carolina*. Hanover, NH: UP of New England, 1990.

Lupton, Ellen. "Design and Production in the Mechanical Age." *Graphic Design in the Mechanical Age: Selections from the Merrill C. Berman Collection*. Ed. Deborah Rothschild, Ellen Lupton, and Darra Goldstein. New Haven, CT: Yale UP, 1998. 50–81.

McBride, Dwight A. *Impossible Witnesses: Truth, Abolitionism, and the Slave Testimony*. New York: New York UP, 2001.

McCaskill, Barbara. "'Yours Very Truly': Ellen Craft—The Fugitive as Text and Artifact." *African American Review* 28.4 (1994): 509–29.

McHenry, Elizabeth. *Forgotten Readers: Recovering the Lost History of African American Literary Societies.* Durham, NC: Duke UP, 2002.

Mitchell, Michele. *Righteous Propagation: African Americans and the Politics of Racial Destiny after Reconstruction.* Chapel Hill: U of North Carolina P, 2004.

Moses, Wilson Jeremiah. *The Golden Age of Black Nationalism, 1850–1925.* New York: Oxford UP, 1978.

Olney, James. "'I Was Born': Slave Narratives, Their Status as Autobiography and as Literature." *The Slave's Narrative.* Ed. Charles T. Davis and Henry Louis Gates Jr. New York: Oxford UP, 1985. 148–75.

Quashie, Kevin [Everod]. *The Sovereignty of Quiet: Beyond Resistance in Black Culture.* New Brunswick, NJ: Rutgers UP, 2012.

———. "The Trouble with Publicness: Toward a Theory of Black Quiet." *African American Review* 43.2–3 (Summer/Fall 2009): 329–43.

Raiford, Leigh. "Ida B. Wells and the Shadow Archive." *Pictures and Progress: Early Photography and the Making of African American Identity.* Ed. Maurice O. Wallace and Shawn Michelle Smith. Durham, NC: Duke UP, 2012. 299–320.

———. *Imprisoned in a Luminous Glare: Photography and the African American Freedom Struggle.* Chapel Hill: U of North Carolina P, 2011.

Ray, Emma. *Twice Sold, Twice Ransomed.* Chicago: Free Methodist Publishing House, 1926.

Reid-Pharr, Robert. *Conjugal Union: The Body, the House, and the Black American.* New York: Oxford UP, 1999.

Rohrbach, Augusta. *Truth Stranger than Fiction: Race, Realism, and the U.S. Literary Marketplace.* New York: Palgrave, 2002.

Roper, Moses. *A Narrative of the Adventures and Escape of Moses Roper, from American Slavery. I Was Born a Slave: An Anthology of Classic Slave Narratives.* Vol. 1. *1772–1849.* Ed. Yuval Taylor. Chicago: Lawrence Hill Books, 1999. 487–522.

Ross, Marlon B. *Manning the Race: Reforming Black Men in the Jim Crow Era.* New York: New York UP, 2004.

———. "The New Negro Displayed: Self-Ownership, Proprietary Sites/Sights, and the Bonds/Bounds of Race." *Claiming the Stones, Naming the Bones: Cultural Property and the Negotiation of National and Ethnic Identity.* Ed. Elazar Barkan and Ronald Bush. Los Angeles: Getty Research Institute, 2002. 259–301.

Rugg, Linda Haverty. *Picturing Ourselves: Photography and Autobiography.* Chicago: U of Chicago P, 1997.

Schneider, Suzanne. "Louis Agassiz and the American School of Ethnoeroticism: Polygenesis, Pornography, and Other 'Perfidious Influences.'" Wallace and Smith, *Pictures* 211–43.

Sekula, Allen. "The Traffic in Photographs." *Only Skin Deep: Changing Visions of the American Self.* Ed. Coco Fusco and Brian Wallis. New York: International Center of Photography/ Harry N. Abrams, 2003. 79–109.

Smith, Shawn Michelle. *Photography on the Color Line: W. E. B. Du Bois, Race, and Visual Culture.* Durham, NC: Duke UP, 2004.

Tagg, John. *The Burden of Representation: Essays on Photographies and Histories.* Amherst: U of Massachusetts P, 1988.

Trachtenberg, Alan. *Reading American Photographs: Images as History, Matthew Brady to Walker Evans.* New York: Hill and Wang, 1989.

Wallace, Maurice O. *Constructing the Black Masculine: Identity and Ideality in African American Men's Literature and Culture, 1775–1995*. Durham, NC: Duke UP, 2002.

———. "Framing the Black Soldier: Image, Uplift, and the Duplicity of Pictures." Wallace and Smith, *Pictures* 244–66.

———. "'How a Man Was Made a Slave': Contraband, Chiasmus, and the Failure of Visual Abolitionism." *English Language Notes* 44.2 (Fall/Winter 2006): 175–79.

Wallace, Maurice O., and Shawn Michelle Smith, eds. *Pictures and Progress: Early Photography and the Making of African American Identity*. Durham, NC: Duke UP, 2012.

Wallis, Brian. "Black Bodies, White Science: Louis Agassiz's Slave Daguerreotypes." *Only Skin Deep: Changing Visions of the American Self*. Ed. Coco Fusco and Brian Wallis. New York: International Center of Photography/Harry N. Abrams, 2003. 163–81.

———. "The Dream Life of a People: African American Vernacular Photography." *African American Vernacular Photography: Selections from the Daniel Cowin Collection*. New York: International Center of Photography; Göttingen: Steidl, 2005. 9–14.

Washington, Booker T. *My Larger Education: Being Chapters from My Experience*. Garden City, NY: Doubleday, Page, 1911.

———. *The Negro in Business*. 1907. Wichita, KS: DeVore and Sons, 1992.

———. "Signs of Progress among the Negroes." *Century Magazine* 59 (January 1900): 472–74.

———. *The Story of My Life and Work*. 1900. Naperville, IL: J. L. Nichols, 1901.

———, ed. *Tuskegee and Its People: Their Ideals and Achievements*. New York: D. Appleton, 1905.

———. *Working with the Hands*. New York: Doubleday, Page, 1904.

Washington, Harriet. *Medical Apartheid: The Dark History of Medical Experimentation on Black Americans from Colonial Times to the Present*. New York: Doubleday, 2006.

Wiegman, Robyn. *American Anatomies: Theorizing Race and Gender*. Durham, NC: Duke UP, 1995.

Wood, Marcus. *Blind Memory: Visual Representations of Slavery in England and America, 1780–1865*. New York: Routledge, 2000.

Wright, Michelle. *Becoming Black: Creating Identity in the African Diaspora*. Durham, NC: Duke UP, 2004.

Young, Harvey. *Embodying Black Experience: Stillness, Critical Memory, and the Black Body*. Ann Arbor: U of Michigan P, 2010.

Richard Wright's Environments
Mediating Personhood through the South's Second Nature

SUSAN SCOTT PARRISH

Critics have often associated Richard Wright with the word *environment*. His adoption of the realist and, still more so, the naturalist genres of writing seem to entail that he believed humans to be products of their environs.[1] In particular, as scholars have attended to Wright's immersion in the work and the methods of the Chicago School of Sociology after his move north in the fall of 1927, they typically transfer those sociologists' understanding of environment in a wholesale way to Wright. Carla Cappetti, for example, describes the relation between the Chicago School and Wright as one of "intellectual grafting" ("Sociology" 255).[2] In a paradigmatic 1925 study, *The City*, the leading practitioners of the Chicago School, Robert E. Park, Ernest W. Burgess, and Roderick D. McKenzie, define their new field of "human ecology" as "a study of the spatial and temporal relations of human beings as affected by the selective, distributive, and accommodative forces of the environment" (63–64). Theorizing that the modern city is a kind of organism that acts on the humans inhabiting it in predictable and ultimately stabilizing ways, Park, Burgess, and McKenzie contend that humans are best understood by their "*position*" (64) within the spatiotemporal development of that organism. Human design of space was secondary to the environment's design of the human. Wright himself, when explaining his youth, frequently uses the term *environment* to connote a social milieu that "claim[s]" its "will-less" subjects by conditioning their habits of thought and behavior (*Black* 104).[3] While it would certainly be justifiable, then, to contend that Wright hewed to contemporaneous sociological theories of environmental conditioning, this point would not begin to tell the whole story.

To put it another way: we have not yet hit the mark in defining Wright's environmentalism. I contend that Wright's uptake of the Chicago School theories of "human ecology" was only partial. Much of their modeling emerged from studies of northern cities—especially the abruptly modernized city of Chicago—in which immigrant and migrant groups seemed to compete for space and resources and adapt their social organization to their new setting. Their theories did not particularly fit the postslavery South, which Wright was busy thinking and writing about while he lived in Chicago from 1927 to 1937. Although phases of competition, accommodation, and stabilization—a sequential model used by Chicago sociologists—may have explained a new city made by vying groups, these terms hardly seemed adequate in describing the long-entrenched and legally mandated racial hierarchy and spatial zoning of the Delta region. Such a contention has important implications for how we understand Wright's life and his life writing. If we can better appreciate his experiences of the natural and built world of the South in his youth, we can read anew how he wrote into being a "self" that developed in relation to that world. Moreover, we can perceive that when fictional characters failed to affect his readers the way he felt they should, Wright turned, again and again, to autobiography to educate his readers on how southern "nature" and the southern "negro" were cognate, though mutually alienated, historical and human-made products. By recovering the importance of the rural environment and its disturbances to Wright, I offer a new reading of Wright's autobiographical work, including the highly canonical *Black Boy*, and I challenge the truism that it was the urban "street" that gave Wright his critical edge.[4]

Skeptical of the fit of "human ecology" for the rural South, he adapted it—and signified on it—in his first piece of autobiographical writing, "The Ethics of Living Jim Crow," as he tried to define the racialized way in which his identity was a function of spatiotemporal "position." By the time he wrote *Black Boy* five years later, though, he had moved still farther away from the Chicago School model. In this text, he fashions others as environmental products while giving to his own self a much more personally willed subjectivity. This subjectivity, moreover, derives its rich emotional repertoire from its contact with "green, growing things" (*Black* 10). If *Black Boy*'s trajectory ultimately follows the path-north-to-authorship model so central to the tradition of African American autobiography, he also grounds his self in a kind of Romantic literacy. To put this point another way: the first encrypted signs he decodes are not alphabetical but instead concern rural nature and the rural built environment. The "green" world makes him relatively impervious to his social milieu; country "nature" fortifies him to face town and city "culture." Another aspect of the Chicago School that Wright bristled against was the fact that its "human ecology" was based on a model of ecology characterized by equilibrium. In such a model, when disequilibrium occurred, it only served to encourage humans to create better social systems of mutual support. Wright's own personal experiences—including witnessing one of the major ecocatastrophes of the twentieth century in the Lower Mississippi Valley—challenged such a model.

Once we notice, then, how Wright engages in his autobiographical texts with the southern nature of his childhood and youth, we begin to perceive Wright's protests anew.[5] We see that Wright was producing a distinct kind of revolutionary materialism, one especially fit for the postslavery southern section of the United States and the world of the twentieth century's imperial "color-line."[6] For Karl Marx, alienation occurred as the rural or industrial laborer under capitalism "sinks to the level of a commodity" (106) as he gives his self to the things he produces; for

Wright, alienation for people of African descent in the South, dealing simultaneously with the alienations of labor *and* race, occurred as a still more profound break between the human and his or her omnipresent bodily and cosmic envelopes. It was Wright's reading of a now-obscure apostate to Freudianism, Trigant Burrow, and his thesis about humanity's "biological recoil" (119) as well as its "image-production" (249) that informed Wright's insights. Moreover, Wright's adaptation of Marx to consider politicized space anticipated the late twentieth-century work of Henri Lefebvre. In short, Wright describes the making not of a naturalist self but rather of a Romantic self who, after his forced "recoil" from biology, must learn to operate in a turbulent "second nature" (Lefebvre 345).

The Ecological Approach

Wright scholars have examined the author's immersion in the scholarship of the Chicago School as well as his connections to individual scholars in that community.[7] Most famously, Wright claims in his introduction to *Black Metropolis*, "I did not know what my story was . . . until I stumbled upon science," after which "I discovered some of the meanings of the environment that battered and taunted me" (xvii). And in *Black Boy*, he explains that sociology's "tables of figures relating population density to insanity, relating housing to disease, relating school and recreational activities to crime" all helped to explain "the causes of [his] conduct and the conduct of [his] family" (278). From this research, Wright, as he puts it, "absorbed some of that quota of inspiration necessary for [him] to write *Uncle Tom's Children* and *Black Boy*" (Introduction xviii).[8] It is certainly true that Wright encountered sociology at a critical juncture in his maturation when its linkages between social conditions and behavior gave scientific validation to his intuition that African American misery ("insanity," "disease," "crime") was not racially inherent but rather socially and historically produced; and, as he states, sociologists provided for him, in Chicago in the 1930s, one of his first intellectual communities.[9] Hearing such testimony from Wright about sociology's heuristic powers, we have tended to let it stand as a simple fact of his own development and a definition of the prime "science" behind all his designs of the self. Wright's attitude about the institutions of the academic sciences, and the extent of their applicability to him, were in fact more equivocal.

Two anecdotes suggest Wright's discomfort with the reification that seemed to accompany institutionalized empiricism. In the early 1930s, while visiting the sociology department at the University of Chicago, Wright first met Horace R. Cayton, the PhD student who, along with St. Clair Drake, would in 1945 write the book *Black Metropolis: A Study of Negro Life in a Northern City*. According to Cayton, when Wright saw the files that Cayton and his advisor, Louis Wirth, were accumulating on "every facet of the city . . . the vast complex of human beings who make up the monster of Chicago," Wright observed, "You've got all your facts pointed, pinned to the wall like a collector would pin butterflies" (qtd. in Rowley 81), a remark that suggests Wright's sense that much was sacrificed as mobile life became "pinned" "facts."[10] Indeed, Robert Park had proudly avowed this disposition of sociology to "dissect" dispassionately when he told graduate students at this institution who were inclined toward racial activism that "their role was to be that of the calm, detached scientist who investigates race relations with the same objectivity and detachment with which the zoologist dissects the potato bug" (qtd. in Bulmer 76).

At the time of his interchange with Cayton, Wright was working as a laboratory assistant in a medical research institute at a prestigious Chicago hospital. As he describes it in *Black Boy*, he and three other African Americans occupied an "underworld position" (303) in the basement, keeping watch over the animal research subjects. The dogs whose vocal cords he helped slit and who "gape[d] in a silent wail" seemed to him a recognizable "symbol of silent suffering" (305). One day, when two of his fellow employees engaged in a brawl, all the cages holding the carefully separated rats, mice, guinea pigs, rabbits, and dogs clattered down and opened. Amid the ensuing chaos, the four men held "a strange scientific conference" (312) about how to restore order to the mayhem of data, for, having been kept intentionally blind to "the meaning of the experiments" (312), they did not know the researchers' principles of categorization. Largely "at random" (312) then, the four reclassified the animal specimens. The white doctors, suspecting nothing, continued to work with these randomized subjects as they painstakingly recorded "findings" (314) on their charts, perhaps giving to "some tested principle . . . a new and strange refinement" due to this "fresh, remarkable evidence" (314). Wright tells the story of this "secret disaster" (314) as an American epistemological and racial allegory, asking: since we were seen as "close kin to the animals we tended" (314)—like them "locked in the dark underworld of American life" (314)—and kept ignorant of the ordering principles and experimental goals of the laboratory work, how could we muster a commitment to producing or safeguarding a knowledge that was so socially and ethically contaminated?

To be sure, a different scene presented itself at the University of Chicago, where a number of African American sociologists were trained in the 1920s and 1930s and mentored by Park, who had worked as Booker T. Washington's secretary for seven years (Bulmer 37). And certainly W. E. B. Du Bois's work in sociology at Atlanta University helped to make it a symbolically significant field for black investigators. Yet I contend that Wright's sense of being—like those "facts," dead butterflies, and other animal subjects, "pinned" and "locked" in America by his racial and class position—made him feel of two minds about the empirical social sciences. Though "science" made manifest to him the truth that social, physical, and mental anguish often resulted from concrete and quantifiable external causes, he knew from experience that the "havoc" (*Black* 310) and "helter-skelter" (312) of life in the "underworld" was not as reducible to "facts," and to theory, as systematizers believed. In fact, he knew that "scientific truth" (314) could "devocalize" (305) subjects, that subjects could "shrewdly . . . cover up . . . evidence" (311), and that "guesswork" (311) entered in, especially when a "vast . . . distance" (314) separated knower from known.

Apart from these issues involving what we would today call the "sociology of science," Wright also demurred from certain assumptions then underpinning the science of sociology. As I noted above, Park, Burgess, and McKenzie used the term *human ecology* to indicate the study of "the spatial relationships of human beings" that are produced by "competition and selection" (64) and evolve over time. Even the ghettos of the Jewish diaspora, according to Park's colleague Louis Wirth, could be seen as a "form of accommodation between divergent population groups," in which "one group has effectually subordinated itself to another"; though, as he notes, the culture group of the ghetto will "[maintain] its integrity" for a time, it will be "transformed by degrees until it blends with the larger community about it" (4–5). Though humans might believe they are consciously designing their habitats and selecting their own positions within these habitats, they are in fact responding to spatial conditions in an inevitably recurring pattern of "disorganization, reorganization, and increasing differentiation" (Park, Burgess, and McKenzie 56).[11]

Directing their methodology was the assumption that neither individuals nor small groups of men willfully created institutions and communities ex nihilo, but that human collectives, like plant groupings, operated according to fairly predictable laws of behavior and change. In particular, as they implemented their "Ecological Approach," these sociologists called frequently upon the work of leading American ecologist F. E. Clements, whose 1916 *Plant Succession* had argued that species in a given area over time evolve progressively toward a climax stage, at which stage they represent a superorganism, a community interconnected and self-balancing enough to be understood as having achieved an integral identity.[12] Though Park and Burgess, in their *Introduction to the Science of Sociology*, define their method as a "science of society" (44) and distinguish it from August Comte's and Herbert A. Spencer's nineteenth-century philosophies of history *as progress*, they nevertheless, in seeking predictive social laws, trusted in Clements's notion of detectable and stabilizing patterns.[13] For, as they argue, "society is an immense co-operative concern of mutual services" (162).

While one might assume that the preponderance of disasters in the early twentieth century might have caused the field to doubt its thesis of ineluctable stabilization, these crises did not upset but instead reinforced the prevailing sociological model.[14] Or, to put it another way, this trust was so strong that it could incorporate and neutralize evidence of human error writ on a tremendous scale. In 1920 sociologist Samuel Henry Prince published *Catastrophe and Social Change: Based upon a Sociological Study of the Halifax Disaster*, which had occurred three years earlier and through which "the City of Halifax ha[d] been galvanized into life. . . . She ha[d] caught the spirit of the social age. This spirit after all means only that the community is just a family on a larger scale, and the interests of each member are interwoven with those of all" (139). Five years later, sociologists Stuart Alfred Queen and Delbert Martin

Mann followed up with *Social Pathology*, arguing that cataclysm invariably brings about a "realignment of social forces which will make for a better organized community working more effectively toward the solution of its various problems" (435–36). According to these sociologists, disasters act as overdue social heuristics, making needs "apparent" and "open[ing] the way for rendering long-needed services" (437). According to Prince, Queen, and Mann, the superorganism comes to know and to fix itself under stress. Equilibrium, then, is the key feature of the universe of ecology and thus of human ecology; periodic disturbance, as this line of thinking argues, exists mainly to adjust and deepen that equilibrium.

Wright and the Mississippi Flood of 1927

When Wright was eighteen years old, living, working, and avidly reading both black and white papers in Memphis, the largest scale disaster ever to occur on the Mississippi River—and by some measures, in the entire United States—took place. As a point of reference, it unfolded with all the elements that became so notorious in New Orleans in 2005: massive and systemic human error, unflagging national and international attention across multiple media outlets, as well as displacement, discrimination, and fatality largely determined by race. Imagine an eighteen-year-old budding author from New Orleans living through the levee disaster of 2005 and *not* having her sense of the world, of nature, of technology, of embodiment, of the media, and of national politics profoundly affected by that experience.

Though Memphis, with its relatively high elevation, was protected in 1927 from direct inundation, it was a central hub in rescue and relief organization, and it was only some 150 miles away from the most scandalous Red Cross camp at Greenville, Mississippi.[15] Wright's constant migrations as a child and his work as a young man for an insurance agent had made him familiar with both the Arkansas and the Mississippi Deltas and with life on the levee—that is, with the social and physical terrain of a great part of the flood zone. What is more, as a reader of the Memphis *Commercial Appeal*, the *Chicago Defender*, and other papers, Wright had the opportunity to see how the flood was taking on meaning in both the white and the black public spheres.[16] Not only did he come into contact with minstrel renditions of black refugees and with Red Cross promotional iconography through these newspapers, but he was also exposed to H. L. Mencken's anti-Dixie editorial and its southern rebuttal as well as a series of articles protesting Jim Crow abuses by all the major African American pundits. Given its immense popularity and its topicality in the spring of 1927, Bessie Smith's "Back-Water Blues" very likely reached his ears and made its way into his consciousness.[17] In short, through this exposure to both black and white flood culture, he came to see that something "natural" and catastrophic could be produced by human agency and that it could be highly political. And he saw that an event in the Delta could command the nation's attention, a nation that, in its fractiousness, attributed utterly contrary meanings to that event. Out of this exposure to a catastrophe that was both anthropogenic and polysemous, Wright produced the 1937 short story "Silt," the 1938 novella "Down by the Riverside," and his first piece of life writing, the 1937 "Ethics of Living Jim Crow," the last two brought together in 1940 in a revised version of *Uncle Tom's Children*. In these texts, either autobiographical or inspired by his own witnessing of disaster and disaster mediation, Wright experimented toward a new mode of environmental writing, a type that we would today associate with the environmental justice movement.[18]

When William Faulkner later called this the "flood year 1927" (20) to indicate its extreme duration, he underestimated the length of time in his point on this year: its full cycle actually lasted from the extreme weather events beginning in August 1926 to the final return of displaced farm laborers to their landlords' properties in the late winter of 1928. After the crest had reached the Gulf, by the late spring of 1927, water covered 27,000 square miles, land in seven states where almost 1 million people lived; thirteen major crevasses occurred; roughly 637,000 people became homeless; and 154 "concentration camps,"[19] where a mostly African American population lived for months, were run by the Red Cross. Death figures are uncertain, but it was estimated that 1,000 people were killed in the Mississippi Delta region alone. And, financially, the disaster had resulted in at least $1 billion dollars in losses (Barry 285–86, 363; Saikku 156–59). Of the flood, Commerce Secretary Herbert Hoover, who was put in charge of rescue and relief operations, said: "Outside the Great War, there has been no such calamity as this flood" (qtd. in Barry 329).[20] Though the whole region was devastated, environmental historian Mikko Saikku summarizes that "the people hardest hit by the 1927 flood—and its predecessors—were black sharecroppers" (157). For it was African American men doing the lion's share of the physical work of flood prevention and cleanup, often at gunpoint; poor African Americans had less opportunity for evacuation and, in fact, were frequently barred from flight by planters concerned about losing their laborers; landlords passed their own postflood indebtedness on to the sharecroppers, rendering them legally bound to the land in a debt-peonage system.

Though, as Saikku notes, overflows are an inherent feature of a river's "disturbance regime," this flood was an anthropogenic disaster brought on by the improvident alteration of the Mississippi River and its watershed over the preceding fifty years through industrial-scale deforestation, wetlands drainage, and agriculture combined with a "levees only" engineering strategy.[21] It moved so slowly and lasted so long that national audiences could be pulled in, through newly quickened and extensive media circuits, to the events as they occurred.[22] American publics, though initially synchronized in their consumption of the disaster reportage, were soon fractured by the meanings they made out of the event. Because the flood moved from north to south, it seemed to white southerners to be a kind of biological re-enactment of the "War of Northern Aggression," resulting from federal negligence and carrying Yankee water. As a white, southern public meditated on this second river-borne assault, northern and western white publics tended to see the rescue efforts they were asked to finance as an opportunity to replay the Civil War, but this time as an "army of rescuers" ("Big"), drawing their needy white brethren back into the national family. Because of the disproportionate environmental vulnerability of black southerners and the Jim Crow management of the Red Cross camps, African American commentators across the nation argued that slavery had returned to Dixie.

It is often noted that Wright attested in *Black Boy* to learning how to use "words as a weapon" (248) from reading H. L. Mencken in 1927.[23] But it is seldom pointed out that his exposure to Mencken occurred in the midst of this flood and in the context of his consumption of a wider print culture involving the catastrophe.[24] Indeed, in the months between the flood and Wright's departure north in November was that period in which, as he put it, a "new knowledge ... was dawning within [him]" (251), a knowledge he carried about within him like "a secret, criminal burden" (252) and that created a "vast sense of distance between [him] and the world in which [he] lived" (253). This knowledge had partly to do with his commencing to read notable American authors, but it also involved the ways in which the flood became a flashpoint in American interracial and interregional relations.

On May 28, 1927, Wright read "Another Mencken Absurdity," an editorial in the Memphis *Commercial Appeal* that was a response to Mencken's own *Evening Sun* editorial of five days earlier, "The Mississippi Flood." In his editorial, Mencken rather blithely put salt in the wounds of the flooded region, declaring that "New Yorkers [would] refrain from sobbing" for the suffering of "the least advanced white people now living in the United States" ("Mississippi Flood"). According to this text, southerners, all being fundamentalist "yokels" and "Ku Kluxers," were not fellow Americans but rather a "hostile tribe on our borders" ("Mississippi Flood"). The editors of the *Appeal*, turning the tables, accused Mencken of "ignorance" and of "pl[ying] the trade of the most credulous of the revivalists who see in every cataclysm of nature, God's visitation for sin" ("Another"). Wright was struck, when reading the *Appeal*'s response, by the "scorn" (*Black* 244) flowing between northern and southern whites, prodding him to wonder: "Were there, then, people other than Negroes who criticized the South?" (244). As Wright recalls in *Black Boy*, it was this discord within American whiteness that opened up for him a rhetorical space and allowed him to begin to imagine belonging to a larger world of print. If mainstream print culture could provoke within itself a public discord, rather than merely project a single ideology, then perhaps he could enter into its fray. Moreover, realizing that there were whites who fiercely opposed the South made what was a private, unspoken revolt against his region feel legitimized by appearing in mainstream, national print.

Beyond this rhetorical model for an antisouthern stance, Wright would have seen, as a frequent reader of the *Commercial Appeal*, an active, white verbal and visual culture of satire, and specifically a surprising kind of minoritarian satire. That

Wright encountered a public discourse of minority resistance in the shape of white southern editorials must have produced in him a strange dissonance: after all, how could his oppressors see themselves as oppressed? As an adolescent, Wright had been mentored in the practice of decoding visual caricature by a "soft-spoken black man" (*Black* 129); thus, his critical viewing skills were presumably honed by the time he was eighteen.[25] Editorial pundits of the white South read the recurrence of devastating Mississippi floods as a supreme indicator of their region's continuous suffering "for no offence it committed and because of no fault of its own" ("Stand"). The flood made manifest to the South its existence as a kind of internal colony, denigrated "tribe," or perpetually disabled white minority within the nation. Wright would have absorbed white southerners' contention that this flood was not an "unprecedented visitation of nature's wrath" but rather a sign of land use negligence on the part of "the whole nation" ("Burden") and poor engineering design by federal planners. The critique of Washington's fake and scanty "SYMPATHY" vis-à-vis a South "crippled" by such negligent assault, as seen in a cartoon of 1 June (fig. 5.1), would no doubt have made Wright not only think about print satire and an intrawhite resentment he believed to have ended with the Civil War but also wonder about how the white South understood and represented its region's suffering within a national realm. In particular, the *Appeal*'s tactic of representing flood suffering through a disabled, white male body must have jarred against awareness within the black community that it comprised the majority of the flood's bodily victims.

Along with resentment about federal negligence, a major element of white flood print culture involved a racialized drama in which whites tended to take center stage as romantic and heroic protagonists while blacks appeared as entr'acte minstrel figures of comic relief. For this black figure, the flood was a godsend, freeing him from work and allowing him to bask in federal munificence. Indeed, Red Cross camps were experienced as an unbeatable tent show, one that did not even charge admission! A front-page cartoon from 21 April would have made it painfully clear to Wright how a mainstream white southern public saw the participation of African Americans within the conversation about catastrophe (fig. 5.2). While the "[white] Public," "Trade," "Farming," "General Business," and "Transportation" huddle under a large sheltering umbrella to strategize and come up with "Relief Plans," "Hambone," a regular comic presence in the daily, has no place in what Queen and Mann called "a better organized community working more effectively toward the solution of its various problems" (435–36). Though the cartoon notes Hambone's exclusion from this process, it also justifies his exclusion as it vocalizes his thinking as a form of subrational folk animism: "Uh! Ef de ole Mis'sippi *is* de 'Father O' Waters,' den Pappy sho done rolled outen he bed!!!" Picturing black incompetence and dependence serves to publicize white organizational mastery and paternalistic munificence.

By contrast with the white print culture that Wright conspicuously engaged with and signified upon, black print culture during the flood, according to Wright's telling in *Black Boy*, had little influence on him: "When I read a Negro newspaper"

Figure 5.1. J. P. Alley, "Saying It with Flowers." *Commercial Appeal*, 1 June 1927: front page. Courtesy the *Commercial Appeal*.

Figure 5.2. J. P. Alley, "Let's Pray for a Drouth!" *Commercial Appeal*, 21 Apr. 1927: front page. Courtesy the *Commercial Appeal*.

in the months comprising the disaster, "I never caught the faintest echo of my preoccupation in its pages" (252). Given that local black papers perhaps could not afford to be critical of Jim Crow southern politics, perhaps this attitude about the local press is not surprising.[26] It is a strange omission, though, that Wright mentions only being enlightened by Mencken's antisouthern polemic during the spring and summer of 1927 but says nothing of being stirred by the constant barrage of flood exposés written by the likes of W. E. B. Du Bois, Ida B. Wells, Walter White, and Jesse O. Thomas in the *Pittsburgh Courier*, the Baltimore *Afro-American*, the *Crisis*, *Opportunity*, and the *Chicago Defender*, papers available in the South and which he otherwise read eagerly.[27]

In the *Defender*, for example, J. Winston Harrington reported frequently from the dysfunctional and racist camp at Greenville, Mississippi, which exhibited, as he put it, "The ugly specter of Race hate [that] has reared its head above the angry waters" (1). A *Defender* editorial opined: "Newspapers said the floods washed away everything in the South. But you know better. You know that the floods, in reality, washed the white South of everything BUT ITS CUSSEDNESS. That was inlaid TOO DEEP for the waters to get at" ("The Week" 1-A1). And Ida B. Wells worked to generate nationwide "protest" against the behavior of the Red Cross and the National Guard. She accused the former of "encouraging and condoning a system of discrimination, of peonage, and of robbery of funds" ("Brand" n. pag.). She became the intermediary for the stories of black male informants caught in the disaster zone, whose narratives asserted that, essentially, slavery had returned to the South. She shamed members of the Colored Advisory Commission (appointed by Hoover), especially Tuskegee's Robert Moton, for keeping their findings hidden. Finally, she insisted, "The only way to bring public opinion to action is for those whose race is suffering to cry aloud, and keep on crying aloud until something is done" ("Flood Refugees" 1-A11). It seems well-nigh impossible for Wright to have been unaware of this commentary and other protest literature, whether he read it hot off the press in the summer of 1927 in Memphis or via faded copies in Chicago in the ensuing years. Indeed, while Wright was working on the drafts of his flood stories and "Ethics" in the midthirties, he lived at 3743 Indiana Avenue in Chicago.[28] The Associated Negro Press, headed by Claude Barnett, a member of the Flood's Colored Advisory Commission who had toured the Red Cross camps, was located just down the street at 3423 Indiana Avenue and would presumably have housed some of the journalistic materials, both black and white, connected with the flood (Work 426).[29]

This flood posed a threat not only to humans and their built environment but also to that cosmological paradigm of *equilibrium* that reigned in ecology and hence in the field of human ecology. In the decades leading up to 1927, silviculture, agriculture, and engineering had presumed that nature's stability was so secure that it would support humanity's large-scale redesign of the Mississippi watershed. But a season of extreme weather producing coincident high water in all the Mississippi's tributaries acted like a dramatic stress test that disproved such a view of nature. Moreover, racism during and after the flood gainsaid any model of catastrophe as a galvanic community reset button. There was, however, academic modeling—in which the operative concept was not equilibrium but instead *risk*—that better explained the events of 1927. Rather than focusing on whole systems, theorists in economics, philosophy, and anthropology producing such risk modeling tended to focus on human and nonhuman agents encountering an aleatory world in a wagering and experimental mode. In the field of ecology, for example, Henry A. Gleason represented a dissenting model from that of Clements's prevailing idea of distinct successional series working toward climax stages. Gleason, in his 1926 article, "The Individualistic Concept of the Plant Association," concludes that "an association is not an organism, scarcely even a vegetational unit, but merely a *coincidence*" (16), one dependent on the seeds' "means of migration, including the various accidents of dispersal" (17). In short, "every species of plant is a law unto itself" (26). For Wright, such a dissenting cosmology—based not on the stabilizing communal organism but rather on the individual who wagers within an unremittent pattern of accidental unfolding—aptly describes the worlds he, and his narrativized selves, inhabited.

The Green Ethics of the White South

In the 1930s, when Wright composed, along with his flood fiction, "The Ethics of Living Jim Crow," he brought to these texts a sense of the ways in which the "green" world was not only a place of inherent natural risk but also one shaped into a still more dangerous political artefact. He recognized that nature can be modified according to human design, and that—in a boomerang gyration—humans could then be affected by this design and by its miscalculations. Not only were white southerners making that point in 1927 (vis-à-vis inept federal flood management), but African American pundits were observing how those dangers were meted out in the Delta unequally according to race. If *Uncle Tom's Children* represented at the time of its publication, as Richard Yarborough has argued, "the most unrelenting and rage-fueled critique of white racism ever to surface in fiction written by blacks directed toward a mainstream American readership" (x), this landmark text also delineated how such racism operated through a strategic white management of the rural built environment and of "green growing things" (1). That Wright chose to open the 1940 revised collection with "Ethics"—after he was dismayed by the uptake of the stories in 1938 as sentimental tearjerkers ("How 'Bigger'" 531)—suggests that he was not only trying to give to his fiction "the documentary solidity of first-hand personal testimony" (Yarborough xxiii) but also inserting commentary on the episodes in his young life as a guiding primer in racialized geography, a primer that might promote in his readership the capacity for critical distanciation. That way, when readers, later in the volume, encountered Big Boy's or Mann's fatal run-ins with white spatial domination, they would know how to approach the plots analytically.

Wright's very "first lesson in how to live as a Negro" (1), as he tells it in "Ethics," involved seeing how Jim Crow environmental design masked itself as nature, even as a picturesque nature. In the opening paragraph, Wright describes the "cinder environment" of the house he lived in for a time in Arkansas: "Nothing green ever grew in that yard. The only touch of green we could see was far away, beyond the tracks where the white folks lived" (1). He "never missed the green growing things" because he believed the cinders paving his yard made excellent combat material for the "nice hot war" (1) that boys in the neighborhood were continuously waging among themselves. One day though, when his gang found itself "engaged in a war" with white boys from that green space across the tracks, he came to see the "appalling disadvantages" (1) of his own environment. The white boys threw broken bottles from behind "fortifications" (1) and "trench[es]" (2) much superior to Wright's and his gang's shelter, that is, from behind "trees, hedges, and the sloping embankments of their lawns" (1). Badly cut in the neck, Wright had to be taken by a neighbor woman to a doctor for stitches. When Wright's mother returned home, rather than offer balms and sympathy, she took this event as an opportunity to be an intermediary for Jim Crow discipline: she beat him until he had a fever of 102. That Wright tells the incident differently in *Black Boy* (both sides have broken bottles, and his mother takes him to the doctor before she punishes him) suggests the symbolic contraction of the anecdote (83). What he wants readers to perceive is not only how black parents are forced to become unwilling administrators of racist violence but also how the rural environment of the South is not natural and is by no means picturesque. Rather, Wright suggests, it was strategically designed by whites to maintain superiority in an unceasing race war. "The green trees, the trimmed hedges, the cropped lawns grew very meaningful" in the wake of his first decisive battle, and "through the years they grew into an overreaching symbol of fear" (3). As signs, "white" and "green" became coiled together.

The ensuing episodes that comprise "Ethics" serve to reinforce and expand this initial "lesson." Wright learns that if he attempted to "exceed [his] boundaries" (7)—spatially and epistemologically—he would be physically violated. The stringent social hierarchy of the Delta was enforced through divisions of space and of knowledge. To be in a white neighborhood after dark was as dangerous as trying visibly to "git smart" (4). As Wright represents it then, southern black boys learned early that not only was the green environment strategically fabricated by whites but virtually all inhabitants of space and knowledge were performed to support a regime of whiteness. Because of the South's own particular environmental history, one represented by its creation and dogged retention of the race-based plantation complex for a period of over three hundred years, any kind of supraplantation nature was almost impossible to glint or to feel within.

Wright's introduction to the spatial protocols of the South establish an exception to the thesis of Park, Burgess, and McKenzie in *The City* that spatial allocation of humans involves predictable, quasi-natural processes, such that "human communities are not so much the products of artifact or design" (64–65) as many suppose. "Ethics" asserts, by contrast, that in a postplantation, postslavery milieu, this model of multiple groups interacting in "competition and accommodation" (Park x) did not pertain;[30] moreover, a dominant group can, to a certain extent, "design" space and do it so that all its advantages accrue to this group. That he names the protagonist of one flood story "Mann" and the planter in another flood story "Burgess" suggests to me that he was signifying on the assurance within sociological theory, produced by the likes of Delbert Mann and Ernest Burgess, that ethnic competition, and even disasters, produce in the end more complex and stable social organisms. Moreover, the Chicago School's practice of analyzing a group based on its spatiotemporal *"position"* ignores what Wright shows to be an overlooked aspect of this model: namely, the dangers of mobility outside one's communal niche. The spatial discipline that Wright shows himself internalizing in "The Ethics of Living Jim Crow" stands as an autobiographical refutation to prevailing sociological theories of the human habitation of space.

Rather than an "intellectual grafting" of the Chicago School, then, Wright's ideas about how space is socially created and inhabited instead anticipates the influential 1970s work of Henri Lefebvre, who understood space as a kind of dynamic "social morphology" (94).[31] Lefebvre, a French contemporary of Wright's who was likewise deeply influenced by Marx, sought to shift what he considered the too-exclusive emphasis in Marxist thought on dialectical change *in time* to an awareness of how dialectical change occurs, or might occur, *in space*. He describes how, increasingly with modernity, "nature's space has been replaced by a space-*qua*-product" (90), a "second nature" (345). He further describes how "hegemony" (11) establishes itself in space by using a "variety of brutal techniques and an extreme emphasis on visualization" (166). In particular, the dominant authority designs space to separate class divisions: "the *social relations of reproduction*" from "the *relations of production*" (32). Such a division is authenticated by being symbolically "displaced onto" the "backdrop of nature" (32). In this scenario, "Nature is imitated . . . but only *seemingly* reproduced: what are produced are the *signs* of nature or of the natural realm—a tree, perhaps, or a shrub" (376). When the fact that this space has been sorted in such a way is "obscured," so that this "second nature" seems natural and "absolute," its "'users' spontaneously turn themselves, their presence, their 'lived experience' and their bodies into abstractions too" such that they cannot "recognize themselves" or "adopt a critical stance" (93). Spatial protocols are internalized as corporeal alienations. Lefebvre avers that despite the ways in which hegemony sorts space, the system that is made is "decidedly open—so open, indeed, that it must rely on violence to endure" (11).

Wright's "Ethics" is an autobiographical telling of processes much like these. It is an autoethnography of spatiality composed some forty years before Lefebvre. Wright notes how nature has been transformed into look-alike "symbols" of itself—hedges, trees, sloping embankments—which become a fortification from behind which Wright's young body is cut open and marked. Nature's impartial and undirected behavior has been reformulated to give partisan support to white victory in an everyday trench warfare enacted across neighborhood color lines. If, for Lefebvre, class is what is primarily enforced in space, for Wright's Delta, whiteness reproduces itself by marking itself off from black production; labor and blackness are yoked together and differentiated from biological reproduction within the white family "through an extreme emphasis on visualization" (Lefebvre 166). As Wright puts it, describing the peril of being caught—even while laboring—in a white neighborhood after dark: "The color of a Negro's skin makes him easily recognizable, makes him suspect, converts him into a defenseless target" (10). Per Lefebvre, Wright, as a "user" of the streets, was trained to see his body as the "abstraction" that white viewers would affix to him as a kind of optic target.

Yet for Wright, inhabiting this "abstraction" did not comprise a total bodily and cognitive alienation but was instead the ongoing performance of a "role which every Negro must play if he wants to eat and live" (13). Wright put on a blank face in the presence of white prostitutes while working in a hotel, looked "as unbookish as possible" (14) in the Memphis library, and generally "exercised a great deal of ingenuity" (15) to pass as this abstraction. Wright could only continue to "recognize," or re-cognize, himself as human by articulating to himself that this behavior in white-dominated space was a "role." Writing "Ethics," then, offered him the opportunity to commit to the public page this previously silent "critical stance," which he had adopted in relation to the southern mise-en-scène of space. He opens up his performance to a much broader audience than the one for whom it was originally staged and by doing so, turns his autobiography into a more Brechtian theatrical space in which Wright the "role" player moves in and out of embodying the "southern Negro" abstraction and analyzes how that abstraction was devised and enforced. "Ethics" was meant to bring public distanciation to the "social morphology" of the Jim Crow South and prepare readers to approach critically the texts that followed it.

Wright's Green Ethos in *Black Boy*

The black male subject whom Wright produces in "Ethics" cannot see "green growing things" (1) as anything but the cultural bulwarks of his enemy. By contrast, eight years later, in the beginning of *Black Boy*, Wright takes his readers back to an earlier epoch in his history, before the move to the "dead"-seeming (10) urban terrain of Memphis and even before the move to the "cinder"-filled lot in Arkansas. He commences his narrative in rural Mississippi, where the "green, growing things"

(10) of his sensual surround have not yet come to adopt someone else's meaning. That he recycles the phrase "green, growing things" suggests that the comparison with his earlier autobiography was intentional. In "Ethics," Wright needed to train his readers to see the southern environment as so saturated with risk that coincidental slips into catastrophe, which occur repeatedly in his texts that follow, make logical and historical sense. *Black Boy* has a different objective and thus a different environmental imaginary.

A major narrative destination of the complete autobiography is Wright's making himself into a cosmopolitan writer. As such, the text follows a common narrative arc ingrained in the African American literary tradition: U.S. slave autobiographies recounted the twin developments of going northward and acquiring literacy.[32] Post-slavery narratives emerging out of the Great Migration and the Harlem Renaissance linked the geographic movement northward with mental and cultural liberation and modernization (Locke 114). Wright had to balance this tradition against what he had absorbed of the Chicago School's "Ecological Approach," which tended to downgrade individual liberation narratives and even individual-centered studies in favor of diagnoses of the social organism's development and its effects on people. In *Black Boy*, Wright resolves this conflict by applying the sociological mode of analysis to those around him—"will-less" peers "wholly claimed by their environment" (104)—while reserving the movement to literacy and northern liberation template for himself.

Wright avers that, growing up in Mississippi, Tennessee, and Arkansas, "my environment contained nothing more alien than writing or the desire to express one's self in writing" (121). His narrative burden, then, is to show how he became exactly that subject which his environment could *not* have made. The valor of Wright's persona inheres precisely in his "pushing against the current of [his] environment" (168) and pursuing that "single aim of [his] living," that is, "knowing how to write narrative" (280). Wright describes a threshold of maturation in the following terms: "[my ability] to [render] unto my environment that which was my environment's, and [render] unto myself that which I felt was mine" (282). Echoing, but importantly altering, the words attributed to Jesus in Mark 12:17—"Render to Caesar the things that are Caesar's, and to God the things that are God's"—about how to get on politically while staying faithful to one's ultimate devotion, Wright casts environmental constraints as a necessary but negotiable evil, while casting his "self" as his most prized sovereignty. In enshrining self-ownership here, he enlists the interconnected legacies of the slave narrative tradition and radical, secular Enlightenment thought, as when Thomas Paine declared in *The Age of Reason*, "My own mind is my own church" (2).

As he tells it, Wright ultimately reaches a state in which his "own inner mood" could function like a compass directing him toward environments that "would complement" (282) that interiority. What is striking though—and critical for our understanding of Wright's environmental thinking—is that, from nearly the beginning of *Black Boy*, Wright associates the making of those "inner mood[s]" with the observation of and immersion in both wild and agrarian nature. His first scenes of reading, in fact, concern not alphabetical literacy but rather decoding the "cryptic tongue" (7) of natural, or at least rustic, occurrences. He describes his coming into a varied emotional repertoire via the "coded meanings" (7) of a countryside he internalizes to decipher. In short, rural nature presented him with his first semiotic puzzles, and his varied emotions arose in the process of puzzling them out. In *Black Boy*, then, unlike in "Ethics," "green" and "white" had not yet become synonymous. Thus, he establishes his *ethos*—his knowledge and character—for the reader by cataloging his rural pedagogy.

In his country environs, he feels "wonder" looking at "spotted, black-and-white horses" as well as "delight" seeing "long straight rows of red and green vegetables"; he experiences a "faint, cool kiss of sensuality when dew came on to [his] cheeks and shins as [he] ran down the wet green garden paths in the early morning"; and he acquires a "vague sense of the infinite" while looking down on the "yellow, dreaming waters of the Mississippi River" (*Black* 7–8). And the list goes on at some length, as Wright shows his acquisition of a complex emotional lexicon, including "disdain," "nostalgia," "melancholy," "desire," "hot panic," "astonishment," "quiet terror," and "love" (8–9). He links each emotion to a rural glyph: landscapes, cultivars, the built environment of the farm, and especially, animals (ants, wild geese, sparrows, crawfish, snakes, beheaded chickens, and slaughtered hogs). He ends this catalog of his rurally inscribed interiority with an ellipsis and an abrupt transition to his city life in Memphis, where, he remembers, the "absence of green, growing things made the city seem dead" (10).

For the Romantics, humans acquired the most elemental, authentic emotional and verbal fluency from nature. William Wordsworth, in his preface to *Lyrical Ballads* (1800), professed that it was in "humble and rustic life," where one finds "the beautiful and permanent forms of nature," that "the essential passions of the heart find a better soil in which they can attain their maturity . . . and speak a plainer and more emphatic language," indeed speak "the best part of language" (102). In a similar vein, Ralph Waldo Emerson contended in his 1836 essay, "Nature," that every word, were we to trace language back to its poetical "infancy" (22), was rooted in a "natural fact" (20). Because every "natural fact is a symbol of some spiritual fact" (20), and Nature is "the present expositor of the divine mind" (42), humans retain their right relation to Intelligence only as they "fasten" self and language to God's "visible things" (23). And according to Emerson, they derive a kind of social or political ethics from this "grand cipher" (23), for even "in the hour of revolution, these solemn images shall appear in their morning lustre, as fit symbols and words" (23). Moreover, "with these forms, the spells of persuasion, the keys of power are put into his hands" (23), a power that will be just because the "laws of ethics" are encoded in nature (24).

Like Wordsworth and Emerson, Wright too connects his "essential passions of the heart," his elemental concepts of the head, and his cosmically informed ethics to "rustic life." The rural hieroglyphs that Wright interprets are somewhat different from his Romantic predecessors though: he not only describes "Nature" (what Emerson termed "essences unchanged by man" [8]) but places equal stress on the humanly altered environment of farm buildings, domesticated horses, and sugar-cane processing; he further emphasizes the violence of this human/nonhuman contact as new-cut grass "bleed[s]" and hogs are "split open" (8–9); and he characterizes divine power not only as "God" (8) but also in less anthropomorphic terms such as "the infinite" (7) and the "cosmic" (9) and imagines this power as equally capable of "joke[s]," "cruelty," and "love" (8–9). As with the Romantics, he becomes properly human through this process of sensing and deciphering the facts and events of rural life, all the while establishing a complex interiority and hence reversing the disenchantment and "corruption" (Emerson 22) of modernization.[33] And yet, because Wright's Mississippi environs comprise for him a more undeniably labor-filled, labor-altered, and mortal agricultural realm, a "self" emerges in this process not wholly consonant with Romanticism but also leaning toward the georgic, the ancient genre that foregrounded the ways in which labor necessitates the worker "shaping and being shaped" (Sweet 422) by nature.[34]

Why does he want to represent himself to readers in *Black Boy* as having this kind of quasi-Romantic core? Why does it replace the "cinder" disaffection that opens "Ethics"? Wright needed a core self that could be the subject of the self-liberating, coming-into-cosmopolitan authorship narrative that he ultimately wanted to tell in *Black Boy*. Though he will, later in the narrative, insert scenes of his reading experiences—digesting comics, fairy tales, detective stories, Mencken's "words as weapons," and so on—he grounds his interpretive capacities *first* in rural phenomena. He locates his ability to push against social environment (where the color line is palpable) in his early experiences in the rural environment (where the color line was, at least in his memory, subdued).

Given this rural grounding, Wright's eventual alienation from all things "green"—as he describes it in "Ethics"—is that much more traumatic because he defined this alienation stemming from the language and experience of self-formation and accessibility to the infinite. As it so happens, at the same time that Wright was reading sociology in the 1930s, he was reading the work of psychologist Trigant Burrow, specifically his 1927 *The Social Basis of Consciousness*, which analyzed precisely this human alienation from an internal and ambient biology. I contend that Burrow's model expresses Wright's sense of the problems of modernity more accurately than do the sociologists of the Chicago School.

Biological Recoil

An analysand of Carl Jung's who had practiced psychoanalysis for some years, Burrow became increasingly dissatisfied with the individualist orientation of psychoanalysis as well as its therapeutic goal of a "normality" he viewed as fully implicated in a "disease process" of repression (11)—a process that parents, education, and the broader culture all tended to substantiate (59, 87). The problem, as Burrow saw it, was that we as a species had acquired consciousness wrongly. Viewed phylogenetically, consciousness in humanity appeared as an unfortunate *self*-consciousness, a "biological recoil" (119), or a recoil away from the continuous biology of life. The human self was constituted on a fiction of biological transcendence and hence a repression of the biology within. Thus, the human being stood "irresistibly arrested before the mirror of his own likeness" (118). In that mirror, humanity saw not a self seamlessly integrated into and made out of a biological process but rather perceived as real her own "substitutive image-production" (249). Burrow sought to redirect consciousness so that humans could avow their nature and experience life as "integral members of an original organic matrix" (115). Burrow rejected not only Cartesian theories of cognition but also Hobbesian theories of individual appetite. Yet he warned that "in the absence of a more societal and inclusive reckoning among us," a "crash" that had been "gathering momentum for centuries" and been "detonat[ed]" in the World War "will descend upon the world with inevitable fatality" (132). Treating individuals would not alter this perilous course; only collective therapy would work, for "the individual cannot be healthy whose consciousness is the outgrowth of an unhealthy social mind about him" (236). Though applied psychoanalysis in its current state was misguided, he believed, it would be through a social application of both Darwin's theory of evolution and Freud's evolutionary theory of mind that humans would find "the entire repudiation of man's image-production and a re-uniting of his organic and conscious life into a single constructive whole" (249).

Much in Burrow's book must have suggested to Wright ways to diagnose his experience: how "image-production" tied in with a visual logic of racial hierarchy and black stigmatization; how history, with the rising fascism of the midthirties, was gathering toward a "fatality" unless a new "social mind" could be collectively brought into being; and how revolutionary art *could* be a "repudiation" of man's dominant "image-production" and a "re-uniting of his organic and conscious life." In particular, Burrow's concept of humanity's "biological recoil" must have helped Wright conceptualize the antebellum plantation history which still hung over his life, a history in which certain biota—sugar, tobacco, rice, cotton, and Africans—were removed from their matrixes, forced into strange and severely dislocated patterns of reproduction, and then made into things whose outward appearances obscured the history of that transmutation. The phrase—"biological recoil"—must also have helped Wright understand his childhood anew as a forced withdrawal from the "green growing" world into a landscape of frightening "symbols." Burrow had argued that "life has its beginnings"—both for the individual and the species—"in a continuous organic medium" (115); "our primary objective experience merges into continuity with inherent feeling" (115); "race or national separation, social or

Richard Wright's Environments

caste distinction have not entered in" (115). Wright's early rural memories evince just such a state in which objective and subjective, inner and outer nature, participate in a "fluid, undifferentiated, confluent mode" (115). But then the landscape that had developed his mind and senses through its encoded mysteries had been made to assume an alien skin. The "green growing things" all around him receded into "only [a] touch of green" (1) visible in the distance, across the color line. Green became the environmental skin of white property.

For Marx, within the industrial capitalism that engulfed both city and country in the nineteenth century, the laborer loses life by investing it in the commodity he produces but does not own. As he works, he feels alien from his body and from that which his body makes as it replaces him.[35] And yet this alienation is not quarantined to the time and place of his work, for, in as much as the laborer must appropriate "the *sensuous external world*" to produce for others, he likewise severs himself from "*nature*" (109). Before his labor had become alienated by capital, Marx notes, "man *lives* on nature—[which] means that nature is his *body*" (112), and through nature, "man really proves himself to be a *species being*" (114). But, Marx concludes, "estranged labor tears from him his *species life*," and hence "his inorganic body, nature, is taken away from him" (114).[36]

In "Ethics," Wright describes a similar alienation from "*species-being*" and from "*nature*" brought about by the historical and social relations of labor in the Jim Crow South. Indeed, though it hardly seems possible to imagine an alienation more total than the one Marx describes, Wright suggests that when a segment of the population is spatially sorted and visually stigmatized as "labor," then the severance from one's natural body and the body of nature occur not only in acts of labor but all the time and in all space. Because whiteness reproduced its privileges by inscribing itself on the skin of nature, appropriating green as white, an African American not only had to experience nature's estrangement as her labor turned cotton plants into a bale for her landlord's weighing but also experienced the "second nature" Jim Crow built as an unavoidable space of "fear." And yet Wright, in the early pages of *Black Boy*, recalls a time in his childhood *before* such estrangements—while being in nature still offered the experience of, in Marx's words, "life-engendering life" (113). Indeed, Wright describes the rural landscape as the very source of his aesthetic and emotional reserves and the origin of his future authorship. By representing this early experience, Wright suggests that coming into the construct of race entailed for him a simultaneous ripping from the fabric of nature at the level of both his body and his environment.

Wright parted ways with the Chicago School sociologists, for whom the social organism was patterned much like the apparently self-stabilizing ecology of the natural world. Instead, he used the individual-centered genre of autobiography, a genre that would allow his injections of commentary on events as they occurred and plot the accidents of an individual negotiating an aleatory world. In particular, he employed autobiography to show how he was both formed by and then alienated from the green world. The country was not a simple, safe haven, but a complex cosmos of "love," "jokes," and "cruelty," which provided him with an ample interior repertoire. Forty years before Lefebvre, he drew attention to how "second nature[s]" can be made as the strategic bulwarks of those in power. By drawing his audience in on the "role" he was forced to play within that "second nature," he hoped to give a potentially naïve audience the tools of distanciation that might block a sentimental identification with the characters of *Uncle Tom's Children*. And finally, by extending Marx's critique of labor's "alienation" to the unremittent bodily and spatial alienation of black subjects in the South, and in the United States more broadly, Wright was advancing a revolutionary materialism more suited to the experiences of non-Europeans living in the multiracial, imperial world of the twentieth century.

NOTES

A version of this chapter has been published as "Richard Wright: Environment, Media, and Race," in *The Flood Year 1927: A Cultural History* by Susan Scott Parrish. Copyright © 2017 by Princeton University Press. Reprinted by permission.

1. Robert J. Butler, for example, describes *Black Boy* as a book that "crystallizes a problem that goes to the core of Wright's vision—how to achieve a human self while inhabiting a deterministic environment" (56). See also Richard Yarborough's introduction to Wright's *Uncle Tom's Children* (xiii).

2. For a more complete treatment of Wright's "sociological imagination," see Cappetti's *Writing Chicago: Modernism, Ethnography, and the Novel*; she argues in this text that writers like Wright "in sociology found the inspiration to become sociological informants and observers of their own neighborhoods" (15). William L. Andrews and Douglas Taylor argue, in their introduction to *Richard Wright's* Black Boy (American Hunger): A Casebook, that "Wright's autobiography was meant to blur the boundaries between sociology and autobiography" by showing the "applicability" of Wright's story to "many African-American men's lives in the early twentieth-century South" (8).

3. Wright speaks of the "will-less" boys and girls who were "claimed wholly by their environment" (*Black* 104); see also his comments on this point on pp. 121, 200, 264, 282. Before publication in 1945, the autobiography was divided into two sections, "Southern Night" and "The Horror and the Glory," and only the first section was published at that time due to pressure from the Book-of-the-Month Club.

4. Wright's naturalist "street" tends to be contrasted with Zora Neale Hurston's apparently idyllic "country." Wright himself called the setting for *Their Eyes Were Watching God* (1937) "'quaint'" ("Between" 23); I would argue that *both* authors concerned themselves with the chance and violence inherent in rural life but exacerbated in the Jim Crow South by anthropogenic environmental change and racist politics. See my chapter, "Zora Neale Hurston and the Environmental Ethic of Risk," in *American Studies, Ecocriticism, and Citizenship: Thinking and Acting in the Local and Global Commons*.

5. When describing Wright as an urban sociological writer, Cappetti defines him as part of a group of authors "from Chicago" who "wrote about a northern industrial immigrant city

and not . . . a rural South" (*Writing* 6). But Wright was from the Deep South and wrote, while in Chicago, a set of stories and an autobiographical essay set in Mississippi and Tennessee.

6. W. E. B. Du Bois famously prophesized that "the problem of the Twentieth Century is the problem of the color-line" (1).

7. Along with Cappetti (*Writing*), see Michael Fabre's *The Unfinished Quest of Richard Wright* (232, 571n38) and Hazel Rowley's *Richard Wright: The Life and Times* (81–82).

8. Wright, in this same introduction (xviii), also mentioned the influence of *Tepoztlan: A Mexican Village*, in which the author, Robert Redfield, does take physical geography seriously but still seeks to render his data into a study of "the general type of change whereby primitive man becomes civilized man, the rustic becomes the urbanite" (14).

9. On this intellectual community, see Rowley (81–82).

10. For an institutional history, see Bulmer.

11. This model of social organization-disorganization-reorganization comes from a preceding Chicago sociologist, W. I. Thomas. Thomas's theory sought to explain how the rules that previously distinguished and controlled a group might be loosened and then reformed; see Bulmer (31, 61).

12. Park, Burgess, and McKenzie's chapter 3 title is "The Ecological Approach to the Study of the Human Community"; for the use of the "climax stage" concept, see p. 77 in *The City*. On Clements, see Worster (3, 4). On the narrative and Darwinian underpinnings of the Clements-Gleason debate, consult Journet.

13. Spencer, who wrote in the mid-nineteenth-century across the fields of biology, philosophy, sociology, and psychology, engaged selectively with both Lamarck and Darwin to propose that, at all scales of life, organisms were evolving toward greater differentiation and complexity, all the while producing an ever more concordant network. Spencer posits that "universally a patient self-rectification" (469) was occurring. As changes internal to organisms and in the outer environment act reciprocally on each other, they would, Spencer notes, eventually achieve an end-state of "harmony" (469) and "equilibrium" (476). On Spencer's theories of "progression towards perfection," see Francis (196).

14. Lowell Juilliard Carr noted, in 1932, that in the United States, "where nature is supposed to be most completely subdued, there were 938 disasters in the forty-eight years from 1881 to 1928" (209); after these, he asserted, came an "eventually renewed equilibrium" (207).

15. For an excellent comprehensive history of the 1927 flood, consult Barry; on the Jim Crow management of the Greenville levee camp, see pp. 314–17 of his book.

16. Wright had been a delivery boy for the *Defender* in 1924 (Rowley 32).

17. Her music and live concerts were also played on Memphis radio stations; see Albertson (41, 43, 45). On "Back-Water Blues" and the 1927 flood, consult Evans.

18. In 1987, the Reverend Benjamin Chavis, executive director of the United Church of Christ Commission for Racial Justice, originated the term *environmental racism* in a report linking the construction of hazardous waste facilities close to communities of color; in 1991, delegates at the First National People of Color Environmental Leadership Summit in Washington, DC, devised the seventeen-point "Principles of Environmental Justice" statement; for a tracing of significant events in environmentalism, see Di Chiro (304). As Adamson, Evans, and Stein put it in their introduction to *The Environmental Justice Reader: Politics, Poetics, and Pedagogy*, "Environmental justice movements call attention to the ways disparate distribution of wealth

and power often leads to correlative social upheaval and the unequal distribution of environmental degradation and/or toxicity" (5). For the intersection of racial and economic inequity and environmental justice issues in the South, see Robert D. Bullard's *Dumping in Dixie: Race, Class, and Environmental Quality* and his edited book, with Beverly Wright, *Race, Place, and Environmental Justice after Hurricane Katrina: Struggles to Reclaim, Rebuild, and Revitalize New Orleans and the Gulf Coast.*

19. Herbert Hoover used this language (Barry 282).
20. Hoover spoke these words at a Rotary meeting in Greenville, Mississippi, in 1927.
21. As Saikku clarifies, "disturbance regime" refers to a "certain type of landscape created and maintained by a disturbance that occurs with characteristic frequency" (23). On the factors contributing to the catastrophe, consult Williams (186–88, 238–43), Saikku (161–62, 221), and Barry (91, 158).
22. Hoover, for instance, established a nationwide radio system in February 1927. In 1926 the Associated Press crowed: "Only minutes now separate readers from the most distant point in the world" (*Associated* 13); the Associated Negro Press was only eight years old in 1927.
23. See, for example, Rolo (27).
24. William Howard was the first and only scholar really to contextualize Wright's flood stories. Howard asserts that "the flurry of journalistic activity attending the flood of 1927 exposed him to alternative points of view (like those of Mencken) that must have spurred his imagination as much as the flood itself" (44). However, this article set out only to establish the connection between Wright and the flood, not to perform close readings of Wright's work in light of such a connection.
25. Wright tells of a carpenter in the neighborhood who made him look carefully at a racist cartoon in a newspaper that the author was selling (*Black* 129).
26. On this point, see *Black Boy* (165–68). Wright's first appearance in print, at fifteen, had been with a local black paper, the *Jackson Southern Register*, and he had received encouragement from its editor, Malcolm Rodgers.
27. When Wright worked for the *Southern Register*, he would ask Rodgers to read the black papers and magazines arriving from around the nation, including the *Chicago Defender*, the *Pittsburgh Courier*, the Baltimore *Afro-American* as well as the *Crisis* and *Opportunity* (Walker 28). All these papers and magazines reported on the flood: see the editorial "Withstanding the Flood"; Thomas's "In the Path of the Flood"; Jones's "Death Stalks in Mississippi Flood Path"; Walter White's exposé, "The Negro and the Flood," was reprinted in the *Chicago Defender* (2 July 1927: A1).
28. Wright typed his address on the typescript draft of "Down by the Riverside." This information may be found in the Richard Wright Papers (Series I. Writings, Books, *Uncle Tom's Children*) housed at the Beinecke Rare Book and Manuscript Library at the Yale University Library.
29. Wright knew Barnett well enough to suggest him as a referee for his Guggenheim application in 1938 and shared drafts of his flood stories with Associated Negro Press reporter Frank Marshall Davis (Rowley 116, 157).
30. As Park puts it, "the city is not merely an artifact, but an organism. Its growth is, fundamentally and as a whole, natural, i.e., uncontrolled and undesigned" (x).
31. Joshua Scott Stone, in his dissertation, "American Ethni/Cities: Critical Geography, Subject Formation, and the Urban Representations of Abraham Cahan, Richard Wright,

and James Baldwin" (2010), makes a similar argument, namely, that Wright differed from the Chicago School's spatial theorization and anticipated Lefebvre (112, 136, 138). Stone describes Wright's "critical urbanism" and argues that Wright was attending to the northern racialization of space, which was especially ineradicable because it was unacknowledged behind a claim of "spatial neutrality" (116).

32. See, for example, Olney (50–51, 55). In his seminal article, he addresses how *Black Boy* and "Ethics" harken back to the slave narrative conjoined trope of "literacy-identity-freedom" as Wright flees his "southern bondage" (65) to "hard-won literacy in a northern, free-state city" where he becomes "the writer we know as 'Richard Wright'"(66). The colonial, black Atlantic autobiographies of enslaved Africans also recounted a movement into literacy, one typically connected with Christian conversion, but the geographic movements were more circuitous and the sites of freedom or manumission were not necessarily northern. See, for example, Carretta's *Unchained Voices: An Anthology of Black Authors in the English-Speaking World of the Eighteenth Century*.

33. Ralph Ellison draws attention to this rural-emotional interlude and how distinct it was from the rest of Wright's experiences: "*Black Boy* presents an almost unrelieved picture of a personality corrupted by brutal environment, [but] it also presents those fresh human responses brought to this world by the sensitive child" (64).

34. Timothy Sweet distinguishes georgic from pastoral in the following way: "In the pastoral movement of retreat and return, we are refreshed and restored, able again to face our alienating quotidian environment. Georgic manifests our laboring, information-gathering, productive behavior. In the 'good strife' of living, registered poetically as early as Hesiod's *Work and Days*, our engagement with nature leaves no space for alienation" because it involves "a process of constant action, of shaping and being shaped" (422).

35. Marx wrote: "The object which labor produces—labor's product—confronts it as *something alien*, as a *power independent* of the producer. The product of labor is labor which has been embodied in an object, which has become material: it is the *objectification* of labor" (108).

36. Scholars have shown that Marx was not only concerned with temporal paradigms but also engaged issues of both space and nature. See, for example, Harvey's commentary on Marx's argument that imperialism could not offer a "spatial fix" to capitalism's social dilemmas (299–300) as well as Burkett's reading of Marx's consideration of the instability of nature and its despoliation by industrial capitalism.

WORKS CITED

Adamson, Joni, Mei Mei Evans, and Rachel Stein. Introduction. *The Environmental Justice Reader: Politics, Poetics, and Pedagogy*. Ed. Joni Adamson, Mei Mei Evans, and Rachel Stein. Tucson: U of Arizona P, 2002. 3–14.

Albertson, Chris. *Bessie*. Rev. and expanded ed. New Haven, CT: Yale UP, 2003.

Andrews, William L., and Douglas Taylor. Introduction. *Richard Wright's* Black Boy (American Hunger): *A Casebook*. Ed. William L. Andrews and Douglas Taylor. Cambridge: Cambridge UP, 2003. 3–24.

"Another Mencken Absurdity." *Commercial Appeal* 28 May 1927: n. pag.

Associated Press: The Story behind the (AP) Story. 1933. Self-published brochure.

Barry, John M. *Rising Tide: The Great Mississippi Flood of 1927 and How It Changed America*. New York: Simon and Schuster, 1997.
"Big New Crevasse Opens in the Louisiana Levees." *New York Times* 4 May 1927: n. pag. *ProQuest Historical Newspapers*.
Bullard, Robert. *Dumping in Dixie: Race, Class, and Environmental Quality*. Boulder, CO: Westview Press, 1990.
Bullard, Robert, and Beverly Wright, eds. *Race, Place, and Environmental Justice after Hurricane Katrina: Struggles to Reclaim, Rebuild, and Revitalize New Orleans and the Gulf Coast*. Boulder, CO: Westview Press, 2009.
Bulmer, Martin. *The Chicago School of Sociology: Institutionalization, Diversity, and the Rise of Sociological Research*. Chicago: U Chicago P, 1986.
"The Burden of Floods: Who Should Bear It?" *Commercial Appeal* 24 Apr. 1927: n. pag.
Burkett, Paul. *Marx and Nature: A Red and Green Perspective*. New York: St. Martin's Press, 1999.
Burrow, Trigant. *The Social Basis of Consciousness: A Study in Organic Psychology Based upon a Synthetic and Societal Concept of the Neuroses*. New York: Harcourt, 1927.
Butler, Robert J. "Seeking Salvation in a Naturalistic Universe: Richard Wright's Use of His Southern Religious Background in *Black Boy (American Hunger)*." *Southern Quarterly* 46.2 (2009): 46–60.
Cappetti, Carla. "Sociology of an Existence: Wright and the Chicago School." *Richard Wright: Critical Perspectives Past and Present*. Ed. Henry Louis Gates, Jr. and K. A. Appiah. New York: Amistad Press, 1993. 255–71.
———. *Writing Chicago: Modernism, Ethnography, and the Novel*. New York: Columbia UP, 1993.
Carr, Lowell Juilliard. "Disaster and the Sequence-Pattern Concept of Social Change." *American Journal of Sociology* 38 (1932): 207–18.
Carretta, Vincent, ed. *Unchained Voices: An Anthology of Black Authors in the English-Speaking World of the Eighteenth Century*. Rev. ed. Lexington: U of Kentucky P, 2003.
Di Chiro, Giovanna. "Nature as Community: The Convergence of Environment and Social Justice." *Uncommon Ground: Rethinking the Human Place in Nature*. Ed. William Cronon. New York: Norton, 1996. 298–320.
Du Bois, W. E. B. *The Souls of Black Folk*. 1903. New York: Penguin, 1996.
Ellison, Ralph. "Richard Wright's Blues." *Antioch Review* 50.1–2 (Winter/Spring 1992): 61–74.
Emerson, Ralph Waldo. "Nature." *Essays and Lectures*. New York: Literary Classics of the United States, 1983.
Evans, David. "'Back-Water Blues': The Story behind the Song." *Popular Music* 26.1 (2006): 97–116.
Fabre, Michael. *The Unfinished Quest of Richard Wright*. Trans. Isabel Barzun. 2nd ed. Urbana: U of Illinois P, 1993.
Faulkner, William. *The Wild Palms [If I Forget Thee, Jerusalem]*. New York: Vintage, 1995.
Francis, Mark. *Herbert Spencer and the Invention of Modern Life*. Durham, UK: Acumen, 2007.
Gleason, Henry A. "The Individualistic Concept of the Plant Association." *Bulletin of the Torrey Botanical Club* 53.1 (1926): 7–26. *JSTOR*.
Harrington, J. Winston. "Use Troops in Flood Area to Imprison Farm Hands." *Chicago Defender* 7 May 1927: 1.1. *ProQuest Historical Newspapers*.
Harvey, David. *Spaces of Capital: Towards a Critical Geography*. New York: Routledge, 2001.

Howard, William. "Richard Wright's Flood Stories and the Great Mississippi River Flood of 1927: Social and Historical Backgrounds." *Southern Literary Journal* 16.2 (1984): 44–62.
Jones, William N. "Death Stalks in Mississippi Flood Path." *Afro-American* 30 Apr. 1927: n. pag.
Journet, Debra. "Ecological Theories as Cultural Narratives: F. E. Clements's and H. A. Gleason's 'Stories' of Community Succession." *Written Communication* 8.4 (1991): 446–72.
Lefebvre, Henri. *The Production of Space*. Trans. Donald Nicholson-Smith. Malden, MA: Blackwell, 1991.
Locke, Alain. "The New Negro." *The New Negro: Readings on Race, Representation, and African American Culture, 1892–1938*. Ed. Henry Louis Gates Jr. and Gene Andrew Jarrett. Princeton, NJ: Princeton UP, 2007. 112–18.
Marx, Karl. *Economic and Philosophical Manuscripts of 1844*. Ed. Dirk J. Struik. Trans. Martin Milligan. New York: International Press, 1964.
Mencken, H. L. "The Mississippi Flood." *Evening Sun* 23 May 1927: n. pag.
Olney, James. "'I Was Born': Slave Narratives, Their Status as Autobiography and as Literature." *Callaloo* 20 (1984): 46–73.
Paine, Thomas. *The Age of Reason*. 1793. London: Freethought, 1889.
Park, Robert E. Foreword. Wirth, *Ghetto* ix–xi.
Park, Robert E., and Ernest W. Burgess. *Introduction to the Science of Sociology*. Chicago: U of Chicago P, 1921.
Park, Robert E., Ernest W. Burgess, and Roderick D. McKenzie. *The City*. Chicago: U of Chicago P, 1967.
Parrish, Susan Scott. "Zora Neale Hurston and the Environmental Ethic of Risk." *American Studies, Ecocriticism, and Citizenship: Thinking and Acting in the Local and Global Commons*. Ed. Joni Adamson and Kimberly Ruffin. New York: Routledge, 2013. 21–36.
Prince, Samuel Henry. *Catastrophe and Social Change: Based upon a Sociological Study of the Halifax Disaster*. New York: Columbia UP, 1920.
Queen, Stuart Alfred, and Delbert Martin Mann. *Social Pathology*. New York: Crowell, 1925.
Redfield, Robert. *Tepoztlan: A Mexican Village*. Chicago: U of Chicago P, 1930.
Rolo, Charles J. "This, Too, Is America." *Richard Wright's* Black Boy (American Hunger): *A Casebook*. Ed. William L. Andrews and Douglas Taylor. Cambridge: Cambridge UP, 2003. 25–32.
Rowley, Hazel. *Richard Wright: The Life and Times*. New York: Holt, 2001.
Saikku, Mikko. *This Delta, This Land: An Environmental History of the Yazoo-Mississippi Floodplain*. Athens: U of Georgia P, 2005.
Spencer, Herbert A. "A Theory of Population, Deduced from the General Law of Animal Fertility." *Victorian Web: Literature, History, and Culture in the Age of Victoria*.
"Stand Together, Pull Together and Victory Is Certain." *Commercial Appeal* 22 May 1927: n. pag.
Stone, Joshua Scott. "American Ethni/Cities: Critical Geography, Subject Formation, and the Urban Representations of Abraham Cahan, Richard Wright, and James Baldwin." PhD diss. U of Miami, 2010. *Open Access Dissertations*.
Sweet, Timothy. "Projecting Early American Environmental Writing." *American Literary History* 22.2 (2010): 419–31.
Thomas, Jesse O. "In the Path of the Flood." *Opportunity* 5 (Aug. 1927): 236–37.

Walker, Margaret. *Richard Wright, Daemonic Genius: A Portrait of the Man, a Critical Look at His Work*. New York: Warner, 1988.
"The Week." *Chicago Defender* 14 May 1927: 1.A1. *ProQuest Historical Newspapers*.
Wells, Ida B. "Brand Ministers in Flood Area as Betrayers." *Chicago Defender* 16 July 1927: n. pag. *ProQuest Historical Newspapers*.
———. "Flood Refugees Are Held as Slaves in Mississippi Camp." *Chicago Defender* 30 July 1927: 1–A11. *ProQuest Historical Newspapers*.
White, Walter. "The Negro and the Flood." *Nation* 124 (22 June 1927): 688–89.
Williams, Michael. *Americans and Their Forests: A Historical Geography*. Cambridge: Cambridge UP, 1989.
Wirth, Louis. *The Ghetto*. Chicago: U of Chicago P, 1928.
"Withstanding the Flood." *Pittsburgh Courier* 28 May 1927: 20.
Wordsworth, William. Preface to the Second Edition. *Lyrical Ballads*. The *Norton Anthology of English Literature*. Ed. M. H. Abrams. Vol. 2. New York: W. W. Norton, 1968. 100–112.
Work, Monroe N., ed. *Negro Year Book: An Annual Encyclopedia of the Negro, 1921–22*. Tuskegee, AL: Negro Year Book Company, 1922.
Worster, Donald. "The Ecology of Order and Chaos." *Environmental History Review* 14.1–2 (1990): 1–18.
Wright, Richard. "Between Laughter and Tears." *New Masses* 5 Oct. 1937. 22–23.
———. *Black Boy (American Hunger): A Record of Childhood and Youth*. 1945. New York: Harper, 1991.
———. "The Ethics of Living Jim Crow." *Uncle Tom's Children*. New York: Harper Perennial, 1991.
———. "How 'Bigger' Was Born." *Native Son*. By Richard Wright. New York: Harper Perennial, 1993.
———. Introduction. *Black Metropolis: A Study of Negro Life in a Northern City*. By St. Clair Drake and Horace R. Cayton. New York: Harcourt, 1945. xvii–xxxiv.
———. *Uncle Tom's Children*. New York: Harper Perennial, 1991.
Yarborough, Richard. Introduction. *Uncle Tom's Children*. By Richard Wright. New York: Harper Perennial, 1991. ix–xxix.

"A Space of Concentration"

The Autobiographical Comics of Richard "Grass" Green and Samuel R. Delany

BRIAN CREMINS

In the January 1986 issue of *The Comics Journal*, Richard "Grass" Green interviewed fellow underground cartoonist Skip Williamson. They talked about Ronald Reagan and Jerry Rubin, Jack Kirby and Shel Silverstein, Frank Sinatra and *Playboy*, Harvey Kurtzman and pocketknives. They talked shop, too, of course—one cartoonist to another—but their conversation eventually turned to their mutual love of Chicago. "You know, an interesting thing happened when he was doing that interview," Williamson told me.[1] "He was recording it, I was in my office at *Playboy*, and I said let's go for lunch, so we stepped out of the building. The building on the block south of the *Playboy* building was the John Hancock Center." Williamson and Green noticed a crowd of people. "Some guy had jumped from the 99th floor," Williamson recalled. After describing his memory of the grotesque scene, Williamson admitted, "It's got nothing to do with Grass except he was with me, you know, and we both were, like, amazed by it" (Williamson).

In that now thirty-year-old *Comics Journal* interview, Williamson and Green discuss the incident in more detail. "You remember," Green says, "the people were packed around us, so we stepped out into the street, and that dirty look that cop gave us—'You guys want to get back on the curb?'" (Green, "Strange World" 63). Williamson does not have much to say about the cops, but he remembers the small crowd. "Surrounded by urban violence," he says, "the people were animated and excited like at a sporting event. These are the things cartoons are made of" (Williamson qtd. in Green, "Strange World" 63). As Williamson said, this scene does not have much to do with the work of Grass Green, at least on its tragic surface. But Green, a prolific cartoonist who died from lung cancer at the age of sixty-three in 2002, is fascinated in his work by the metaphysical density of urban spaces like Chicago. He's a careful observer of small gestures—the sudden glance, a passing conversation with a stranger. In his later work, Green often drew himself into his stories, notably in the photocopied series of *Un-Fold Funnies* he produced in the early 1980s. In this chapter, as I discuss the autobiographical nature of Green's work and its relationship to comics written by Samuel R. Delany, I am also interested in exploring, to borrow a phrase from Williamson, what Green's "cartoons are made of" (Williamson qtd. in Green, "Strange World" 63).

For both Green and Delany, two African American artists working in a complex medium that in the last twenty years has become a major focus of academic study in the United States, comics enable the writer or artist to explore a self shaped by contact with the outside world, especially the form of contact described by Jane Jacobs in *The Death and Life of Great American Cities* and Delany himself in *Times Square Red, Times Square Blue*. Although these sudden, unexpected encounters between the self and the other might appear insignificant, Jacobs argues persuasively that they are "not trivial at all. The sum of such casual, public contact at a local level—most of it fortuitous, most of it associated with errands, all of it metered by the person concerned and not thrust upon him by anyone—is a feeling for the public identity of people, a web of public respect and trust, and a resource in time of personal or neighborhood need" (56). In my analysis of Green's autobiographical comics and Delany's graphic novel *Bread & Wine: An Erotic Tale of New York*, the story of his love affair with his partner Dennis Rickett, I will return frequently to this idea of contact as I explore how both writers employ the medium of comics to shape and define an autobiographical self. While other scholars have written on the autobiographical impulse in Delany's work, Green remains an obscure figure, even in the twin worlds of comics studies and comics fandom.[2]

During our conversation, I asked Skip Williamson about Green's life and legacy. "Well, as a person," Williamson told me, echoing Green's other friends and acquaintances, "he was a gentle soul, and that was very evident in him at all times. As an artist," Williamson added, "I liked that he could run with several genres at the same time and weave in and out of them" (Williamson). Best known for his superhero parodies, Green also drew stories featuring horny ghosts, time-traveling cats, stoned freaks, and Elvis-impersonating lounge singers.[3] He produced some of his best work in the early 1980s, when his comics took a more autobiographical turn and he began writing, drawing, and photocopying the *Un-Fold Funnies*.[4] These self-published works of comic art, which Green shared with friends or sold through mail order and at comic book conventions, anticipate the storytelling of contemporary autobiographical cartoonists from the United States including John Porcellino, Carrie McNinch, and Whit Taylor. In these minicomics, Green reflects on his life, his art, and his everyday concerns, from battling the common cold to rehearsing with his band to buying a new pair of glasses. As Green's cartoon avatar explains to a friend in "Grass vs . . . Criticism!" from *Un-Fold Funnies* no. 12, he believes these delicate, black-and-white, one-page comics reveal an intimate, sometimes serious, often hilarious world to readers: "I mean, it ain't er'ry *day* whitey gets 'into' the mind of a black dude, man! Sure," he points out to his friend, "*you* know me to a great extent, but I been lettin' *other* fans in on the phenomenon of my fantastic inimitable mental machinations!" ("Grass vs . . . Criticism!").

Green is at his most dynamic and compelling when he explores the "interclass contact" that Delany describes in *Times Square Red, Times Square Blue* (198). Like Jane Jacobs, Delany, whose fiction and nonfiction have had a tremendous influence on contemporary comics innovators such as Edie Fake, argues that contact is essential to the vitality of diverse urban spaces.[5] This form of social interaction, which Delany calls "the lymphatic system of a democratic metropolis" (*Times Square* 198), is a form of community built on chance encounters in which open discourse crosses boundaries of race, class, and gender. These brief but significant moments, Delany explains, can take place while "standing in line at a movie" or "sitting at a bar" or even "coming down to sit on the stoop on a warm day" and often "involve some form of 'loitering' (or, at least, lingering)" (*Times Square* 198–99)—all casual interactions, often with strangers. Delany sums up his argument with a statement that informs my understanding of Green's work: "Contact and its human rewards are fundamental to cosmopolitan culture, to its art and its literature, to its politics and its economics; to its quality of life" (199).

I imagine this chapter as a space in which I am initiating other forms of contact: first, between the reader and these two African American artists, one obscure but significant, the other celebrated not for his comics but for his fiction and his essays. I hope other scholars take an interest in Grass Green's large body of work. If we do so, we will have a more complete picture of the history of comics in the United States in the late twentieth century. At the same time, scholars of African American literature will find that Green's comics, from his superhero parodies to his raunchy stories for underground publishers like Kitchen Sink Press, exist in the same comedic tradition as Moms Mabley, Redd Foxx, Richard Pryor, and James Wesley Jackson. Like those other African American storytellers, Grass Green employs humor as a means of social critique and as a form of memoir.

What I will also argue for here, then, is a closer relationship between comics scholarship and African American studies. As I briefly discuss later in this chapter, several important scholars, including Michael A. Chaney, Qiana J. Whitted, Marc Singer, and Rebecca Wanzo, have already begun to map the connections between these two fields of inquiry. My study of Richard "Grass" Green's work locates its theoretical and methodological models in the archival research undertaken by scholars of African American studies in the late 1960s and early 1970s. Just as the narrative of U.S. literary and cultural history is not complete without discussions of innovators such as Oscar Micheaux, Zora Neale Hurston, or Jean Toomer—to name just a few significant but once forgotten African American artists—narratives of the history of comic books and graphic novels will remain fragmentary without archival projects such as Nancy Goldstein's recent book on cartoonist Jackie Ormes. As Whitted has argued in recent essays and blog posts that seek to define a tradition of African American comic books, African American studies offers a set of theoretical models to the growing field of comics studies.[6] At the same time, those working in African American studies will find that the world of comics includes many stories that have yet to be told. Green's life and art are significant not only in themselves but also for what they can tell us about the communities of which he was part.[7]

In *On the Real Side*, his classic study of African American comedy, Mel Watkins argues that what made Richard Pryor's work, for example, so distinctive was the comedian's ability "to introduce and popularize that unique, previously concealed or rejected part of African-American humor that thrived in the lowest, most unassimilated portion of the black community" (550). In their comics, Green and Delany also document communities otherwise ignored or forgotten: while Green tells the story of an African American cartoonist working in Fort Wayne, Indiana, in the last few decades of the twentieth century—through his use of a distinctly midwestern voice, both welcoming and deeply suspicious, sometimes lonely and isolated— Delany and artist Mia Wolff invite readers to imagine a love story set in a New York that, by the late 1990s, no longer looked and felt like the city Delany remembered from the 1960s and 1970s. Just as Pryor found inspiration in what Watkins describes as an "unassimilated portion of the black community" (550), Green and Delany observe and remember other neglected stories, those of African American neighborhoods in the Rust Belt of the Midwest or of queer communities devastated by AIDS and by gentrification under Rudy Giuliani's administration. I read Green and Delany as artists whose autobiographies serve as records of contact and whose work communicates the psychological and phenomenological density of casual, unexpected, but telling urban encounters.

When I use the word *density* here, I have in mind philosopher George Yancy's use of the term in his recent book, *Look, a White! Philosophical Essays on Whiteness*, and Thierry Groensteen's discussion of *densité* from *Bande dessinée et narration: Système de la bande dessinée 2* (2011), which was recently published in an English translation by Ann Miller as *Comics and Narration*. Before I consider *density* and its relationship to the forms of urban contact described by Jacobs and Delany, however, I would like to discuss briefly a few theories of autobiographical comics that guide my readings of Green's *Un-Fold Funnies* and of Delany's *Bread & Wine*.

Comics and Autobiography

Michael A. Chaney's 2011 collection, *Graphic Subjects: Critical Essays on Autobiography and Graphic Novels*, is an excellent introduction to the subject of autobiographical comics narratives. The book collects several of the major texts in the field, including some of Marianne Hirsch's groundbreaking work on Art Spiegelman's *Maus* along with more-recent essays by scholars including Hillary L. Chute and Bart Beaty.[8] Chaney himself is an important figure because of his work on autobiographical comics and on African American comics. In his introduction, he offers readers a general definition of how to read (or how to *see*) the "I" in autobiographical comics

"A Space of Concentration" 149

narratives. Following a brief discussion of Leigh Gilmore's essay on Marjane Satrapi's *Persepolis*, Chaney argues that once

> the "I" of autobiography is explicitly stylized as a kind of cartoon, the result is a brazen departure from the "seemingly substantial" effects of realism that traditional autobiographies presume. The larger consequences of this tension between objective and subjective truths in creating realistic fictions of the self prod us to reconsider what is at stake in telling our life stories in pictures and how it is that we have come to visualize identity in particular ways and according to particular sociohistorical contexts. (Chaney, Introduction 7)

I would add that "this tension between objective and subjective truths" suggests a divide between the self on display in these comics—the cartoon image of the author—and the reader, who makes contact with these speaking subjects and enters into a dialogue with them. For example, in his discussion of Harvey Pekar's autobiographical comics—narratives produced in collaboration with a number of artists including R. Crumb—Charles Hatfield argues that a "cartoon self-image" might "offer a unique way for the artist to recognize and externalize his or her subjectivity. In this light," he continues, "comics autobiography may not be alienating so much as radically enabling" (*Alternative Comics* 115). The tension that Chaney describes, then, might be essential for creators and for readers of autobiographical comics. "*Seeing* the protagonist or narrator," Hatfield argues, "in the context of other characters and objects evoked in the drawings, objectifies him or her. Thus the cartoonist projects and objectifies his or her inward sense of self, achieving at once a sense of intimacy and a critical distance" (*Alternative Comics* 115).

W. E. B. Du Bois's notion of the Veil, as we shall see, might be useful in complicating Hatfield's description of that "inward sense of self" so familiar to readers of autobiographical comics. What shape does the autobiographical self take once it enters, to borrow a phrase from Du Bois, "a world that looks on in amused contempt and pity" (3)? Autobiographical comics, as Hatfield implies here, are often about the relationship between the artist and the reader. This complex give-and-take between the autobiographical subject and the reader sometimes leads to the page density that Thierry Groensteen describes (*Comics* 44–45). Consider, for example, the ornate pages of artists such as Lynda Barry or Chris Ware (whose best-known work, strictly speaking, might not be autobiography but includes autobiographical traces). Not all autobiographical comic artists work in a dense style, of course. Some, like John Porcellino and Keiler Roberts, achieve their effects with simple images and clean, uncluttered drawings. Green, however, works in a much more complex, detailed style in order to convey both a "sense of self" (Hatfield, *Alternative Comics* 115) and, perhaps more significantly, a consciousness shaped by interaction—*contact*—with others. With Hatfield's and Chaney's arguments in mind, I would like to turn to a discussion of George Yancy's examination of the *"lived* density of race" (17) in chapter 1 of his recent book.

In the following passage, Yancy specifically refers to the writing and teaching of philosophy, but I think his argument has larger implications for the practice and the study of cartooning: "When it comes to a deeper, thicker philosophical engagement with issues of race," Yancy argues, "the medium has to change to something dynamically expressive, something that forces the reader/listener *to feel* what is being communicated, to empathize with greater ability, to imagine with greater fullness and power" (30). I find an affinity here between Yancy's discussion of density and Groensteen's points on page design in chapter 3 of *Comics and Narration*. For Groensteen, *densité* involves "the variability in the number of panels that make up the page" (Groensteen 44).[9] Consider, for example, as Groensteen does later in the book, Ware's page designs in *Jimmy Corrigan: The Smartest Kid on Earth* (Groensteen 47–50). The *densité* of a comic book page, Groensteen argues, is an important "criterion" in "the critical appreciation of page layout" (44), especially as that layout contributes to the overall meaning of the book of which it is a small part: "It is obvious that a page composed of five panels will appear less dense (as potential reading matter) than a page that has three times as many" (44). For Groensteen, page design is essential to a story's "basic beat, its fundamental rhythm, which structures the narration" (45). While Green's pages, inspired by cartoonists Jack Kirby and Harvey Kurtzman, are often densely packed with panels, figures, and word balloons, Mia Wolff's compositions in *Bread & Wine* are more spacious, therefore giving the reader a sense of openness and possibility.[10]

Groensteen's theories of page layout need not be limited to discussions of design and composition. I am interested in how the density that Groensteen describes might be understood in the context of Yancy's analysis of the phenomenology of race in his chapter "Looking at Whiteness: Finding Myself Much like a Mugger at a Boardwalk's End" in *Look, a White!* (Yancy 17–50). As he speculates on what that "deeper, thicker philosophical engagement with issues of race" might look like, Yancy borrows an image from the world of comics to narrate his experience of hearing white drivers, parked or stuck in traffic, lock their car doors when they see him approaching. Those white drivers, Yancy writes, have "created a false dichotomy: an outside (the blacks) as opposed to an inside (the whites)" (Yancy 31). Yancy imagines this scene, a sudden moment of contact between himself and the white subject locking the doors of his or her car, as a cartoon: "Once next to the car (or once whites 'see' my black body approaching), though physically separated from it, I find myself 'over there' floating like a phantasm in their imaginary—much like a thought bubble. Yet I am also 'alongside' myself as I catch a glimpse of me through their gaze—I have become a predator, *their* predator" (35).

If this scene from Yancy's chapter were a four-panel comic strip, it might look like this: an establishing shot of Yancy (or a cartoon version of the philosopher) waiting at an intersection. The expression on his face tells readers that he has made eye contact with something—another pedestrian? A light? Maybe he's reading a sign, or his iPhone, or trying to figure out how long it will take him to cross. In the next panel, a white driver, startled and uneasy, waits for the light to change. In the third panel, Yancy hears a "click"—a sound effect, bold and jagged. (In his work, Yancy italicizes those repetitive *clicks* for emphasis; see pages 30–34, for instance.) I am not sure how to imagine the final panel of this sequence. Do we see Yancy's reaction? The driver's? Or do Yancy and the driver stare at each other in silence, the windshield of the car acting as a barrier between them? If I have space for one more panel, I might draw this moment of stasis: the driver, so obsessed with what he *thinks* Yancy might do, fails to turn into the intersection, while Yancy, imagining how the driver sees him, pauses, and fails to cross the street. Yancy and the driver remain locked in place, sharing only a sudden and unwelcome exchange of glances.

By figuring this moment as a cartoon, Yancy highlights the absurdity and the complexity of this interaction. His description of this incident clearly alludes to Du Bois's definition of double-consciousness, that sense of "always looking at one's self through the eyes of others" (Du Bois 3), but Yancy offers readers another set of images to describe this sensation. First, he is a ghost, a "phantasm in their imaginary," but he also appears for a moment as "a thought bubble" (35). This cartoon reference urges readers to imagine and experience the *density* of this moment. That density is tied to a moment of contact, much like the ones Green illustrates in his comics.

For Green, the autobiographical self is linked inextricably to forms of contact made possible on city streets, in intersections, at crosswalks. The density of Green's comics, however, also celebrates his affection for artist Jack Kirby, one of the most important and influential comic book artists of the twentieth century (Spurgeon 32). While Kirby, like Green, is perhaps best known for his superhero comics—notably the role he played in creating or co-creating familiar characters (and now lucrative Hollywood properties) including Captain America, the Hulk, and teams such as the Avengers and the X-Men—he, like other artists of his generation, was fascinated by urban landscapes. In Kirby's comics, as in Green's work, density is tied to a sense of place, to a specific geographic location. Just as Green's work often takes its inspiration from Chicago, Kirby frequently returned to the Lower East Side of New York as a setting for his comics.[11]

The Art of Richard "Grass" Green

In a 1983 interview with cartoonist C. C. Beck, best known as the co-creator of the popular 1940s character Captain Marvel, Will Eisner asks the Minnesota-born artist to speculate on the relationship between a sense of place and the act of cartooning. Eisner is curious to learn more about Beck's midwestern origins, including the time the artist spent training at the Chicago Academy of Fine Arts in the late 1920s. As Eisner explains, "The reason I'm questioning you about that is that I believe geographic origin impinges on style of art considerably" (55). Beck does not comment on Eisner's theory, but the question remains an interesting one. For Green, as we shall see, Chicago is both a destination and a point of departure.

Although Green is often associated with other Chicago-based underground cartoonists including Williamson and Jay Lynch, and although critic Tom Spurgeon and zinemaker Jake Austen remember Green as a fixture at Chicago-area comic book conventions in the 1980s and 1990s (Spurgeon 33), he spent most of his life in Fort Wayne, Indiana, where he was born in 1939. Green, encouraged by his mother, began drawing when he was a child (Schelly 151). He shared an interest in comics with classmate Ronald Foss, who, as comics historian Bill Schelly points out, gave Green the nickname "Grasshoppa" (151–52). Foss, another important figure in what Bart Beaty has described as "the second wave of organized comic book fandom" (154) in the United States, soon began writing and drawing stories with his friend. After completing their service in the Air Force, the two continued to pursue their interest in comics and contributed to the fanzines of the era (Schelly 152). Foss published Green's "Da Frantic Four" in a 1962 issue of *The Comicollector*. Bill Schelly notes that, after the publication of "Da Frantic Four," Green "quickly became known as a humor artist of remarkable ability" (152).

Green went on to draw other Marvel and DC superhero parodies including "Bestest League of America Meets Da Frantic Four," which he created with Roy Thomas for the fanzine *Alter Ego* in 1964 (Schelly 152; Thomas and Schelly 75–84). Green developed a lifelong friendship with Thomas, who, as an editor at Marvel Comics, tried to find assignments for the Indiana-based cartoonist. In Tom Spurgeon's 2002 obituary in *The Comics Journal*, Thomas described his admiration for Green's work: "I was always in awe of Grass'[s] talent . . . and frustrated because I couldn't find the right place (or chance) to use it at Marvel" (Thomas qtd. in Spurgeon 32). As Spurgeon also points out, however, Green drew The Shape for the first issue of *Charlton Premiere* in 1967 and went on to produce other comics for the Connecticut-based company, including stories for *Go-Go Comics* and *Abbott & Costello* (Spurgeon 32).

Green also created a comic strip for Fort Wayne's African American community newspaper *Frost Illustrated* (Spurgeon 32) and, in the early 1970s, wrote and drew stories for Kitchen Sink titles including *Bizarre Sex* and issue no. 2 of *Teen-Age Horizons of Shangrila*, which includes work from influential underground cartoonists Justin Green and Trina Robbins (Spurgeon 32). In 1972 Kitchen Sink published *Super Soul Comix* no. 1, featuring Green's hero Soul-Brother American. Over the course of his long career, Green returned again and again to superhero comics, most notably the Afrofuturist shapeshifter Xal-Kor the Human Cat, who made his debut in the fanzine *Star-Studded Comics* in 1964 (Schelly 153).

While he remained a prolific artist for most of his career, Green was unable to support himself with his comics. In letters he sent to fellow fanzine writer, artist, and self-publisher Bruce Chrislip and other friends in the late 1970s and 1980s, Green describes some of his day jobs, which included a sales position at an automobile dealership and design work for a Chicago-based mail order company. "You thank it's easy-livin' in Chicago?" Green jokes in a letter from March 1984. "Then you try bringin' *yo'* ast here to live by freelancin' you think it's so easy, you dumb-ast!!!" (Green, Letter to Bruce Chrislip et al.).[12] In addition to working gigs as a musician, Green designed and sold blue-line drawing paper to other comic book artists. Cartoonist Russ Maheras, a frequent contributor to Alan Light's *The Buyer's Guide for Comic Fandom*, recalls ordering paper and minicomics from REGco, Green's small-press imprint (Maheras; see also Schelly 154). In the late 1980s and early 1990s, as Green continued to write and draw superhero parodies in *Wildman Comics & Stories* for Megaton Comics and for Miller Publishing Company, he produced erotica for the Fantagraphics imprint Eros Comics. He published his final collection of Xal-Kor the Human Cat stories with TwoMorrows in 2002 just a few months before his death (Schelly 154; Spurgeon 33).

As this brief summary of his life suggests, Green produced a large body of work for a variety of publishers. Throughout his career, from his superhero parodies to his minicomics and his erotica, Kirby remained his greatest influence. In the early 1960s, just as he was gaining a reputation in comics fandom, Green wrote Kirby a letter filled with technical questions, notably about the size of original comic book pages. Kirby's reply, published with an introduction by Bill Schelly in Roy Thomas's comics history magazine *Alter Ego* just a few months before Green's death, is detailed and generous. "In regard to comic magazine pages," Kirby explains, "I rule mine to a size of $12\frac{1}{2} \times 18\frac{1}{2}$ and divide them in thirds. The size of the individual panels should depend on the artist's dramatic sense. Actually, you will find that scenes with the most movement will demand larger space" (Kirby 25). Kirby's letter provided Green with a lesson in how the density of word and image on a comic book page can produce startling effects.

What Skip Williamson has described as the "madness" of Green's work also reveals the cartoonist's debt to Harvey Kurtzman's *Mad* (Williamson). In his conversation with me, Williamson explained that often in Green's comics "a character will leap across the panel with a grimace on his face, kind of leaving the Kirby world and going into Kurtzman world" (Williamson). In his *Comics Journal* interview with Williamson, Green praises Kurtzman as "the lay out master. There are probably people who can't stand Harvey Kurtzman's work," he continues, "but for people like me he's been a major influence, I think the man can do no wrong" (Green, "Strange World" 74). Green, Kirby, and Kurtzman are artists whose work expresses the anxieties and wonders of the urban contact that both Jane Jacobs and Samuel Delany describe.

"I come from Fort Wayne," Green says in his interview with Williamson. "Nobody comes to Fort Wayne, and very few people leave. Paupers are left. Now Fort Wayne's dead" (Green, "Strange World" 64). Williamson places the blame on Ronald Reagan, but Green saves politics for later in the interview. He still wants to talk about place: "But I love Chicago," he continues. "I love walking down the street with my portfolio, whether I've got work or not I just love being here, because I know this place, and art is all over" (64). When Green says, "I know this place," and when he contrasts Fort Wayne with the streets of Chicago, he might be describing scenes from *Xal-Kor the Human Cat* no. 1, published by New Media Publishing in 1980.

In the comic, Green tells the origin of Xal-Kor once again. According to the text, the hero is one of the Felinians from Planet Felis, a race of "proud, powerful" aliens who, despite their desire for peace, find themselves at war with the Rodentites, citizens of Planet Rodens (Green, *Xal-Kor* 18). Before they take over the rest of the universe, the rat people decide to subjugate the Felinians. Unlike earthbound rats, the warriors of Rodens are a time-traveling, shape-shifting species. "Naturally," the narrator informs us, "the Felinians don't dig the idea worth a sh t [*sic*], and the result is . . . . WAR!" (Green, *Xal-Kor* 18). After being defeated by the Felinians, the Rodentites flee to Earth. Xal-Kor pursues them and, disguised as newspaper reporter Colin Chambers, uncovers their plans for world domination. Xal-Kor, like his Rodentite adversaries, is also a shapeshifter, one who can change his form and his race at will as he does in issue no. 8 of *Wildman Comics & Stories* from 1989.

The final panel on page 24 of the 1980 edition of *Xal-Kor* shows the hero surveying his new home (fig. 6.1). Now in his "basic cat form," he stands on the roof of a building and studies the human beings he sees below him. The cityscape, Xal-Kor realizes, "*is* striking" and "strangely *beautiful*!!" (Green, *Xal-Kor* 24). In this image, readers see the shadows of enormous skyscrapers. A cross draws the reader's attention to the lower right-hand corner of the panel. Green follows this ecstatic moment with the wide-screen drawing that introduces the next page (fig. 6.2). A caption informs us that "Xal-Kor sees and studies all the various peoples from many different walks of life, listening to the talk, learning the myriad expressions" (25). Suddenly this is no longer a superhero comic. Xal-Kor and the reader both observe this carefully rendered street scene. This large, single panel provides the reader the space and time to study each figure: the white executive in the suit and tie; the woman clutching her purse; the black man in the sport coat and the open-collared shirt; the long-haired kids on the corner, one on the stoop and the other with his hands in his pockets; the kid on the skateboard; a police officer, the hydrant, a stop sign, the sidewalk, an iron railing. The images first, then the word balloons, scraps of conversation: "But I'm happy with my job . . ." and "Do you think he'll propose tonight?" and "That kid needs a good *whuppin*'!" (said with a smile) and "*Whee!*" If movement, as Kirby advised Green, demands more "space," it also demands *density* of word and image, especially when an artist is depicting a street scene such as this one.

Rather than using a grid of separate panels to express motion, Green fills every corner of this large, rectangular panel with figures and details that evoke Xal-Kor's wonder at these strange creatures. In the caption that introduces the page, Green points out that the Felinian warrior "studies" these humans carefully. Their liveliness

Figure 6.1. Xal-Kor, disguised as an ordinary cat, surveys his new home on page 24 of *Xal-Kor the Human Cat* no. 1 (New Media Publishing, August 1980). Script and pencils by Richard "Grass" Green and inks by Howard Keltner. © 1980 Richard "Grass" Green.

Figure 6.2. Xal-Kor observes his fellow citizens, in a scene that echoes the work of Jack Kirby, in the first panel of page 25 of *Xal-Kor the Human Cat* no. 1 (New Media Publishing, August 1980). Script and pencils by Richard "Grass" Green and inks by Howard Keltner. © 1980 Richard "Grass" Green.

attracts and fascinates him. Panels like this one display Green's debt to Kirby and to Kurtzman as well as his mastery of drawing dynamic figures and placing them in carefully rendered urban scenes. While Green's cartoon alter ego might not appear in this story, a reader familiar with his other work will recognize a pattern emerging. Even in a panel such as this one from his genre work, Green's fascination with how characters interact with one another, and how those sudden interactions shape consciousness, is evident. Green employs these characters as compositional elements to express the joy and wonder of these moments of urban contact.

In order to interact more closely with these humans, Xal-Kor adopts a new identity as a newspaper reporter, that time-tested profession for superhero alter egos. Not long after Xal-Kor takes on a human appearance as Colin Chambers, Green introduces a new visual strategy: rather than filling a large panel with a series of extras like the ones in a Will Eisner comic (or, for that matter, in a Jacques Tati film), he includes two portraits of a young woman and a long-haired young man (fig. 6.3). Colin Chambers, Xal-Kor's alter ego, also appears in the story's final panel, but I will focus my attention on these two unnamed characters.

Colin Chambers, in this panel, reflects on his ongoing conflict with his enemies. Green includes the two portraits of the young man and woman to silence the hero's racing thoughts. The artist ends the story without further spectacle or violence. It's just another moment of quiet contact. These two character studies have no relationship to the absurd, often humorous science fiction adventures of Xal-Kor and his war with the Rodentites. The two portraits look instead like studies from an artist's sketchbook. The young woman wears a floral print blouse and large hoop earrings. The long-haired man wears a bandana and looks forward as all three walk toward the lower left-hand corner of the image, slowly moving out of the frame. While Xal-Kor's adventures offer the reader plenty of spectacle, they also include these subtle moments, ones in which Green expresses a longing for sudden but fleeting urban encounters. "When I come to Chicago," Green told Williamson, "talk to you, and then I go back, boom, man, I'm just swell up. I'm ready to draw, draw, draw, and I get back and start drawing, and then it poops out and I got to come back and refuel" (64). Green discusses his creative process in more detail in issue no. 5 of *Un-Fold Funnies* from 1981, a comic in which another chance meeting on a sidewalk leads to a long conversation on subjects ranging from racism in the workplace to the art of cartooning.

The *Un-Fold Funnies* include some of Green's most innovative and hilarious work. Thus far, I have found nearly twenty issues, each one printed on a single 8½ by 11 sheet of paper, almost like a broadside. These self-published comics are an essential part of Green's story. While his superhero parodies are more widely available — at least through online sellers and some comic book shops specializing in back issues — these photocopied narratives provide the autobiographical, self-published counterpoint to Green's work for companies like Charlton and Kitchen Sink.[13] Issue no. 5, "Ga-rass Ga-ripes," begins with a panel of Green's cartoon avatar talking to himself

"A Space of Concentration" 157

Figure 6.3. Xal-Kor, now disguised as reporter Colin Chambers, walks down the street of his new city, while Grass Green offers two portraits of a young man and a young woman, in the final panel from page 31 of *Xal-Kor the Human Cat* no. 1 (New Media Publishing, August 1980). Script and pencils by Richard "Grass" Green and inks by Howard Keltner. © 1980 Richard "Grass" Green.

(fig. 6.4). Like Colin Chambers, Green is on the sidewalk. The composition of this first panel echoes that of the final image from the Xal-Kor story I discussed earlier, only this time, there are two figures instead of three. Green's style here is looser than in his underground comix or in *Xal-Kor*. In issue no. 12 from 1981, in fact, Green explains the difference between these more personal stories and his superhero parodies. When a friend suggests that Grass do another "superhero strip," the cartoonist responds, "Now jus' *how* th' hellamy gunna get a superhero strip into these tiny-ass panels, *ha?*—*You* know this's a *bitch* of a format!" (Green, "Grass vs . . . Criticism!"). This "small size," as he describes it in the next panel, suits these smaller stories:

Figure 6.4. We meet Grass Green on the street in the first two panels of *Un-Fold Funnies* no. 5 (Pokey-Press, 1981). Script, pencils, and inks by Richard "Grass" Green. © 1981 Richard "Grass" Green.

"The only thing that's made it all worthwhile is doin' my *quik-art*! Now, *you* think I should bust my ass an' try t'do *super-heroes*?!?" ("Grass vs . . . Criticism!").

In "Ga-rass Ga-ripes," as in *Xal-Kor*, we're back on the street, this time with one of Grass's friends. Unlike that final Xal-Kor image, which is more static, the opening image of *Un-Fold Funnies* no. 5 prepares the reader for a world filled with motion: Grass's friend waving to him; Grass turning his head; his friend catching up with him. Background details in the second panel are sparse. More important, Green seems to suggest, are the *movements* of these figures—Grass turning his head, a friend reaching out and initiating a conversation. The *Xal-Kor* panels, filled with buildings, street corners, and pedestrians, are about observation. The *Un-Fold Funnies*, featuring Green's "*quik-art*" ("Grass vs . . . Criticism!"), allow for more personal reflections, stories in which the artist can share secrets with a small circle of friends and acquaintances.

Over the next two pages, Grass talks about his coworkers, "jealous," he says, "as 3 mu-fuggahs," just a bunch of "dumb-ass honkies" who have given him trouble ("Ga-rass Ga-ripes"). His friend is surprised to hear that Grass has a day job. Wasn't he doing OK as a freelance cartoonist? Not really. He missed too many deadlines. He needed a regular job to support his comics. "But then," he says, "a funny thing happent! Suddenly, er-ry nite after work, I was going' home drawin' like a *mu'fugga*!— And the nights I'd go home *pissed* is when I'd *really* whail on 'at ol' drawin' board! The loot started pourin' *in* again!" ("Ga-rass Ga-ripes"). If *Xal-Kor* is about silent observation, the *Un-Fold Funnies* are about dialogue. Even in those panels where Grass is alone, he addresses the reader directly about issues ranging from money troubles to the flu. The backgrounds are less elaborate than in Green's other work, but his mastery of cartoon portraits remains. In "Ga-rass Ga-ripes," he draws himself in close-up in the second panel of section 4 (fig. 6.5). Chance encounters, like the one with his friend, animate these stories. Having abandoned the spectacle of his superhero narratives in these minicomics, Green offers a different kind of contact, one more direct and less mediated by genre conventions.

In the *Un-Fold Funnies*, Green draws on his lifetime of experience as a musician. Green's protégé and friend Seitu Hayden, who began his career as an artist by inking Green's comic strips for *Frost Illustrated*, remembers his mentor's musical side: "Grass was a funny[,] self-deprecating guy," Hayden noted. "He would talk to the audience, tell a joke or two and go into 'Johnny B. Goode' or something similar. I never saw his act but he described it to me as another outlet for his talent and more importantly— EXTRA INCOME!" (Hayden). Green, Hayden remembers, played standards and rock-and-roll oldies for audiences in Indiana.

The different stages of Green's long, multifaceted career—from his parodies and superhero stories to his autobiographical minicomics and back again—reflect the slow transformation of comic books as an art form in the United States in the late twentieth and early twenty-first centuries. Due in no small part to the success of Art Spiegelman's *Maus*, comics are now the focus of a great deal of academic attention

Figure 6.5. Grass Green's self-portrait from *Un-Fold Funnies* no. 5 (Pokey-Press, 1981). Script, pencils, and inks by Richard "Grass" Green. © 1981 Richard "Grass" Green.

in the United States. As scholars including Qiana J. Whitted have argued, with the ascendancy of comics studies also comes an opportunity for collaboration, notably with other disciplines such as African American studies. Tremendously gifted and prolific, Green is an artist whose comics provide scholars from both fields an opportunity to study the relationship between genre work and more intimate narrative forms such as autobiography and memoir. As Hayden suggests in his recollection of

Green's musical performances, the fanzine artist, underground cartoonist, and comic book entrepreneur knew how to work a crowd, a skill that's less about art and more about magic. But, then again, maybe that's what Samuel Delany has in mind in his essays about Times Square: the magical qualities of a utopian urban space.

Delany's Bread & Wine

In the introduction to *The Motion of Light in Water*, his 1989 autobiography, Samuel R. Delany describes the limits of memory as he recalls the circumstances of his father's death. He cautions the reader against thinking of the book as a definitive statement of his life. In his introduction, Delany invites readers to trust the emotional reality of his sense impressions, those ghosts of memory and experience. He leaves the work of facts and figures to his biographers:

> I hope instead to sketch, as honestly and effectively as I can, something I can recognize as my own, aware as I do so that even as I work after honesty and accuracy, memory will make this only one possible fiction among the myriad—many in open conflict—anyone might write of any of us, as convinced as any other that what he or she wrote was the truth. (Delany, *Motion* 15–16)

In *Bread & Wine*, Delany includes several voices other than his own: those of his partner Dennis Rickett and artist Mia Wolff, of course, but also that of poet Friedrich Hölderlin, whose poem "Brod und Wein" provided the book's title and, Delany explains in a recent interview, "a wonderful retelling of the whole story at an interesting cultural distance" (Delany and Wolff, *Bread & Wine* 51).[14] In the same conversation, Wolff—who has produced autobiographical visual narratives of her own, notably the 1994 children's book *Catcher*, about her experiences as a trapeze artist—discusses the nature of this collaboration, one that echoes Delany's earlier work in comics with artists including Dick Giordano on *Wonder Woman* and Howard Chaykin on the book *Empire* in the 1970s. "I like partnerships," Wolff explains. Alluding to her experiences as a circus performer, Wolff adds, "With Chip I was flying after the ink and he was more grounded. It's a very satisfying state" (Wolff qtd. in Delany and Wolff, *Bread & Wine* 51). Later in the interview, Delany discusses this collaborative process in more detail, especially as it relates to the relationship between a writer and an artist creating a comic book or graphic novel. Like Chaney and Hatfield, Delany emphasizes the visual qualities of these narratives: "When you write comics captions," he explains, "you want to use all the senses *except* the visual—you leave that to the artist" (*Bread & Wine* 53).[15] In this portion of the conversation with Wolff and Rickett, Delany alludes to an earlier interview in which he discusses the role played by the reader in shaping and understanding comic book narratives.

In the late 1970s, Delany spoke with Denny O'Neil and Gary Groth about the nature of this visual medium, one, he argues, quite distinct from painting, film, or television.[16] Delany uses opera as an example: "You know, I distrust people who 'read' comics—in the same way I distrust people who go to 'see' an opera." Just as one should go to "*hear* an opera," Delany explains, one must "*look* at a comic book" (Delany, "Refractions" 91). This act of looking, Delany argues, is an act performed in solitude: "The intense and committed silence with which one *looks at* a comic—or even the cursory silence with which one *looks through* a comic . . . that range of silences is terribly important" (92). This experience of silence raises an important question about both contact and density. What happens in those silences—those spaces, for example, between two panels of a comic book, or, for that matter, between Yancy and the driver who locks the car door?[17] If I revise my earlier comments on Yancy, what I might say is this: a critical assessment and expression of density is impossible without the silence Delany describes in the following passage (which gives my chapter its title).

> The noisy genres, entertaining as they are, as they fill up the space of looking with sound—words, music, the noise of crashing cars, the susurrus of breath that halts, suddenly, in anticipation of mayhem or violence—do so at the price of suppressing a certain inner dialogue, a certain internal critique, a space of concentration and criticism, which, I might add, our society desperately needs. ("Refractions" 92)

The silence that Delany discusses here is not that of wordless visual narratives like the novels of Lynd Ward or the comics of contemporary artists including Marnie Galloway and Norwegian cartoonist Jason (John Arne Sæterøy). Filled with dialogue, narration, and passages from Hölderlin's poem, *Bread & Wine* is not a silent comic— that is, one without words. Nonetheless, by practicing an "intense and committed silence" while engaging with the text, the reader might enter that "space of concentration and criticism," one that encourages self-reflection. Delany's comic book autobiography, in other words, urges the reader to recognize and cherish these moments of contact between the self and the other.

Take, for example, the first two pages of *Bread & Wine*. The text begins with what in a superhero comic would be called a *splash page*, one with a single image designed to attract the attention of the reader while also introducing the hero or protagonist. Dennis Rickett stands alone on a New York street. Except he's not alone: we see him from Delany's perspective. Wolff has designed the page in such a way that, as a reader, I can imagine myself walking toward Rickett. Maybe I'm in Delany's shoes. Maybe I'm another pedestrian, standing behind Delany. What at first appears to be a lonely image of a man standing beside a blanket covered in books is now a small community of Delany, Wolff, the reader, even Hölderlin, whose opening lines from "Brod und Wein" appear in an English translation in the lower right-hand corner of the drawing (fig. 6.6).

Figure 6.6. The reader meets Dennis Rickett on the first narrative page of *Bread & Wine: An Erotic Tale of New York*. Script by Samuel R. Delany and art by Mia Wolff (Fantagraphics, 2013). © Samuel R. Delany and Mia Wolff, courtesy Fantagraphics Books.

Figure 6.7. Delany and Rickett watch a PBS documentary during their first night together, on pages 26 (*above*) and 27 (*right*) of *Bread & Wine: An Erotic Tale of New York*. Script by Samuel R. Delany and art by Mia Wolff (Fantagraphics, 2013). © Samuel R. Delany and Mia Wolff, courtesy Fantagraphics Books.

"A Space of Concentration" 165

> **Outside it was still raining...**
>
> **I offered to take him back uptown in a cab.**
>
> **OK**
>
> **TAXI**
>
> **Want me to let you off at 72nd street?**
>
> **A couple of blocks before. That'd be better...**
>
> **At 68th street, I told the cab driver to pull up.**
>
> **Dennis got out.**
>
> **I saw him step under the red awning of a fancy Chinese restaurant.**
>
> **...then the cab started uptown to take me back to my apartment.**
>
> Later in my journal (January 21, 1990) I wrote: "Dropped him, with knapsack and sleeping roll, off in a cab at 68th and 10th— he wanted to be let out a few blocks before 72nd. The rain began to pound like hail as he slid out, dragging his gear. I saw him, in his long hair and grey woolen hat, hurry over to a doorway. And rode home through the wet morning."
>
> Near the entry are some notes on de Man's reading of Hölderlin's *Bread and Wine*.
>
> I figured that was the end of it. I'd see Dennis again—we'd still be friends. But I was certain that was the end of anything physical between us. I wondered what it *would* have been like to have him up in Amherst.

The page includes several layers of text: two awnings that advertise a nail salon and a Japanese restaurant, narration that introduces Rickett, and the first six lines of Hölderlin's poem. Rickett, his hands in his pockets and a braided ponytail just visible under a knit cap, stands to the left. Wolff implies a kind of density here with the grid-like structure of the sidewalk. The books on Rickett's blanket also tell a story. In fact, they look like ten empty panels, without words or titles or figures. Three parking meters lead the eye to the drawing's vanishing point. In discussing this first page, I cannot ignore the blank one that precedes it, black in the new Fantagraphics edition and white in the Juno Books version from 1999. The darkness of the facing page resonates with and frames Wolff's portrait of Rickett. For a moment, as I look at Wolff's drawing, I am standing where Delany once stood, and I am seeing the books and the nail salon and the sidewalk. But what is Hölderlin doing here?

The passages from "Brod und Wein," Delany explains, also "supply any sense we wanted of heightened diction" (Delany and Wolff, *Bread & Wine* 53). The presence of Hölderlin's "heightened diction," borrowed from a poem in which the speaker expresses a desire for, to use a phrase from Michael Hamburger's English translation, "a wine-cup more full" and "a life more intense and more daring" (Hölderlin 153), introduces another voice to Chip and Dennis's love story. On page 27 of *Bread & Wine*, Delany further explains the link between the poem and this narrative in a discussion of a journal entry from 21 January 1990, the day after he and Rickett spent their first night together. Meanwhile, pages 26 and 27 document the beginning of this relationship (fig. 6.7).

The two pages are almost mirror images of each other. On the left-hand side, we see Dennis and Chip lying in bed and floating through a series of constellations. The two lovers are watching a PBS documentary about "the formation of the Universe with spiraling, flaring images of planets, comets, and stars" (Delany and Wolff, *Bread & Wine* 26). The image on page 27 is much more mundane and suggests the possible limits of their relationship. Wolff draws the taxi in roughly the same shape as the bed. On page 27, however, the stars have disappeared, replaced by heavy rain and two smaller panels on either side of the taxi itself. Dennis wants to return to the streets, at least for now. On page 26, they talk about a possible future — will Dennis join Chip in Amherst? — but, as they watch a Universe taking shape (we see it, too, on the TV screen of their room), they do so, as the caption tells us, "silently, almost in awe" of the documentary.

In contrast, page 27 begins with rain falling on the hood of a taxi. There is no room on page 27 for possibility. The visual clutter here — the two smaller panels, the speech balloons, the white streaks of rain on the inky, black background — implies the distance that remains between the two men. The next three panels also mirror the three panels at the center of page 26: we see Dennis leaving, then moving away from Chip, then a final image of solitude and disappointment. On page 27, Wolff varies her pacing by eliminating the final, three-panel grid structure that concludes page 26. She ends this sequence with a block of Delany's text: a passage from his journal, an allusion to Paul de Man's essay about "Brod und Wein," and Delany's memory of Dennis's farewell.

Wolff's decision to conclude with a passage from the journal reinforces Chip's sense of disappointment and confusion. "The rain began to pound like hail as he slid out, dragging his gear," Delany writes. "I saw him, in his long hair and grey woolen hat, hurry over to a doorway. And rode home through the wet morning"

(Delany and Wolff, *Bread & Wine* 27). The next line in this caption reminds us that what we have just read, what we have just *seen*, is not a page from Delany's diary. What we see is a passage that Mia Wolff has copied from the journal itself or, perhaps, from Delany's script: "Near the entry are some notes on de Man's reading of Hölderlin's *Bread and Wine*" (27). This page, like the book itself, comes from multiple sources—a journal, a set of notes, a poem, a memory. Delany explains, "I figured that was the end of it" (27). He thought for certain they'd "still be friends" (27). Despite his disappointment, Delany still "wondered what it *would* have been like to have him up in Amherst" (27). A few pages later he gets to find out, but the solid black border that ends page 27 suggests that, at least for now, that future is not certain and perhaps not as limitless as the constellations that introduce page 26.

"A Space of Concentration and Criticism"

I want to return to the point that Will Eisner made in his conversation with C. C. Beck in 1983. Is there a link between "geographic origin" and a cartoonist's style? What role does region play in the imaginative life of the artist? In a recent interview, Chicago-based cartoonist Marnie Galloway described the city's "tongue-in-cheek distrust of institutions, a kindred feeling of aggressive outsiderness" (Galloway). Richard "Grass" Green is part of this tradition and remains a significant if underrated figure for a number of reasons. His entrepreneurial spirit lives on in underground comics micropresses and the online world of digital comics. I wonder what Green's comics might have looked like had he lived to see Tumblr. Green's legacy of enthusiasm and inclusiveness also remains. As Denis Kitchen told Tom Spurgeon, "Many cartoonists are loners who skulk around the edges of parties, but Grass was invariably surrounded by a group and in animated conversation" (Spurgeon 32). Green's sensitivity and generosity of spirit animate his comics, a rich body of work that invites close, engaged readings. In this chapter, I've conducted an experiment: how does a reading of Green's work change when juxtaposed with Delany's *Bread & Wine*? What might Green and Delany (and Wolff and Rickett and Hölderlin and the other voices in this chapter) tell us about the nature of comics, of narrative, of autobiography?

I find possible answers to these questions in the comics and the letters that Green left behind when he died in 2002. In his letter to Bruce Chrislip from December 1979, Green asks for some flexibility on an upcoming deadline: "The reason I'm warning you right now is cuz my current job (car-sales) demands that I spend LOTSA time at the office (to compensate for the fact that Dec sales are very slow, and I gotta be there if I wishes to make any loot), which means coming home tired and reluctant sometimes to throw myself at the drawing board" (Green, letter to Bruce Chrislip).[18] Just two years later, in *Un-Fold Funnies* no. 5, Green refers again to his day job and its relationship to his work at the drawing board. This time, however, he seeks to document those day-to-day experiences as best he can. The petty slights, the casual racism, the veiled threats, the "lil' stunts they do to try to keep a nigga upset . . . *you know, like treatin' ya like yer stupit, or, callin' ya 'boy' an' shit like dat!*" ("Ga-rass Ga-ripes")—these moments, he explains to his friend, form the basis of the work he's now producing: "Them jealous, rat-faced mu'-fuggahs keepin' me *pissed* is my *motivation!*" As he walks away in the final panel of the comic, Grass's friend thinks, "Crazy artist-ass mu-fuggah" ("Ga-rass Ga-ripes"). Green challenges his readers and his fellow cartoonists. What does it take to write autobiography? The cartoonist might be implying that the reader, in truth, is the "crazy" one for wanting to know all these intimate details in the first place.

I asked earlier about Hölderlin's presence in *Bread & Wine*. As Delany explained, the poem is "a wonderful retelling of the whole story"—that first meeting with Dennis Rickett, the process of falling in love (Delany and Wolff, *Bread & Wine* 51). For Delany and for Green, autobiography has nothing to do with telling an original story. Rather, each one tells a tale so familiar—about love, work, friendship—that it resonates strongly with readers. As Michael A. Chaney points out, autobiographical comics urge us "to reconsider what is at stake in telling our life stories in pictures" (Introduction 7), but his choice of pronouns—"telling *our* life stories" (emphasis added)—is interesting. Green and Delany invite readers to join them in this conversation, this moment of contact, which soon becomes a memory, an intimate one shared by strangers.

NOTES

Thank you to the following for sharing their memories of Grass Green: Jake Austen, Bruce Chrislip, William H. Foster III, Seitu Hayden, Russ Maheras, Jim Main, Roy Thomas, Bill Schelly, Tom Spurgeon, and Skip Williamson. Thanks also to Eric Reynolds at Fantagraphics for his assistance with the images from *Bread & Wine*. I presented an early version of this chapter under the title "The Art of Richard 'Grass' Green" at the International Comic Arts Forum (ICAF) at The Ohio State University on 14 November 2014. I would especially like to thank Bruce Chrislip for attending that session and sharing his copies of Green's correspondence with me.

1. Unless otherwise noted, my quotations from Skip Williamson come from a phone interview I conducted on 25 October 2014. For other resources on American underground comix, Patrick Rosenkranz's *Rebel Visions: The Underground Comix Revolution, 1963–1975* and Leonard Rifas's "Racial Imagery, Racism, Individualism, and Underground Comix" are useful introductions to the history of comic books and the U.S. counterculture of the 1960s and 1970s. Both make passing references to Green. Comics scholar and historian William H. Foster III has also spoken about Green in his presentation "The Forgotten Black Kings of Underground Comix," delivered at the New York Comics and Picture-Story Symposium in New York City in the fall of 2013 (New York). While used copies of Green's comics can be found online at auction sites such as eBay, very little of his work is currently in print. A great

deal of archival work still needs to be done on Green so that we can assemble a more complete picture of his life and his art.

2. For more on Delany and autobiography, consult the scholarly work of Long, Noya, Smith, and Tucker. Michael Bronski's short article from *Publishers Weekly* provides a brief introduction to Delany's *Times Square Red, Times Square Blue*. Delany wrote the script for issues 202 and 203 of *Wonder Woman*, which were published by DC Comics in September–October 1972 and November–December 1972. *Empire*, his collaboration with artist Howard Chaykin published in 1978 by Byron Preiss, is no longer in print but easy to find from used booksellers.

3. For ghosts, read "The Haunted Mansion" in *Teen-Age Horizons of Shangrila* no. 2, published by Denis Kitchen's Kitchen Sink Enterprises in 1972. The issue also features Grass Green's ad for Stone Bleu Ltd., a head shop in Minneapolis. I describe Green's time-traveling cat, Xal-Kor, later in this chapter. Green tells stories of playing in a band and working with an Elvis-impersonating lead singer in *Un-Fold Funnies* no. 13, which features the story "Grass Green; [*sic*] Musician!"

4. There are a number of sources on the history of fanzines and zines in the United States including Duncombe, Spencer, and Radway. Anne Elizabeth Moore's "Be a Zinester: How and Why to Publish Your Own Periodical," from *Fall of Autumn* (www.fallofautumn.com), provides a good history of fanzines in the United States in the twentieth century and explains their gradual evolution into zines and minicomics. Moore has also posted a copy of this essay on her website (www.anneelizabethmoore.com).

5. In February 2013, on the closing night of his show *Memory Palaces* at the Thomas Robertello Gallery in Chicago, Edie Fake discussed the influence of Delany's *Times Square Red, Times Square Blue* on his work. In his animation, his comics, his zines, and his drawings, Fake imagines queer utopian urban spaces inspired in part by the idea of contact defined by Jacobs and Delany. Fake's graphic novel *Gaylord Phoenix* (2010) and *Memory Palaces* (2014), a collection of paintings from the 2013 Robertello show, are essential introductions to his art. I discuss Fake's innovations and his relationship to other queer artists including filmmaker Jack Smith in "Bodies, Transfigurations, and Bloodlust in Edie Fake's Graphic Novel *Gaylord Phoenix*."

6. In posts for *Pencil Panel Page*, a scholarly comics blog, Whitted speculates on how comics scholarship and African American studies might share resources and methodologies ("How Does" and "What"). Toni Morrison's *Playing in the Dark* is an important point of origin for Whitted's work, notably her essay "'And the Negro thinks in hieroglyphics': Comics, Visual Metonymy, and the Spectacle of Blackness."

7. For other discussions that gesture toward a theory of African American comics, consult Singer's "'Black Skins' and White Masks: Comic Books and the Secret of Race," Wanzo's "Wearing Hero-Face: Black Citizens and Melancholic Patriotism in *Truth: Red, White, and Black*," and Whitted's "'And the Negro thinks in hieroglyphics': Comics, Visual Metonymy, and the Spectacle of Blackness." In his 2009 essay "Is There an African American Graphic Novel?," Chaney argues that "at the intersection where the politics of identity collide with the aesthetics of form and genre, there are graphic novels produced by artists who self-identify as black that convey diasporic histories and experiences at the level of both subject matter and manner of expression" (74).

8. There is now a large and growing body of work on autobiographical comics. In addition to Hatfield's *Alternative Comics* and Chaney's *Graphic Subjects*, Hillary L. Chute's *Graphic Women: Life Writing and Contemporary Comics* and Elisabeth El Refaie's *Autobiographical*

Comics: Life Writing in Pictures are important recent studies. Two early and influential works on the subject include Joseph Witek's *Comics Books as History: Jack Jackson, Art Spiegelman, and Harvey Pekar* and chapter 1 of Marianne Hirsch's *Family Frames: Photography, Narrative, and Postmemory*. Hirsch elaborates on her earlier thoughts on *Maus*, comics, and memory in the first chapter of her recent book *The Generation of Postmemory*. In that chapter, she expands on her earlier analysis from *Family Frames* by discussing both Spiegelman and the late German poet, novelist, and essayist W. G. Sebald.

9. In the French edition of Groensteen's book, he discusses *densité* on pp. 44–45.

10. Consult Green's *Comics Journal* interview with Williamson for his comments on Kurtzman (Green, "Strange World" 74). Art Spiegelman describes Kurtzman's impact on underground cartoonists in his conversations with Hillary L. Chute in *MetaMaus* (especially pp. 191–92).

11. Hatfield's *Hand of Fire* is an essential study of Kirby's art.

12. Green mailed this letter, dated 5 March 1984, to Bruce Chrislip and other friends. Copy of the letter courtesy of Bruce Chrislip.

13. As Qiana J. Whitted points out in a recent blog post about studying titles published by independent African American publishers, one of the obstacles that scholars face is tracking down comics that were published in limited print runs (Whitted, "How Does"). Scholarship on filmmaker and novelist Oscar Micheaux might provide a useful model for the study of Green's work. Like Micheaux's novels, Green's later work was largely self-published. And like Micheaux, Green was an entrepreneur who sought to balance self-expression with business. Both Micheaux and Green found ways to distribute and sell their work by interacting directly with consumers. Thulani Davis, Pearl Bowser, and Louise Spence have argued that Micheaux's novels and his films might be read as an experiment in autobiography, one that documents both his subjective experience and the concerns and aspirations of his community (Davis xv–xvi; Bowser and Spence xvii–xxii). Once obscure and neglected, Micheaux is now an important figure in the history of African American film. His ascendancy, however, would not have been possible without the diligent archival work of scholars including Bowser, Spence, Thomas Cripps, and J. Ronald Green.

14. In this chapter, I refer to the 2013 Fantagraphics edition of *Bread & Wine*, which includes a new interview with Delany, Rickett, and Wolff. The original 1999 Juno Books edition, which features a different cover, is no longer in print but is still available online from used booksellers. The Juno Books edition, with its stars and planets on the cover, alludes directly to the PBS documentary that Chip and Dennis watch on their first night together, the scene on pages 26–27 that I discuss in this chapter. The dust jacket of the Fantagraphics edition from 2013 features another Wolff painting, this time a portrait of the two men, with Delany looking mischievous and affectionate and Rickett smiling and content. While the original cover alludes to the promise at the start of their relationship—we see only their hands clasped and resting on a blue planet—Wolff's painting for the Fantagraphics edition suggests the wholeness they have found with each other. Beneath the dust jacket are two portraits, one of Delany on the front cover and another of Rickett on the back of the book.

15. Anyone who has read Alan Moore's scripts knows that not all comics writers leave the visuals entirely to the artist. Moore's detailed scripts are closer in spirit to Eugene O'Neill's plays with almost novelistic descriptions of characters and action. Moore does, however, leave many decisions up to his artists. See, for example, the script for his first

Marvelman story, published in the now out-of-print *Kimota! The Miracleman Companion*, edited by George Khoury (57–65).

16. In this chapter, I reference the expanded version of this interview that Delany includes in *Silent Interviews: On Language, Race, Sex, Science Fiction, and Some Comics* from 1994 ("Refractions"). The original version appears in *The Comics Journal* no. 48 (Aug. 1979), pp. 37–43, 70–71.

17. Scott McCloud discusses "closure" and the work readers must do between comic book panels in chapter 3 of *Understanding Comics*, especially pp. 64–69.

18. Green dated this letter to Bruce Chrislip 14 Dec. 1979. Copy of the letter courtesy of Bruce Chrislip.

WORKS CITED

Beaty, Bart. *Comics versus Art*. Toronto: U of Toronto P, 2012.

Bowser, Pearl, and Louise Spence. *Writing Himself into History: Oscar Micheaux, His Silent Films, and His Audiences*. New Brunswick, NJ: Rutgers UP, 2000.

Bronski, Michael. "Samuel Delany: Ghosts of Time [*sic*] Square." *Publishers Weekly* 12 July 1999: 68–69.

Chaney, Michael A., ed. *Graphic Subjects: Critical Essays on Autobiography and Graphic Novels*. Madison: U of Wisconsin P, 2011.

———. Introduction. *Graphic Subjects: Critical Essays on Autobiography and Graphic Novels*. Ed. Michael A. Chaney. Madison: U of Wisconsin P, 2011. 3–9.

———. "Is There an African American Graphic Novel?" *Teaching the Graphic Novel*. Ed. Stephen E. Tabachnick. New York: Modern Language Society of America, 2009. 69–75.

Charlton Premiere vol. 2, no. 1 (Sept. 1967). Derby, CT: Charlton Comics Group.

Chute, Hillary L. *Graphic Women: Life Writing and Contemporary Comics*. New York: Columbia UP, 2010.

Cremins, Brian. "Bodies, Transfigurations, and Bloodlust in Edie Fake's Graphic Novel *Gaylord Phoenix*." *Journal of Medical Humanities* 34.2 (June 2013): 301–13.

Davis, Thulani. Foreword. *Writing Himself into History: Oscar Micheaux, His Silent Films, and His Audiences*. By Pearl Bowser and Louise Spence. New Brunswick, NJ: Rutgers UP, 2000. ix–xvi.

Delany, Samuel R. *The Motion of Light in Water: Sex and Science Fiction Writing in the East Village*. Minneapolis: U of Minnesota P, 2004.

———. "Refractions of *Empire*: The *Comics Journal* Interview." *Silent Interviews: On Language, Race, Sex, Science Fiction, and Some Comics*. Hanover, NH: Wesleyan UP/UP of New England, 1991. 83–126.

———. *Times Square Red, Times Square Blue*. New York: New York UP, 1999.

Delany, Samuel R., and Mia Wolff. *Bread & Wine: An Erotic Tale of New York*. Seattle: Fantagraphics, 2013.

Du Bois, W. E. B. *The Souls of Black Folk*. New York: Bantam Classics, 2005.

Duncombe, Stephen. *Notes from Underground: Zines and the Politics of Alternative Culture*. Bloomington, IN: Microcosm, 2008.

El Refaie, Elisabeth. *Autobiographical Comics: Life Writing in Pictures*. Jackson: UP of Mississippi, 2012.

Eisner, Will. "C. C. Beck." *Will Eisner's Shop Talk.* Milwaukie, OR: Dark Horse Comics. 52–75.
Fake, Edie. *Gaylord Phoenix.* New York: Secret Acres, 2010.
———. *Memory Palaces.* New York: Secret Acres, 2014.
Galloway, Marnie. Interview with the author. 22 Sept. 2014.
Go-Go vol. 1, no. 5 (Feb. 1967). Derby, CT: Charlton Comics Group.
Goldstein, Nancy. *Jackie Ormes: The First African American Woman Cartoonist.* Ann Arbor: U of Michigan P, 2008.
Green, Grass. "Ga-rass Ga-ripes." *Un-Fold Funnies* no. 5 (1981). Fort Wayne, IN: REGco/Pokey Press.
———. "Grass Green; [*sic*] Musician!" *Un-Fold Funnies* no. 13 (1981). Fort Wayne, IN: REGco/Pokey Press.
———. "Grass vs . . . Criticism!" *Un-Fold Funnies* no. 12 (1981). Fort Wayne, IN: REGco/Pokey Press.
———. "The Haunted Mansion." *Teen-Age Horizons of Shangrila* 2 (Nov. 1972). Milwaukee: Kitchen Sink Enterprises.
———. Letter to Bruce Chrislip. 14 Dec. 1979. Courtesy of Bruce Chrislip.
———. Letter to Bruce Chrislip et al. 5 Mar. 1984. Courtesy of Bruce Chrislip.
———. *Super Soul Comix* no. 1 (October 1972). Milwaukee: Kitchen Sink Enterprises.
Green, Grass (writer, penciller), and Par. Holman and Mike Vosburg (inks). *Wildman Comics & Stories* vol. 2, no. 8 (1989). Watseka, IL: Miller.
Green, Grass (writer, penciller), Howard Keltner (inks), et al. *Xal-Kor the Human Cat* no. 1 (Aug. 1980). Largo, FL: New Media.
Green, Richard "Grass." "The Strange World of Snappy Sammy Smoot." *The Comics Journal* 104 (1986): 50–74.
Groensteen, Thierry. *Bande dessinée et narration: Système de la bande dessinée 2.* Paris: PU de France, 2011.
———. *Comics and Narration.* Trans. Ann Miller. Jackson: UP of Mississippi, 2011.
Hatfield, Charles. *Alternative Comics: An Emerging Literature.* Jackson: UP of Mississippi, 2005.
———. *Hand of Fire: The Comics Art of Jack Kirby.* Jackson: UP of Mississippi, 2012.
Hayden, Seitu. "Grass Green." E-mail message to the author. 6 Nov. 2014.
Hirsch, Marianne. *Family Frames: Photography, Narrative, and Postmemory.* Cambridge, MA: Harvard UP, 1997.
———. *The Generation of Postmemory: Writing and Visual Culture after the Holocaust.* New York: Columbia UP, 2012.
Hölderlin, Friedrich. *Selected Poems and Fragments.* Trans. Michael Hamburger. New York: Penguin, 1998.
Jacobs, Jane. *The Death and Life of Great American Cities.* New York: Vintage Books, 1992.
Kirby, Jack. Letter to Richard "Grass" Green, January 1962. Reprinted in Bill Schelly, "Presenting Grass Green's 'Da Scavengers.'" *Alter Ego* 3.15 (2002): 25–30.
Long, Thomas Lawrence. "Tales of Plagues and Carnivals: Samuel R. Delany, AIDS, and the Grammar of Dissent." *Journal of Medical Humanities* 34.2 (2013): 213–26.
Maheras, Russ. "Richard 'Grass' Green." E-mail message to the author. 9 Sept. 2014.
McCloud, Scott. *Understanding Comics.* New York: HarperPerennial, 1993.
Moore, Alan. "Alan Moore's Script for *Miracleman* #1." *Kimota! The Miracleman Companion.* Ed. George Khoury. Raleigh: TwoMorrows, 2001. 57–65.

Moore, Anne Elizabeth. "Be a Zinester: How and Why to Publish Your Own Periodical." *Fall of Autumn*. N.d.

The New York Comics and Picture-Story Symposium. "The New York Comics Symposium: Prof. William H. Foster III on 'The Forgotten Black Kings of Underground Comix.'" *The Rumpus*. 18 Oct. 2013.

Noya, José Liste. "Memory in Motion: The 'Double Narratives' of Paul Auster's *The Invention of Solitude* and Samuel R. Delany's *The Motion of Light in Water*." *Selves in Dialogue: A Transethnic Approach to American Life Writing*. Ed. Begoña Simal. New York: Rodopi, 2011. 133–58.

Radway, Janice. "Zines, Half-Lives, and Afterlives: On the Temporalities of Social and Political Change." *PMLA* 126.1 (2011): 140–50.

Rifas, Leonard. "Racial Imagery, Racism, Individualism, and Underground Comix." *ImageText: Interdisciplinary Comics Studies* 1.1 (2004): n. pag.

Rosenkranz, Patrick. *Rebel Visions: The Underground Comix Revolution, 1963–1975*. Seattle: Fantagraphics, 2002.

Schelly, Bill. *Founders of Comic Fandom: Profiles of 90 Publishers, Dealers, Collectors, Writers, Artists and Other Luminaries of the 1950s and 1960s*. Jefferson, NC: McFarland, 2010.

Singer, Marc. "'Black Skins' and White Masks: Comic Books and the Secret of Race." *African American Review* 36.1 (2002): 107–19.

Smith, Stephanie A. "A Most Ambiguous Citizen: Samuel R. 'Chip' Delany." *American Literary History* 19.2 (2007): 557–70.

Spencer, Amy. *DIY: The Rise of Lo-Fi Culture*. New York: Marion Boyars, 2008.

Spiegelman, Art. *MetaMaus*. New York: Pantheon, 2011. Print.

Spurgeon, Tom. "Pioneering Underground Cartoonist Grass Green Passes Away at Age 63." *The Comics Journal* 247 (2002): 32–33.

Teen-Age Horizons of Shangrila no. 2 (Nov. 1972). Milwaukee: Kitchen Sink Enterprises.

Thomas, Roy, and Bill Schelly. *Alter Ego: The Best of the Legendary Comics Fanzine*. Raleigh, NC: TwoMorrows, 2008.

Tucker, Jeffrey Allen. "The Window of Autobiography: *The Motion of Light in Water*." *A Sense of Wonder: Samuel R. Delany, Race, Identity, and Difference*. Middletown, CT: Wesleyan UP, 2004. 150–98.

Wanzo, Rebecca. "Wearing Hero-Face: Black Citizens and Melancholic Patriotism in *Truth: Red, White, and Black*." *Journal of Popular Culture* 42.2 (2009): 339–62.

Watkins, Mel. *On the Real Side: A History of African American Comedy from Slavery to Chris Rock*. Chicago: Lawrence Hill Books, 1999.

Whitted, Qiana J. "How Does What's in Print Affect Comics Studies?" *Pencil Panel Page / The Hooded Utilitarian*. The Hooded Utilitarian. 24 Apr. 2014.

———. "'And the Negro thinks in hieroglyphics': Comics, Visual Metonymy, and the Spectacle of Blackness." *Journal of Graphic Novels and Comics* 5.1 (2014): 79–100.

———. "What Is an African American Comic?" *Pencil Panel Page / The Hooded Utilitarian*. The Hooded Utilitarian. 30 Jan. 2014.

Williamson, Skip. Interview with the author. 25 Oct. 2014.

Witek, Joseph. *Comics Books as History: Jack Jackson, Art Spiegelman, and Harvey Pekar*. Jackson: UP of Mississippi, 1989.

Wolff, Mia. *Catcher*. New York: Farrar Straus Giroux, 1994.

Yancy, George. *Look, a White! Philosophical Essays on Whiteness*. Philadelphia: Temple UP, 2012.

Born into This Body

Black Women's Use of Buddhism in Autobiographical Narratives

TRACY CURTIS

How Three Black Women Find Buddhism

As far back as 1992, as Bruce B. Lawrence points out, bell hooks, a practicing Buddhist, decried the fact that black Buddhists were absent from any discussion of immigrant Buddhism or American converts to Buddhism (85). In fact, black people have consistently engaged with Buddhism as dabblers, adherents, and scholars. The writers examined in this chapter—Faith Adiele, Angel Kyodo Williams, and Jan Willis—illustrate this range of connections with Buddhism in the African American community while also allowing readers to discover a unique chapter in the history of black American women's autobiography. Their explorations into Buddhism result from the aftermath of the civil rights movement. Access to education led to worldly exposure and the opportunity for travel and study that would not have been available to a woman a generation earlier. Their writing about these experiences and the resulting discoveries and beliefs, however, place them squarely within a tradition of African American women's spiritual autobiography. Unfortunately, this tradition includes deeming unnatural and detrimental to the community black women who speak of individual religious experiences.[1] Although much of the tendency toward extreme condemnation has passed, these three women still write about and analyze the same anxieties over community and its concerns. Their forays into Buddhism offer both isolation that allows them to put their concerns into perspective and the opportunity to write about often-ignored issues that are specific to African American women's lives.

American black women have encountered Buddhism as both a spiritual and a political tradition. According to Carol Cooper, "in the half-century since Buddhism re-entered American pop culture ... more and more black females—children of the civil rights movement, champions of black nationalism, feminist iconoclasts, and intellectuals—have been finding their way to Buddhist practice." Cooper goes on to refer to Dr. Martin Luther King Jr.'s nomination of Buddhist Thich Nhat Hanh for the Nobel Peace Prize and his adoption of a Hindu practice of nonviolence as some of the most prominent examples of how Eastern religions can complement black American life. Author, professor, and Buddhist practitioner Charles Johnson similarly connects King's embrace of nonviolence and Buddhism:

> In his Nobel Prize acceptance speech, Dr. Martin Luther King, Jr. said that civilization and violence are antithetical concepts. I link King with Buddhism because his statements are very close to the idea of dependant [sic] origination. He talked beautifully about how the world we live in is one of mutuality in which we are all equally dependant [sic] on each other. King embodies both social change and spiritual growth. That's what made his 14-year public ministry—from the Montgomery bus boycott until his assassination in Memphis—as a leader so important.

Because King made his religious and social philosophies explicit and public parts of his activism, the connections that he made to Eastern philosophies and spiritual leadership of movements around the world were available for individuals in the African American community to discover. Much of the detailed information about what he incorporated into his activism has faded from memory even though his image has not. This set of circumstances makes him an ideal example to present to black Americans curious about Buddhist practice.

Buddhism pushes new practitioners to examine their ways of connecting their interior lives to the external world. Such encouragement helps ease the minds of black people who may worry about indoctrination. The beginnings of Buddhist exploration can act as a self-assessment or self-examination that feels empowering. Angel Kyodo Williams sees Buddhist principles as aids in helping people become responsible for their own spiritual health ("'Revolutionary'"). Meditation teacher Ralph Steele and Shu Shin priest Joseph Jarman cite examples from their own lives. Steele used meditation alongside other forms of therapy to recover from flashbacks he suffered after serving in the Vietnam War (qtd. in Pintak). Jarman, also a military veteran, reports that his own service in the United States Army Special Forces during the late 1950s was so traumatic that it left him mute for a year, until he was given a book on Buddhist teachings by a librarian who had observed his silence. Then Jarman encountered a Buddhist priest while recovering in a Milwaukee hospital (qtd. in Pintak).

This reintroduction of Buddhism in the United States was sparked in part, as Cooper asserts, by the Beats but also by a loosening of restrictions on Asian immigration, by Martin Luther King Jr.'s public adoption of Eastern practices, by Americans' increased travel to Asia for reasons other than missionary work, and by the movements of the 1960s and 1970s that were interested in the religion and its practices as they spread throughout segments of the U.S. population. Those practitioners who remained dedicated spread news of the methods' effectiveness, either by example or by explicit recommendation. As in other cultural movements, black people participated, but as is common, their presence was often overlooked or undercounted.

The first five years of the twenty-first century saw the publication of several works by black women about their connections with varying forms of Buddhism. Faith Adiele's *Meeting Faith: The Forest Journals of a Black Buddhist Nun* (2004), Jan Willis's *Dreaming Me: An African American Woman's Spiritual Journey* (2001), and Angel Kyodo Williams's *Being Black: Zen and the Art of Living with Fearlessness and Grace* (2000) appeared at a time when the subjects black women were willing to engage publicly expanded.[2] They wrote works based less on their place among community and family and more on individual interests and goals. While this choice should not seem unusual in the wake of women's and self-actualization movements, black women's literary work has changed slowly. These books are part of a shift in the kind of subjectivity depicted in black women's autobiographical writing.

The texts of these three black women illuminate issues central to African American women's autobiography. This chapter examines Adiele's, Willis's, and Williams's works and explores the ways in which these narratives address temporary ordination, a life that culminates in both the study and the teaching of Buddhism, and in the understanding of advice for applying Zen principles to black life, respectively. I owe a great deal to Sidonie Smith and Julia Watson's *Reading Autobiography: A Guide for Interpreting Life Narratives* for assistance in crafting an explanation of what these works bring to autobiographical writing. They observe that "life narrative and its multiple genres have been foundational to the formation of Western subjects, Western cultures, and Western concepts of nation as well as to the ongoing project of exploration, colonization, imperialism, and now, globalization" (108–9).

African American women, writing autobiographical material in the early twenty-first century, are both quintessential American subjects and objectified persons in perpetual battles for an elusive combination of community and autonomy. This dual and contradictory status makes black women's writing a particularly useful indicator of the state and possibility of autobiographical utterances. The works studied here speak to the varying levels of privilege of the American abroad, to the lingering solidity of racial notions, to the failures of ideas pertaining to universal womanhood, and to the place spiritual investigation holds in the life narratives of all their intersectional identities.[3]

While these women write about Buddhism—a topic often considered outside the norm for their demographic—their narratives should be read and understood alongside other African American writing. One of the earliest forms written (or orally delivered) by people of African descent in English is the spiritual autobiography (Andrews 1). While African Americans are generally linked with the Judeo-Christian religious tradition, there is a long tradition of black writing about non-Western or hybrid forms of religion and spirituality. The earliest cited autobiographical narrative by a black woman in the Americas is a petition transcribed from the oral testimony of a formerly enslaved woman named Belinda (Douglass-Chin 1; Foster 44). In

Born into This Body 177

both versions of her petition, she called on West African Orisa, believing Christianity to be the refuge of hypocrites who used it to defend slavery (Douglass-Chin 1). Her exclamations in court, requesting salvation from the god she knew, may have been the first on North American land.[4] Though the black women who followed her immediately focused their narratives on Christianity, the nondogmatic parts of their work could be said to focus on the individual soul's importance over questions of traditional obedience (Andrews 10, 17).

The three works I study here take that concern with the individual's well-being seriously even as community concerns arise. The writers move toward a balance between caring for themselves and dealing appropriately with others. They also follow these early spiritual autobiographies in at least one other important way. As women writing about individual spiritual experience in a religion not considered properly theirs, they run the risk of exacerbating their outsider status. In his book, *Preacher Woman Sings the Blues: Autobiographies of Nineteenth-Century African American Evangelists*, Richard J. Douglass-Chin argues that during the early nineteenth century, African American women's autobiographical writing split into two paths, the sentimental traditions that obscured unpleasant truths and the blues traditions that spoke them aloud (10–11). He puts the black female preacher into the latter tradition and notes that, like the blues performer, these preachers were deemed unnatural (10–11).

This chapter considers how the introduction of Buddhism into these particular twenty-first-century narratives helps the writers address demands of conformity that weigh heavily on black women and how this particular exploration adds to an understanding of the ways in which expectation weighs on autobiographical narratives. The addition of Buddhism allows the writers to address doubts about whether American black people ever engage cultural forms stemming from outside the United States and outside Africa, and by extension whether activities considered atypical for black people are accepted from within or outside the community. The women contradict the assumption that their engagement with Buddhism results from a desire to separate from black communities, with two of the writers highlighting how the practice complements and facilitates external commitments. Although Willis's and Adiele's training takes them to Asia and Williams's early practice finds her in rural retreats, each author writes through the study and practice to address circumstances more common to black women, including physical and emotional vulnerability often compounded by achievement and the resulting opportunities that take them outside realms of safety.

Meeting Faith's central figure, Faith Adiele, is a biracial woman with a Scandinavian American mother and a Nigerian father who was raised among her mother's family in rural Washington. Her narrative focuses on when Adiele returns to Thailand a second time as part of an anthropological project while she is a Harvard student. She makes her first visit to Thailand during high school when she wins a place in the Rotary Club International Exchange Program. Although she has tested highly enough to merit her choice of assignments, she is pushed to go to Thailand in an effort to save the organization's partnership with that country. All previous participants had failed to adjust to the language, food, and culture found in Thailand. The Rotarians see her scores as proof that she is smart and hope that she is also adaptable. After learning the language and excelling in her high school year abroad, she returns to Thailand seeking both comfort and a grand anthropological study to redeem her floundering college career. During the second visit, she plans to study with Buddhist nuns but decides that ordination will help her create a more thorough project.

Jan Willis, the author of *Dreaming Me: An African American Woman's Spiritual Journey*, was among the first American scholars of Buddhism, the first African American scholar/practitioner of Buddhism, and is one of the foremost experts on Indo-Tibetan Buddhism in the country. Her book details her early childhood in Docena, Alabama, where she and her family faced pressure from the local Ku Klux Klan, her love of education and resulting scholarship to study at Cornell, and her eventual choice between remaining in the United States to work on nationalist causes and pursuing Buddhist instruction in Nepal. Willis takes readers through her initial immersion in Buddhist study and practice, discussing, among other topics, how her early experiences of racial violence and resulting low expectations affect how she approaches the Buddhist instruction she is given.

Angel Kyodo Williams's *Being Black: Zen and the Art of Living with Fearlessness and Grace* differs from the other two texts in that this narrative contains fewer traditionally autobiographical elements. Williams mentions a few scattered incidents from her life to illustrate Zen lessons. However, this work is not a life narrative. The text primarily provides instruction in Buddhist practices alongside ways one might connect them to a variety of common black experiences. Including this text in an investigation on Buddhism in black women's autobiography opens up an opportunity to analyze how limited self-disclosure and the use of the first-person plural allows readers to ease into an acceptance of African American women's engagement with Buddhism.

My approach to these texts focuses on specific autobiographical elements. The narrative, the central character, and innovations found in each text drive this inquiry. Buddhism provides a juncture among the three writers and a point of novelty, introduced into narratives plagued by expectations of the routine. For all three of these writers, the religious practice involves a change in setting. Adiele and Willis write extensively of time abroad, a context that briefly removes them from the black/white and black/black dynamic so often central to black American women's narratives. By upsetting the customary, these writers prevent their narratives from being used as metaphors for others' experiences and demand that readers examine the presented experiences closely. These innovations highlight not only the spiritual challenges common to narratives but physical experiences specific to black, or black American, women.

In at least one way, these narratives are typical; the writers discuss pioneering experiences. While many autobiographical works by African Americans have been created because the writers are the first among this ethnic group to achieve a particular position, questions of authenticity underlie many expectations surrounding these firsts. While venturing out into the wider world has been construed as brave, it is most easily read as such when the protagonist does so on behalf of family or community and returns to share any resulting benefits or wisdom. Disconnect, whether calculated or not, can be viewed as betrayal. This possibility of censure for such a departure is especially prevalent for African American women, as their departure from their expected roles destabilizes so many people's sense of security.

All the women mark their entry into Buddhist practice as a move they predict will be met with suspicion. Adiele, who reports that she fails to discuss her ordination for years afterward, remarks: "In truth, Buddhism seemed fertile with shame. It wasn't a black religion, after all. God knew my connection to black America was tenuous enough, given my mixed, African parentage, Scandinavian immigrant upbringing, and privileged college life. Spending a year developing an interior life seemed like a luxury reserved for students with trust funds and time to burn. How would indulgent endeavors uplift the race?" (27). This statement encapsulates the anxieties. Engaging in an act not perceived as black or communal has the potential to separate her from other black people. The fact that Buddhist practice demands a focus on the interior exaggerates this vulnerability. Meditation emphasizes a different relationship to community than religious practices typically associated with African Americans. The congregational and witness-oriented functions that have spread from African American Protestant churches to secular realms do not exist in the *wat* where she lives.[5] Additionally, it is significant to point out that other black Americans are not to be found in this environment. The fact that her ordination and study take place in Asia enhances the separation effect that Adiele already feels between herself and the rest of the African American community.

Adiele writes about an anxiety that conflates self-focus and selfishness. Here the luxury of a trust fund has a pejorative connotation, as does introspection. Almost as a preemptive strike against those who would criticize such a choice, she devalues her ordination because she cannot draw an immediately obvious benefit for any segment of the African American community. It makes sense that she does so because this backlash is predictable.

Spotlighting Less Common Choices in African American Women's Autobiographical Writing

For a long time, black American women writers elided differences in their autobiographical projects. For many, the bulk of the writing concerned childhood, a place where they most often shared experiences considered demographically typical. This practice reinforced expectations of sameness from both inside and outside the community, rendering significant portions of some of this writing targets of indifference at best and targets of scorn at worst. Writing about Marian Anderson's autobiography, *My Lord, What a Morning*, Nellie Y. McKay connects Anderson's writing to one of Zora Neale Hurston's texts while arguing that the persona Anderson creates must alienate some black readers: "As a narrative of a black woman in white America, *My Lord, What a Morning* is as troublesome to some as Hurston's *Dust Tracks*. Between her birth at the turn of the century, and its publication just past its midpoint, Anderson lived through momentous world events that must have seriously affected her outlook on life, but that she never mentions in *My Lord*" (102). McKay points out that Anderson's choice to remain silent about slights and discrimination violates enough expectations to become disturbing to many readers. Given the gap between *My Lord*'s publication date (1956) and the publication date of McKay's essay (1998), the ongoing nature of this upset is striking. Anderson's iconic status as a woman who maintained a dignity above that of her abusers and the symbolic resonance from the various forms of apology offered for her treatment have rendered her a black American heroine. Yet readers remain frustrated with her refusal to engage this discrimination emotionally. Instead, she focuses on her artistic journey. Although McKay's larger point is about Anderson's narrative strategy rather than the audience, I would argue that the frustration arises because what she refuses to engage is exactly where many African American readers might have common ground with her. This absence emphasizes her separation from her readers. If readers cannot forgive Marian Anderson, Adiele's anxiety about their being unable to forgive her is well placed. Among the three writers I investigate here, Adiele presents her anxiety about this rejection most prominently as she contextualizes her narrative.

Willis echoes this pattern of concern when she writes about choosing to study Buddhism. During college, she participates when black students take over the student union and finds herself attracted to black nationalist politics. At the same time, she, like Adiele, recalls being intrigued by the quiet strength displayed by Vietnamese Buddhist monks who protest the war with self-immolation. As she graduates from college, her advisor and department offer her a choice between immediate entry into graduate school and a fellowship for a year abroad. At the same time, her political experiences on the Cornell campus lead her to explore joining the Black Panther Party. After meeting with some Panthers in California, she decides to go to Nepal, claiming, "Amid the revolutionary timbre of the times, I was tossed and pushed along, it seemed inevitably, toward guns and violence. But then, just before taking the fateful step, I bolted. My whole being—mind, body, and soul—bolted" (129). Although she waivers seriously before electing to leave the country, she does not express the same reservations as Adiele. Regarding the decision to go abroad, their narratives work differently despite their ostensible similarities—in part because Willis foregrounds her radical and risky protest activities, but also because both her own expressions of certainty and historical reality help to reframe the elements of the decision that could be seen as too self-indulgent. Willis's framing, unlike Adiele's, brings the narrative back into the realm of the familiar. Although Willis's prose is that of an observer with both temporal and emotional distance from the events she recounts, she provides a setting that allows other black American readers to find themselves on familiar narrative ground and to project their own set of emotional responses onto Willis's life. Although the reading habit of self-substitution does not often lead to real comprehension of the situation presented, by encouraging readers to continue, it opens up the possibility of such understanding later.

When Willis recounts her choice to go to Nepal, she incorporates two narrative elements that lead her away from the disapproval Adiele fears. One way she manages how she is perceived is to write about all the factors she weighs when making the decision and to couch her choice as instinctive rather than intellectual. She writes: "'To thine own self be true,' the saying goes, and my sister, San, had always said, 'Trust your *first mind*'" (129). Drawing on folk wisdom and a family member momentarily removes the emphasis Willis could have placed on Buddhism, travel, and privilege. This choice in her narrative also adds an air of fate to the decision, in some ways marking her as a person who is part of a larger plan rather than someone willfully choosing to abandon a role as a supportive player in the revolution. Readers, at this point, can substitute any belief they have in fate for whatever they imagine she might express. This scene is a moment of narrative seduction.

The second significant narrative element of her text is the deliberate sequencing of specific events found in her autobiography. Her decision to go to Nepal rather than join the Panthers precedes the murder of Black Panther member Fred Hampton by only a few months. Her reporting of it as part of her narrative accomplishes important textual work in at least two ways. First, it supports the assertion that the instinctive part of her decision was correct. She is not fated to be a part of the Panthers. She is meant to live longer. Perhaps she is even blessed in making this decision to go abroad. Second, it places her in a position that seems like an extraordinarily reasonable one for a woman. She had met Hampton during her time as a student activist, noting, "his handshake was warm and firm, his smile infectious" (126). Although she would not have been with him when he was shot in his bed, she could have accompanied him or another Panther elsewhere when they were targeted. She could even have become a target herself if she continued working with the Panthers. Suddenly the option of travel to Nepal, one that she recognizes will worry her parents and by extension other African American parents, becomes so much less dangerous than what could happen in her home country.

This danger to Willis if she stays home is further emphasized by the fact that she describes a childhood filled with regular encounters with the Ku Klux Klan. Once, as a result of news being published about Willis receiving a scholarship, the Klan rides into her neighborhood looking for their family home while her father works the graveyard shift. Willis writes:

> Then, peeking through the bedroom window, no lights on inside, we saw the cars come to a stop, one by one, on the street in front of our house. My mom had already

grabbed her .22 caliber pistol. "Get on the floor; try to get under the bed," she whispered. I was glued to a corner of the window. I could not take my eyes off what I was seeing; a crowd of enrobed whites—men, women, and *children*—was amassing. (69–70)

Willis recalls that while her mother's impulse is to grab a firearm and hide the children, hers, even during childhood, is to teach the hooded people about their common humanity (70). As she returns to this memory in her text, this impulse, peace over a piece, expresses extraordinary confidence in the transformative power of reason (129, 124). Even as she mocks the Klan in her narrative to some degree, Willis carefully considers the destructive power that this group and the entire constellation of associated treatment has had on black people's lives: "None of the blacks who lived in Docena [her home town] were spared the Klan's reminders. On a fairly regular basis, there were drive-throughs and cross-burnings in the Camp. This unimaginable psychic terror crippled my self-esteem and the self-esteem of many black people. I am witness to our scars" (19). Here she chooses words such as "psychic terror," "scars," and "crippled" to illustrate the consequences so many suffered. This description links Willis with an all-too-common racial experience, even as she introduces readers to a much less common one. She recalls harassment by the Klan as an experience routine enough that black residents created jokes about Klan leadership, yet sufficiently terrorizing to have scarred multiple generations. In addition to linking her experiences to those of other black people in the United States, this passage also links her narrative to others' experiences through a common trauma that shapes her identity, the identities of her community, and those of many members of her audience (Balaev 160).

It certainly will not be lost on her readers that Willis, a scholar writing in the twenty-first century, feels herself shaped by an organization and a past that many Americans would like to relegate to the nineteenth or early twentieth century. This recollection of episodic terror comes early in the book, alongside other recurring elements of Willis's life. These include dreams of lions, neighbors remarking on her light skin and hair when she is a child, a fear of snakes, and a love of school, among others. While the dreams, the fear of snakes, and the love of school can be seen as features of her personality, her neighbors' attention to her skin color and the emphasis on the Klan's role in their community immediately mark her life as one affected early by the world outside her household. Foregrounding the Klan's presence before narrating her experiences with Buddhism helps her readers view her as a comprehensible figure even as she embarks on a novel journey.

Willis marks herself as both victim and observer of Klan terrors, meaning that while she has suffered trauma due to her interaction with this organization, she has subsequently emerged as a person strong enough to bear witness for other victims needing someone to attest to the power of the unimaginable. The latter role, necessarily filled by one who must be outside the circle of trauma, provides a service to those people from Docena who might otherwise be considered simply left behind by her. This discussion also helps shift the notion that traumatic experience is necessarily impossible to articulate.[6] This strength, which she makes obvious even as she acknowledges the effects of Klan terror, marks the idea that recovery is possible and indicates that Buddhism, even though some may consider it to be outside the realm of most African American readers' experience, might bring about the strength to view this history at a calm distance. In a sense, through her narratives of violence, she leads her readers who are familiar with such violence more gently into her discussions of Buddhism than is possible with Adiele's narrative of choice within the context of a less dire threat.

Williams substitutes belief systems and their applications for narrative in most places throughout her book. Yet she does so while giving the same care that Willis does to black American readers. Considering her advice for applying Zen Buddhist principles to African American experiences helps illuminate the point behind Willis's recollection of the Klan. At the beginning of her chapter "Fearlessness: Claiming Your Warrior Spirit," Williams offers the following observation: "Fear has been and still is one of the great plagues of people of color. For a variety of reasons, we exist in a state of constant fear" (*Zen* 166). This notion of fear echoes Willis's statements about the Klan without providing specific details that might limit the common ground to particular locations or generations. Williams continues:

> It has been said many times for many years that it is the racist-minded white people that hold black people back and keep us from moving forward. In many ways that is still very true. But it is also true that we have lived so long with so much fear deep within us that we may be unable to tell if we do not move forward because we cannot or because *we will* not. The fear that lives within us is like a dirty little secret that we carry in our pockets everywhere we go. Some of us are aware of the fear and carry it inward, sheepishly struggling to keep it to ourselves. Others are less aware and direct it outward, sometimes in the form of aggression. The stereotypical angry black man isn't just angry; he is often enveloped and drowning in fear. (*Zen* 167–68)

Williams locates this particular description of fear's corrosive effects in a chapter about the practice of fearlessness. Like Willis, Williams emphasizes common black experiences, acknowledging the effects of outside forces before pointing to the impact that a learned acceptance of constant fear might have on the black community. Her language here matters. She uses the word *sheepishly*, a term not frequently associated with black people, to undermine commonly held beliefs that hostile actions or attitudes are spurred primarily by responses to the outside world. Williams insists that readers focus on black people's internal state by giving descriptions of black fearfulness as a nearly congenital trepidation coupled with a persistent sense of shame. The dirty little secret of fear, according to Williams, does not need to be kept because so many outside the self-consciously fearful believe it to be possible.

However, Williams anticipates this passage with a set of circumstances that certainly inspire fright. The chapter begins with discussions of the continued denial of full-citizenship rights, of underemployment, and of the stereotypes associated with those conditions (*Zen* 167–68). The scenarios Williams uses are vague enough to fit some aspect of most of her readers' lives. Fear is a nearly universal experience; emphasizing the disproportionate number of fear-inducing situations to which black people might be subjected solidifies her point about fear's constancy in some lives. By looking broadly at both those who internalize their fear and those who express it through aggressive behavior, Williams covers nearly everyone. Her use of "we" and "us" leads readers who identify with these fearful types to understand her statements as sympathetic and empathetic rather than accusatory. Her introduction of the topic using common tropes allows her to advocate the practice of fearlessness not for those who want to confront individual bullies or the nodes of institutionalized racism but to return to "show[ing] affection without a sense of restriction as most of us did during childhood" (172). In some ways, this advice is buried within the chapter amid situations more common to African American narratives. The expected pairings of individual, society, environment, and oppressive persons are all present. Yet in the center, Williams advocates spontaneous demonstrations of love—advice so largely unexpected that perhaps without the familiar trappings, its potential efficacy in the lives of those she addresses would be misunderstood as doubtful.

This tactic reflects Williams's narrative strategy throughout her book. Although a distinct writer's voice and a personality are present, the autobiographical impulse is atypical, even among women's narratives that tend to emphasize the role of the community in forming and supporting the subject. The details she gives fall short of the amount necessary to formulate a standard broad narrative of individual identity. For instance, she uses *we* much more than *I*. However, as Kenneth Mostern argues, "There is no semantic reason to presume that auto-reference could not be to a group of people who form a collective subjectivity" (32).[7] She couches her particular narratives in a way that emphasizes how she could be any one of us.

Williams recounts some of her early experiences learning meditation, which mostly involve her engagement with family and community. Although Buddhist precepts do not direct her to such involvement specifically, Williams keeps the people around her in the text as a way of showing that a strong Buddhist practice does not require retreat or isolation. When she illustrates fearlessness using a specific narrative, she does so not with her own behavior but with that of her father, who is a New York City fireman. She notes his courage by recounting an exemplary incident in which she arrives home from school to see a neighboring building, a home to children and teenagers with special needs, ablaze. She wonders whether her father is involved in the effort to quell the blaze, then sees him come from the building and head in her direction as the firefighters under his command continue to fight the fire. As he reaches her, he receives a radio message that someone is still inside. He rushes in only to discover that the report was incorrect. When he emerges, he smiles. Williams takes special note of that smile. She writes:

> He doesn't do it because he's crazy or reckless or careless about his life. He doesn't do it because he is just not afraid. He has chosen to know as much as he can about the danger involved, about what makes the situation as scary as it seems to someone like you and me. Armed with that awareness, he acts with warrior-spirit and does it anyway. (*Zen* 171)

The smile takes her father beyond stoicism or a simple bravado to the reasoned bravery described by the Heart of Wisdom Sutra that serves as the epigraph for this chapter: "With no obstacles in the mind, no obstacles therefore no fear" [*sic*] (*Zen* 166). Here she focuses on her father, a man with a well-regarded, physical, and often desired job, and she prevents her readers from interpreting this scene as a possibly repellant example of New Age expression. Individuals sometimes associate the imprecise, umbrella term *New Age* with weakness and impracticality. Williams portrays her father as loving his job in a way that allows him to work with pleasure and give to others without regard for reward or personal danger. He operates well in that position because his knowledge has allowed him to forego fear. As Michel Clasquin-Johnson writes, "Buddhism is a philosophy, in the oldest and truest sense of the word as 'love of wisdom.'" The poise his wisdom gives him can be a beacon to the community that Williams wants to reach. Her father is a member of a profession associated not only with bravery, public service, and a stable income but also, for black people, with a difficult fight for job access.

Williams's deflection of fearlessness from herself to her father exemplifies a narrative humility that draws readers into both her exercise of a Buddhist precept and this brief glimpse of her childhood. In this way, she introduces the ability to quell fear through learning. She integrates Buddhist teachings and principles seamlessly.[8] One of the most notable responses to her work is a kind of reciprocal gesture, a hip-hop compilation, also called *Being Black*. The 2003 compact disc shares the book's artwork in its U.S. release and includes artists such as Bahamadia, Blackalicious, DJ Jazzy Jeff, Jurassic 5, and Mystic, among others. Ursula Rucker reads selections from the book over beats as interludes between songs. In many ways, Willliams sets herself up for such a response. The title of the disc printed in white letters on a largely black cover refers to a state of being rather than to her individual identity directly. The Japanese characters, printed in shiny black over matte black, become visible only as one holds the book closely. She invokes Dr. Martin Luther King Jr. on the first page of the first chapter and recalls Angela Bassett as Tina Turner chanting in the film version of *What's Love Got to Do with It?* (*Zen* 1, 5). Both King and Turner embraced Eastern philosophies and practices to some degree. King used those practices to help shape his nonviolent strategy and to teach people internal coping mechanisms, while Turner adopted Buddhism as she was escaping her abusive marriage. Many readers might have seen the movie, which was the first indication many had that Turner had begun meditation and chanting. The quotation Williams uses as her book epigraph complements both the aggregate of King's messages and the lessons we might take from the Tina Turner biopic:

> Do not believe in anything simply because you have heard it. Do not believe in anything simply because it is spoken and rumored by many. Do not believe in anything simply because it is found written in your religious books. Do not believe in anything merely on the authority of your teachers and elders. Do not believe in traditions because they have been handed down for many generations. But after observation and analysis, when you find that anything agrees with reason and is conducive to the good and benefit of one and all, then accept it and live up to it. (*Zen*)

Although her work is the most didactic of the three considered here, Williams sets her text up to be the most easily accepted work by the African American audience she wants to address. She presents an epigraph that is perfect for a skeptical member of the hip-hop generation.

With this beginning, readers are prepared to receive her presentation of basic Buddhist ideas because they are not asked to accept new practices without proof that they are good, not only for them as individuals but also for the wider community. In the liner notes for the compilation, Williams declares that although she has done nothing to prompt the creation of the compact disc, it represents a wish of hers because she wants to reach people within the African American community who do not necessarily read much and because she is a hip-hop fan. Anticipating questions around the connection between hip-hop and Zen, and perhaps by extension, those about blackness and Zen, Williams alludes to the title of the film on Tina Turner's life. In a statement from November 2002 that appears on the CD cover, Williams writes, "What's hip-hop got to do with Zen? If you know your Zen, you know that it has everything to do with it. At Zen's core is Dharma: the ancient, universal teaching of realizing Truth that brings you to your own freedom. Not someone else's truth or freedom, but your own" (*A Musical*). This approach allays possible suspicion by setting her up as an insider both to the familiar world of hip-hop and the unfamiliar world of Zen Buddhism.

This notion of one's own truth helps Williams present Zen as a tool to assist community members in meeting their own goals rather than as a didactic system meant to order and direct their lives. This presentation invites readers into Williams's reality and makes it easier for her to write about incidents in her life alongside basic versions of the principles to showcase the practices. She exposes her connection to Buddhism as a way to guarantee for readers that she only wants to show how Zen practice can work for them and those around them. Key to her approach is the idea, both lived and advocated by Williams, that Zen need not be practiced in isolation. Her account of one of her earlier spiritual choices echoes a number of her recollections of her practice. Here and in those early remembrances, she highlights the differences from those around her. While on retreat, she hears a teacher call the most devoted monks home-leavers. Reeling from her discomfort with the fact that she was becoming a person who abandoned home and relationship responsibilities for isolated study and practice, she writes, "Spirituality and responsible living are not objects that can be found somewhere outside yourself. . . . As long as you're looking toward anything but yourself, you'll always be headed in the wrong direction" (*Zen* 32). Williams recognizes a truth in that statement; she need not change her context or her company to begin a Zen-based life. Her immediate decision to shift her practice to focus on finding enlightenment without leaving her home marks her as different from the other practitioners on the retreat but ultimately more like the African American community, those with jobs, families, and friends, whom she wishes to reach in her autobiography.

This approach and her insistence on a nearly constant reference to black Americans as a group rather than to her individual experience help illustrate how this engagement with Buddhism allows for unexpected character development. The figure who meditates is the same one who cares for family members and has to shop for groceries. The personal decisions she recalls, though they mirror ones that might be advocated by more-traditional Christians, Muslims, teachers, and others who work or volunteer for improving the community, become steps in her personal growth rather than markers of her willingness to sacrifice herself for others. This inclusion of community helps her to show Buddhism as something that does not threaten personal ties.

In a number of ways, her emphasis on principle over story separates her book from Adiele's and Willis's narratives. While the "Angel Kyodo Williams" she creates on the page often recedes from the text, Adiele's and Willis's protagonists are left more individually vulnerable, Adiele's especially so. First, because both leave the country to study, they find themselves in relative isolation. But it must be noted here that each marks several differences from her community, which I outline below, that precede the decisions to live abroad for a time and to practice Buddhism. Interestingly enough, the physical isolation from other African Americans and the travel to Asia seem to be both the cause and the effect of a vulnerability based on race and gender that each woman recalls as being present in her life long before the possibility of Buddhist practice.

Reflections on Isolation and Danger: Or, What the Women Share with Other Black Women

The differences between Adiele's and Willis's path toward Buddhism and Williams's is evident in the information that emerges when each describes her childhood. While we encounter no obvious statement of such from Williams, both Adiele and Willis mark themselves as hypervisible during childhood. Adiele describes a beginning that includes being the only black applicant for her area's Rotary Club International Exchange Program and being expected to field questions about whether she could handle expectations outside the country that *American* equals *white* (14–15). While Willis does not have to contend with being the only black child most people around her will ever see, she does have to cope with being teased because of her light skin as well as with hearing the suspicion of infidelity cast upon her mother in the time before her father's family and the neighbors meet her light-skinned maternal grandfather and before she starts to resemble her father (6–7, 10).

Both women write extensively about learning to compare themselves to white girls at early ages. For Willis, this comparison comes from the double sting of being on the receiving end of a slur, then having to sit through her father's attempt to inoculate her retroactively against such attacks. The assault comes from a child, one less powerful than Willis in every way except racially. The offending child is younger, smaller, dirty, and barefoot. After Willis cries while reporting what happened, her father talks to her and her sister about racial hierarchy: "Now it seems that you girls and the little white girl are different, doesn't it? . . . Well, she's not *any* different, not any *better* than you two" (54). Describing the talk as devastating and ineffective, Willis argues for childrearing practices focused on daily affirmations of children's worth that are strong enough to prepare them for the inevitable attacks. On this point, Willis writes, "I would rather children be told every day, from the time they can understand the language, how special, bright, talented, and all-around wonderful they are" (55). She places this statement adjacent to her aforementioned talking-to by her father. The moment interrupts the chronology of the narrative yet fits thematically. By the time she concludes that children need daily affirmation, she has felt that and more from Lama Yeshe. Because this acceptance happens concurrently with her study, it temporarily supplants the acceptance from her father for which she yearns. Thus, her study provides her with a personal buffer on the way to higher self-regard and a path to maintain it without external affirmation.

Adiele's discussion of her difference from the white girls and women around her comes in multiple, battering waves. She writes of attempting Farrah Fawcett's hairstyle in junior high school and of other efforts at being more like her schoolmates (109). Yet none of this is more striking than the declared—and relatively late—realization that she is not someone thought worthy of protection. When she encounters students from Minnesota's St. Olaf College, a school offering an exchange program in Thailand, one she and her friends consider relatively insular and lax, she associates St. Olaf students with girls from the Christian high school in her Washington hometown. This high school's "primary function seemed to be the protection of the fair-haired daughters of the Dutch dairy owners and German cattle barons. What they required protection from was vague and varied, ranging from crazy evolution talk to the smoldering attentions of the sons of Mexican field hands" (105–6). Her tone implies contempt for the girls and their families' prejudices. She notes that the families push their boys toward careers that take them into the wider world while they also work to contain the girls. But her response to the girls' separation from the sons of the Mexican field hands must be read as much more complicated. The tone derides her neighbors' implied biases. Yet, given the context, Adiele seems to be expressing wonder at girls considered so precious that they are guarded against advances, even before more substantive encounters can occur. She describes that memory of the sequestered girls as coming to her like an LSD flashback (105). The subsequent stream-of-consciousness series of connections exposes a dilemma persistent in twentieth- and twenty-first-century black women's autobiography. The women are rarely seen accurately; invisibility, hypervisibility, and the perception of invulnerability dog them. Reflective practices are often occasions for recalling particular experiences of these states.

Adiele's narrative moves from a flashback of her life in her town to another flashback inspired by the St. Olafers' disappearance in a "flash of blonde." During Adiele's first class trip to Mexico, the students and their guardian go to a nightclub. Once again, Adiele is the only black person present. At the club, Adiele realizes all at once that the Mexican boys have partnered with all the American girls except her, leaving her alone with their chaperone, who seems to feel sorry for her. This experience is followed by another one on the same trip in which a man molests her on the subway, "leaving a circle of liquid, cold and white, soaking through [her] pants and causing her to cry in a knot of stunned American girls" (112). Notable here are how Adiele is gendered differently from her classmates because of race, how none of the white girls recognize that they benefit from being deemed worthy of protection, desire, and respect, and how they automatically tend to assume themselves—usually correctly—as safe. She recalls that the desirability she was learning at sixteen was that of "someone you take from behind standing up, not caring who sees, like a slave" (112). Her use of the term *slave* emphasizes that although her status as the daughter of a Scandinavian American mother and a Nigerian father does not give her a bloodline connection to chattel slavery in the United States, her experience growing up in the country binds her to its legacy nonetheless.

This assessment of her worth as measured through the actions of an abusive stranger follows the disregard in the nightclub. Then the narrative cycle revolving around invisibility, hypervisibility, and vulnerability begins again. On the very next page, she recounts that while ordained and living in the *wat*, she learns that Cathy, one of the St. Olafers who has also come to the *wat*, had been dating an appealing Thai man, a political intellectual, a principled artist, and a kind revolutionary; she is heartbroken at their separation (113). The factors Adiele imagined would matter for dating in Thailand, including her own successful efforts at understanding Thai culture and speaking the language, never garner her a single date (113). In the book, narratives of these realizations are surrounded by Adiele's journal entries, which appear in the margins. In one incident, the atmosphere during her seclusion seems to mirror the separation she feels from the outside world. She writes that as two monks pass her, they hug their side of the path, going single file (111). These men treat her as a potential contamination of their purity. This action parallels her conclusion that the women who orchestrate their practice in the *wat* may have discarded the ends for the means, indicating that she considers only perfect practice rather than insights or states of being that may result. Early in her ordination, Adiele clearly relishes the end points more, in part because disappointing endings have come to occupy her thoughts.

The temporary isolation from the outside world allows Adiele to reflect on what her South Asian experience has been outside of her mastery of the Thai language and the completion of an extraordinary academic project. Reflecting on a particular episode from her trip preparations, she discloses how much worse were the experiences she has had beyond simple datelessness. Keeping in mind that the anecdotes in this and the preceding paragraphs are placed within a few pages of each other in Adiele's text, note the next episode she recounts. In preparation for this trip, she attends a standard workshop on safety abroad in which she finds herself watching a tall blonde at the front of the room refusing to be seduced (114). The instructor stages scenarios so that the students who volunteer can work through potential responses with help from those in the audience. Adiele recognizes one scenario involving a long motorcycle ride to the countryside and declarations of love because during her first trip to Thailand, it happens to her. She describes her panic during that exercise, remembering, "The basement room was hot, cold, hot again, and I had to remind myself that I was in Madison, Wisconsin, that I was in my twenties, no longer seventeen, that I hadn't known, hadn't known, hadn't known" (115). After she entertains this thought, the narration shifts immediately to the incident in her life that matches the staged scenario. Adiele remembers being given alcohol, people around her and the man who assaults her disappearing, bewilderment that she was not, in fact, being taken home.

Much of Adiele's description of that classroom scene bears repeating in detail as it speaks to her second understanding of the incident, paving the way for a look here at the third. The role-playing mirrors her earlier Thailand experience, thus forcing her to reexamine her life's events, her treatment at the hands of others, and the way she sees herself.

> What I had excused to myself as a passion, an exotic first time, turned out to be something else entirely, so trite it was in the manual, word for word. Which was worse—getting fucked or learning that you've been fucked?
> "Are you okay?" Bob [the instructor] asked, and I couldn't even pretend.
> "That happened to me," I whispered, still mesmerized by the girl at the front of the room, who was insisting on being driven back to town. So easy for her! "Everything, down to the last word."
> "Whew!" Bob shook his head, looking sympathetic. "How did you get out of it?"
> For the first time, I looked away from the tableau unfolding before me and stared at him, stunned again, this time by his assumption. Perhaps it was having to admit you were fucked that's worse, having to become the victim. (115–16)

In a sense, there are three iterations of the textbook seduction that Adiele is unwilling to call a rape. The first, implied and dimly recollected, is that of a seventeen-year-old crafting a self-protective narrative. The story she tells herself fits her aspirations and the image of herself as an invulnerable girl with a bright future. But her placement of it here, amid tales of sleights and abuses, renders it suspect immediately. The second iteration, when placed in the context of other treatment she receives during her youth, rings more true. Her availability and lack of protection are taken for granted. She finds herself alongside people more secure than she. They offer bewildered sympathy. She feels overexposed, angry, and humiliated.

But in this last case, the classroom setting means that even while she begins processing this new understanding of her life's events, she finds herself attending to others' responses. The skit goes on through her initial upset. The questions she asks herself before reaching the conclusion that the public admission is the worst part of the entire ordeal focus mostly on other people. Even the realization one might think of as her own is prompted by the classroom exercise. Although she does not mark this set of revelations as coming from meditation, the relative isolation of the *wat* enables her to assemble this assessment of her experiences to that point. Adiele calls herself a poor meditator, one hard-pressed to ignore physical sensations and balance intrusive thoughts; however, she manages to build up to fifteen hours a day of various static and dynamic meditations (152). She makes the most of her beginning stages of meditation, producing a basic understanding of part of her history that will allow her to move forward postordination. In many ways, the path to understanding provided by the connection episodes in Adiele's "American Girls" chapter is emblematic of the potential that the introduction of Buddhist practice into an autobiographical narrative has to spark a character's reshaping. Placing these incidents together in a single chapter, preceded by an excerpt from Willis's book as an epigraph, recasts the central figure midnarrative while maintaining her connection to common black American women's experiences. In the passage that Adiele excerpts, Willis laments that she was initially unable to admit to her Buddhism teacher that slavery and racism have marked and damaged her. Willis writes, "I suffered. . . . I had come seeking help in coping with feelings of inadequacy and shame" (105). Because Willis writes of Buddhist practice as essential to her healing process, Adiele's use of it at the beginning of her chapter implies both deep pain and a possibility of restoration.

Adiele notes that her vulnerability in the classroom setting shocks both her peers and the experienced instructor and also seems to shock her. Defenselessness is contrary to the image she has built for herself and contrary to the images of strength, invulnerability, and toughness that seem to be so broadly applied to black American women. Her stories address both her vulnerability and the inability of others to see it. In terms of an autobiographical narrative centered on a Buddhist ordination, Adiele's juxtaposition of these incidents matters a great deal. She writes, "Buddhism knows. Open your mouth and start the cycle of *dukkha*, unfulfilled craving that leads to life's dissatisfaction" (134). The incidents she recounts indicate a cycle of thwarted desire and dissatisfaction. In her early stages as a meditator, the elements of the cycle that are particularly hers become clearer.

Regarding both her friend Cathy's dating in Thailand and the volunteer student's ability to escape the predatory man in the skit, Adiele asks a question that the placement of Buddhism within these books helps to answer: whether such ease in the world, such safety, can really be so simple. The answer to that question seems to be an elaborate version of "it depends." It is simple for Cathy; she arrives with the St. Olafers in an aura of solicitous care (113). She also has Adiele's assistance when she moves into the *wat* as a layperson (122). During no point in the narrative is it simple for Adiele, who suffers in part due to an image of black women that has been cultivated and appropriated worldwide. It seems that the men she encounters have no qualms or fear of retribution for their attacks on her. Patricia Hill Collins argues convincingly that American images of sexual violence and exploitation, no matter the race of the woman depicted, stem from the ways that black women's bodies were displayed during the antebellum era (138).

Yet in many people's minds, black women remain prototypes for such images, ones not projected easily into other roles. Men in Mexico and Thailand fail to see Adiele as someone with rights whom they must respect; she certainly does not merit courtship in their eyes. Cathy, on the other hand, operates with a whiteness that acts as privilege and protection without which she might become the object of property as black women did (C. Harris 1721). Willis and Williams, the more experienced practitioners, offer paths toward the ease Adiele seeks. As Willis looks back on her childhood, she focuses largely on prophylactic applications of Buddhist principles that could have prevented or alleviated some of her early pain. Williams offers teachings and practices that could play a part in palliative care. For example, she names "lovingkindness" (*Zen* 145) as a way to approach not only other people but also oneself. Adiele, on the other hand, gives us a figure at a crossroads, using dislocation, isolation, and meditation to form an understanding of her identity that may afford her ease someday. She shows details of the pain that initially arises from mediation, highlighting a physical vulnerability also documented in the other two books.

Willis recalls being forbidden as a child from rolling down the car windows and having her mother respond to her question about the command with "because mean white men like to throw acid in little black children's eyes" (57). This single line encapsulates the constant, mundane discomfort of a southern child unable to enjoy the breeze during the pre-air-conditioning era. But it also indicates the constant vigilance that matches the regular attacks and the decisions of parents who give their children the worst possible expectations of the world out of a desire to protect them. Following this memory, Willis writes of white men breaking a black boy's arm at a birthday party while he screams on his own porch with his parents and neighbors powerless to help him (68–69). These circumstances illustrate what could have happened to Willis and perhaps what she could have become had her responses to her circumstances differed.

In her chapter on self-acceptance, Williams recalls being repeatedly molested by an employee of the apartment building where she lives, then carrying guilt because she does not stop it from happening:

> In what now seems like a bizarre turn of events in a fitful dream, he was close, pressing me up against the cold, dank basement wall.... As an adult, I can still feel the loneliness and abandonment that had become a part of my life once my father had my new stepmother, sister, and new baby brother to give attention to and he and I were no longer as close as we had been.... But all that time I carried with me a deep sense of guilt, because I'd allowed those meetings to take place even though I knew I didn't want to be there. (*Zen* 149)

Her victimization and the guilt she carries about it go unnoticed even though she is only ten years old when the molestation occurs. No one protects her. Williams reports that she represses those memories of the incidents for years until they resurface again during meditation. She had been so successful in obliterating them from her conscious mind that when scenes arise during meditation, she does not initially recognize the experiences as her own. Eventually, she decides to stop avoiding the images of the molestation that arise during her meditation. The practice allows her to watch the scenes unfold without feeling that she is reliving them. She writes, "Safe from the accusations and judgment, the young girl that I had been stepped out of the shadows and shared her fear and confusion with me" (150). This step provides a basis for self-forgiveness that a person reluctant to share such information can begin on her own.

Each writer's use of meditation and retreat shows her move through pain into understanding. The isolated self-focus enabled by the time in solitary practice momentarily disallows conflict with others and prevents all of these writers' immediate responses from being about what others might think of them. Blame and confrontation cannot happen. The woman has temporary safety from disempowerment, overburdening, or further attack. With this hiatus, life stories can fall out of the realm of trauma into that of normal memory. The women's history thus has less potential to function as an intrusive symptom.[9] Hopefully, an understanding of the women at the center of these life narratives revises depictions that flatter their circumstances to suit readers' needs and allows these women to be seen in their full complexity.

NOTES

An earlier version of this chapter was published as "Born into This Body: Black Women's Use of Buddhism in Autobiographical Narratives," *a/b: Auto/Biography Studies* 27.1 (2012): 183–210. © 2012 The Autobiography Society. Reprinted by permission.

1. For a discussion of the assertion that early black women writers of spiritual autobiography were unnatural, see Douglass-Chin.

2. The subtitle of Adiele's book was changed for the first paperback edition to *An Inward Odyssey*. The subtitle of Willis's book was changed to *Black, Baptist, and Buddhist—One Woman's Spiritual Journey* for the paperback edition. Both this book and Adiele's text also included photographs of the writers in editions published after the hardcover.

3. For references to the exploration of differences among women, see Smith and Watson.

4. Consult S. Harris (69–79) and Pitcher for additional information on Belinda's petition.

5. *Wat* is the Thai word for the site where the ordained reside and one of a few Thai words that Adiele uses instead of an English translation.

6. For further discussion of theories around trauma and representation, see Balaev.

7. Mostern makes this point in connection to a larger one when *I* can be taken to represent a collective.

8. During Williams's stop at Eso Won, a Los Angeles bookstore that carries products relevant to African Americans, the capacity crowd discussed the principles, bought books enthusiastically, and waited in line for signatures in an event that lasted more than an hour and a half. This reception highlights the point that Williams effectively incorporates Buddhism into her texts without isolating or distancing herself from the African American community.

9. For additional commentary on traumatic response as a symptom of history, see Caruth.

WORKS CITED

Adiele, Faith. *Meeting Faith: The Forest Journals of a Black Buddhist Nun*. New York: Norton, 2004.

Andrews, William L. Introduction. *Sisters of the Spirit: Three Black Women's Autobiographies of the Nineteenth Century*. Ed. William L. Andrews. Bloomington: Indiana UP, 1986. 1–22.

Balaev, Michelle. "Trends in Literary Trauma Theory." *Mosaic* 41.2 (2008): 149–65.

Caruth, Cathy, ed. *Trauma: Explorations in Memory*. Baltimore: Johns Hopkins UP, 1995.

Clasquin-Johnson, Michel. *Common or Garden Dharma: Essays in Contemporary Buddhism*. Vol. 1. Smashwords.com, 2012. Kindle edition.

Collins, Patricia Hill. *Black Feminist Thought: Knowledge, Consciousness, and the Politics of Empowerment*. 2nd ed. New York: Routledge, 2008.

Cooper, Carol. "Guess Who's Coming to Dharma: Black Women Embrace Western Buddhism." *Village Voice* 3 July 2001: n. pag. *CarolCooper.org*. 2001.

Douglass-Chin, Richard J. *Preacher Woman Sings the Blues: The Autobiographies of Nineteenth-Century African American Evangelists*. Columbia: U of Missouri P, 2001.

Foster, Frances Smith. *Written by Herself: Literary Production by African American Women, 1746–1892*. Bloomington: Indiana UP, 1993.

Harris, Cheryl I. "Whiteness as Property." *Harvard Law Review* 106.8 (1993): 1701–791.

Harris, Sharon M. *Executing Race: Early American Women's Narratives of Race, Society, and the Law*. Columbus: Ohio State UP, 2005.

Johnson, Charles. "Buddhism Is the Most Radical and Civilized Choice." Interview by John Malkin. *Shambhala Sun*, 2008: n. pag.

Lawrence, Bruce B. *New Faiths, Old Fears: Muslims and Other Asian Immigrants in American Religious Life*. New York: Columbia UP, 2002.

McKay, Nellie Y. "The Narrative Self: Race, Politics, and Culture in Black American Women's Autobiography." *Women, Autobiography, Theory: A Reader*. Ed. Sidonie Smith and Julia Watson. Madison: U of Wisconsin P, 1998. 96–107.

Mostern, Kenneth. *Autobiography and Black Identity Politics: Racialization in Twentieth-Century America*. Cambridge: Cambridge UP, 1999.

Pintak, Lawrence. "'Something Has to Change': Blacks in American Buddhism." *Shambhala Sun*, 2008: n. pag.
Pitcher, E. W. "A 'Complaint' against 'The Petition' of Belinda, an African Slave." *Early American Literature* 31.2 (1996): 200–203.
Smith, Sidonie, and Julia Watson. *Reading Autobiography: A Guide for Interpreting Life Narratives*. 2nd ed. Minneapolis: U of Minnesota P, 2010.
Williams, Angel Kyodo. *Being Black: A Musical Compilation Inspired by the Angel Kyodo Williams Classic*. Waxploitation, 2003.
———. *Being Black: Zen and the Art of Living with Fearlessness and Grace*. New York: Viking Compass, 2000.
———. "'A Revolutionary Practice': Angel Kyodo Williams, Author of 'Being Black,' Talks about Meditation, Racism, and the True Nature of American Buddhism." Interview by Jenny Kinscy. *Beliefnet*, n.d.
Willis, Jan. *Dreaming Me: An African American Woman's Spiritual Journey*. New York: Riverhead, 2001.

From Blog to Books

Angela Nissel, Authorship, and the Digital Public Sphere

LINDA FURGERSON SELZER

In *The Structural Transformation of the Public Sphere*, Jürgen Habermas focuses attention on the concept of the public sphere by arguing that the print culture of the Enlightenment mediated between the public and the state, providing a means through which the public's voice could be heard by the state's administrative powers. He thus conceived of the public sphere as a space that enables democracy by facilitating an exchange between the state and face-to-face deliberations among citizens. Habermas also pointed out, however, that in late modernity the public sphere was in danger of being manipulated by state power such that it became proscriptive rather than deliberative. The tension between these alternative readings of the possibilities and dangers of the public sphere energizes much contemporary work on the challenges posed by the more recent turn from a print to an electronically mediated public sphere: does the rise of digital technology and new media create new spaces for democratic deliberation and creative self-expression or more extensive structures for proscriptive power and commercialization? What is the impact of such changes on the production of literature? In particular, what challenges and opportunities are created by the digitalization of the public sphere for African Americans writers, for whom literature—and especially autobiography—has long served as both an artistic medium and an important means to redefine their social status?

    Black Americans, of course, were always aware that the public sphere was more complicated than Habermas's romanticized description of Enlightenment deliberations might suggest. Living under social institutions of slavery and segregation, African Americans were intimately acquainted with the cultural and legal exclusivity of the public sphere. In reaction, they created alternative public spheres more responsive to their needs, from hush harbors to segregated churches to an oppositional black press to hip-hop clubs. Alternative public spheres such as these comprise an essential feature of African American life. At the same time, black activism in the "mainstream" public sphere has been a feature of the country's history—from the moment Africans were first forced to experience radically different lives on the continent, to African Americans' active participation in abolitionism in the nineteenth century (in which black autobiography played an important role), to the successes of the mid-twentieth century's civil rights movement, one well recognized for its effective mobilization of mainstream communications. But the success of black people at integrating mainstream media has led ironically to a growing sense that such integration has come at a price: the late twentieth century was marked by the failure of a number of long-standing black presses and journals and thereby by the diminishment, some argue, of an alternative black public sphere. As Adolph Reed comments, "The demise of *Black World* and atrophy of *The Black Scholar* both fuel and reflect the shriveling of an autonomous domain for black debate" (34).

Just as a number of articles were lamenting the collapse of a separate black public sphere, however, digital technologies were in the process of creating public spaces with radically new dimensions. A public sphere in the sense of a space for face-to-face negotiations as described by Habermas was being joined by—or, some feared, was being *replaced* by—electronically mediated social networking sites. Reactions to such changes, especially as they relate to the interests of black Americans, have been deeply ambivalent. On the one hand, cultural critics such as Mark Anthony Neal argue that digitized spaces provide new alternative black public spheres—if virtual ones. In *What the Music Said: Black Popular Music and Black Popular Culture*, Neal argues specifically that the digitalization of public space may offer a means for fostering black community "within a nontraditional public sphere, much the way barbershops did a century ago" (166). The burgeoning number of networking sites designed with African Americans in mind—on subjects ranging from finance to shopping to history to dating—seems to support Neal's contention. (Such sites are so numerous that one now finds online directories to electronic sites and suggestions for how to choose the best networking sites for African Americans.)[1]

On the other hand, some observers are highly suspicious of the opportunities for community and creativity that digital space seems to offer. Some commentators point out that the explosion of the Internet in the 1990s was tied to commercial designs that can quickly co-opt new media's creative energies. In "Exer(or)cising Power: Black Bodies in the Black Public Sphere," Paul Gilroy laments "the decay of . . . precious oppositional public institutions and the growth . . . of novel patterns in which counter-culture becomes something that is consumed rather than simply used" (22). The digitalization of book publishing deepens this ambivalence by offering opportunities for new forms of aesthetic experience at the same time that it threatens to change the relationship between authors, publishers, and readers in unforeseen ways. Does digitalization signify the "death of the book," or does it promise the democratization of publishing and an expansion of writers' creative possibilities?

The life writing and publishing history of Angela Nissel are uniquely positioned to provide insights into the ways in which the opportunities for fashioning a self—both in prose and in life—are being altered by the new digitized public sphere. By writing about her personal experience in a blog, Nissel gained access both to the traditional publishing establishment and to other media, eventually leading to her current position as a Hollywood screenwriter and producer. During her senior year at the University of Pennsylvania, Nissel began to write a blog about the tribulations of being a broke college student. Started in 1997, Nissel's blog appeared only three years after what is widely considered to be the first weblog.[2] After Nissel graduated from Penn in 1998 with a degree in medical anthropology, the blog continued to circulate informally via readers' e-mails and eventually made its way to an editor who contacted Nissel about the possibility of turning the blog into a book. *The Broke Diaries* was published in 2001 by Villard, an imprint of Random House. Nissel's distinctive sense of humor eventually gained her the attention of Hollywood producers. As I will discuss in more detail below, she became first a staff writer and later a producer for the television show *Scrubs*. In 2006 Nissel published a more serious (but still humorous) autobiography that focused specifically on her experiences growing up as the daughter of a black mother and a white father. *Mixed: My Life in Black and White* was published simultaneously in paperback and electronic format. The trajectory of Nissel's career—from hard-up college student and electronic blogger to successful Hollywood screenwriter and producer—provides a rather stunning example of the manner in which authorship in the twenty-first century's digitized public sphere is being influenced by the rapidly increasingly interpenetration of "new media" and "old publishing."

An analysis of the book Nissel created from her blog and the autobiography she later published demonstrates the manner in which new media both facilitated Nissel's success and influenced her life writing. Primarily what one might classify as a popular writer, Nissel enthusiastically moves across various new media and traditional genres and technologies, something like the line-drawn, curly-haired avatar of herself, who moves comfortably from promotional websites to appearances on the printed pages of her first book. With precursors in the diary, letters, autobiography, and confessional writing, the blog from its inception has been a notably hybrid form. Since its arrival in the mid-1990s, blogging has expanded to include political commentary, reviews, advertising, and travel writing, among other subjects, and to feature sound, art, and video. The origin of the term *blogs* is often attributed to the "online diary" or weblog, shortened to blog. Nissel's blog book pays tribute to this heritage by including the word *Diaries* in her title and by her attribution of the book's origins to the diary that she kept during college on "a personal website" (*Broke* 212). Nissel's comment underscores the fact that the electronic diary is a hybrid genre in another sense as well, since unlike private diaries, blogs must be considered a form of self-publishing. Originally appearing on a "personal" website that was also public, Nissel's electronic entries occupy a space that complicates traditional divisions between private and public spheres.

Immediately available for public reading, the blog is not as public as traditionally published autobiographies that are disseminated through the well-established collective processes of reviewing, editing, and marketing. One collective feature of blogs, however, is that they invite online responses from readers. Although personal blogs have the potential for wide distribution—and even the potential for a *wider* distribution than the traditionally produced autobiography—their readership, in the majority of cases, grows slowly. So although blogs are published immediately for any reader surfing the net to discover, they in fact often debut to a small audience. Nissel's own blogs were originally read by a small circle of friends. As with much online writing, blogs often exhibit the features of spontaneous rather than carefully edited writing: sentence structure and diction may be less conventional and more conversational, paragraph development less logical and more stream of consciousness. Or, as Biz Stone makes clear, "blogging is the Wild West of publishing—a place where everyone gets unlimited ammo as long as they have something to say" (68). Correctness is of less concern than the immediacy of expression. These elements of the genre are reflected in Nissel's own description of the blog that inspired *The Broke Diaries* as a series of "typo-filled entries" (*Broke* 212). The blog's electronic origins also influence its form, in that blogs usually follow *reverse* chronological order, beginning with the current entry and moving backward in time as readers scroll down through previous entries.

As is well recognized in contemporary criticism, traditional autobiographies do not simply present the facts of a particular life but fictionalize those facts in the process of creating a compelling narrative. The contemporary "memoir" claims even broader latitude for artistically refashioning one's materials. In the "Author's Note" that precedes the first entry in *The Broke Diaries*, Nissel specifically addresses the relationship of fact and fiction in her work:

> The characters in the book are real, but it bears mentioning that I have used pseudonyms for a number of them in order to protect their privacy, and in a few cases I have gone a step further by altering their descriptions just to cover my ass even more. Though this is a work of nonfiction, I have taken certain storytelling liberties, particularly having to do with the timing of events. Where the narrative strays from strict nonfiction, my intention has been to remain faithful to the characters and to the essential drift of events as they really happened. (vii)

By self-consciously linking autobiographical facts to "storytelling liberties" and by insisting that whenever she strays from "strict nonfiction" she does so in the service of better capturing the "essential drift" of events, Nissel lays claim both to the authority of her own experience and to authorial control of her materials. Her reference to revising the "timing of events" is especially significant, given that *The Broke Diaries* undoes the reversal of the chronology of her blog by narrating the events in chronological order, with entries dated from 7 October to 27 July. Although the year is not stated (perhaps in order to give the book a longer shelf life), the later entries focus on Nissel's graduation from the University of Pennsylvania at the cusp of the millennium.

As she fictionalizes her experience, Nissel also draws freely on several other literary genres—including autobiography, the picaresque, and self-help literature—as well as other popular forms, and especially on performance genres such as stand-up comedy and open-mic poetry. The subtitle of her blog book, *The Completely True and Hilarious Misadventures of a Good Girl Gone Broke*, identifies the work as a comedy, a point reinforced by the endorsement from Chris Rock that appears on the cover and links the book to black performance comedy traditions. The subtitle also intentionally recalls the picaresque and confessional traditions of "the misadventures" of a good girl "turned bad." Indeed, somewhat reminiscent of *Moll Flanders*, Nissel's book narrates in episodic fashion the petty "crimes" she commits in order to make it through an expensive Ivy League college as a broke African American student, focusing on "the scandalous things she does to make ends meet" (*Broke* ix). The narrator's "crimes" range from pretending to be a graduate assistant in order to "score" free textbooks to dating a chicken farmer simply to have access to free food. Beginning with descriptions of her being so broke that she schemes to get free food and ending with her successful landing of a job postgraduation, *The Broke Diaries* also clearly recalls the self-help tradition of American letters in general and the category of African American tales about "getting ovuh" in particular.

The introduction to the book establishes the first-person narrator as "Ang," a nickname for Nissel that places the author and reader not simply on a first-name basis but on one even more intimate. Not surprisingly, the book is written in the informal, personal style and confessional voice of many blogs. Ang freely mixes levels of diction, jumping from the vernacular to more formal expressions (including the Latinate), as she does in the first entry when she describes herself both as "jonesing" for a textbook and as being in a state of "broke bibliomania" (4, 5). The structure of the book is episodic, with separate diary entries introducing a particular situation that Ang confronts as a result of being broke (although some situations are developed over the course of more than one entry or are returned to in later entries in the book). There is little attempt at traditional character development over the course of the entries, the unity of the book depending instead on the force of Ang's distinctive voice.

The Broke Diaries is in fact notable for showcasing Ang's comedic skill. In particular, her voice effectively melds the semiconfessional, personal voice of the blog with various forms of public performance comedy. Sometimes Ang spins out one-liners as though in response to an unstated question. For example, she answers the question "How broke were you?" with "My checks were so rubber, I had to get them rotated and balanced" (ix). Ang is also able to turn a comedic phrase, as she does when she explains that because people such as bank tellers utter sighs when they see her coming, she has become expert in "Sigh Language" (36). At other times, Ang's entries provide the opportunity for her to elaborate on a subject somewhat in the fashion of a stand-up comedian, as she does in a section responding to a personal finance book's advice to hold a yard sale to raise money by riffing on the fact that she doesn't have a yard and that she would surely get arrested if she set up a table to sell stuff in front of her apartment building. The entries themselves often develop a comic structure by introducing an everyday situation that grows increasingly out of control. For instance, because she doesn't have enough money to do her laundry, one day Ang goes without wearing underwear under her jeans. This dilemma becomes a more significant problem later in *The Broke Diaries* when she faces having to change clothes in the common dressing room of a discount shop.

One characteristic of Ang's comedic blog book is especially relevant to Nissel's later career as a screenwriter. Throughout the narrative, Ang occasionally interrupts her own adventures with an imagined comic scenario. When faced with the exorbitant price of textbooks, for example, she imagines a scene in which she hires a thug to scare the professor who has assigned textbooks he himself has written:

> Thug [knocking Petri dish to the floor]: Yeah, I knocked over your little dish! You wanna do something about it?! Huh, do you??!
> Professor [cowering in corner]: Please sir!!! Leave me be!! Is it money you're after? I don't have any money in here! Just fetal pigs!
> Thug: Sure you don't have any money! We know you're getting kickbacks from the publishing companies for assigning these overpriced books!! And how are you going to assign a book you wrote your own damn self?!! Why I should—
> Professor: Please, take all the drugs you want! In fact, I'll make you some drugs! Please, go!
> Thug [punches hole in Periodic Table of Elements Chart]: I'll be back. (*Broke* 3–4)

After this scene, Ang remarks, "Oops. I didn't mean to start writing a screenplay" (4). Yet writing a screenplay is precisely what Nissel moves toward as she revises her blog into a book that incorporates many such scenarios relying primarily on dialogue and action. Their inclusion in the narrative of Ang's senior year is especially salient given the fact that Nissel is eventually hired by the television comedy *Scrubs*, a show known for interrupting its action with fantasy sequences based on the imaginary thoughts of particular characters, and especially those of medical intern J. D. Dorian (played by Zach Braff). Because J. D.'s fantasies not only include fellow cast members but often incorporate video and musical sequences with iconic cultural significance (such as the dancing gangs from *West Side Story*), the television show's use of fantasy sequences gives the production a sense of the hypertextual; that is, at any moment the action being played out in Sacred Heart Hospital might be expanded to follow a cultural link outside the episode being dramatized. Both blog book and television show thus demonstrate a heightened awareness of increased possibilities for media crossing in the contemporary public sphere. Nissel's inclusion of mini-screenplays in *The Broke Diaries* figures as a significant part of her life writing, a feature that likely resonated with *Scrubs* producers. Given the outline of Nissel's career, *The Broke Diaries* is noteworthy both for pointing back to its electronic origins in Nissel's blogging *and* for anticipating her eventual career in television.

Another performance genre important to *The Broke Diaries* is open-mic poetry, the object of Ang's satire in a series of entries and the inspiration for her to include her own poems in the book. Ang goes to an open-mic performance one night when she looks for some free entertainment, although she suspects that what is *"always* free can't be too good" (103). The evening provides an opportunity for Ang to showcase an aptitude for developing satiric types. The first performer to appear is a "revolutionary poet," who paces back and forth across the stage before screaming at the audience, "YOU'RE NOT READY FOR THE REVOLUTION" (105). He moves next into what Ang calls a "call and response Revolution," during which he scares a middle-aged woman. Not impressed by the revolutionary poet's dated rhetoric or by his politics (in part because he never explains what he is revolting against), Ang comments that she learned all about revolution from her mom, who was around in the 1960s and 1970s, and who, she also adds, still has "a rotary phone." Her mother, Ang concludes, "needs a phone revolution" (139). Her comment clearly positions Ang not as part of *the* revolutionary generation but as part of a new, *technologically* revolutionary generation.

After attending open-mic night, Ang decides to include her own poems in *The Broke Diaries* based on her experiences as a broke student. One, titled "Ode to Mr. Store Owner," draws on an encounter with a local store owner who refuses to let her make a purchase when she came up short, even though she is a regular customer. As she writes in two lines from the poem, "Mr. Store Owner, why can't you hook me up? / You know I always buy yo' shit, this time I'm short a buck" (111, ll. 1–2). In lines from another poem, Nissel draws on her experience with student financial services: "Loans for the hungry, loans for the poor / I'm like little Oliver, 'Please, sir, give me more!'" (152, ll. 19–20). Here Ang takes pleasure in alluding to Dickens while spinning off rhymed couplets that reinforce the performance quality of her voice. Her love of language play also surfaces when a friend loses the "O" of her car's insignia for "FORD." While her friend wants to search for the missing "O," Ang is struck by the opportunity for "potential comedy with the 'O' sound" (131), and she and another friend, in rapper fashion, try to cap one another in producing sentences ending in the sound, including "go," "no," "mo," "bro," "fo'" (for four), and "sto'" (for store). Melding the personal disclosures characteristic of blogs with hybrid cultural allusions and language play drawn from African American vernacular genres, the striking performance quality of Ang's voice figures as one of the primary tools for self-fashioning in *The Broke Diaries*.

Also important to Nissel's shaping of her autobiographical materials in her blog book, however, is the thematic positioning of Ang on the border between the permanently poor and the temporarily poor, a position that is developed against both the privileged students at the University of Pennsylvania and the permanently poor people who live near the university. As a broke African American student attending an Ivy League institution, Ang often brings a street-wise perspective to the college scene. In the "December 1" entry she proposes a "Broke Student Union" to advocate for the rights of poor students in response to the actions of student organizations that she finds impractical and effete. For example, Ang criticizes privileged students who "walk drunk and shirtless at 3 AM through city streets with an open wallet dangling from their left nipple" and then complain if they are robbed (56). The university should not cater to their new demands for additional safety measures, she argues, but should suspend students for their own risky behavior: "someone who walks through the inner city wearing a 'Wharton' shirt, when he has the option of having a university van pick him up and take him wherever he needed to go, deserves some time off" (67). Rather than making broke students pay for increased fees for more security, pictures of students who engage in risky behavior, Ang suggests, should be published with the label "Easy Targets" (57).

But Ang does not completely identify herself as a member of the permanently poor, either. She demonstrates in several entries her awareness that, as a student at an Ivy League institution, she has a promising future. Although she is currently a "struggling sis," Ang is "putting herself through college" (23) and at times seems confident that one day she will "be middle class" (33). In one entry, she worries whether bouncing a check will affect her anticipated future as a "soccer mom" (36). Her unsettled status among the temporarily poor is effectively captured by the image Ang paints of herself as a patron of a particular kind of bookstore. Because she can't afford to buy books, she goes to stores that allow customers to read books in the café without buying them. Her interest in self-help and personal-finance books reflects both her present status and her potential for upward mobility. Interestingly, in the introduction to *The Broke Diaries*, Ang imagines (in a direct address to her audience), her own readers as occupying a similar social space: "Thing is, everyone has a broke diary. Maybe you never wrote yours down, perhaps your broke diary is just a collection of memories from college, or all those low-paying jobs you had. Maybe your broke diary is no memory, 'cause you're broke as hell right now and sitting in that bookstore chair planning on reading my whole book over a latte and a scone instead of buying it" (ix). The conception of a readership who is "broke as hell" expressed here seems more congruent with her own experience of being temporarily poor than with the actual situation of the permanently poor. The audience is positioned, like Ang herself, as individuals who read books for free rather than buying them, who have struggled to attend college, and who have developed a taste for lattes and scones. Although here Nissel broadens her readership from the group of fellow college students and acquaintances who were the original audience for her blog, she clearly identifies her potential audience in terms that fit the category of "temporarily" rather than "permanently" poor.

In fact, her precarious position "*teetering on the edge* of this temporarily broke / permanently poor dividing line" remains a source of constant anxiety for Ang (37; emphasis added). To some extent, Ang's status among the temporarily poor makes her sensitive to the difficulties that the permanently poor have in obtaining basic needs such as food and transportation. One entry focuses on how something as ordinary as being asked to take one's "turn" at bringing the dessert to an office party can pose a crisis for those who struggle to afford their own food. In another entry, Ang attends a funeral largely for the free food served at the reception. A number of entries comment on the difficulties faced by the poor in obtaining reliable transportation. When her car—a vehicle only capable of going twenty miles per hour on the freeway on a good day—breaks down, Ang finds herself reduced to riding the bus and feels herself teetering over the edge into the category of the permanently poor. As a tour bus passes her, she imagines the passengers staring at her as though she were an inner-city sight-seeing attraction: "Ladies and gentleman, if you'd look to your left, you'll see a young lady waiting on the 42 bus. She's only going ten blocks, but it will take her an hour. . . . You don't have to look at her too closely, we can go get some refreshments, see the Liberty Bell, and homegirl will still be standing right there when we get back" (95). As Ang summarizes, "going from working car back to the bus stop is, like, the ultimate status drop" (96).

If her position as temporarily poor distances her from those better off, however, her status also distances Ang from the permanently poor. At one point, reflecting that "broke people love lawsuits," she worries whether a woman she confronts in a Walmart might "sue her for future earnings" (15). In other parts of her text, Ang emphasizes that even though she too is broke, she never dances "nude" to make ends meet like some of the other women she knows (48). And in a long comedic section that describes her first experience at a "Check-Cashing joint," Ang distances herself from the other people who are reduced to using its services. The woman on one side, who initially appears to be a "nice old lady," turns out to be "effing insane" (40, 41). The overweight man who crowds her on the other side constantly invades her space in an attempt to read what she is writing. (In order to discourage him, Ang writes, "*My husband is one dead man*" [42].) Most revealing, while at the check-cashing joint, Ang is struck by an attack of "poor claustrophobia" (39). As she explains, "It's not the poor people, it's the poor atmosphere. I don't want it clinging to my shirt, following me home, and plopping on my sofa with a drink" (39). Ang's reactions in the check-cashing joint are clearly shaped by her recognition that it is "one of the major poor portals"—a door to becoming permanently poor (37). Although she narrates her "misadventures" in a comedic voice, because Ang is "teetering on the edge," her narrative is clearly shaped by anxieties about the ease with which she could cross the tenuous line between temporarily and permanently poor.

Because what a writer leaves out of the narrative she constructs of her life is as important a tool for self-fashioning as what she includes, Nissel's omissions are also highly informative. *The Broke Diaries* concludes as Ang graduates from Penn and lands a job at an "Internet start-up." As she comments, the "thing about the Internet is that it never shuts down. It's open 24/7" (201). Even so, Ang states, she "like[s] her job and [has] accepted the long hours" (201). Over the course of the narrative, Ang has thus moved from struggling college student and committer of petty crimes to hard-working member of the new media. But as her second book will make clear,

Nissel does in fact leave much of her experience out in order to shape her tale. In fact, limiting the time frame of the book to the same period that was covered by her blog (her senior year) enables Nissel to omit such details as her bout with depression in her freshman year and her experience dancing in a strip club after graduation. An equally significant omission from *The Broke Diaries*, however, is a discussion of the practical means through which Ang lands her position at the dot-com. Rather than focusing on the media training and the personal and professional contacts that helped her to succeed, Ang designs the narrative to center squarely on her comedic misadventures.

The "About the Author" note that appears after Ang's last entry provides more insight into the specific means Nissel uses to "get ovuh," however. There readers learn that Angela Nissel is "no longer broke" and is the successful co-owner and site manager for Okayplayer.com. Hinting at the path to her success, the note also points out that although Nissel graduated with a degree in medical anthropology, "she used to cut class to learn more about building websites." As this comment suggests, Nissel's media-crossing expertise is not limited to her revision of her blog into a book and her subsequent writing of an autobiography but also includes her early creative work in website development. For as she was writing *The Broke Diaries* (in the period before she moved from Philadelphia to Hollywood), Nissel cofounded Okayplayer.com with Ahmir (Questlove) Thompson, drummer of The Roots, the well-known hip-hop group. (In 2001, the website won Best New Website at the Online Hip-Hop Awards.) Envisioned as an alternative online musical community, Okayplayer.com brings to mind Neal's argument that digitized spaces may provide alternative public spheres. More recently, The Roots formed a new record label based on the website, an expansion Gail Mitchell describes as a "partnership with Decon, a multimedia/design entertainment company." Although Nissel's work on Okayplayer.com preceded this 2004 development—one that may call to mind Gilroy's concern about the degree to which commercial forces shape black creativity in the contemporary electronic public sphere (23)—the digital expertise Nissel demonstrated in helping to build a site that includes blogs, music reviews, streaming video, member chat, news, and hyperlinks speaks to the new media sophistication that contributed to her rapid transformation from broke student to Hollywood producer. (Like Nissel, The Roots themselves eventually moved to television, when the successful hip-hop group became the house band for *Late Night with Jimmy Fallon* on NBC in 2009.) If Benjamin Franklin has often been singled out as one of the first Americans to make his fortune through letters, we might say that Nissel provides a contemporary example of a rising generation of individuals who are making their fortunes by negotiating the multiple opportunities afforded them by the late twentieth- and early twenty-first-century restructuring of the public sphere.

Like her work in digital networking, other positions that contributed to Nissel's growing media sophistication are mentioned only in passing in *The Broke Diaries*, including those in both new and old media. One entry refers to an interview with a disk jockey "for a magazine a friend runs" (a description, perhaps, of her work with Ahmir Thompson); another mentions an internship at the established *Dateline NBC* (170). Later in the text, Ang comments, "All of my internships have been in media" (166). Because she does not develop these experiences in any detail, her rise in *The Broke Diaries* appears to result from her own "pluck," keeping the focus of self-fashioning on Ang's comedic voice. Similarly, Nissel attributes her success as an author largely to the moment of "luck" when her blog landed on the desk of Melody Guy, the Villard editor, who asked her to adapt her blog for a book. Because Nissel chooses not to narrate the story of her multiple internships and other media experiences in *The Broke Diaries*, growing expertise remains the hidden key to Ang's—and Nissel's—success.

While Ang's comedic voice is not absent from Nissel's second book, *Mixed*, it is newly tempered. Several serious topics either omitted or left undeveloped in *The Broke Diaries* are taken up by the autobiography, including Nissel's treatment for depression and, as its title suggests, her experience growing up as the daughter of a black mother and a white father. A comparison of the covers of the two books suggests that *Mixed* offers a more serious autobiographical effort than her first book. The cover of *The Broke Diaries* features a young woman dressed in a short tank top and jeans. The picture cuts the figure off at the neck, hiding the face of its apparent narrator and centering instead on the fact that she is turning out the pockets of her jeans to show that they are empty. The race of the figure is indistinct. The effect positions the author as youthful and hip, with the previously discussed endorsement by Chris Rock serving as imprimatur. The cover of *Mixed*, on the other hand, features a picture of Nissel's own face—that of a lightly colored African American woman, with freckles and curly, reddish-tinged hair. By featuring an image of Nissel herself, the cover underscores the book's status as autobiography at the same time that it provides a visual reminder of Nissel's mixed ancestry. Halle Berry, the award-winning actress and herself the child of an interracial couple, provides the primary endorsement for this book by declaring *Mixed* to be "deliciously enlightening and heart-rending."

The book covers Nissel's childhood in the late seventies to her college years (six years at Penn, from 1992 to 1998) to her eventual move from Philly to Los Angeles in 2001. Significantly, *Mixed* does not include Angela's senior year at Penn, the period covered by *The Broke Diaries*, an omission that effectively ties the two books together and indicates that they comprise—with Nissel's blog—developing parts of a single life narrative. Written in short chapters usually running between six and eight pages, *Mixed* includes two longer chapters that treat Angela's experience with depression. The book is more polished, further removed from the personal style of Nissel's blog, and narrated by a more mature "Angela." Also indicating greater distance from the blog, Nissel structures the narrative in chapters rather than by diary entries. Most importantly, rather than playing primarily for laughs, Nissel's second book consistently relates her personal experience to larger social issues. Accordingly, each chapter begins with an epigraph that connects the narrative of Angela's life to events in the broader culture. For example, the second chapter, "Primary Colors," begins with an item posted on a Crayola.com site: "1992: The Crayola Company introduces sixteen-count Multicultural Crayons. These crayons give a child a realistic palette to color the people of the world" (qtd. in *Mixed* 9). The chapter itself narrates a grade school experience of Angela's in which a white nun holds up various crayons next to her face in order to find the "right" shade for her to use to color in a self-portrait before she is allowed to hand it in. Taken together, the two passages comment on how supposed "advances" in racial sensitivity can become occasions for reinscribing racial hierarchy.

Most importantly, in her second book and her third publication of life writing (counting the blog), Nissel's previous focus on Ang's precarious position on the edge of the temporarily poor and the permanently poor is left largely behind for an in-depth examination of Angela's difficult life growing up on the edge of the American cultural divide between black and white. During her childhood, a period when Angela is transferred from one school to another by a divorced, single mother who seeks the best education she can for her daughter, Angela's experience of being mixed is often reduced to repeated attempts to find a community where she can fit in, a project complicated by her repeated rejection for being either "Not White Enough" or "Not Black Enough."

Nissel conveys Angela's experience of being not white enough throughout the book by including several scenes in which white people read her mixed-race ancestry as "too Black." As a girl, she endures taunting about being a "Zebra" and having hair that feels "like a Brillo pad" (37). Her position as not white enough is made sharper one day when she brings a black Barbie along to play with three little white girls, one of whom reacts by moving her own Barbie away from Angela's doll and exclaiming, "Ewww! That's not Barbie" (37). Angela's own reaction to the incident reveals the degree to which she has already inculcated white American standards of racial categorization: as Angela reflects, "I agreed with Michelle. . . . Anyone who watched television could tell Black Barbie wasn't as important as White Barbie. White Barbie dominated the commercials: She was the one cruising the coast in a Corvette; she was the one taking the elevator to the second floor of the Dream House. Black Barbie appeared only in a still shot behind White Barbie for about two seconds before the commercial faded to black" (37). Demonstrating that child's play is not simply about play, Angela's comment ties the racial categorization that the young girls have already internalized—and the race privilege that the white girls are already policing—to media conditioning in the larger culture. The details included in the Barbie commercial are especially significant in relation to the emphasis in Nissel's work on achieving success: in this scene, Ang learns both that she can't *play* with white girls unless she denies her blackness, and also, as white Barbie's success implies, that it doesn't *pay* to be black in America.

If in *The Broke Diaries* Ang's position on the edge of poor and temporarily poor sometimes leads her to exhibit an ambivalence toward the permanently poor, in Nissel's second book, Angela develops a similar ambivalence toward black culture, as we can see in the second chapter, which narrates Angela's "Third Grade Chitlin Inquisition" (14). The same nun who will not allow her to hand in the self-portrait she draws until she colors in her face with the correct crayon asks the students in her class to read aloud a report they have written (15). Because she knows she can "outspell and outread everyone," Angela welcomes the opportunity to read a research paper she has written on the food eaten by slaves (11). But the white teacher sidetracks Angela's report on slavery by stopping her at the pronunciation of the word *chitlins* (12). As she laughs at the young girl, the nun corrects, "It's chit-ter-lings, Angela. Break it into syllables" (12). After making Angela repeat the individual syllables one-by-one, the nun explains to the class that chitterlings are "pig's intestines"— to which the class reacts with predictable disgust. She then asks each black child in turn if her or his family eats chitterlings. In shame, all four black students deny it, including Angela. Illustrating the authority the white teacher assumes over a culture she knows little about, Angela's inquisition over a seemingly small matter effectively undermines her ability to demonstrate her own abilities, inculcates ambivalence over aspects of traditional African American culture, and reinforces her status as "Not White Enough."

As Angela moves from one school to another, including inner-city schools, black suburban schools, private schools, public schools, magnet schools, and, finally (and most happily) the Philadelphia School for Creative and Performing Arts, she also has several experiences that teach her that she is "Not Black Enough." Although her mother tells her that in America "one drop of black blood makes you black," certain incidents repeatedly call Angela's blackness into question, as when, for instance, she demonstrates that she does not know how to fix her hair, dance, or skip Double Dutch. At one point, Fat Pam, an older girl whom Angela's mother hires to babysit, tells Angela, "You ain't nothing but a white girl" (195). Subsequently, Fat Pam takes on the task of instructing Angela how to be "a real black person" (90). For example, when Angela's experience with bullies at the integrated magnet school she attends turns quickly from taunts by a pair of popular black girls that she is a "light skinned bitch" (91) to physical threats, Ang asks Pam to help her learn to fight. Pam tells her, "Protect your face.... When I fight light-skinned girls, I always go for the face" (96). Attributed by the text partly to colorism in the black community, the bullying that Angela receives at school eventually escalates to the point that one girl throws Angela's schoolbag in front of a subway train—and another attempts to push Angela in afterward. When her mother later decides to move her to an all-black suburban school, Angela wonders if she does so because "she knew it would cause my fear of black girls to disappear" (109). Angela's experience of "not being black enough" growing up therefore complicates her racial identification with black people.

At college, Angela's fears of "not being black enough" are in part the reason why she begins to date a black Muslim student, Mah, with whom she makes future plans to set up a free school for black children. During her freshman year, she learns more about racist events in the nation's history (such as the Tuskegee experiments). With Mah, she also watches tapes titled "The Goddamn White Man" about "all the destruction caused by—well, the goddamn white man" (130). As Angela says, "It made sense to me" (130). Already predisposed to dislike white men because of her troubled history with her own white father and her own lived experiences of not being white enough, Angela is told, "Don't let them white boys get in your head. They just want to drug you" (130). When a speaker on one of the tapes asks his audience to "show [him] one good white person," Ang reflects, "I couldn't think of one . . . not my non-child-support-paying dad, and certainly no one so far at the University of Pennsylvania" (130). Angela's experience thus fosters a deep ambivalence toward both sides of her ancestry, black and white.

The narrative also complicates any attempt to resolve the twin problems of "not being black enough" or "not being white enough" by claiming a positive mixed-race identity. When Angela is a girl, her mother attempts to prepare her for the racism she might suffer by telling her, "You've got two beautiful races in one package" (9). But by watching a discussion of mixed-race children on television, Angela soon learns instead that the attitude of the world is that she "should never have been born" (21). The subject of interracial couples appears frequently on shows like *Phil Donohue* as Angela is growing up. "Invariably," she finds, "the topic turned to 'What if the couples decided to have sex (the horror!) and gave birth to flawed, confused-race children?'" (22). At one point, knowing that her daughter is looking for a community to fit into, her mother joins a group for biracial families called "Rainbow Connections." But Angela's mother turns out to be the only black woman in the group, and it appears to her that the other families are trying to define themselves as multiracial largely to avoid defining themselves as black. Angela's experience as neither black enough nor white enough eventually leads her to wish that she were anything but mixed: "I didn't want another race lesson or an analysis of how crazy everyone else was and how special I was. I wanted out of the race game. It seemed that every time I learned the rules, someone changed them on me. . . . I was tired of fighting. I wanted to be purebred" (99).

The relationship of being mixed to Angela's depression, part of her life story omitted from *The Broke Diaries*, is complex. One of the factors contributing to her illness is a breakup with the supposedly conservative Mah, whom Angela learns has been "sleeping with other women at parties" (135). She also learns that he has another girl on the side, one who is a "real black person" with the "perfect brown toast color [she had] been trying to achieve by all [her] hours at Sun on the Run" (135). As Angela comments, "That was the straw that broke the depressed black woman's back" (135). But it is Angela's miscommunication with a white customer service representative that leads to her initial admittance to the psychiatric ward of a local hospital. In order to receive insurance coverage for the Prozac that has been prescribed by a local physician, Angela has to receive approval from her insurance company. The company's customer service representative explains that he has a number of questions he must ask her over the phone before he can give approval. After making his way through a long list of required questions, he asks, "Do you have thoughts of suicide? . . . Right now?" (138). When Angela answers, "Yes. Because of how long this phone call is taking" (138), the representative ignores her humor and moves into high gear: before their conversation has ended, the police are at Angela's door. As with the representative, they must follow a set protocol in their response, and Angela soon finds herself on a gurney being taken to the hospital, where she spends eight hours in the "seclusion room" (148).

Angela's stay in the hospital in fact crystallizes for her several issues regarding race. As a black woman, Angela is especially shamed by her emotional troubles. She remembers the historical suffering that black women have borne without breaking down, including the troubles of her grandmother, who scrubbed white women's floors. Angela recognizes that she has little to complain about, because, unlike her grandmother, she attends "a posh Ivy League school with rich white girls who grew up having their floors cleaned" (149). For Angela, being depressed is a white person's disability, and she scolds herself: "This is what your Mom marched on Washington for: so you could vote and have a mental breakdown right with the white crazy people" (149).

But Angela is also aware of the racism in her own treatment as a patient, made clear when a white Penn PhD student, Anne, arrives to give her Thematic Apperception and Rorschach tests. When the student explains that that TAT test is basically a "storytelling game" (160), Angela at first takes some pleasure in spinning out stories about each picture—until she is shown a card with "white people leaning on a back porch with what looked like cotton fields stretched out before them" (161). When Angela inquires whether there are any black people at all represented on the cards, Anne responds, "No," and Angela is left to reflect on how Anne would feel if she were depressed and shown a series of cards featuring black people (161, 162). Later, Angela learns that the doctors interpret her TAT responses as revealing that it is she, rather than they, who demonstrates "a preoccupation with issues of race" (165).

Another incident in the hospital, however, points Angela in the direction of an answer to the prompt on Mah's tape, "Show me one good white person." After Angela checks herself out of the hospital, she returns voluntarily after only ten hours to find herself welcomed by Rose and her "white old lady friends" (167). On her fourth night back, a white male patient, Gus, approaches her and makes inappropriate comments, including "I'd like to stick a banana in your tailpipe" (168). When Gus begins to rub his hand up and down Angela's arm, she slugs him. Afterward, the nurse and security guards refuse to take her side against the "white guy," and Angela yells at them. She is then sent to floor 2, with the more "dangerous" patients— who are all black. Recognizing that "when black people show distrust of the system . . . they are . . . labeled as delusional" (170), Angela discovers a new interpretation of the relationship between race and mental illness. Two days later, however, Angela is allowed to move back downstairs, where she learns that Rose and her friends had refused "to eat until they brought [her] back downstairs" (170). The fact that the women had gone on "a hunger strike" for her provides the response to the prompt on Mah's tape. Sitting down next to "her new friends," Angela realizes that the "uncomplicated act of sitting where [she] wanted to sit felt . . . powerful" (171). Angela's depression, then, both deepens her feelings of racial shame at "not being black enough" and increases her understanding of the racism practiced toward those who are not white enough. Her experience also contributes, however, to a growing sense that racial categorizations may not be completely inflexible.[3]

Like the conclusion of *The Broke Diaries*, the ending of *Mixed* moves quickly, following Angela from Philly to California in search of her fortune. By the autobiography's end, Angela's search for community is partly satisfied, as she begins to tutor black junior high school students, starts an African American literary club in Los Angeles, reestablishes a relationship with her white father, and, most important, marries a "black identifying," mixed-race husband (220). A more mature Angela realizes that although she will not be able to escape the "race game"—not even for "just one day" (225)—she will be able to survive it and to find contentment. The autobiography concludes with a scene that depicts an irate white driver pulling up next to the car in which she and her husband are riding and yelling at them to "go back to Mexico!" To the man's consternation, both Angela and her husband break out laughing at the man's attempt to insult them by identifying them with "one of the few ethnicities [they] have no ties to" (226). Dramatizing the power of humor, the scene underscores Nissel's decisive rejection of a "tragic mulatto" framework for her narrative about growing up mixed. Although the autobiography focuses on Angela's being "on the edge" between races and includes material about her depression, a tragic outcome in fact never seems probable, possibly because the work is enlivened throughout by the comedic sensibility developed for Ang in *The Broke Diaries*.

As in *The Broke Diaries*, readers learn more about the practical means of Nissel's eventual success in Hollywood from the short "Acknowledgments" and "Author's Note" that follow the book than from the autobiography itself. There we learn that Nissel originally went to Hollywood "to pursue writing full time" at the urging of people who "call themselves producers" and promise to get her a job writing a screenplay of her book. When this plan fails, Nissel reports, she lists some of her possessions on eBay to raise money. An executive at Warner Brothers familiar with *The Broke Diaries* bids on one item and subsequently puts Nissel in contact with an agent who circulates her blog book to studios looking for comedy writers. Taken together, the "Acknowledgments" and "Author's Notes" of Nissel's two books comprise another narrative of her rise—one that rests on two lucky incidents made possible by electronic media, the first event when Nissel's blog lands on the desk of Melody Guy at Villard, the editor whom Nissel credits with "chang[ing] her life with one email," and the second when the unnamed executive comes across Nissel's items on eBay ("Acknowledgements," *Mixed*).

It is not simply by providing an electronic space where her luck unfolds that new media contributes to Nissel's success, however, but also her mastery of what Aaron Barlow has termed "neteracy," or the "new set of skills that do not replace literacy, but [are] increasingly necessary as more and more human activities acquire Web-connected aspects" (xi). From the blog she began in 1997, her work as site manager for Okayplayer.com, and her media internships to her more traditional authorship and her eventual work in Hollywood, Nissel proves herself an adept negotiator of a public sphere characterized by the increasing interpenetration of various forms of media, something in the manner that Nissel's official webpage leads visitors from links to her NPR interview to links for marketing ads for her books to links for video streams of her appearances on the *Tyra Banks Show* to links for the websites for *Scrubs*, *Dumpster World*, and Okayplayer.com. Nissel's career as blogger, writer, screenplay writer, and television producer illustrates the ways in which authorship is becoming hypertextual in the digital age.

When she began self-publishing her life writing by blogging in 1997, Nissel may not have anticipated the directions the undertaking would lead, but her "luck" was also tied to changes in book publishing occasioned by the linkage of new media and mainstream publishing. Melody Guy's discovery of Nissel was not simply accidental or a matter of luck, it should be noted. As mainstream publishing has become more competitive, and as the interest in works by African American authors has risen, editors have increasingly begun to search online and for self-published works as sources for acquisitions. In 2001, the year that *The Broke Diaries* appeared, Guy also launched a new imprint for Villard, Strivers Row, named after the famous neighborhood in Harlem and focused specifically on African American works. In talking with Robert Fleming, Guy describes her method for finding works, explaining that she looks for "new voices" by "finding books that were initially self-published." In "Black in Print," Guy further explains the manner in which self-publishing, a practice with a long history in the black community and one that has been supercharged by digital technologies, can function as a screening ground for large publishing firms: "Self-publishing is an underground kind of activity . . . [but] it can be an avenue to commercial publication" (qtd. in Mabe). Although Guy's comments refer explicitly to her work with the new imprint, the connection to her "lucky" discovery of Nissel's self-published blog is unmistakable.

Given the increasing degree of their interpenetration, breaking the public sphere into "alternative" and "mainstream" seems to ignore the very electronic forces that are working to efface such distinctions. The question of whether the electronic public sphere provides a greater latitude for self-expression or a greater concentration of corporate power assumes an opposition that may not account for the blurring of borders that is one characteristic of an emerging public sphere in which the same electronic media are increasing opportunities for self-publishing and for corporate access to that expression. On the one hand, as Stone suggests, blogging is the "first real democratization of the Internet . . . a social revolution" (68). On the other, as

Robert W. McChesney says, the increased commercialization and corporatization of communications "leave us with a very small number of massive firms dominating the communication landscape" (TBS). In the face of such divergent viewpoints, Lisa Nakamura suggests that we should not adopt either a "utopian or [a] pessimistic view" on this issue but should focus instead on the "ideological and cultural work" accomplished in the new digital public sphere (xiii).

As I argue here, the ideological and cultural work accomplished by Nissel's life writing includes at least three significant elements. First is the manner in which the decision to go electronic with her life writing becomes a path to her eventual success as author and Hollywood producer. In an interview with Lisa Levy, Nissel says of her decision to write her blog book, "If you can get paid for being broke, you can get paid for doing anything. . . . It's capitalism at its finest." Nissel's comments unabashedly identify writing not only as a means for creative self-expression but also as a means for "getting ovuh." As I suggest, one essential feature of Nissel's own rise is the media literacy she draws on in a twenty-first-century public sphere increasingly characterized by the interpenetration of old and new media. Equally important, Nissel uses her authorship to assert the legitimacy of her mixed-race identity. Although some academics argue that mixed-race identity is "little more than a fad" (Spencer), Nissel's second book speaks forcefully to her own experience growing up mixed. Because Nissel firmly roots her story in the immediacy of her first-person account, her text makes an appeal to a phenomenological warrant. Part of the ideological work accomplished by Nissel's life writing, then, is to provide what, as a girl, she found missing on television, in children's books, and in cultural products like dolls: representations of people who look like her.

The cultural work of Nissel's life writing is not limited to representation, however, but also includes the manner in which her work contributes to the very creation of the community that Angela seeks in *Mixed*. Combining with the work of other mixed-race authors in a new public sphere in which electronic networks link people with similar experiences, Nissel's life writing joins the creative work of others who speak about their lives as "mixed" in the increasing number of blogs, books, and films that proliferated in the first decade of the twenty-first century, including websites such as mixedraceamerica.blogspot.com, the Mulatto Diaries of YouTube vlogger Tiffany Jones, and blogs such as mixedchickschat.com. In 2008 Nissel received the Loving Prize for "inspirational dedication to celebrating and illuminating the Mixed racial and cultural experience" ("Loving Prize") from the Mixed Roots Film and Literary Festival, a national group of mixed-race artists, filmmakers, and families that maintains its own website and holds annual conferences. The growth of such communities is another form of cultural work being fostered by the digital public sphere. Nissel's life writing, then, not only charts her personal success but also provides insight into the changing nature of authorship, asserts the legitimacy of her personal experience growing up "mixed," and joins the cultural work being undertaken by a number of Americans who are forming new, digitally based communities at the beginning of the twenty-first century. By going electronic with her life writing in 1997, Nissel propelled herself from student "on the edge" to fully networked author.

NOTES

An earlier version of this chapter was published as "Angela Nissel from Blog to Books: Authorship and the Digital Public Sphere," *a/b: Auto/Biography Studies* 27.1 (2012): 127–52. © 2012 The Autobiography Society. Reprinted by permission.

1. Such electronic guides are too numerous to mention individually, but Black-Network.com, BlackPlanet.com, and BlackNetworking.com are three of many that provide lists of particular electronic networking sites.

2. The question of the identity of the "first blogger" is open to debate. Understood in terms of use of the web to post personal reflections, Justin Hall's blog, begun in 1994, is considered by many to have been the first, but others point to precedents in the personal weblogs that grew up hand in hand with the new technology at computer companies and universities. For more information, see McCullagh and Broache.

3. Appearing near the end of *Mixed*, the narration of Angela's experience as a seminude dancer in a strip club is another aspect of her life that Nissel omits from *The Broke Diaries* (which in fact contains Ang's somewhat smug comment about *not* taking up nude dancing like other broke girls she knows). The incident is highly racialized, clarifying the recent college grad's attitudes toward white men and emphasizing the degree to which sexual fantasies are imbricated with race—and racial fantasies are imbricated with sex. Angela presents her auditioning for the strip club in *Mixed* as an "adventure" and as "serious karma" for being judgmental earlier of her friends who danced (196, 187). Drawing self-consciously on the literary genre of the passing narrative, Angela has to "forget she is black" to strip (186)—first because a white girl in the costume shop outfits her in the role of a more racially ambiguous "exotic" and later because the strip club will permit only four black girls to perform on any particular night. As her friend Morgan explains to the club's house mom so Angela can audition, she is "not black! She's Puerto Rican, Asian, and . . . Irish" (192).

Initially Angela seems to find her performance liberating. She has often been put in the role of the exotic by white people who ask her "Where are you from?" in an attempt to locate her racial identity without asking directly. At first, the performance of the exotic other provides Angela with the sense that for once she is in control of the racial fantasy. Over the course of four hours, she pretends to be "Russian, Sicilian, Papua New Guinean, Mexican, and Jewish" (199). Similarly, Angela feels initially empowered by her sexual influence over the white men. Remembering that "there was a time [she] couldn't even speak to white men; they terrified [her]," she wishes her therapist could see her looking "a grown white man in the eye" (198). In reaction to the men who are "clapping and hooting and looking at [her] like [she] was the pop star they'd had hanging on their wall since they were fourteen," then, Angela initially feels strong, "smiling and enjoying her power" (196).

But Angela's own fantasy ends abruptly when she is called over to a table of men, the "leader" of whom encourages her to give a lap dance to a member of the group to "loosen him up." The "alpha male," as Angela calls him, then lapses into "the best slave accent he could master," saying, "hoo-hoo, honey chile, how did you get such a black ass? How much to buy that?" Suddenly, Angela realizes that she is not in control of anyone's racial fantasy, including her own: recognizing that she is "half naked with dirty dollar bills sticking out of [her] shorts," she suddenly finds it "hard to feel powerful" (200). Morgan's reaction to her friend's unnerving predicament is to tell Angela, "You just have to get used to that. The guys in here think they own you" (200). She further advises Angela to "num[b] herself and just pla[y] along with whatever people want [her] to be" (202). Realizing that fulfilling the racial expectations of others is precisely what she has had to do "every damn day," Angela decides that she will no longer let people define her (202). She decides to quit passing, both in the strip club and in life, or "trying on different races and religions in response to people's perceptions of [her]" (222).

WORKS CITED

Barlow, Aaron. *Blogging America: The New Public Sphere*. Westport, CT: Praeger, 2007.
Fleming, Robert. "Strivers Row Imprint Makes Its Debut." Rev. of *The Dying Ground: A Hip-Hop Noir Novel*, by Nichelle D. Tramble. *BookPage* Feb. 2001.
Gilroy, Paul. "Exer(or)cising Power: Black Bodies in the Black Public Sphere." *Dance in the City*. Ed. Helen Thomas. New York: St. Martin's, 1997. 21–34.
Habermas, Jürgen. *The Structural Transformation of the Public Sphere*. 1962. Trans. Thomas Burger and Frederick Lawrence. Cambridge, MA: MIT P, 1991.
Levy, Lisa. "Surfing for Broke." *Entertainment Weekly* 16 Apr. 2001.
"Loving Prize." *Mixed Roots Film and Literary Festival*. New York Foundation for the Arts, 29 Dec. 2010.
Mabe, Chauncey. "Black in Print." *Race Matters*. Lighthouse Ministries of Boca Raton, 9 Feb. 2001.
McCullagh, Declan, and Anne Broache. "Blogs Turn 10—Who's the Father?" *CNET* 20 Mar. 2007.
Mitchell, Gail. "Roots Launch Okayplayer Records." *Billboard* 22 Jan. 2004.
Nakamura, Lisa. *Cybertypes: Race, Ethnicity, and Identity on the Internet*. New York: Routledge, 2002.
Neal, Mark Anthony. *What the Music Said: Black Popular Music and Black Public Culture*. New York: Routledge, 1999.
Nissel, Angela. *The Broke Diaries: The Completely True and Hilarious Misadventures of a Good Girl Gone Broke*. New York: Villard, 2001.
———. *Mixed: My Life in Black and White*. New York: Villard, 2006.
Reed, Adolph. "What Are the Drums Saying, Booker? The Current Crisis of the Black Intellectual." *Village Voice* 11 Apr. 1995: 31–36.
Spencer, Ranier. "Mixed Race Chic." *Chronicle Review* 29 May 2009: B4.
Stone, Biz. *Who Let the Blogs Out? A Hyperconnected Peek at the World of Weblogs*. New York: St. Martin's, 2004.
TBS Symposium. "Corporatization of the Media." *Transnational Broadcasting Studies* 6 (Spring/Summer 2001).

Grafted Belongings
Identification in Autobiographical Narratives of African American Transracial Adoptees

MARINA FEDOSIK

> Too often a perversion of caring for the world means that this care morphs into a violence based upon caring for these children, or for ones who will be like them. . . . For that, these children must more or less literally put their own lives on the line.
>
> VIKKI BELL,
Culture and Performance

Even though according to Albert E. Stone "nearly every segment of black life has found a voice through the art of personal history" since the publication of W. E. B. Du Bois's *Dusk of Dawn* and Richard Wright's *Black Boy* in the 1940s (171), narratives of African American adoptees raised by Caucasian families in the second half of the twentieth century remain relatively unknown to the public. Around twelve thousand transracial adoptions of African American children that took place between 1948 and 1975 practically vanished from the public eye after the National Association of Black Social Workers' "vehement stand" against transracial placements resulted in a significant drop in their numbers (777).[1] Protesting against the social perception of transracial adoption as a cure for racial divisions in American society, the NABSW raised concerns over the ability of white adoptive parents to provide transracial adoptees access to culturally transmitted identifications and social skills necessary for surviving in a racist society. Although the ongoing public discussions of transracial adoptions informed the implementation of the Multiethnic Placement Act (1994),[2] and there have been numerous studies of transracial adoptees' adjustment over the decades following the boom in transracial placements, these inquiries relied on a limited understanding of transracial adoptees' experience—an understanding informed primarily by the need to determine the social value and viability of transracial adoption.[3]

In recent years, however, the often-neglected adoptees' side of the story has found its way into representation through adult transracial adoptees' narratives. These narratives have become available to the public as informal and research interviews (such as those included in Sandra Lee Patton's important study *Birthmarks*) as well as the aestheticized published accounts of transracial adoptees' experiences that are the subject of this chapter. Conversing with the reductionist understandings of transracial adoption as a universal good or a threat to a habitable identity, two adult African American transracial adoptees' memoirs discussed below—Catherine E. McKinley's *The Book of Sarahs* and Jaiya John's *Black Baby, White Hands*—question identification trajectories of kinship and race that are widely perceived as natural by bringing attention to common undifferentiation of culture and race in public perceptions of the transracial adoptee's identity. A comparison of these two narratives reveals how definitions of "whiteness" and "blackness" are complicated in the life writing of African American transracial adoptees, who expose the dependence of their identity formation simultaneously on essentialism and the performative/discursive practices lodged in the politics and economies of American kinship, American cultural imaginaries shaped by racial formations, and pan-Africanism.

Through the practice of life writing, McKinley and John seek to restore their private histories in the public memory as they speak of growing up in white adoptive families, searching for a racial identity, reuniting with their birth parents, and coming to terms with genealogies that straddle both sides of the color line. Among other topics, these adoptees-authors explore possibilities for black-white kinship; limits to cultural acceptance of their hybrid subjectivities; legitimacy of their white, African American, and African identifications; and the consequences of being biracial in the United States. The aesthetically formalized autobiographical adoption narratives (re)produce and question representations of the transracial adoptee's identity that resonate not only with American kinship ideals and established public perceptions of adoption but also with "narrative paradigms, stylistic and linguistic practices—which had to have been given in advance in order for that particular text to be produced in its unique historical specificity" (Jameson 42). McKinley's and John's memoirs draw on at least two life writing traditions—adoption-search narratives and black autobiography—to contextualize and aestheticize the complexities of their identification process at the junction of American kinship and race.

African American transracial adoptees' autobiographical writing often follows narrative trajectories shared by adoption-search narratives and black autobiographies. Discovery of difference (adoptive and/or racial) and experience of loss/displacement orient the narrator toward identification routes that lead from bondage to freedom, dependence to autonomy, ignorance to knowledge, and exile to return. Such texts often present themselves as narratives of resistance and self-reinvention inspired by a quest for wholeness, be it a search for a dialectic solution to "Du Bois's 'twoness,' this inability to achieve wholeness of spirit and vision" (Gomez 177) or the adoptee's simultaneous and often conflicting identifications with adoptive and birth cultures and families—or both. The recovery of wholeness in such narratives is often imagined through a return to a site of natural belonging, where someone's essence is difference no more.

Among typical concerns of adoption-search narratives is the issue of regaining control over adoptee-authors' personal histories obliterated by the institutions that regulate transnational adoption and subsumed by the histories of adoptive families. The search memoir—a specific kind of adoption narrative that emphasizes the centrality of searches and reunions with birth families to the adoptee's selfhood—became the prevalent form of the representation of adult adoptees' experience in American literature by the turn of the twenty-first century. The majority of search narratives published to date have been authored by adoptees who joined their adoptive families in the 1950s to 1970s—a period in American adoption history when silencing the adoptee's pre-adoption past was culturally acceptable and legally enforced. While the complicity of the search narrative in reaffirming culturally endorsed forms of kinship is hard to deny, the first search narratives authored by matched, domestic adoptees appeared in the 1970s as a practice of resistance to contemporaneous adoption practices.[4] Articulating their identity struggles through the language of trauma and loss, domestic adoptees-writers of the 1970s protested against the policy of closed records that regulated American domestic adoptions at the time.[5] The policy was implemented in the middle of the twentieth century to protect the privacy of the parties involved in adoption. It denied adoptive and birth families legal access to any information about each other and denied adoptees, specifically, access to their original birth certificate and complete medical history. In their life writing, adoptees commonly positioned unrestricted knowledge of their genealogy and a reunion with the birth family as solutions to genealogical confusion that precluded them from feeling "whole." And yet search narratives often reveal that besides a potential connection with the birth culture and family and, often, a reinforced relationship with the adoptive family, newfound genealogical knowledge exposed adult adoptees to the limits of their belonging at both sites.

The culture of secrecy associated with adoption was consistent with the prominent bias against child illegitimacy and preference for biological families in American culture of the time. Following these cultural ideals of kinship, adoptive parents were trying to raise their adopted children as their own, often disregarding the adoptees' pre-adoption histories. In the case of transracial adoption, adoptive parents tended to ignore even the adoptees' racial difference. Colorblind parenting approaches, combined with the lack of ethnic diversity in the white adoptive families' neighborhoods, often complicated transracial adoptees' identity formation. The adoptive parents' avowal, "You are our daughter/son," could hardly orient a transracial adoptee living in the economy of differently valued bodies toward a satisfactory identification route. Hence, the search memoirs written by transnational and transracial adoptees that appeared at the turn of the twenty-first century raise a significant set of issues. These autobiographical narratives brought to the fore the transracial adoptee's alienation from the adoptive family and culture due to racialization, inability to identify unconditionally with her or his birth family and/or culture due to lack of exposure to birth culture and language, and estrangement from histories of ethnic communities in America combined with cultural pressure to identify in relation to such communities.

The clash between the transracial adoptee's experience of racialization and the adoptive parents' inability or refusal to incorporate the adoptee's racial heritage into the adoptive family's collective history shaped the transracial adoptee's identification—a process that "entails discursive work, the binding and marking of symbolic boundaries" (Hall 3)—in very specific ways. Transracial adoptees' searches for racial identities and biological kin became tightly intertwined because their identification was contingent on simultaneous negotiation of adoptive and racial differences. Transracial adoptees' life writing, therefore, often reveals that the identity of a transracial adoptee depends as much on discovering private genealogy as on appropriating racial heritage.

Both McKinley and John explore their racial difference from their adoptive families as a cause for the psychic condition of nonbelonging that fuels their desire to search for roots. John writes that even though "at the base of [his] being, next to Mom was the place [he] wished to belong and be accepted" (62); "as [his] life evolved into a processing of constant racial messages and interactions," he increasingly felt that his adoptive mother could not "underst[and] the totality of what [he] was beginning to choke upon" (65). Lacking experience in dealing with overt and latent racism, she could not be a "conductor, explainer" (65) and the protector he needed to navigate self-identification in a predominantly white environment. John remembers experiencing his identity formation as dependent on the racializing gaze of the larger American culture: he learned to "deriv[e] [his] sense of belonging largely from how others who looked like [him]—. . . in books, television, and movies—were accepted or rejected" (136).

As John's double consciousness develops, his awareness of the contingency and uncertainty of his membership in his hometown community increases. Although he feels accepted as a transracial adoptee—a "subject of a collective and benevolent agenda" (287)—John understands that this acceptance depends on his demarcating himself from manifestations of blackness perceived as threatening by white people. Resisting a further split of his identity, which has already been destabilized by his adoptive status, he envisions such partial erasure of the "racial ingredient of [his] persona" (287) as "a denial of [his] essence" (138), a form of indirect violence that fosters his invisibility and social blindness to a definitive part of his selfhood. The pressure to carry on the impossible, simultaneous performances of acceptable blackness and membership in a white kinship structure prompts John to seek refuge from the multiple incongruent identification trajectories in a strong black identity solidified by boundaries drawn against the white racist other. John's search for inclusion in the African American collective becomes his strategy of resistance to racist discourses and a path to empowerment in the racially stratified American society.

While the adoption-search narrative blueprint is apparent in John's memoir—the text relies on information that could have become available only through a deliberate search for adoption papers and inquiries about birth parents—this narrative pattern is overridden by the aesthetic of the conversion narrative typical of "black spiritual autobiographies, which exhibit a similar threefold pattern of death, conversion, and rebirth" (Lionnet 115). Several chapters at the end of his memoir are dedicated to his reunion with his birth parents, but these reunions do not seem central to John's search. Rather, they confirm and reinforce the black identity that he has created for himself by appropriating African American collective experience and immersing himself in African American culture. Such a departure from the emphasis on the birth mother and the adoptee reunion, recurrent in adoption-search memoirs authored by women and present in McKinley's text, marks John's narrative as an autobiographical text that follows "male pathways to selfhood via escape, literacy, and public activity" (Stone 189) typical of male black autobiography.

Following the logic of the conversion narrative, John's memoir begins with a symbolic death of his old life. As an adult, he rides a bus through his hometown devastated by a fire. Seeing his old family house in ruins, John imagines the Great Spirit saying, "'You may go forward now, my son'" (3). The destruction of his house, "the trigger for [his adoptive family's] memories" (4), signals to him freedom from the adoptive family's narratives of his past and prompts his decision to articulate "new truths" about his adoption experience. The opening scene communicates that while as a child and a teenager John could only intuit racialization that inscribed a racial identity onto his body, as a young adult he possesses the agency to control his own identification. The scene is also a declaration of his authorial power over his life story—the power to choose how to represent himself.

The conversion narrative paradigm enables John to forge a unified black identity and claim an empowered membership in the black community. Within this paradigm, John reframes his search as a recovery of his lost identity and focuses on (re-)creating its continuity.[6] By placing biographical information about his birth parents (both black), their encounter, his birth, and his initial nine-month placement with a black foster mother at the beginning of the narrative, he marks the beginning of his black identity formation. Having thus established a chronological frame for his identity narrative, he imagines himself "dislocated, muted, and a betrayer of all who came before [him]" (301). His focus is therefore on reconnecting with his essence—repressed by the transracial adoption—through a spiritual awakening. Adoption papers proving that for eighteen months "he was immersed in . . . rhythms, sounds, voices, words, emotions, energy, scents, routines, and the social influx" (30) in African American homes become authenticating documents for his primary identification as black. By imagining his identity formation as predating his birth, John naturalizes his socialization into African American culture and implies that his inculcation into the ways of a white adoptive family is secondary and reversible.

The success of John's project depends on the "marking of difference and exclusion" (Hall 4) as an identity-building strategy; therefore, he represents his racial identity as dependent on reunification with the essential black self and disidentification with the white racist other. The unifying thrust of the conversion narrative seems to serve John's purpose better than the adoption-search narrative format. Adoption-search narratives typically seek to explore and piece together an identity defined by "intersectionality," or the adoptee's ability to identify or be identified with (at least) two cultures and two families: adoptive and birth.[7] Even though adoption-search memoirs may end in avowals of adoptees' newfound "wholeness," such closures frequently appear forced. Often, they serve to contain the adoptee's confusion brought on by the discovery of the limits of belonging with either culture or family. In other words, due to its open-ended character, the search narrative may not be the most suitable form for writing into being a coherent and stable autobiographical subject. If anything, this form of autobiographical adoption narrative compels the writer to acknowledge the liminality of the transracial adoptee's position.

Granted, in his pursuit of a unified identity, John does not fully suppress the complexity of the transracial adoptee's subjectivity. He remembers feeling intimidated by contact with African Americans and thinking that he is not "black enough." In choosing a college, he says, he deliberately avoided historically black schools because he "was not ready to immerse [him]self in Blackness" yet (236). He admits that ironically "the first reassuring step on the journey to [his] Black heritage occurred when [he was] sure [his] two White roommates accepted [him]" (239). Noticing that racism is not only an individual prejudice but also a "kinetic force stowed away in whatever hue of skin it chose to inhabit" (263), he acknowledges racial prejudice that exists in black communities and mentions, albeit in passing, his concern about colorism among African Americans. And yet, even though he writes that a reunion with his birth parents and a strong racial identity have brought him closer to his adoptive family, the narrative shows little ambiguity about his identification.

His spiritual quest to (re)claim his black identity begins with the decision to "get far away from New Mexico" (236) and attend college in a place with a more substantial African American presence. John writes that his racial identity is gradually strengthened by his friendships with African Americans, knowledge of African American history gained in college, his engagement in an African American activist group on campus, his initiation into the barbershop culture, and his experience of the communal character of African American kinship. By the end of college, he claims, he feels strengthened enough by the "circle of Black kinship and White persons who explicitly honored that bruised Black part of [him]" not to feel crushed by racism (254). Several years later, following a two-year-long debilitating illness brought on by the stress of reinventing his identity and kinship, he relinquishes his adoptive family name. John imagines the disease as the death of his old self and declares that Jordan Jaiya John—his new name revealed to him by God—marks the end of his "lifelong spiritual bondage" (305). Speaking of his adoption experience through the trope of slavery, John avows his autonomy and "the power to determine the text of his own life" (Andrews 4). At the end of his narrative, his racial identification is unmistakably black.

The contingency of satisfactory identification in the reappropriation of African American collective experience—central to John's memoir and frequently explored in life narratives of transracial adoptees—brings into focus forces that control African American transracial adoptees' identification in a culture with a history of organizing social empowerment along color lines. Racial identification of transracial adoptees is often culturally understood as a matter of individual choice, but the discursive formations that make this choice inevitable remain obscured. For instance, Sandra Lee Patton claims that research supportive of transracial adoption relies on "race as a fixed category," limits inquiry to the "individual and familial levels," but ignores "institutional, cultural, social, economic, and political contexts within which such families are constructed and maintained" (5). Autobiographical narratives that represent the process of the transracial adoptee's identity formation from the adult adoptee's perspective, however, demonstrate that race, endorsed as a cultural, legal, and social axis of identification, is not entirely a matter of free choice for the transracial adoptee. Within the framework of American identity politics, an African American child brought up by Caucasian adoptive parents often feels compelled to identify as black by the logic of culture(s) and/or a social order averse to hybrid black-white identifications. Under such conditions, the "transmission of [African American] culture within a racially stratified social structure" (Patton 5)—the main concern of transracial adoption critics—becomes a survival issue for transracial adoptees whose place in hierarchically organized cultural and social structures is contingent on their race.[8]

McKinley, for instance, remembers having an acute awareness of the hypo-descent imperative as a teenager. When her white adoptive brother unwittingly called her "half-Black," she shouted back, overcome with anger: "I am BLACK! . . . In America, if you have one drop of Black blood, you are BLACK!" (81). Similar to John, as a teenager and a young adult, McKinley resorts to accepting and reinforcing her blackness as a survival strategy in an environment in which she is expected to identify as an African American. But while McKinley shares John's desire for a strong black identity, she probes the limits of racial categories more rigorously than John, who significantly essentializes his identification process. McKinley challenges the perceived homogeneity of the black subject by raising issues that John may not have had to address or chose to suppress in his attempt to produce a relatively linear (masculine?) narrative of a coherent racial identity. McKinley's visible biracialism—she has a Jewish birth mother and an African American birth father—exposes her to experiences and challenges that John, whose birth parents are both black, may not have encountered. Consequently, their identification pathways and ways of narrating them diverge at the point where the concept of authentic homogenous blackness is brought into question. John, like McKinley, has to negotiate a certain hybridity of identity; he has been raised in a white adoptive family, after all. Given his embodied blackness, however, his hybridity is lodged primarily in the cultural, the performative. McKinley, though, has to contend with the essentializing discourses of black authenticity that determine her access to "'the Black community' which has tightly drawn boundaries in terms of admittance" (Tate 151).

Autobiographical practice typically necessitates at least partial suppression of the autobiographical subject's heterogeneity, since identification "operates across difference" and "requires what is left outside, its constitutive outside, to consolidate the process" (Hall 3).[9] And while identities emerge "within, not outside representation," the structure of the resulting identity is determined not only by the autobiographer's desire but also by "discourses and practices which attempt to 'interpellate,' speak to us or hail us into place as the social subjects of particular discourses" (Hall 4–5). McKinley's and John's narrative choices are subject to overlapping but also distinctive, identifying, discursive formations determined by their racial genealogies. John's identification against the white other is facilitated by the color of his skin and the race of his birth parents. McKinley's mixed genealogy, however, complicates the definition of her racial other and engenders a more open-ended narrative focused less on the "constitution of a social identity [as] an act of power" (Ernesto Laclau qtd. in Hall 5) and more on understanding where she "fit[s] into The Story of Race in America" (McKinley 13).

Like many adoptee-authors of search narratives, McKinley begins with an avowal of her alienation from the adoptive family. In the opening chapter—a story of her adoptive family's trip to Scotland—she draws on the trope of return shared by both slave and transnational adoption-search narratives.[10] Return trips frequently become literal and symbolic journeys to places of imaginary belongings. McKinley, however, makes it clear that her family's trip is their "return," not hers. It is, she writes, "a journey back through the McKinley's narrative of Scotch-Irish and English migrations" (3–4). The trip underscores her adoptive and racial difference and amplifies her insecurities about belonging with her adoptive family. Every new bit of discovered familial history makes her "feel oddly cold" and weak to the point of experiencing "emotions of an asthma attack—the kind of terrible struggle you feel when your body cannot take in the air that freely surrounds you, while the people you hope will save you look on from the outside, perversely gulping it in" (5, 11). She ponders her family's desire to distance itself from other people (is her family embarrassed by her presence?) and feels unable to partake in activities her adoptive parents and white adopted brother enjoy, "spending hours at times in an intensely fixed threesome" (8). The insight that she gleans from this "return" is her family members' inability to comprehend the depth of her alienation from the culture and kinship relations they take for granted.

Growing up with a white adopted brother, she knows the varying effects of racializing discourses that determine her and his acceptance by the adoptive family and larger culture: "There were adopted children, such as my brother, who were free of public curiosity and scrutiny—and there were transracial adoptees, who could never escape it" (53). Skin color conceals her brother's adoptive difference and amplifies hers, inviting people's frequent questions about her origins. Even though she accepts that such questions may be prompted by a genuine desire to know her, people's curiosity seems to her more a veiled request "to affirm the politics of the 'one drop' law of Blackness" and the "baseline assumptions about who any of us are" (24). With her membership in a white adoptive family constantly questioned, McKinley experiences herself as "an appendage" to her adoptive family's life, a "not-too-friendly organism that joined a larger body, the host accommodating . . . leaving the thing to nurse undisturbed" (104, 83, 77). Her adoptive parents' refusal to admit that their whole family is transracial—"a white and Black family" that has to "be attuned to particular things"—leaves her one-on-one with a racist society while they hide behind their whiteness and "naïveté" (83) about American racial formations.

The trip to Scotland, though devastating to her sense of belonging with her adoptive family, brings McKinley a brief encounter with her own "roots." At a pub in Edinburgh, she observes a group of Nigerian students "soaking up their languor" (4), admiring their afros, bright scarves, and unusual, beautiful dresses. Comparing the tartan of the McKinley kilt she is wearing to the bright fabric of the Nigerian women's scarves, she feels drawn to the scarves that are "reweaving the dull, familiar textures of that world, of home, where the only sight of Africa was an occasional face floating behind the windshield of a passing car, always en route to somewhere else" (4). This brief encounter with the Nigerian students is one of her own moments of self-discovery, one that she structurally juxtaposes to her family's. Another such moment is her watching reruns of Alex Haley's *Roots* while her parents and brother spend time engrossed in their shared hobbies. The show nurtures her attachment to the fantasy of Africa as a place of "natural" belonging and orients her toward seeking inclusion in an African American community.

McKinley's identification process seems to follow a route similar to the one that has led John to the security of an unambiguous racial identity protected by the firmly set boundaries against the white other. McKinley's evolving identification along the black/white binary, however, is shattered during one of her first encounters with black Americans. The complexity and vulnerability of her racial identification are exposed at a service in the black church she has just started attending. A black child she hugs and kisses (the usual church greeting) "wipe[s] his cheek in disgust" and says to his mother that he does not want "no white lady kissing [him]" (63). McKinley's "fear of not being able to control how others perceive her" (54) is exacerbated by the fact that the boy who does not recognize her blackness has a biracial adopted sister. Caught between "different meanings in [the] simultaneous embodiment" (Bell 26) of her blackness and whiteness, McKinley experiences her position as marginal, boding arbitrary acceptance, nonbelonging, and "being imagined as especially different, good or bad, and often the Only One" (62).

Since the corporeal ambiguity complicates her unconditional belonging with any racial group, McKinley seeks to reinforce her desired black identification by learning how to "be" black. She tries to "master [her African American friend's] Black-girl-ness—her attitude and phrases . . . sound and posture" (66). Her friend, she writes, would "coach" (67) her on how to dress and act to fit in with other black teenagers and then take her out to practice her new skills. This narrative moment in McKinley's autobiography, like no other, exposes the role of culture as a racializing tool and the performative aspect of culturally inscribed racial identities. Yet McKinley feels that "performativity cannot itself make a promise in disembodied form" (Bell 5). Lacking in embodied blackness herself, she invents a black mother, whose body could authenticate her racial identification. At a Black Liberation Day festival, she takes a picture of an unknown black woman who, she imagines, could be her "real" mother. She names the unknown woman Mattie after the "archetypal Black mother[s]" she has read about in "narratives of Southern childhoods" (30). In college, McKinley keeps the framed photo on her dresser, and when her white adoptive parents visit her, she introduces them as guardians. McKinley successfully harnesses cultural assumptions about embodied racial difference: McKinley's friends take a picture of a black woman as a more likely index of her racial identity than a white couple.

The picture secures her belonging with the group of black students who "polic[e] a strong Black line of social identity" (30), but McKinley is still aware of the precariousness of her position. The group has accepted her, she writes, because "our number was so small, who could afford to cast off a ('phoney' was the word we always used) half-breed? But I knew I needed a definite sign of my legitimacy. I knew that old saying *Mama's baby, papa's maybe*. Mattie was the sign" (30). McKinley's fantasy grows out of her desire for the birth mother known to many adoptees raised in a culture that favors biological lines of descent. Yet, simultaneously, it is a fantasy that taps into American racial imaginary, in which mulatto/mulatta genealogies are inflected with rape, matrilineal racial descent, socially constructed illegitimacy, and violent disruptions of black motherhood.

The search for her birth mother, which McKinley undertakes as an adult, is inseparable from her search for black racial identity. She hopes that a reunion with her black birth mother will "naturalize" her arbitrary and unstable race and kinship identifications. When her search finally reveals that her biological mother is Jewish and white, McKinley feels "the lines of [her] imaginings shift again" because there is "no room in [her] imagination for a white birth mother" (36). This new genealogical knowledge and her subsequent search for her black birth father force her to reinvent her personal history in the context of a "post–Black Power, post-segregation transracial adoptee's consciousness" (55).

An encounter with the National Association of Black Social Workers further enhances her awareness of her unique subject position and the need to develop her "own consciousness living inside transracial adoption's contradictions" (102). As part of her research on transracial adoption history, she visits the NABSW headquarters and talks to several social workers. She is compelled to do it because her "anger and struggles with [her] family, and some of [her] personal truths" (98) have been built on the Afrocentric and black nationalist philosophies underpinning the radical position of the NABSW. The interviews reveal to her, however, that such a position may foreclose possibilities for identifications that she finds equally important. While she is grateful to the NABSW for being "the only voice that answered [her] need for a clear politicized analysis of transracial adoption" instead of color blindness or the use of a political antisegregation statement, she feels that she cannot "reconcile [her] upbringing with their absolute position" (100). "As I held on to that radical posture," McKinley writes, "I began to feel like I was betraying my family and myself, and some of my more interesting and attractive contradictions" (100). Talking to social workers about possibilities to "work together," she realizes that she is "not the transracial adoptee [they] nee[d]" because she cannot "ultimately say that [she is] against transracial adoption" and because the needs of adult transracial adoptees are not on their agenda (100).

The complexities of her identity become more and more pronounced as McKinley tries to reconcile its multiple contexts with the exclusionary visions of black authenticity. Although she keeps "looking for a way to find [her] own story within the larger story of African Americans" (61), the dimensions of her history become clear only after she connects with the Afro-German women she meets at the memorial service for Audre Lorde. Their experiences, she writes, "like Jackie Kay's and Thelma Perkins's and Isha McKenzie-Mavinga's, were in some ways closer to [hers] than those of most African Americans" (60).[11] "Worn out from trying to cast [her]self within the very narrow conventions in narratives of Blackness" (61), McKinley looks for identification in contexts beyond white American patrilineal mulatto/mulatta genealogies and imagines herself a product of "African American men's segregation-era sexual crossings of racial lines, which ha[ve] created a whole international community" (61). She gives her identity diasporic dimensions, following in the footsteps of Jackie Kay, a writer and a black Scottish adoptee with a Nigerian birth father who stated in an interview that her selfhood had been shaped by her desire to "tak[e] different things from Black culture, different Black cultures around the world, and lin[k] them up to [her] own identity" (qtd. in Gish 179). McKinley thus invites the reader to contextualize the identity of an African American transracial adoptee not only by private histories of birth and adoptive families or the history of African Americans in the United States but also by more-recent transnational histories of black people and, specifically, transracial/transnational adoptees.

Imagining her identity as diasporic allows McKinley to expand its structure beyond the black/white binary. Living in Ghana and traveling around Africa prompt her to position her black identification as hybrid, characterized by "the interaction of 'the Black same' and 'the black other'" (Tate 128). By participating in the daily lives of people in Ghana, McKinley gradually gains communal acceptance, but she writes that to Ghanians she is always a foreigner, a "half-caste," an "obruni."[12] She is furtively touched in the street by strangers curious about her origins, and while she notices no malice in their touches and questions about her genealogy, their curiosity nevertheless "bring[s] back a powerful sense of the outsidership that [she] had often felt at home" (17). She must face the fact that in the land she had invested with the hope of reinforcing her blackness, she is compelled yet again to revise her racial identification: "At the end of my search for self-definition, I have become a rich, white woman. A stranger. . . . If I offer explanations—that I am an African American—people respond with comments that betray their sense of the incongruity of my Blackness. . . . None of what matters to American social sorting, to one's identity at home, counts for much here" (286–87). Thus she is introduced to "the great conundrum" of the African diaspora: "the unattainable nature of the polarities: Africa, once lost, has yet to be recovered; whereas America, as an ideal, has yet to become home" (Gomez 177).

While the ending of McKinley's narrative is similar to John's text in that she develops a strong African American identification and finds solace and a place to belong within a community of black people, she embraces the condition of not fully belonging anywhere. Above all, McKinley searches for an awareness of the forces that shape her identity and claims the right to "sit down in someone else's paradigms and try to figure [her]self out" (286–87). Her narrative, more so than John's life writing, probes the dialectic of essentialism and hybridity in a transracial adoptee's racial identity to confirm Shirley Anne Tate's claim that "'race' is unstable and can be transformed through hybridity, whilst hybridity depends on essentialism to emerge" (76). McKinley's "blackness" is constituted not only by drawing boundaries against the white racist other but also by dis-identifying with what Tate calls the "Black same" or the idea of blackness lodged in "exclusionary Afro-centric thinking" (2, 75). At the same time, her hybrid blackness is inflected by her refusal to let go completely of her "white" identifications. "An African American woman without any discernable roots, with barely any melanin, with a Jewish birth mother, adopted to and raised in a WASP nest" (61), she refuses to cast away parts of herself that may be perceived as incompatible with and within exclusionary identifications. In other words, McKinley frames the problem of the transracial adoptee's identity formation by demonstrating that the adoptee rarely experiences an ontological certainty about who the "self" and the "other" are. Unlike John's text, her narrative is not a project focused on writing into being an "authentic" self but rather "an orphan text that attempts to create its own genealogy by simultaneously appealing to and debunking the cultural traditions it helps to redefine" (Lionnet 116).

The autobiographical "truth" that emerges at the end of McKinley's narrative is that, for an adoptee, there is never an "authentic" self. Adoptees, Patton holds, "write [their] identities through the trope of difference" and "cope" with nonbelonging by "develop[ing] techniques for appearing to fit anywhere" (8). It may seem that such a postmodernist ability to switch subject positions promises an adoptee greater freedom of identification and an increased autonomy from identity-anchoring discourses operating in the larger society. Both John and McKinley demonstrate, however, that in the case of transracial adoption, the potential of such an eternally performative self is limited. In a culture that favors biological, "legitimate lines of descent," all adoptees may feel as if they "occupy a particular social location" (Patton 6), but in-racial adoptees do have more freedom to choose and/or manipulate their (dis)identifications. For the transracial adoptee, whose embodied difference is constantly invoked and contextualized by the histories of racial relations in the United States, performances of certain kinds of whiteness or blackness often become impossible. The identity of the transracial adoptee is a mode of being lodged in both the embodied and the performed, characterized by what Tate calls a "strategic form of hybridity" (163). The conflict of such an identity is, therefore, "not to be comprehended as between the real and the acted, the before and the after, but between different simultaneous modes of embodiment as the body moves through necessarily different sets of relations" (Bell 26).

No less importantly, the differences in McKinley's and John's approaches to the representation of their searches for selfhood signal that transracial adoptees cannot be understood as a homogenous group any more than transracial adoption can be understood as an unequivocally beneficial or tragic experience. The narrative choices that McKinley and John make are indeed choices between the homogeneity and the multiplicity of the autobiographical subject, whose articulation in each case is contingent on determinate conditions of existence and discursive practices that orient the adoptee's life narrative toward specific gender, race, and kinship identification trajectories. Ultimately, McKinley's and John's narratives demonstrate that transracial adoptees' identities depend on (to rephrase Hall slightly) "'who [they] are' or 'where [they] came from,'" *as well as* "what [they] might become, how [they] have been represented, and how that bears on how [they] might represent [them]selves" (4).

NOTES

An earlier version of this chapter was published as "Grafted Belongings: Identification in Autobiographical Narratives of African American Transracial Adoptees," *a/b: Auto/Biography Studies* 27.1 (2012): 211–30. © 2012 The Autobiography Society. Reprinted by permission.

1. In this chapter, I use *transracial* in reference to adoptees who are identified by adoption facilitating institutions or self-identify as African American and have been brought up by Caucasian adoptive parents. The first official placement of an African American child with a

Caucasian adoptive family was recorded in Minnesota in 1948 (Herman). Transracial placements, however, gained momentum only at the beginning of the 1960s.

2. The Multiethnic Placement Act was aimed at promoting adoptions of the growing number of non-Caucasian children in foster care by curtailing racial and ethnic matching policies. The implementation of this act followed heated public debates in the 1980s over "crack babies." For a discussion of the "crack babies" controversy and its implications for adoption policies, see Perry.

3. Informed by popular imaginings of adoptees as children, the studies predominantly focused on transracial adoptees' childhood and adolescence. As the adoptees grew older, attrition of families participating in the studies increased, which compromised the accuracy of findings. Also, evaluations of adoptees' adjustment were often based on reported outcomes without due attention to daily lived experience. See, for example, Brooks and Barth for a more detailed discussion of the scope and limitations of transracial adoptees' adjustment studies.

4. Regarding the role of the search narrative, see, for instance, Barbara Yngvesson's and Sandra Lee Patton's discussions of the sociocultural mechanisms that compel adoptees to search for their birth parents as a way to find out who they "really" are. Both authors point out that American culture, similar to other Western cultures, endorses and favors exclusive, biological kinship. "Matching" is the practice that assures visual resemblance between adoptive parents and adoptees. Examples of domestic search memoirs that challenged the policy of closed records are Fisher and Lifton.

5. Previously, since the beginning of the twentieth century, domestic adoptions were open or regulated by the confidentiality policy, which denied public access to adoption records but allowed it to the adoption triad members. The policy of closed records is still applied today in the majority of states; however, since the 1970s it has been successfully challenged in several states by adoption triad members seeking to reunite. Given the growing popularity of open adoptions in which birth and adoptive families maintain some form of contact, the closed records policy has become a choice rather than a rule in current adoptions.

6. Buckley mentions a possible focus of conversion autobiography on recovering the lost identity (53).

7. See Minow for a discussion of the "intersectionality" of identities, that is, possibilities to identify simultaneously with different groups or experience oppression along multiple trajectories (e.g., race and gender).

8. Consult, for example, Hollingsworth as well as Bradley and Hawkins-Leon.

9. Smith and Watson write about the colonizing potential of the autobiography's universalizing tendencies.

10. Adoptees' "return" trips to birth countries have become popular among transnational, especially transracial, adoptees and their adoptive families since the 1990s, when the importance of recognizing the adoptee's racial and cultural heritage became widely accepted by adoption experts and adoptive parents.

11. These are the names of British biracial adoptees-writers born to white mothers and black fathers from Nigeria and Trinidad.

12. McKinley explains that "obruni" is a "person with lighter than dark brown skin or any person of any color from the West, or anyone who is not a native-speaking Ghanian" (16).

WORKS CITED

Andrews, William L. Introduction. *African American Autobiography: A Collection of Critical Essays.* Ed. William L. Andrews. Upper Saddle River, NJ: Prentice Hall, 1994. 1–7.

Bell, Vikki. *Culture and Performance: The Challenges of Ethics, Politics and Feminist Theory.* Oxford: Berg, 2007.

Bradley, Carla, and Cynthia G. Hawkins-Leon. "The Transracial Adoption Debate: Counseling and Legal Implications." *Journal of Counseling and Development* 80.4 (2002): 433–41.

Brooks, Devon, and Richard P. Barth. "Adult Transracial and Inracial Adoptees: Effects of Race, Gender, Adoptive Family Structure, and Placement History on Adjustment Outcomes." *American Journal of Orthopsychiatry* 61.1 (1999): 87–99.

Buckley, Jerome H. *The Turning Key: Autobiography and the Subjective Impulse since 1800.* Cambridge, MA: Harvard UP, 1984.

Fisher, Florence. *The Search for Anna Fisher.* New York: A. Fields, 1973.

Gish, Nancy K. "Adoption, Identity, and Voice: Jackie Kay's Inventions of Self." *Imagining Adoption: Essays on Literature and Culture.* Ed. Marianne Novy. Ann Arbor: U of Michigan P, 2004. 171–92.

Gomez, Michael A. "Of Du Bois and Diaspora: The Challenge of African American Studies." *Journal of Black Studies* 35.2 (2004): 175–94.

Hall, Stuart. Introduction: Who Needs Identity? *Questions of Cultural Identity.* Ed. Stuart Hall and Paul DuGay. London: Sage, 1996. 1–17.

Herman, Ellen. "Transracial Adoptions." *Adoption History Project* 11 June 2007. U of Oregon.

Hollingsworth, Leslie Doty. "Symbolic Interactionism, African American Families, and the Transracial Adoption Controversy." *Social Work* 44.5 (1999): 443–53.

Jameson, Fredric. *The Political Unconscious: Narrative as a Socially Symbolic Act.* 1981. New York: Routledge, 2006.

John, Jaiya. *Black Baby, White Hands: A View from the Crib.* 2nd ed. Silver Spring, MD: Soul Water Rising, 2005.

Lifton, Betty Jean. *Twice Born: Memoirs of an Adopted Daughter.* New York: McGraw-Hill, 1975.

Lionnet, Françoise. "Autoethnography: The An-Archic Style of *Dust Tracks on the Road.*" *African American Autobiography: A Collection of Critical Essays.* Ed. William L. Andrews. Upper Saddle River, NJ: Prentice Hall, 1994. 113–37.

McKinley, Catherine E. *The Book of Sarahs: A Family in Parts.* New York: Counterpoint, 2002.

Minow, Martha. *Not Only for Myself: Identity, Politics, and the Law.* New York: New Press, 1999.

National Association of Black Social Workers. "Position Statement on Trans-Racial Adoption, September 1972." *Children and Youth in America: A Documentary History.* Vol. 3. Ed. Robert H. Bremner. Cambridge, MA: Harvard UP, 1974. 777–80.

Patton, Sandra Lee. *Birthmarks: Transracial Adoption in Contemporary America.* New York: New York UP, 2000.

Perry, Twila L. "Transracial and International Adoption: Mothers, Hierarchy, Race, and Feminist Legal Theory." *Yale Journal of Law and Feminism* 10.1 (1998): 101–64.

Smith, Sidonie, and Julia Watson. Introduction. *De/Colonizing the Subject: The Politics of Gender in Women's Autobiography.* Ed. Sidonie Smith and Julia Watson. Minneapolis: U of Minnesota P, 1992. xiii–xxxi.

Stone, Albert E. "After *Black Boy* and *Dusk of Dawn*: Patterns in Recent Black Autobiography." *African American Autobiography: A Collection of Critical Essays*. Ed. William L. Andrews. Upper Saddle River, NJ: Prentice Hall, 1994. 171–95.

Tate, Shirley Anne. *Black Skins, Black Masks: Hybridity, Dialogism, Performativity*. Aldershot, UK: Ashgate, 2005.

Yngvesson, Barbara. "Going 'Home': Adoption, Loss of Bearings, and the Mythology of Roots." *Social Text* 21.1 (2003): 7–27.

Reading Signs of Crazy

Pam Grier, a Black Feminist in Praxis

KWAKIUTL L. DREHER

> Pam Grier is an incredible actress!
> LEIGH KOLB,
> "The Unfinished Legacy of Pam Grier"

> Pam Grier has phallic charisma, [and] we gain a sense of her as both a *phenomenon of consumption* (consumed by audience-consumers) and a *phenomenon of production* (produced by industrial institutions like American International Pictures).
> MIA MASK,
> *Divas on Screen: Black Women in American Film*

> Pam Grier [is] the Mocha Mogul of Hollywood.
> JAMAICA KINCAID,
> "Pam Grier"

Anyone who watches, for the first time, a film starring Pam Grier comes away with a vivid memory of experiencing the actress in this medium. It is not surprising, then, that a wide range of individuals have recalled and/or committed to print their visceral reactions to Grier, or what we may refer to as "I remember when I first saw Pam Grier" narratives. Not only does the actress typically evoke reactions such as "I was blown away" or "why isn't she in everything?"—the latter written by the contemporary blogger Leigh Kolb—but her appearances onscreen, on television, on the red carpet, and in print/visual interviews command wonder and respect. Even Pam Grier reacts emotionally to "Pam Grier" when discussing her personal life and career in the filmmaking industry. As demonstrated in this chapter, the actress's use of linguistic ribaldry in interviews and within *Foxy: My Life in Three Acts* (written with Andrea Cagan) intersects with the concerns of her life.[1] Is it any wonder, then, that Quentin Tarantino, one of the most formidable filmmakers/directors in Hollywood, wrote *Jackie Brown* (1997) for her and thus reaffirmed her legacy in film? Here I offer my "I remember when I first saw Pam Grier" narrative to begin evaluating *Foxy* by this complex and engaging actress.

I shuddered. Not in awe of her, as many viewers had, but in my memories of hearing assessments of her physical appearance as "phine," good looking, and "stacked" coming from the young men in high school. "Man!!! she's got a body!" one exclaimed in ecstasy as he mimed her curvaceous figure. All the young men gathered on this occasion applauded his assessment of Grier with a round of high-fives. Unlike these young men, however, I only could *imagine* instead of participate in this discussion on Grier's body because my parents declined my every heartfelt plea to view her films or any other movie playing during the film era known as blaxploitation.

Before I continue, it is necessary to pause to mark the genesis of this term. According to film historian Ed Guerrero, the production of *Superfly* (1972) instigated the backlash against this burgeoning film genre as "black civic dissatisfaction with the genre and that film in particular reached a crescendo" (101). Junius Griffin, then president of the Beverly Hills–Hollywood branch of the National Association for the Advancement of Colored People (NAACP), coined the term *blaxploitation*. In August 1972 *black* and *exploitation* appeared in a headline that read "NAACP Takes Militant Stand on Black Exploitation Films" in the *Hollywood Reporter*. This article summarized Griffin's "declaration of militancy" address to the branch's general membership on Hollywood's perpetuation of stereotypes concerning individuals of African descent and the presence of racial inequality in the film industry. Griffin merged *black* and *exploitation* into the popular term *blaxploitation*, defining it as "proliferating offenses" against blacks in the film industry in his expressions of frustration ("NAACP" 1, 10). A month before Griffin criticized blaxploitation, however, Rev. Jesse Jackson, president of his new organization, People United to Save Humanity (PUSH), spoke out against the genre. He promised to "raid studios [and] take on those films of vulgarity, violence and vanity, those films that project into the minds of our children the images of killers rather than healers, of dope pushers in the vein rather than hope in the brain" (qtd. in Delaney 39).

Griffin's dread mirrored that of Rev. Jackson's when he stated in his address, "We will not tolerate the continued warping of our black children's minds with the filth, violence[,] and cultural lies that are all pervasive in current productions.... The transformation from the stereotyped Stepin' Fetchit to Super Nigger on the screen is just another form of cultural genocide" (qtd. in Guerrero 101).[2] Critical assessments of this genre combined with opinions circulating in my community by filmgoers about blaxploitation no doubt contributed to the consternation harbored by my parents. According to several individuals in the black community, blaxploitation film was dangerous. In their minds, it extended no messages of racial uplift, and, worse, this type of film preyed on the young generation whose minds had been nourished by the print media of the civil rights movement.

Fast forward to the 1990s. I had forgotten about blaxploitation until Grier reentered my life during my graduate studies. When I first saw her in *Coffy* (1974) and

Foxy Brown (1974), I shuddered as I began to understand why my parents were firm regarding their decision not to allow me to view Grier's films in the 1970s. I marveled, in the on-campus media room, nevertheless, at Grier's athleticism and strength; at how well she fit into her bell-bottomed pants; at the yellow and red halter dresses she wore that accentuated her curves; at the *comfort* and *confidence* she projected in disrobing in front of the camera; and at the ease in which she participated in scenes of lovemaking with her men, namely, Howard (Booker Bradshaw) in *Coffy* and Michael (Terry Carter) in *Foxy Brown*. These images projected from the video taunted the picture of a rail-thin, very insecure teenager who came to the forefront of my adult mind as I screened these movies, and I shuddered. I immediately reached in to protect her (me) from an image to which the young men coming of age in the 1970s no doubt compared her. I thought, as I floated through memory, how could I, a black female teenager, have found a connection to this baadasssss woman, one who appeared so self-assured in her own body in her films? Even Link Brown (Antonio Fargas), Foxy's brother, declares in the film *Foxy Brown*, "That's my sister, baby, and she's a whole lotta woman!" Notably, Brown's comments on his sister being a *woman* and not a *lady* link to my parents' decision to prevent me from viewing Grier's films at a young and vulnerable age. Perhaps they intuited that such a representation of black womanhood would assault my underdeveloped and fragile self-esteem and confidence. Instead of immediate praise and awe, my initial reaction to Grier bordered on anger entangled with confusion over exactly how to make sense of the sociocultural meaning and significance of the actress and the characters she played in the films. This unique reflex baffled me more, given the remarks on Grier by young black males and that the actress's reputation begged a kind of heroine *worship* of her; my reaction, then, defied the logic of Grier. It was, in effect, *crazy*!

Fortunately, I had matured in my own self-confidence by the time I entered higher education, and I therefore concentrated on the story lines in the films she starred in: a black woman protecting her community from peril and, in each case, the menace of drug culture. *That* kind of woman I knew via Angela Davis, Coretta Scott King, Fannie Lou Hamer, and the majority of women in my community, among others, who ferociously challenged racist practices in the United States. In the process, these women held their own as black women in the presence of threat and danger. Suddenly, my engagement with the black/feminist movements and their politics, ideologies, and narratives fine-tuned as well as revised the lens through which I viewed Grier and her presence in several films. With this new understanding, Pam Grier/Coffy/Foxy Brown *made sense*, and my eventual understanding of her in the context of revolutionary black women in the 1960s and 1970s ushered the initial reaction of crazy out of my mind.

In 2010 Grier contributed to the memoir boom and published *Foxy: My Life in Three Acts*.[3] This memoir undeniably expanded my vision of her as an actress and, more importantly, as a person. In this study of her memoir, my research continues the interrogation of the lives of black celebrities writing autobiography. In *Dancing on the White Page: Black Women Entertainers Writing Autobiography*, I maintain that "the revelation of [a woman's] interior life as she fights for self-preservation is one of the most compelling features of [celebrity] autobiographies" (13). Grier's text offers an account of a celebrity writing about her life, and I designate autobiography to her text as a standard definition of an account of a person's life written by that person or recorded by someone else. Furthermore, her "autobiographical 'I' connects with the collective black literary community by narrating her journey of harrowing familial persecution" (Dreher 24), among other life experiences. Also, by disseminating her story to the general public, the actress "creates [a history] that expose[s] the complexity of black life as lived" (24) as a member of the entertainment community.

Shortly after the text appeared in print, *Foxy* enjoyed a hefty number of book reviews and book signings often intertwined with interviews about Grier's life. Practically all reviewers remark on Grier's sexy sassiness in blaxploitation—that is a given—yet they offer fair observations of her written work. Jack Feerick, for instance, notes, "When you lay out the particulars of Grier's life, it's a kind of dilettante fairy tale.... But she approaches every twist in circumstance with respect." Felicia Lee, writing for the *New York Times*, observes, "'Foxy' reveals a darker personal life, including, for the first time, the details of her sexual assault at 6. It also recounts the diagnosis of cervical cancer Ms. Grier received in her late 30s and the untimely deaths and suicides of family members and friends." The film and television industries, in tandem with print media, have also taken notice of the memoir. Imprint Entertainment optioned the rights to the book, and Michael Becker, president and CEO of Imprint Entertainment, employed screenwriter Eunetta Boone to adapt the memoir into a screenplay (Franklin). Additionally, Orpah.com published an excerpt, titled "Stunt Work," from the memoir, and the late Josh Strauss, programmer for the Film Society of Lincoln Center, sponsored *Foxy: The Complete Pam Grier*. Strauss's *Foxy*, which took place March 15–17, 2013, included screenings of Grier's films, a book-signing event, and a facilitated question-and-answer period, titled "Conversations with Pam Grier."

Despite the publicity and popularity of *Foxy* as well as its contribution to the memoir boom and black life writing, scholars have yet to examine this important text. The academic void is puzzling given the popularity of *Jackie Brown* (1997) as well as her work in Showtime's *The "L" Word* (2004), among other recent and publicly visible projects. At the time of publication, academic journals such as the *Journal of Blacks in Higher Education*, in its section "Black Digest of Literature" (94), and *Black Camera*, in "Recent Publications in Black Film" (182), referenced *Foxy*, but contributors have yet to provide more extensive commentary or even a review of the memoir in these types of publications.

Prior to the publication of *Foxy*, however, scholars have mostly focused on Grier's place in studies on blacks in film as well as her roles in blaxploitation films. For instance, Donald Bogle mentions her in *Toms, Coons, Mulattoes, Mammies, and Bucks* (251–52) and *Brown Sugar: Over 100 Years of America's Black Female Superstars* (193, 194,

195, 303), both of which are encyclopedias of blacks in film. Guerrero includes a brief discussion of her in his chapter, "The Rise and Fall of Blaxploitation," in *Framing Blackness: The African American Image in Film* (98–100). Mia Mask's *Divas on Screen: Black Women in American Film,* Stephane Dunn's *"Baad Bitches" and Sassy Supermamas: Black Power Action Films,* and Yvonne D. Sims's *Women of Blaxploitation: How the Black Action Film Heroine Changed American Popular Culture* assess Grier's value in blaxploitation. Interestingly, Grier appears on the covers of both *Divas* and *Women of Blaxploitation*. In his article "Wham! Bam! Pam! Pam Grier as Hot Action Babe and Cool Action Mama" (2005), Chris Holmlund examines the ways in which the actress "offers a salutary counter model to the white hard body hardware heroines of the 1980s" (97). Given that most scholarship on Grier has focused on her place in black film and that academic journals have recently only mentioned the publication of her memoir, it is critical, then, to investigate closely *Foxy: My Life in Three Acts,* and the operative term here is *life.*

Commentary on Grier up to the publication of her memoir has centered also on her body, its performance and athleticism as a baadasssss heroine—even including her skin tone. In the famous article in *Ms.* magazine (1975), for example, Jamaica Kincaid describes Grier's facial features in painstaking detail, almost to the degree of insult. She writes:

> Pam Grier is the most winning example of a miscegenated person I have ever seen. . . . Her skin is the exact color of the pancakes in the Little Black Sambo book. Her nose is the kind that was meant to flare when someone disgusts her. She has the kind of lips that look comfortable smiling, pouting, or pursing. She has big, dark, almost almond eyes, dark hair, long legs and long arms. She has the sort of body that press agents like to promote as a sex symbol. (50)

Kincaid's pancake and Black Sambo references offer a "backhanded slap" of a compliment; and the allusion to Grier's body wefts the sex symbol into her remarks. The titles of the texts referenced above—such as *"Baad Bitches" and Sassy Supermamas*—similarly conjure images of the uber-athleticism of women in the genre of blaxploitation in general, and Grier in particular. Holmlund's title, "Wham! Bam! Pam! Pam Grier as Hot Action Babe and Cool Action Mama," appoints the syntax used to describe the actress's sexual prowess. In other words, according to these accounts, Pam Grier *is* all physical sans a life.

Feminist critic Catherine Cucinella's work on the poetics of the body facilitates an understanding of Grier considered *as body* and her execution of the same on-screen. She asserts, "This focus on the body runs the risk of reducing everything to biology or, more specifically, to a biological determinism" (14). As Grier admitted in an interview in *Ms.* magazine, the policy of American International Pictures (AIP), the film studio that made her a star, "is to give the niggers shit. They don't like me but they want to work with me because I make them money. They don't like it that

I talk about the cheesy way they work or that I say the movies that I did for them were jerk jobs" (qtd. in Kincaid 53). This chapter recognizes the feminist transmission of Grier's onscreen, disciplined choreography that catapulted her to celebrity; however, to frame Grier as her body and its performance as black sex goddess ultimately obscures Pam Grier, the person, just as the moguls at AIP preferred to manufacture then circulate her image for the salacious pleasure of the film audience. This project moves beyond the physical and investigates some of the constructions and representations of her private self that she has made available to the reader on the white pages from her memoir. As I maintain in *Dancing on the White Page*, celebrity autobiography "illuminates the performance; it brings out its color and bestows on the viewer a cloak of understanding the visual cannot give. . . . Behind the glitter and the glamour that are part and parcel of entertainment, behind every character on celluloid, and behind every publicity shot are battle scars—even grave sites—that tell stories of each woman's survival" (189).

Participating in this vein of celebrity life writing, *Foxy* invites the reader to bear witness to Grier's stories of survival and to understand the inadequacy of the visual to accommodate them via her venture into the genre of celebrity autobiography. We take pleasure in her beauty; we consume every inch of her nude body exhibited with poise in her films. Grier's written words, however, infer a mandate to her fans and admirers, claiming: as you look on me, you shall be made aware of the emotional, psychological, and *physical* costs I have had to endure in my life.

In constructing her narrative, Grier deliberately pays homage to the black/women's movements of the 1970s in general and the *Black Women's Manifesto* in particular. Published by the Third World Women's Alliance (based in New York) in 1970 and signed by black feminists Gayle Lynch, Eleanor Holmes Norton, Maxine Williams, Frances M. Beal, and Linda La Rue, the manifesto, in part, reads as follows:

> It is not right that the black woman's existence should be validated only by the existence of the black man. The black woman is demanding a new set of female definitions as a . . . companion, and confidant, not a matriarchal villain or a step stool baby-maker. . . . Role integration encourages a broader mental and emotional growth in black women and men as they share the responsibility of working towards liberation. . . . *Neither of them should have their potentiality for self-determination controlled and predetermined by the opposite sex.* . . . That is a *form of bondage* which is an integral part of the racist and capitalist system which black women and black men must work to oppose and overthrow. (Lynch; emphasis added)

In her memoir, Grier identifies the manifesto as the primary resource she consulted during her journey of self-determination. The document may be understood as the black woman's resistance to the trammels of racism and capitalism and, in Grier's case, from the constraints of patriarchy. In the latter, that "form of bondage" appraises her only as a "matriarchal villain" or reduces her to maternity subjugated under the heel of male oppression. These characterizations not only impede progress between black females and black males; each one also perpetuates the legacies of domination and tyranny. Black women, according to the document, must insist on and, when necessary, battle for gender equality to form holistic relationships that heal psychic and physical wounds after experiencing the traumas from the institution of slavery and segregation in the United States.

Curiously, Grier published the manifesto in her memoir in the account of her relationship with Kareem Abdul-Jabbar (aka Ferdinand Lewis Alcindor Jr.). The iconic actress introduces the text as a complement to her observations on student activism on the campus of the University of California at Los Angeles (UCLA) when she dated Abdul-Jabbar. On the UCLA campus, she engaged with black politics. She writes, "For me walking around UCLA was pure nirvana. . . . I was in awe of the black student union. . . . The women's movement . . . was alive with wisdom and messages from the likes of feminists Angela Davis, Coretta Scott King, Gloria Steinem, Betty Friedan, Germaine Greer, and Bella Abzug" (86–87). These entries lay bare Grier's initiation into the ideals of the black feminist movement and, specifically, her application of the *Black Women's Manifesto* as a guide or blueprint for her management of romantic relationships. Grier's narratives about her love interests, in particular, highlight clearly a missive of the manifesto: "It is not right that the black woman's existence should be validated only by the existence of the black man" (Lynch). These influential and provocative movements, I maintain, gave her the necessary tools to *read* the signs of "crazy."

In this chapter, I use the term *crazy* to name Grier's textual assessments of the responses made and actions carried out by her and her lovers. My reading of Grier's text, then, refrains from the common, clinical definition of crazy—that is, one who demonstrates expressions of being deranged, psychopathic, or insane; rather, I use the term *crazy* as it operates in the black vernacular, and I take my cue from Geneva Smitherman and Henry Louis Gates Jr. Consider these imagined speech acts: "Abdul-Jabbar gave you only two hours to decide to marry him?? Pam, he must be *crazy* to even put you through that!" or "Pam, Freddie was out of his mind with *crazy* for trying to get you pregnant!" or "Pryor ain't got not one lick of sense! He crazy! And you crazy for staying with him!" Smitherman would cite these examples as "represent[ations of] an alternative or a different reality through language—through a *language which is based a lot on irony*, on ambiguity . . . a double sort of meaning" (6, 7; emphasis added). The impulse to "humanize an often harsh world, and to do so with honesty, with toughness, and often humor" (Gates, "Vernacular" 4) resides in Smitherman's "double sort of meaning." In the imaginative speech acts above, the speaker(s) know that Grier, Abdul-Jabbar, and Pryor are not clinically crazy; also, the judgments made by them are not literally true. However, in the context of friendship, each speech act signifies humor coupled with concern and support for Grier even in her and her lover's enactments of crazy: the nonsensical, the foolish, the ludicrous, the illogical, and even the absurd.

That Grier uses her heterosexual pairings to read the signs of crazy emphasizes the strength of black feminism to hone a vibrant self-determination—a sense of self she vigorously honors and a self that came of age during the blaxploitation era in the 1970s. Grier also illustrates that her *neglect* to read the signs of crazy compromises her black feminism in praxis. Yet, as I examine in the section on Grier's relationship with Richard Pryor, the life writer indirectly addresses a blind spot in the *Black Women's Manifesto*'s creed. In her appeal for equal rights in her romantic liaisons, I analyze Grier's success in reading the signs of "crazy" and her release of crazy that her lovers manifest during this particular historical time. In moments of personal crisis, though, my close reading of the *Black Woman's Manifesto* unearths no direction on how to press on or where to find sanctuary when either the black man or the black woman fail each other in the work for liberation. My analysis, furthermore, uncovers that Grier unwittingly discloses this shortcoming in the manifesto in the parts of her narrative that document her relationship with comedian Richard Pryor.

Throughout *Foxy*, Grier not only reflects on her life but works to control her image, one that the executives and producers at American International Pictures consistently promoted as sexy, sensual, and athletic. Grier, in her life writing, maps onto herself the black action heroine of blaxploitation, namely, the characters she played in films such as *Coffy* (1973), *Foxy Brown* (1974), *Friday Foster* (1975), and *Sheba, Baby* (1975).[4] She constructs her self, in her memoir, based on each woman's baadasssss posings, not in an entirely "I am invincible" way but one that suggests that the life writer models herself narratively, to a certain degree, from the characters she played onscreen. These women, she comments in the memoir, "claim[ed] the right to fight back[.] My roles were written as vanguard personalities who were the first to defend themselves against violence and prejudice. At the same time, they were determined to bring peace to a situation rather than engage in the draconian ways of war in the lower income communities" (141).

Grier's commentary on her strong characters questions the legitimacy of the largely negative commentary on the blaxploitation film genre—a genre that black spokespersons vilified and the NAACP as well as the Congress on Racial Equality (CORE) railed against. Roy Innis, national chairman of CORE, remarked, in a 1972 ABC News conference, for instance, that black actors and actresses enacting revenge on the white establishment failed to translate their actions off-screen into effective change in the political and legal system of the United States. He stated, "Once you get through that vicarious thrill of seeing a black man beat up a white man on the screen you go back and you face the same evil system that you faced before you went there. We should always deal with reality and not fantasy" (qtd. in *BaadAsssss*). This type of criticism reached far into the community of black actors as well. Beah Richards (*Guess Who's Coming to Dinner*, 1967) and Cicely Tyson (*Sounder*, 1972) blasted the genre of film. "Everybody is tired of the skin game," said Richards, and Tyson agreed: "There is nothing realistic about any of these films. They're fantasy: super-this and super-that. . . . The psychological effects I'm concerned about are the ones on the kids. They are being affected by these negative images" (qtd. in Mason 66). Film historian Yvonne D. Sims and film director Isaac Julien, however, locate the weak points in these critical evaluations. Sims maintains, "It is significant that critics would blindly dismiss Grier's roles because of their violence and weak plotlines while ignoring the fact that she developed strong characters" (74). According to Isaac Julien, director of the documentary *BaadAsssss Cinema*, "the black bourgeoisie was vaguely embarrassed about these films[.] Unfortunately, the discussion of how these films work cinematically and artistically never gets beyond the question of whether they show positive or negative images of black characters" (qtd. in Lambert).

In her memoir, the icon answers Sims's and Julien's indirect/implicit call to deconstruct her roles, and her reflections on her films and her characters embrace each character's positive, feminist spirit and the social movements that influenced them. Grier finds in her memoir that blaxploitation films were "shadowing the [black/]women's movement, where women were demanding equal rights to men in art, business, family, and all aspects of life" (141). In essence, Grier exposes the freedoms instead of the limitations these black, feminist texts afforded her, and the reflections in *Foxy* may be understood as evidence of the fruits of those labors. In the process, *Foxy* reminds the contemporary reader of the artistic and dynamic decade of the 1970s too often parodied in film and visual culture. *I'm Gonna Git You Sucka* (1988), *Leprechaun in the Hood* (2000), *Undercover Brother* (2002), *The Hebrew Hammer* (2003), and *Black Dynamite* (2009) all spoof the era as well as the genre. The parody of the genre has made it to broadcast television as well.[5]

However, the 1970s, Grier argues in her book, permitted artistic freedoms determinately won in the realm of film and visual culture for black women/actresses. During this period, the black action heroine eventually became successful enough to carry a feature film, even though in the B-movie genre. The dramatization of these characters conveyed the power and influence of black women onscreen and, by extension, the focus on improving the conditions found in their communities. In fact, Sims rightly proclaims, "The emergence of the action heroine in mainstream popular cinema began with Pam Grier" (72). Grier's entire franchise of films during blaxploitation, states Jamaica Kincaid, "are the only films to show us a woman who is independent, resourceful, self-confident, strong, and courageous. Above all, they are the only films to show us a woman who triumphs!" (52). When she retired her gun and demolished the menace of drugs in her community, she *lived* to see the fruits of her own labors rather than to experience death as a martyr.

In the process, Grier asks the reader to reflect on her life as lived. As Felicia Lee notes, Grier loads her memoir with gripping stories of overcoming rape by her male cousins at the age of six and by an athlete as a young adult; the impact of racism on her family; the devastating loss of her father via divorce; and her bout with cancer, along with insights on her performances on film and stage (Lee). Her narratives on romances with two iconic celebrities in comedy, Freddie Prinze Sr. and Richard

Pryor, and sports icon Kareem Abdul-Jabbar, I posit, validate the authenticity of the *Black Women's Manifesto* published and celebrated by women of color in the 1970s.

In order to grasp fully the sociocultural value of *Foxy*, it is worth noting that Grier published her memoir in 2010, a year before Oprah Winfrey's retirement from her highly successful television show. Her memoir appeared at a time when black women in entertainment consistently "enrolled" in self-actualization "seminars" made popular by Winfrey, Iyanla Vanzant, and the late Maya Angelou. In ways similar to the *Black Women's Manifesto*, these women attempted to heal the psychic wounds that have plagued (and currently plague) women and women of color in particular. The 1990s chapbook movement, an extension of the black women's literary renaissance, complemented these sessions.[6] During this flourishing literary period, black women published a plethora of pocket-sized books containing daily meditations for people of color and expanded the genre of traditional pocket-sized meditation literature, which typically included the New Testament, the *Upper Room*, and the *Daily Word*, among others. In 1993, for instance, Vanzant published *Acts of Faith: Daily Meditations for People of Color*. In her pages for daily reflection, Vanzant sought to "assist the children of the earth in the redevelopment of their minds, bodies, and spirits. Who are the children of the earth? They are the children of a darker hue. For they are the ones born of the first Father and Mother, . . . the ones who . . . have the secret of the beginning and the end buried deep in their souls" (1). In the search for the secrets "buried deep in their souls," Vanzant argues that people of color can find their way to health and wholeness through recognition of their place in history.[7]

Like Vanzant, Winfrey participated in the contemporary self-help movement. In 1997 the famous talk-show host held a pajama party in the home of Angelou to launch Oprah's book club selection of *The Heart of a Woman* (1981). A segment of the meeting featured them lounging in pajamas, during which Oprah received advice as a "daughter" from her "mother" Angelou. Oprah opened the show with the comment, "One of the most important lessons I ever learned from you . . . is *when people show you who they are, believe them*" ("Oprah Recalls"; emphasis added). Responding to Winfrey, Angelou reaffirmed her message:

> Yes! Absolutely! A person says to you, "I'm selfish" or "I'm mean" or "I am unkind." . . . Believe them! They know themselves much better than you do. But no! More often than not those of us who don't trust life say, "Don't say a thing like that; you're not really crazy . . . you're not really unkind . . . you're not really mean," and as soon as you say that the person PAP! And shows you I told you. I told you I was unkind. So now, why are you angry? ("Oprah Recalls")

Though Angelou offered this piece of advice on Oprah's television show, the cautionary folktale "The Scorpion and the Frog" registers in her commentary to Oprah's audience. The frog's second-guessing of the scorpion's ability to sting eventually results in the death of both of them in the river. Nevertheless, Angelou embeds in her language persuasive encouragement for women to develop critical listening skills that include "purposeful attention to accuracy and consistency of a speaker's message" (Keaton, Keteyian, and Bodie 85). The act of listening compels the hearer to "evaluate and critically assess messages" (Keaton, Keteyian, and Bodie 85) received from the speaker. Crucial to the act of listening is *belief* in the speaker's self-account, as Angelou makes clear, and this factor must play a part in the evaluation of the speaker to offset the second guess. The latter, Angelou implies, places a woman in a vulnerable position to be "stung" by "crazy" if she fails to receive, interpret, and act on the aural messages ("Oprah Recalls"). *Listening* assists her in "acquiring the perspective of the other person" (Keaton, Keteyian, and Bodie 9); *belief* in the information she has heard further provides the listener with the choice to love herself, which bell hooks views as a "move towards freedom, to act in ways that liberate ourselves" (*Outlaw* 250).

More compelling, in the year following Angelou's appearance on the show, Vanzant's presence as a guest on Winfrey's show augmented the former's message. During this show, Vanzant offered a more detailed strategy for *listening* and *believing* when the urge to fix overcomes the desire to accept a person. She cautioned:

> Most of us have a death urge; and we see the guy comin' warning slapped right in the middle of his head and we say, "ohh I'mmo fix it . . . ," but we've gotta understand love doesn't have to fix you . . . change you; when you see crazy comin', cross the street! Don't stay there and say, "come on crazy, let me give you some therapy! . . ." You see love is so real . . . it's already patient . . . it's already kind, it's already enduring. . . . So when you get somebody to love and you gotta start fixing them, understand that you are in your lust . . . you are out of your mind, and you have to go back in[side yourself]. ("Iyanla")

Whereas Angelou's commentary appears to be influenced by folklore, Vanzant takes her inspiration from the apostle Paul in his first Letter to the Corinthians, chapter 13, verses 4–5. This text reads, "Love is Patient. Love is Kind. [Love] seeks not its own way. Love bears all things, . . . endures all things" (King James Study Bible). The desire to contort someone into one's image, Vanzant maintains, contradicts the apostle's theory of love and, instead, verifies an intense but selfish craving to satisfy lust. Vanzant, however, challenges women to *see crazy*—meaning to "read the signs of crazy"—or else experience the "death urge" in the effort to dispense therapy on the crazed.[8]

These television shows and products from the culture of self-help similarly form the contexts within which Grier frames her life writing. Ultimately, Grier does identify and *believe* the dysfunction that comes to light in her relationships with Abdul-Jabbar, Prinze, and Pryor, as Angelou cautions, but she reveals in her memoir that, contrary to the advice offered by Vanzant, she invites "crazy" and attempts to offer therapy, namely, in her documented relationship with Prinze and Pryor. The actress confides in her book the tendency to wrangle love into saving men, or in Vanzant's theory, to *fix* the man with unhealthy and life-threatening habits, and to *fix* her own *self* to accommodate the wishes of her lovers—the latter with Abdul-Jabbar. Therefore, the publication date of her memoir reveals the *result or application* of the lessons outlined for black women in the preceding century. The practice of the lessons in the most volatile of situations stands as convincing proof of the success of counsel and therapy given by black women to black women. In essence, Grier *is* self-help in praxis, and she submits that the ideals of the black women's movement of the 1970s and the wisdom of the 1990s have not died in the twenty-first century, despite the representation of women whom bell hooks calls those "out-for-what-she-can-get . . . bitch goddess[es]" (*Salvation* 41) featured on contemporary, "reality" television shows such as *The Real Housewives of Atlanta* (Bravo 2008), *Basketball Wives* (VH1 2010), and even on Tyler Perry's *For Better or Worse* (TBS, OWN 2011). The exploration of Grier's memoir, moreover, points to a critical directive to her contemporary readers: black women/men would do well to cultivate a disciplined adherence to the *Black Women's Manifesto* as well as to those missives laid out by Angelou and Vanzant even though popular culture, as hooks notices, seemingly advises otherwise.

Foxy advances the ideal of self-love, and when nourished, the text claims, self-love will take root in the interior and/or psyche, even in the chaos of racial oppression. For instance, Grier writes about how, at the age of five, she witnessed housing discrimination:

> When we arrived [at the base in Columbus, Ohio] we had been awarded a lovely place . . . to live, because they thought Dad was Caucasian. But before we ever moved in, they discovered their mistake and told us that since we were Negroes, we had to make other living arrangements. . . . We lived in an apartment off base that was shockingly inferior. You felt the humiliation, embarrassment, and sting of segregation. . . . We had to make sure we didn't look at someone the wrong way—it was a constant tension—or we could end up having our lives threatened. . . . It was so bad that just chatting with white people could get us in trouble, so we avoided it. (5–7)

She attributes bypassing the sting of inferiority brought to bear by racial discrimination to the closeness of her family and the fact that her parents "made sure [they] had good manners and morals" (7). These parental guides instill in Grier a healthy interior driven by self-love, and any reader of her memoir will surmise that when she reaches for the same, this notion of self-love *always wins* in every situation that compromises it. For Grier, self-love *seeks its own way* and thereby lifts her up into its "hands" lest she stumble into the muck and mire of self-destruction.

Throughout her narrative, Grier inspires the contemporary reader to have an intimate knowledge of the power of self-love coupled with the imperative to act on self-love to sustain psychological, emotional, and physical well-being. Implied in the reflections on each of her relationships is that self-love will save a woman's life. Using the *Black Women's Manifesto* as a pedagogical model, Grier reminds her readers of the hard-won, sociocultural lessons each woman can retrieve from the civil rights and women's movements, black history, and contemporary popular culture. These historical lessons, Grier makes clear to her readers, stress the importance of a woman's relationship to her society but her relationship to her*self* as well. When Abdul-Jabbar pressures her to marry him, for example, Grier declines, explaining, "I have to give up too much of myself. . . . I just can't do it" (121). Or when Pryor solicits her to take over his finances, she informs her reader that she had turned him down, remarking, "I have a career too. . . . I need to focus on myself" (167). bell hooks would applaud Grier's tenacity, for she states, "When we have healthy self-love, we know that individuals in our lives who demand of us self-destructive martyrdom do not care for our good, for our spiritual growth" (*Salvation* 41).

Grier testifies to the power of self-love when she narrates her love affairs with three of the most popular men in U.S. visual culture from the 1970s and 1980s: NBA star Kareem Abdul-Jabbar, and two of the most talented stand-up comics/actors of color, Freddie Prinze Sr. and Richard Pryor. Curiously, Grier's attraction to each man parallels the way in which Joe Starks captivates Janie in Zora Neale Hurston's novel *Their Eyes Were Watching God*. In Hurston's seminal text, the narrator describes Starks as "a citified, stylish dressed man with his hat set at an angle [wearing a] shirt with the silk sleeveholders [that] was dazzling enough for the world" (27). Yet when Janie decides she will suffer Joe's physical and verbal abuse no longer, she opens her mouth and "rob[s] him of his illusion of irresistible maleness that all men cherish" (79). Grier does not represent herself as bold as Janie, but she does lift the veil of illusion to reveal the man behind what the dazzle and glitter proficiently hide. When Grier first meets these celebrities, their good looks and the confidence they exude attract her to them; plus her down-to-earth personality entices them to her. Each man's desire to transform her from the independent working woman into a subservient and loyal housewife/caretaker/mother or someone who will assume responsibility for his health, finances, and literacy, however, provide prime opportunities for Grier to enact her black feminism not in the realm of theory but in praxis.

Ferdinand Lewis Alcindor Jr. (Kareem Abdul-Jabbar)

> It is not right that the black woman's existence should be validated by the existence of the black man.
>
> *Black Women's Manifesto*

Grier writes that she met Alcindor at a bar called the Maverick's Flat in the Crenshaw District after leaving Colorado for Los Angeles during the summer before his relocation to Milwaukee, Wisconsin, to begin his career as an NBA basketball player. "I'd been watching him dance[;] he had great rhythm and he knew all the moves" (85), observes Grier, and she informs readers that they started dating when they met again at a frat party at UCLA. According to the text, he invited her to campus often, and there Grier took advantage of the political climate at that educational institution by listening. Grier surmises that she and the soon-to-be NBA star had much in common. She writes:

> As an army brat, I'd lived in England and my father had exposed me to jazz, classical music, and opera. We both loved ... travel, exploration, books, culture, anthropology, and Egyptology. We also shared a love of art, architecture, photography, and filmmaking. And we both loved the martial arts. I'd studied karate and jiu-jitsu when I was young, and Lew and I loved watching Bruce Lee films. We must have watched Kurosawa's *Seven Samurai* ... at least a dozen times. (87)

These commonalities, Grier explains, bonded the sports figure and the actress. Despite their gap in education, Grier states that she believed in her own curriculum of life experiences, and her own regard for them created a smooth interaction with Alcindor.

Compellingly, her education outside the walls of academia, Grier assures the reader, could match those of Alcindor's academic pursuits. As the relationship progressed, Grier established her own ground rules, she also reveals, making clear to the athlete her main goal, "to go to school, so [she] did not want the heartbreak and malaise that so often accompanied love to distract [her] from what [she] needed to accomplish" (88). Alcindor's agreement to her terms sets the stage for him and Grier to enjoy a romantic liaison for the summer because the up-and-coming basketball player "was leaving for Milwaukee within the year" (88) to start his career with the Bucks. What is notable in this part of the narrative is that Grier makes no mention of Alcindor helping her apply to college, even after she discloses to him that "[she] came to [Los Angeles] to try and get into UCLA" (86). Instead, she relished having found someone with whom she could communicate, her narrative reports. "Nothing beat just being in his company and sharing our stories and dreams," she writes (88). Here Grier sets the *Black Women's Manifesto* in action, calling for and receiving the complementary recognition of man and woman as equals, as seen in her use of the word *our*.

Eventually, the socialization of patriarchy in the form of religion compromises the Alcindor-Grier relationship. In 1971 Alcindor officially changed his name to Kareem Abdul-Jabbar; very carefully thereafter, Abdul-Jabbar converted to Islam. This juncture in the relationship, according to Grier, "would change both of [their] lives dramatically," even though Abdul-Jabbar assured her that there was "'nothing to worry about,'" insisting, "'You don't have to convert or anything like that'" (89). However, as the life writer states, he encountered difficulty with Grier working as a

DJ at the Sports Page in West Hollywood. Grier worried about this dilemma especially since she adored Abdul-Jabbar, but the answers to the questions she posed to the athlete about women's roles within Islam align with the *Black Women's Manifesto*'s "role of integration" that she successfully managed to lay out from the onset of the relationship. It was less about the conversion of the athlete, Grier states, and more that he pushed aside her hopes for an education, to which he replied, "'[If] we get married, you don't have to get an education. I'll take care of you'" (92). As the memoir makes clear, Grier countered with the following:

> I really can't have anyone taking care of me. . . . That's the master/slave syndrome, and I refuse to ever be oppressed or manipulated. . . . We all know that being educated is the only way to be free in this world . . . the only way a woman can be responsible for herself. Don't forget, not that long ago it was against the law for a slave to have a book on their [*sic*] person. You're a basketball star; you already have an education. I don't. (93)

Here Grier not only "demand[s] a new . . . female definition," as articulated in the *Black Women's Manifesto*; moreover, she acknowledges that her "existence [shall not be] validated by the existence of a black man" by deliberately referencing early black history to drive her point. Abdul-Jabbar may have relied on the principles of Islam and the Koran to construct his self, but Grier, in this part of her memoir, positions her *self* in relation to the history of enslaved African peoples and their quest for freedom. Her reply to him also underscores her knowledge of slave codes and the measures installed by southern legislators that made it illegal to teach a slave to read. Consider, for example, the South Carolina Act of 1740, which, in part, reads:

> Whereas, the having slaves taught to write, or suffering them to be employed in writing, may be attended with great inconveniences; Be it enacted, that all and every person and persons whatsoever, who shall hereafter teach or cause any slave or slaves to be taught to write, or shall use or employ any slave as a scribe, in any manner of writing whatsoever, hereafter taught to write, every such person or persons shall, for every such offense, forfeit the sum of one hundred pounds, current money. ("Acts")[9]

The suggestion that Abdul-Jabbar would "take care of her," Grier surmises, threatened her freedom. To agree with him would leave her totally dependent on him for her socioeconomic security. Her description of his "generosity" framed along the lines of the master-slave dynamic conveys an acute fear of the danger of *ownership* of her very being and points to her awareness of the gravity of the implications of this union. She relentlessly interrogates Abdul-Jabbar on his vision of marriage with her thorough questions, such as: "why is the woman, even in the 'new Islam,' supposed to walk behind the man?" "Why can't I walk around without a chaperone?" and "Why can't I work?" (93). She remarks that she has learned, though, that a "small contingent of modern Muslim women was beginning to emerge ... who were getting educated" (93). Yet, Grier discloses, "Kareem never told [me] about them. Either he didn't know or he didn't want [me] to know" (96).

Grier's "reading the signs of crazy," or *seeing* crazy or the illogical/nonsensical, forces her to surmise finally that a marriage to Abdul-Jabbar would mean "once a woman converted to Islam and got married, she gave up her individual rights" (95). In any event, Grier's reading of the *Black Women's Manifesto*'s theory of "role integration [that] encourages a broader mental and emotional growth" (Lynch) undergirds her desire for persuasive reassurances from Abdul-Jabbar. At the time, the athlete had earned the NBA's Most Valuable Player Award and certainly was equipped economically to support Grier after marriage, but the life writer senses this threat. Thus, she calls into question her perception of black women's roles within Islam and opts instead to strive for the opportunities that the black/women's movements had made available to women. That primary opportunity was the choice for a woman to make her own decisions. She writes,

> Gloria Steinem and the late Bella Abzug ... as well as Shirley Chisholm and the late Barbara Jordan ... supported women in breaking down the walls between them and making decisions for themselves, instead of letting men decide things for them. They showed me that I had choices, that I could get married or not, that I could have children or not, and that society does not have the right to judge me as inferior because I don't have a husband or live in a more traditional manner. (277)

For Grier, this "breaking down the walls," as encouraged by the feminist figures referenced above, meant choosing independence by creating a financially secure future for herself on her own terms. After the demise of her relationship with Abdul-Jabbar, Grier adds, she "looked forward to focusing on acting and making more money for my future than [she] ever had before" (102). Grier's grasp of this opportunity for independence invalidates Abdul-Jabbar's ideas for her existence through marriage.

Freddie Prinze Sr.

> The black woman is demanding a new set of female definitions and a recognition of herself as a ... companion, and confidant, not a matriarchal villain or a step stool baby-maker.
> *Black Women's Manifesto*

If Grier ever formed a romantic partnership with a man who intends to make her into a "step stool baby-maker," she fashioned that partnership with comedian Freddie Prinze Sr. As a "fine-featured Latino [with a] striking demeanor and a sophisticated polish [who] held doors open for [her]" (139), he impressed Grier the most, as she sets forth in her memoir. She and Prinze, she also writes, "enjoy[ed] [their] ascension to stardom" (141), and their popularity in mainstream entertainment served as the common denominator for Grier's gravitation toward him. They met in the mid-1970s when she and Prinze appeared on the *Irv Kupcinet Show*, and after careful observation, she realized that "he was a true gentleman who respected women" (139). Consistent with her blueprint for dating, she insisted on courtship before the consummation of the relationship. She writes:

> Before we ever got into bed together, I insisted we get to know each other. . . . He loved my stories about the Black West, and he wanted to come to Colorado and meet my family. I found that romantic, and so was going to Catalina Island for dinner one evening. . . . We checked out the town and ate in a great Italian restaurant for which Catalina was famous. We spent a lot of time talking about our dreams, where we had come from, and where we wanted to go. (142–43)

Among other interactions, Grier reports that she and Prinze helped each other choose clothes for business meetings in order to maintain the look of movie stardom. What is more, Grier deems, in her book, that her life stories were just as meaningful as Prinze's own life stories, as evident in the above quote. Her construction of romance adds value to the time she spent with him, all the while giving her a defense for establishing a romantic link with him. Over the course of their relationship, however, Prinze coerced Grier to partake of drug culture. Consequently, Grier began to read the signs of Prinze's crazy during their lovemaking. "A pattern was emerging," she recalls. "He would start wrestling me, the energy would get sexual, and he would want to have sex without contraception," promising always to "pull out" (146). Her persistent interrogation of him exposed what she viewed as Prinze's crazy plan, and he admitted to what Vanzant refers to as trying to fix the actress. Grier reports that Prinze stated, "'I *am* trying to get you pregnant. I love you, and I'm afraid you may not marry me. You may want out . . . but if you have my baby, I'll have a connection to you that will never go away'" (147). Grier reminds Prinze, "'You need to be as committed to your work as you are to me'" (147). After he has failed to persuade her to indulge in drug culture ("'I have to keep my mind clear,'" she writes [147]) so that he can have a partner in paranoia and in "capricious" behavior such as "acting rude and unrestrained with no filters to his language, . . . losing all track of time, [and being] undependable" (146), Prinze, Grier notes, plans strategies to entrap her via pregnancy. He "forgets" contraception in the gamble that Grier will give in to the sexual energy between them—all to ensure a lifelong relationship with her. His plans to subordinate her run counter to the part of the *Black Women's Manifesto* that reads, "Neither [males or females] should have their potentiality for self-determination controlled and predetermined by the opposite sex" (Lynch).

Prinze's enterprise to make Grier a "step stool baby-maker" (Lynch) fails to compromise her own self-determination to protect herself from the comedian's self-destructive actions. After close readings of Prinze's harmful behavior patterns, Grier states, she remained loyal to the tenets of the manifesto by ending the relationship. "I finally realized there was no place for me [in Freddie's life]," she concludes. "Freddie," she continues, "insisted I was being dramatic, but I held my ground.... 'I love you ... but I can't let you get me pregnant'" (148). As a result, she deliberately sidestepped the possibility of a maternal "form of bondage" (Lynch) along with a type of control by Prinze. She leans, instead, on the manifesto as well as on her persistence and talents to give her strength as she moves forward in her work in film. As she writes, "I distanced myself [from Freddie] by filming *Foxy Brown*, an action/adventure film [and] I took roles that appealed to me and did the best I could with them" (148–49).

Richard Pryor

> When you see crazy comin', cross the street! Don't stay there and say, "Come on crazy, let me give you some therapy!"
>
> IYANLA VANZANT

Compared to her commentary on Abdul-Jabbar and Prinze, Grier invests more textual space to how she designed a plan for healthier living for Pryor, which included literacy, breaking drug addiction, and new eating regimens. On the one hand, Abdul-Jabbar and Prinze attempted to control Grier via religion and/or sex. In her romance with Pryor, on the other hand, Grier essentially invites crazy over for therapy in an all-out effort to *fix* him and to provide *therapy* for him so that he can improve his life. In this relationship, Grier ventures to be the caretaker of a man who, like Prinze, became engulfed in drug culture yet fed off Grier's own health in a desire to be released from his addiction. Interestingly, she met Pryor through Prinze when he bet his colleague that he knew Grier and would be able to bring her to his house. Upon meeting her, Pryor shouts to Prinze, "'Motherfucker, ... you *do* know the bitch'" (159). Though Grier refuses to stay and watch "two grown men get stupid on cocaine" (159), Pryor insists that she stay as his guest. No matter how much he tries to coax her, however, Grier informs the reader that she tells Prinze to take her home. Implicit in her rejection of Pryor's invitation to be his guest is Grier's insistence on her own agenda. She stands on her own tenuous experience with Prinze and drugs and intuits that he, along with another man who has called her a "bitch," and his use of drugs could jeopardize her control over herself and her life.

Grier and Pryor begin their relationship after Melvin Van Peebles cast them in *Greased Lightning* (1976). At first glance, this pairing may seem like an unlikely couple, and in his second greeting of Grier, Pryor fails to redeem himself when he first sees her on the set. According to Grier, Pryor states through his blurry eyes, "'Pam Grier, you're just a farmer. A hick'" (160). His refusal to acknowledge her celebrity status or her constructed persona via film uncovers a curious aspect of Pryor, the man who "loved his family, [had] pride in his success, and . . . humility about his career" (160). That each experienced rape at an early age—Grier at six years old and Pryor at ten by "both a neighbor and a priest" (157)—eventually becomes the common denominator between the entertainers. The incidents of rape, then, lift the veil of celebrity, and Pryor and Grier begin to *see* each other while working in entertainment.

In this relationship, Grier appoints herself as Pryor's caretaker, one coming to rescue him from the world of drugs. As she notes,

> We'd met at a time in Richard's life when his body was starting to rebel against so much abuse. He was having physical symptoms—his skin and his scalp were broken out, he was losing sleep—and he desperately wanted a way out of the drug culture. . . . He'd hoped (as I did) that he could conquer his addictions and we could be together indefinitely with a deep commitment and dedication to each other and our relationship. He was banking on my strength and will to help him stay away from the wrong people. (161)

Grier's belief in her and Pryor as a couple—instead of individual celebrities—reflects the *Black Women's Manifesto*'s call for black men and women to "share the responsibility of working towards liberation" (Lynch); in this case, it is an all-out effort to break Pryor's drug addiction that Grier observes was a product of celebrity culture in general and the city of Los Angeles in particular. Pryor, she detects, was "yet another comedian caught up in the glitz and speed of a dangerous game of Russian roulette called 'Drugs'" (157). This culture preyed on brilliant black men who were making headway in a mainstream entertainment culture that privileged whiteness. More specifically, Grier's narrative about Pryor's drug habit addresses the cocaine epidemic in Los Angeles in the 1970s that reached its height in the 1980s. According to journalist Gary Webb, this "exotic South American drug" had been rediscovered after the "drug-soaked 1960s" (23). "Coke stayed up in the penthouses, nestled in exquisitely carved bowls and glittering little boxes," he writes. "It came out at private parties, or in the wash rooms of trendy nightclubs. . . . Street cops almost never saw the stuff" (24).

While drug culture certainly impacted poverty-stricken communities such as South Central Los Angeles, Grier's narrative on her relationship with Pryor affirms that the epidemic infiltrated the celebrity community. She writes,

> I hated the fact that my relationship with Richard was based on whether or not he was getting high. . . . One afternoon, . . . I saw a pile of cocaine sitting on the mirror

next to a razor blade and a rolled up $100 bill. Richard acted like he hadn't been indulging . . . but I . . . saw the signs—his bloodshot eyes, the lines of coke, the half-smoked joints, and the nearly empty bottle of Courvoisier. (166)

Given this context, the effect of Grier's role as savior preserves—for a while, at least—a segment of black entertainment culture from self-destruction. She writes, "[Richard] was a great talent, a brilliant man, and I hated that drugs were stopping him from attaining real success" (161). Pryor's drug addiction, she sensed, could sabotage the comedian's career, thus robbing him of opportunities to circulate his talent. Because of his comedic gifts, Pryor, in the 1970s, was a critical and commercial success, and the white entertainment industry was recognizing his talents. His appearance on *The Ed Sullivan Show* in 1966, when he performed his stand-up routine "Being Cool," laid the foundation for him to achieve mainstream success, a path first charted by the black comedian Flip Wilson, who gained fame in the 1960s. (In 1970 *The Flip Wilson Show* premiered on NBC.) In 1973 Pryor received an Emmy nomination for the category Outstanding Writing Achievement in Comedy, Variety or Music; in 1974 he won the Emmy for Best Writing in Comedy-Variety, Variety or Music for his album *That Nigger's Crazy*. He also wrote for the most popular comedy shows starring blacks, in particular *The Flip Wilson Show* and *Sanford and Son*. The influential actor, director, and producer Mel Brooks hired Pryor to collaborate with him on the screenplay for *Blazing Saddles* (1974), and, by 1976, when he and Grier were romantically involved, Pryor had won three Emmy accolades for Best Comedy Recording and another box office hit for *Silver Streak*, wherein he costarred with Gene Wilder and Jill Clayburgh. A year later, in 1977, *The Richard Pryor Show* premiered on NBC.

Given all of Pryor's success, Grier's effort to preserve the black comedian's "genius" (166) coincides, once again, with her *service*, if not *obligation*, to follow the mission of the *Black Women's Manifesto*, particularly for "black women and men [to] share the responsibility of working towards liberation" (Lynch). In the Pryor–Grier connection, the actress writes that she recognized Pryor's sociocultural currency among urban youth:

When you consider contributions in the seventies that changed the way people talked about life, comedian Richard Pryor comes to mind. . . . "The establishment" judged his urban comedy as vulgar. But to the youth movement, urban was hip and Richard was the king of hip. His audiences got a charge out of hearing him say the words *dick* and *pussy* in public, and they loved to hear him talk about drugs. "Hey," he famously said, "cocaine ain't addictive. I've been using it since I was thirteen, and I ain't addicted." (157)

Pryor *was* worth saving because "he had power coming to him that was unprecedented in the world of black comedians," Grier makes clear to readers (161). She, therefore, organized a health-and-fitness regimen to include the preparation of healthy food recipes, exercise (tennis, bicycling), and a consistent sleep schedule (early to bed and early to rise) for the comedian.

The key project she supported in this initiative, however, was to bring literacy into Pryor's life. "He learned all of his lines phonetically with the help of a few intimate acquaintances," Grier recalls, "and more than anything in the world, he wanted me to teach him to read" (162). Pryor's desire for literacy underscores his acknowledgment that talent would get him only so far in a trendy and fickle industry, as well as his appreciation of the limits of celebrity. That Grier agreed to bring literacy into Pryor's life signifies her place in a group of black women who have used their *elite* position to effect change in the lives of others in the black community. Jacqueline Jones Royster would agree that Grier utilized her own privilege as a star to uplift the race, so to speak. Even though she writes about black women and literacy, Royster's examination of well-accomplished black women helps in understanding Grier's cultural project in her memoir. Royster writes, "These women had access to power and influence, and *because of their elite status*, they also had the luxury, the class privilege, and the time to use this access in their own interests and *in the interest of others*" (7; emphasis added). Indeed, celebrity culture afforded both Grier and Pryor the privilege of leisure time to *sit* and to *practice* literacy; Grier's *interest* in Pryor, in essence, moves her to perform a kind of community outreach initiative and complements part of Alice Walker's definition of womanism. Grier, according to Walker's language, may be understood as being "committed to [the] survival and wholeness of entire people, male *and* female" (xi; emphasis added). As Grier brings to light in her text, her personal management pays off, and Pryor "graduate[s]" to becoming a healthy individual poised to live life without drugs; under her tutelage, Grier confides, Pryor makes "great strides in his reading [with her], coaching him along the way" (162). The curriculum for health and literacy, then, positions both stars to "work . . . towards liberation" (Lynch) from the menace of drugs and the social stigma of illiteracy.

But Pryor, Grier reports, did not completely invest in and commit to this outline for health for the long haul. While Abdul-Jabbar had moved to control Grier via religious conversion, and Prinze had sought to manipulate the actress through pregnancy, Pryor, in a different manner, infects her. He ingests, according to the memoir, so much cocaine *after* his stint in what I call "the Pam Grier Clinic" that the drug actually makes its way into her vaginal walls. Her doctor, the text states, warns her to use a condom or "[she could] become sterile . . . might have a hysterectomy, and was going to be a very sick woman" (169). Pryor refuses, explaining, "'I hate condoms. I can't feel anything'" and simply that he will not talk to her doctor at her request (170). Pryor can/will not sustain his own healthy lifestyle as he, like Prinze, dismisses Grier's anxiety over her own health; these concerns require Pryor's collaboration in ensuring Grier's well-being in staying faithful to the *Black Women's Manifesto*'s emphasis on "sharing in the responsibility for liberation" (Lynch) from illness and disease. However, Pryor's refusal essentially nullifies the "contract" initially made by both of them. She works diligently to restore Pryor to health, but, she discloses, Pryor adamantly rebuffs the invitation to restore *her* health—if only for a moment until she heals. Pryor's stance may be understood by what bell hooks would refer to as a psychological "lovelessness" fueled by patriarchal privilege that "affirmed that males d[o] not have to answer to females" (*Sisters* 22). Pryor's reaction to Grier's request registers as a violent act in the domestic space; that Grier allows him to engage in unprotected sex with her stands as an example of a sexual battering of her body and, yet more radical, a misogynistic act on her body and self. When all is said and written, Grier realizes that she has invited herself over to crazy's pad to give him some therapy. More critical, Grier chooses to ignore the tenets of the *Black Women's Manifesto* almost to her disadvantage. She manages, nonetheless, to bring herself back to its precepts, as I demonstrate later in this chapter.

Surprisingly, Grier relents to Pryor because she admits, "I loved Richard [and] we women always think in the back of our minds that the guy might change" (170). That Grier's text makes known her decision to put her own health at risk creates a puzzling moment for readers; even more suspect is her leaving of Pryor's world not because of his drug abuse and its effects on her body but because of a near-death mishap involving her beloved pony, Ginger.[10] Grier's quick thinking saved Ginger, but the episode brought her to the conscious awareness that she "couldn't save Richard" (173). Grier's risk-taking runs counter to the tenets in the *Black Women's Manifesto*, and its authors would surmise that a lack of regard for the principles invites a type of psychic death or, in the words of Vanzant, a death urge. Grier's preoccupation with Pryor ultimately undermines her focus on herself and her consistent use of the tenets from the manifesto in other parts from her memoir.

Patricia Hill Collins's theory on "The Power of Self-Definition" generates a helpful insight into Grier's reckless behavior and, I would argue, a blind spot in the *Black Women's Manifesto*. A black woman's labor in fashioning self-determination, Collins writes, is "a series of negotiations" that "creates a peculiar tension" (99, 100). The lack of regard for her own signs of crazy points to Grier's reliance on the success—though short-term—she garners bringing Pryor to a life of fitness, health, and literacy. Her plan *works* for a "few good months" (165). Pryor, then, may be understood as Grier's *investment* with the possibility of yet another return "with a deep commitment and dedication to each other" (161). This logic hopes that, in all likelihood, Pryor will find the "love" inside him to *listen* to her, and they can draw up another "contract" whereby they both strive together for liberation from sickness to health.

These negotiations, however, betray the pressures and strains on the actress. At her weakest point, she refuses to find any support system other than Pryor. Sole reliance on the comedian reinforces Collins's comment on a "peculiar tension"; Grier's "slip" in the *Black Women's Manifesto* involves the lack of a "social space where [Grier] can speak freely[, and this social space] is a necessary condition for Black women's resistance" (100). Collins identifies the requisite "social spaces" as "extended families, churches, and African-American community organizations" and describes them as "important locations where safe discourse potentially can occur" (100–101). The absence of institutions such as these at this particular period in Grier's life ultimately hurts her. Even though the manifesto maintains that black men and women must work together to end oppression, the Pryor–Grier relationship, as revealed in the memoir, invites the reader to witness the hazardous effects when a woman tarries in a life-threatening liaison with a man without regard for her own condition. Grier's story of her relationship with Pryor uncovers the patriarchal stronghold in the black community that produces this impulse, and its iron grip fails to elicit love, protection, compassion, understanding, and a collaboration for liberation. Yet, even though Grier makes no mention of involving herself within the *external* "social spaces" listed by Collins, she places front and center her *interior* space as her exclusive personal savior in all her intimate associations. She remembers, "When I look back, I can say without hesitation that I have stepped up and met my challenges with as much courage as I could muster. . . . I have survived as a human being and a woman as I lived up to my strengths and my imperfections" (275).

Grier's narrative closure conveys her faith in the teachings of the *Black Women's Manifesto*, Angelou, and Vanzant, even when she has strayed from it or them in the past. This narrative closure, at heart, celebrates her victories while recognizing her human frailties. By extension, Grier's memoir settles nicely on the continuum of black women writing and talking about the value of self-help most notably in the company of her readers. By moving through "The Early Years," "'Fros and Freaks" (Abdul-Jabbar, Prinze, and Pryor), and "Finding Balance," the three acts of life as listed in her table of contents, then, Grier honestly recounts, in detail, her engagement with the *Black Women's Manifesto*. Her appreciation of these acts makes it clear that for the black woman of the twenty-first century, the manifesto—along with Angelou's and Vanzant's warnings—is viable *and* sustainable, if not *mandatory* for surviving and *living* life.

As I end this chapter, I recall the remarks at the end of *Dancing on the White Page*: "The technology of writing for black female celebrities is the means to construct again and again their own life stories at different moments in time" (201). Grier is known as the quintessential black action heroine whom Tarantino brought to popular memory in *Jackie Brown* (1997), his cinematic tribute to her. No actress except, *maybe*, Zoe Saldana, Halle Berry, or Angelina Jolie has yet to overturn successfully her cultural value and significance. While Grier played the baadasssss characters during the blaxploitation era in films such as *Coffy*, *Foxy Brown*, *Friday Foster*, and *Sheba, Baby*, she inhabited them all while drawing on her experiences growing up in a segregated U.S. society as well as her coming of age during the black/women's movements. What can be gleaned from *Foxy: My Life in Three Acts* is that for all the courage and bravery demonstrated by her characters, Grier, the woman, *is* a black feminist in praxis; she shows her contemporary readers in her memoir that if women graft the blueprint of the *Black Women's Manifesto*, absorb the recommendations of Winfrey, Vanzant, and Angelou, among others, and read the signs of "crazy," we can realize our greatest gift: "the freedom . . . to wake up each day and take it as it comes [and to] continue to create our art until we take our last breath" (Grier 278).

NOTES

1. This type of language is especially present in her recounting of her relationship with comedian Richard Pryor.

2. Samuel Z. Arkoff, head of American International Pictures (AIP) from 1954 to 1980, discloses in his autobiography, *Flying through Hollywood by the Seat of My Pants*, that the films produced in his studios instigated the anger among members of black organizations. He writes, "As sensitive as we tried to be, the black films in general, including our own, came under repeated attack. The leader of one black organization, while pleased that the new film genre was providing work for many black actors, called me and complained, 'These films don't depict black families. All you're showing is cops and criminals'" (201). He reveals also that while the black intelligentsia was incensed over the portrayals of blacks, "Pam Grier went to bat for us. . . . She repeatedly told the press that she took those roles because they showed black women in positions of power. According to Pam, our pictures depicted black women in a positive light" (203). Her comments to Kincaid in *Ms.* magazine, however, tell a different story.

3. See Julie Rak's *Boom! Manufacturing Memoir for the Popular Market*, wherein she describes the memoir boom as "a period roughly spanning the first decade of the twenty-first century, when the production and public visibility of American and British memoirs by celebrities and by relatively unknown people sharply increased" (3).

4. Grier's characters, specifically Coffy, Foxy Brown, Friday Foster, and Sheba Baby, all sidestep law enforcement officials and carry out vigilante justice to rid communities of drug dealers and pimps. As Coffy, Grier plays a nurse whose sister becomes catatonic after ingesting contaminated heroin. To avenge her sister's addiction, Coffy hunts down the drug dealer and, at gunpoint, forces him to inject himself with his own heroin. In *Friday Foster*, Grier plays an ex-model-turned-photographer with the same name who witnesses the murder of her best friend, Clorils Boston (Rosaline Miles). She, along with detective Colt Hawkins (Yaphet Kotto), join forces to uncover a political conspiracy called Black Widow. Foxy Brown goes undercover to expose the drug lords who killed her boyfriend Michael Anderson (Terry Carter). In *Sheba, Baby*, Sheba Shayne returns home from Chicago to Louisville, Kentucky, only to find that she and her father (Rudy Challenger) have to fight mobsters trying to take over the family's business.

5. See, for instance, the conclusion of the *Seinfeld* episode "The Wig Master," and the episode "Happy Valentine's Day . . . Baby?" from the television show *Girlfriends*.

6. The black women's literary renaissance matured in the 1970s. Hortense J. Spillers regards this literary movement as one that formed from the "continuing urgency of black women writing themselves into history" (249). Henry Louis Gates Jr. maintains that Toni

Cade Bambara's anthology *The Black Woman* [1970] "heralded an effort by black women to define themselves" ("Contemporary" 918) within this contemporary period.

7. Vanzant's work in television after *Acts of Faith* also complements Grier's life writing. From 2001 to 2002, Vanzant hosted her television show, *Iyanla*, and the ABC network introduced her as "syndicated TV's next great hope: she is equal parts counselor, spiritual guru, girlfriend and most of all, survivor" ("Move"). Continuing her role as an advisor, Vanzant, from 2003 to 2006, appeared as a life coach on *Starting Over*, a reality television show that featured women who wanted to turn their lives around after having faced and endured life-changing difficulties.

8. Winfrey expanded this continuum of self-affirmation with the debut of two major programs on the *Oprah Winfrey Network* (OWN), both of which appeared on New Year's Day in 2011. Grier's memoir anticipated these inspirational programs: *Life Class Lessons* and *Super Soul Sundays*. Some of the themes featured on *Super Soul Sundays* include "The Healing Power of Love" with the Omega Institute founder Elizabeth Lesser; "Falling into Grace" with spiritual teacher Adyashanti; and "Finding Devotion," with best-selling author Dani Shapiro. These programs advocated for health and wellness and featured experts in the field in an effort to educate and encourage people to find their best selves.

9. Grier may have been familiar with the Virginia Revised Code of 1819 as well. This code reads: "That all meetings or assemblages of slaves, or free negroes or mulattoes mixing and associating with such slaves at any *meeting-house* or houses, &c., in the night; or at any SCHOOL OR SCHOOLS *for teaching them* READING OR WRITING, *either in the day or night*, under whatsoever pretext, shall be deemed and considered an UNLAWFUL ASSEMBLY" (Goddell 320).

10. Burt Sugarman, producer of *The Richard Pryor Show*, presented Pryor with a miniature chestnut horse named Ginger. Grier became attached to the horse, and she made Ginger her sole responsibility because she "was thrilled to have [her] own little horse to raise and train" (171). Grier gave strict instructions to the housekeeper and to Pryor to "never [let] the dogs out in a pack around the horse. They would tear her from limb to limb . . . and Ginger, a miniature, was not large enough to kick them away like a bigger horse would do" (171). The housekeeper failed to heed her warning, and the dogs attacked the pony to near death (171).

WORKS CITED

"Acts against the Education of Slaves South Carolina, 1740 and Virginia, 1819." *The Slave Experience: Education, Arts, and Culture*. PBS.

Arkoff, Sam, with Richard Turbo. *Flying through Hollywood by the Seat of My Pants*. New York: Carol Press, 1992.

BaadAsssss Cinema: A Bold Look at 70's Blaxploitation Films. Dir. Isaac Julien. New Video Group, 2003.

"Black Digest of Literature." *Journal of Blacks in Higher Education* 67 (2010): 93–97.

Bogle, Donald. *Brown Sugar: Over 100 Years of America's Black Female Superstars*. New York: Continuum, 2007.

———. *Toms, Coons, Mulattoes, Mammies, and Bucks*. 4th ed. New York: Continuum, 2007.

Coffy. Dir. Jack Hill. Perf. Pam Grier, Booker Bradshaw, and Robert DoQui. AIP, 1973.

Collins, Patricia Hill. *Black Feminist Thought: Knowledge, Consciousness and the Politics of Empowerment.* New York: HarperCollins, 1990.

Cucinella, Catherine. *Poetics of the Body: Edna St. Vincent Millay, Elizabeth Bishop, Marilyn Chin, and Marilyn Hacker.* New York: Palgrave, 2010.

Delaney, Paul. "A Job Drive Is Set by Jesse Jackson: Rights Leader Lists the Film Industry as First Goal." *New York Times* 30 July 1972: 39.

Dreher, Kwakiutl L. *Dancing on the White Page: Black Women Entertainers Writing Autobiography.* Albany: State U of New York P, 2008.

Dunn, Stephane. *"Baad Bitches" and Sassy Supermamas: Black Power Action Films.* Urbana: U of Illinois P, 2007.

Feerick, Jack. "Popdose: Pam Grier's 'Foxy: My Life in Three Acts.'" *Kirkus*: n. pag.

Foxy: The Complete Pam Grier. Film Society of Lincoln Center. *YouTube* 12 Apr. 2013. https://www.youtube.com/watch?v=oX8nyOPytaM.

Foxy Brown. Dir. Jack Hill. Perf. Pam Grier, Antonio Fargas, and Peter Brown. AIP, 1974.

Franklin, Garth. "Pam Grier Gets a 'Foxy' Biopic." *Dark Horizons*: n. pag.

Friday Foster. Dir. Arthur Marks. Perf. Pam Grier, Yaphet Kotto, and Godfrey Cambridge. AIP, 1975.

Gates, Henry Louis, Jr. "Contemporary Period." *The Norton Anthology of African American Literature.* Gen. ed. Henry Louis Gates Jr. and Valerie A. Smith. 3rd ed. New York: Norton, 2014. 913–29.

———. "The Vernacular Tradition." *The Norton Anthology of African American Literature.* Gen. ed. Henry Louis Gates Jr. and Valerie A. Smith. 3rd ed. New York: Norton, 2014. 3–11.

Goddell, William. *The American Slave Code in Theory and Practice: Its Distinctive Features Shown by Its Statutes, Judicial Decision, and Illustrative Facts.* New York: American and Foreign Anti-Slavery Society, 1853. Library of Congress.

Grier, Pam, with Andrea Cagan. *Foxy: My Life in Three Acts.* New York: Springboard Press, 2010.

Guerrero, Ed. *Framing Blackness: The African American Image in Film.* Philadelphia: Temple UP, 1993.

"Happy Valentine's Day . . . Baby?" *Girlfriends*. UPN, Los Angeles. 10 Feb. 2003.

Holmlund, Chris. "Wham! Bam! Pam! Pam Grier as Hot Action Babe and Cool Action Mama." *Quarterly Review of Film and Video* 2.2 (2005): 97–112.

hooks, bell. *Outlaw Culture: Resisting Representations.* New York: Routledge, 1994.

———. *Salvation: Black People and Love.* New York: William Morrow, 2001.

———. *Sisters of the Yam.* Cambridge, MA: South End Press, 2005.

Hurston, Zora Neale. *Their Eyes Were Watching God.* 1937. New York: Harper Perennial, 2006.

"Iyanla Vanzant: 'When You See Crazy Comin', Cross the Street!'" *Oprah Winfrey Show* 9 Apr. 1998. *YouTube* 19 May 2014. https://www.youtube.com/watch?v=cGRKnaJUzG4.

Keaton, Shaughan A., Robert V. Keteyian, and Graham D. Bodie. "Bivariate and Multivariate Associations between Trait Listening Goals and Trait Communicator Preferences." *International Journal of Listening* 28.2 (2014): 82–97.

Kincaid, Jamaica. "Pam Grier: The Mocha Mogul of Hollywood." *Ms.* August 1975: 49–53.

The King James Study Bible. Ed. Barbour Staff. Uhrichsville, OH: Barbour Press, 2011.

Kolb, Leigh. "The Unfinished Legacy of Pam Grier." *Bitch Flicks* 27 Feb. 2013.

Lambert, Craig. "The Blaxploitation Era." *Harvard Magazine* Jan.–Feb. 2003: n. pag.

Lee, Felicia. "Pam Grier's Collection of Lessons Learned." *New York Times* 10 Apr. 2014: n. pag.
Lynch, Gayle, et al. *Black Women's Manifesto*. New York: Third World Women's Alliance, 1970.
Mask, Mia. *Divas on Screen: Black Women in American Film*. Urbana: U of Illinois P, 2009.
Mason, B. J. "New Films: Culture or Con Game." *Ebony* Dec. 1972: 60–68.
"Move over Oprah, It's Iyanla." *ABC News* 10 Aug. 2010. http://abcnews.go.com/GMA/story?id=126780.
"NAACP Takes Militant Stand on Black Exploitation Films." *Hollywood Reporter* 10 Aug. 1972: 1–10.
"Oprah Recalls One of Her Favorite Life Lessons from Maya Angelou." *YouTube* 27 Oct. 2011. https://www.youtube.com/watch?v=BTiziwBhd54.
Rak, Julie. *Boom! Manufacturing Memoir for the Popular Market*. Waterloo, ON: Wilfrid Laurier UP, 2013.
"Recent Publications in Black Film." *Black Camera* 2.1 (2010): 180–87.
Royster, Jacqueline Jones. *Traces of a Stream: Literacy and Social Change among African American Women*. Pittsburgh: U of Pittsburgh P, 2000.
Sheba, Baby. Dir. William Girdler. Perf. Pam Grier, Austin Stoker, and D'Urville Martin. AIP, 1975.
Sims, Yvonne D. *Women of Blaxploitation: How the Black Action Film Heroine Changed American Popular Culture*. New York: McFarland, 2006.
Smitherman, Geneva. "African-American English: From the Hood to the Amen Corner." *Center for Writing*. U of Minnesota.
Spillers, Hortense J. "Cross-Currents, Discontinuities: Black Women's Fiction." *Conjuring: Black Women, Fiction, and Literary Tradition*. Ed. Marjory Pyrse and Hortense J. Spillers. Bloomington: Indiana UP, 1985. 249–61.
Vanzant, Iyanla. *Acts of Faith: Daily Mediations for People of Color*. New York: Fireside, 1993.
Walker, Alice. *In Search of Our Mother's Gardens*. Boston: Mariner, 2003.
Webb, Gary. *Dark Alliance: The CIA, the Contras, and the Crack Cocaine Explosion*. New York: Seven Stories Press, 1999.
"The Wig Maker." *Seinfeld*. NBC. Los Angeles. 4 Apr. 1996.

Contributors

LYNN A. CASMIER-PAZ is an associate professor in the Department of English at the University of Central Florida. She has published several articles on slave narratives and is currently working on a longer book manuscript about condemned African American criminals and their autobiographical confessions that were published in the eighteenth century.

BRIAN CREMINS earned his PhD at the University of Connecticut and is an associate professor of English at Harper College in Palatine, Illinois. His essays on comic books and graphic novels have appeared in publications including the *Journal of Medical Humanities*, *Studies in American Humor*, *Los Angeles Review of Books*, and in the collection *Comics and the U.S. South* (2012). *Captain Marvel and the Art of Nostalgia*, forthcoming in 2017, is his study of the comics of C. C. Beck and Otto Binder. He lives in Chicago.

TRACY CURTIS's research interest is African American autobiography, and she is working on two books, "The Artist Project," which explores artists' creative processes and the resulting work, and "On Being Haunted," which considers shifting roles of black intellectual work in the academy, communities, and broad public contexts. She is also working on a project called "Dark Meat" exploring foodways given short shrift in mainstream outlets. She is the author of *New Media in Black Women's Autobiography: Intrepid Embodiment and Narrative Innovation* (2015).

KWAKIUTL L. DREHER is an associate professor of English and ethnic studies at the University of Nebraska–Lincoln. She conducts research in African American studies, including auto/biography, film, visual and popular culture, and mass-marketed popular literature. She is the author of *Dancing on the White Page: Black Women Entertainers Writing Autobiography* (2008). She has also published "Don't Slap Yo' Gran'Momma: Tyler Perry and Madea," in *Screening Motherhood in Contemporary World Cinema*; "I Really Need a Maid: White Womanhood in *The Help*," in *Movies in the Age of Obama: The Era of Post-Racial and Neo-Racist Cinema*; "'Scandal' and Black Women in Television," in *African Americans on Television: Race-ing for Ratings*; "A Eulogy for Tyrell Musgrove: The Disremembered Child in Marc Forster's 'Monster's Ball,'" in *Film Criticism*; and "'It's My Body and I'll Show It If I Want To': The Politics of Language in the Autobiographies of Dorothy Dandridge, Diahann Carroll, and Whoopi Goldberg," in the *Popular Culture Review*, among other scholarly articles. Her blog, *The Dreher Report*, expands the dialogue on visual culture beyond its entertainment value. Each post considers the sociocultural and historical contexts within which visual culture operates, advances entertainment as an art, and offers a stimulating opportunity for readers to "tour" its forms.

MARINA FEDOSIK is a lecturer at Princeton University. Her interdisciplinary research on representations of kinship in American literature, film, and culture reveals the potential for new knowledge offered by the adoption studies perspective. Among her publications is "Genealogical Ambiguity and Racial Identity: Adoption and Passing in Kate Chopin's 'Desiree's Baby' and Jessie Redmon Fauset's 'The Sleeper Wakes,'" an article published in *America and the Black Body: Identity Politics in Print and Visual Culture* (2009). Another article, "*Orphan* and *The Member of the Family*: Disability and Secrecy in Narratives of Disrupted Eastern European Adoption*," published in the third volume of *Adoption & Culture*, draws on crossovers between adoption and disability studies in order to examine the tendency of American culture to imagine transnational adoption as rehabilitation.

ANTHONY S. FOY teaches African American literature and culture at Swarthmore College, where he has also directed the Black Studies Program. His research examines the impact of discourses of race, class, and visuality on African American autobiography after Reconstruction. His articles have appeared in *American Literary History* and *a/b: Auto/Biography Studies*, and his essay on the origins of black celebrity autobiography will be published in *A History of African American Autobiography*, edited by Joycelyn K. Moody.

LINDA FURGERSON SELZER is an associate professor of English at Pennsylvania State University. She is the author of *Charles Johnson in Context* (2009) and the coeditor of *New Essays on the African American Novel* (2008). Her work on African American literature and culture has appeared in a number of scholarly and theoretical collections and in journals such as the *African American Review*, *Callaloo*, *MELUS*, and the *Massachusetts Review*. In 2003 she received the Darwin Turner Award for the year's best essay in *African American Review*.

ERIC D. LAMORE is an associate professor in the Department of English at the University of Puerto Rico at Mayagüez, where he teaches courses in African American, United States, and Caribbean literatures. He is the coeditor of *New Essays on Phillis Wheatley* (2011) and the editor of *Teaching Olaudah Equiano's Narrative: Pedagogical Strategies and New Perspectives* (2012). His scholarly and editorial work has also appeared in a special issue of *a/b: Auto/Biography Studies* (27.1 [2012]) devoted to African American life writing.

JOYCELYN K. MOODY is a professor of English and the Sue E. Denman Distinguished Chair in American Literature at the University of Texas at San Antonio, where she teaches courses on early African American literature and culture, U.S. slavery, and U.S. black autobiography. She is currently completing the edited volume *A History of African American Autobiography*. With John Ernest, she coedits the reprint series Regenerations: African American Literature and Culture.

SUSAN SCOTT PARRISH is a professor in the Department of English and the Program in the Environment at the University of Michigan–Ann Arbor. Her research addresses the interrelated issues of race, the environment, and knowledge-making in the Atlantic world from the seventeenth to the mid-twentieth century, with a particular emphasis on southern and Caribbean plantation zones. Her second book, *The Floor Year 1927: A Cultural History*, is forthcoming in 2017.

Index

Page numbers in italics indicate illustrations.

Abdul-Jabbar, Kareem (aka Ferdinand Lewis Alcindor Jr.), 238, 242–43, 244–47, 252
Abdur-Rahman, Aliyyah, 44
abolitionism, 93, 95, 112n9, 196–97. *See also* slaves/slavery and slave trade
action heroine, Grier as, 234, 239, 240, 249, 254, 255n4
Adiele, Faith. See *Meeting Faith: The Forest Journals of a Black Buddhist Nun* (Adiele)
adoptees, transracial. *See* transracial adoptees' lives and life narratives
adoption-search narratives, 217–18, 221, 229n4
African Americans: genealogical research, 11, 15nn9–11; genetic mapping, 11, 15n9, 15n12; as term of use, 111n11. *See also* black(s); comics narratives, autobiographical; life narrative(s); literature, African American; lives/life writers/writings; men, black; women, black
African cultural customs and identifications, 66, 71–72, 217, 224, 227, 229n12
Afro-British subjects, 69, 74, 77, 84n21
Agassiz, Louis, 94, 95
agency: in criminal confessional literary narratives, 19, 22, 23, 27; human-made ecological disasters and, 122, 123, 140n21; in transracial adoptees' lives/narratives and, 219
"age of Obama" assessment, 3, 10, 13
Alcindor, Ferdinand Lewis, Jr. (aka Kareem Abdul-Jabbar), 238, 242–43, 244–47, 252
alienation: from adoptive families/culture, 218–19, 223; human, 118–19, 132, 135, 137, 141nn34–35
Alryyes, Ala, 13n3
American Colonization Society, 77, 80
Anderson, Alexander, 73, 74–75, 83nn14–16
Anderson, Marian, 180

Andrew (Ofodobendo Wooma) memoir, 10–11, 14n8
Andrews, Charles C., 70, 71, 75, 77, 80
Andrews, William L., and topics: antebellum African American life narratives, 13n3; Arthur's criminal confessional literary narrative, 37n5; autobiographies of African Americans, 91; institutions and uplift, 97, 112n15; *Life . . .* (Jea) as conversion to Christianity narrative, 47; postbellum frontispiece portraits, 112n11; Wright's autobiography and sociology, 138n2
Angelou, Maya, 241–43
antebellum literature, 4, 5, 14n4, 42. *See also* postbellum era
antebellum slave narratives, 4, 13n3, 19, 22, 91, 96, 112n11. *See also* slave narrative(s)
Appeal to the Coloured Citizens of the World (Walker), 5, 14n4, 41, 42, 45, 58
archival works and research, 10–11, 15n11, 147
Arkoff, Samuel Z., 255n1
Arthur's criminal confessional literary narrative: overview of, 4–5, 19–22, 37; agency in, 19, 22, 23, 27; antebellum slave narrative context for, 19, 22; blackness in, 36; the body in, 19, 20, 21, 23, 25, 32–33, 35, 37; colonial masculinity and black body relationship in, 20, 23–24; dandyism in, 31, 36, 38n10; and dignity, personal, 28; escape or "steal themselves" activity in, 20, 23–24, 26–27, 31, 32–33; humanity affirmation in, 21, 23, 37; and language, retaliatory, 32, 38n12; as life narrative, 20, 37n6; manhood as expressed in, 19, 23, 27, 29, 31; masculine heterosexual activities in, 21, 24, 26, 27, 29; Native American women relations in, 26, 27–28, 36; and persona,

Arthur's . . . narrative (*continued*)
    black, 19, 28, 36; rape act in, 26, 33–35; and rapists, racist stereotype of, 22, 35; sartorial self-fashioning, 21, 24–25, 26, 27, 28–30, 31, 38n10; scholarship on, 20, 37n5; slavery and enslaved status in, 21, 23, 26–27; social order in colonial America and, 35–36, 38n12; subjectivity in, 23, 26, 31–32, 37; survival strategies in, 30; and visibility, black, 19, 22–23, 25, 26, 32; white women's sexual relations in, 27, 29, 32, 33–35
auction block as spectacle, 93, 94, 95, 111n8, 112n9
Austen, Jake, 152
autoadaptations, 71, 83n13
the autobiographical self, in autobiographical comics narratives, 145–46, 147, 148–49, 156, 157, *158*, 159, *160*, 161
autobiographies, by men: overview and history of, 91, 216; abolitionism in, 112n9, 196–97; biographies compared with, 20, 37n6; the body and text relationship in, 90, 97; with buildings, photographs of, 97, 112n14, 112n16; citizenship, 96; collaborative autobiography and, 74–75, 84n18; Jim Crow era, 90, 91, 92; photographs in, 89, 91; of postbellum era, 96, 109; in postslavery era, 90, 99, 101, 109, 117–18; readership's interests and, 90; self-representation in, 89, 90, 96, 97, 99; slave narratives as, 37n11; sociology and, 138n2; transracial adoptees' life narratives as, 219; in Tuskegee culture, 98–100; uplift in, 89, 90, 98. *See also* comics narratives, autobiographical; criminal confessional literary narratives; spiritual autobiographies of men; visibility, black; *and specific authors and titles*
autobiographies, by women, 179–80, 199–200, 217, 219, 235. *See also* Buddhist lives/life narratives of women; *Foxy: My Life in Three Acts* (Grier); Nissel, Angela

Bailey, Julius H., 60n7, 62n27
Bambara, Toni Cade, 255n6
Barry, Lynda, 149
Beaty, Bart, 148, 152
Beck, C. C., 151, 152
Becker, Michael, 235
Being Black: Zen and the Art of Living with Fearlessness and Grace (Williams): overview of, 8, 174, 176, 178, 193; community and individual's relationship in, 177, 183–87, 194nn7–8; fear/fearlessness in, 183–85; geographic locations or changes in settings in, 178, 186–87; individual vulnerability in, 177, 192–93; interiority in, 175; solitary practices in, 177, 184, 186, 193; and stereotypes, racist, 183, 184; subjectivity in, 184
Belinda's petition, 176–77
Bell, Vikki, 216
Benjamin, Walter, 108
Berry, Halle, 206, 254
Biographical Sketches and Interesting Anecdotes of Persons of Colour (Mott), 79, 83n11, 85n23
biographies, compared with autobiographies, 20, 37n6
"biological recoil" of humans, 119, 136–37
biopolitics, 21
biracial (mixed-race) people, 177, 198, 206, 207–9, 214n3, 222
birth parents' reunions, 217, 219, 220
Black Baby White Hands: A View from the Crib (John): overview of, 9–10, 217, 227–28; agency in, 219; autobiographies and, 219; birth parents' reunions in, 220; blackness in, 219; color lines and, 217, 222; community and individual's relationship in, 219, 220, 221, 227; as conversion narrative, 220–21; cultural imaginaries in, 220, 221–22; double-consciousness in, 219; hybridity in, 221, 222, 223; identity formation in, 219, 220, 223; kinship in, 219, 221; racial differences and, 219; racial identity/identities in, 221–22, 224; racism in, 219, 221
Black Belt life, 91, 102, *103*, 104, 105, *106*, 107, *107*, 108, 113n18
Black Boy (Wright): overview and description of, 117, 119, 138n3, 139n8; childhood experiences in, 117, 130, 137, 138n3; decoding skills in, 125, 134; equilibrium critique, 118; human ecology theory in, 119; print culture participation by minorities in, 124, 125, 128, 133; Romanticism in, 118; rural environment in, 118, 132–34, 138n1, 141n33; sociological experiments as racial allegory in, 120–21; spatio-temporal position in, 129–30; subjectivity in, 118
Black Metropolis . . . (Cayton and Drake), 119
blackness: confessional literature and, 19–20, 36; frontispiece portrait as image of, 96; racial knowledge production of, 90; in transracial adoptees' lives/life narratives and, 217,

222–23, 224, 225, 226–27; in visual properties of black autobiographies, 90. *See also* whiteness

black(s): alienation of, 118–19, 132, 137; and Atlantic literature, black, 66, 67; and black power movement, 42, 226; and black quiet theory, 111n3; black/white binary and, 224–25, 226–27; in blaxploitation films, 233, 235–37, 239–40, 255n1; and the body, female, 196, 233, 234, 236–37, 239; citizenship for, 90, 96; as dandies, 30–31, 36, 38n10; engagement with Buddhism by, 174–77; flood culture and, 122, 123, 124, 125, *127*, 128, 139n17; gender roles' intersection with race and, 42, 44, 58; and ideography, black, 92, 96, 97, 98, 101, 109; Native Americans' relationships with, 26, 27–28, 36; and persona, black, 19, 28, 36; rape in colonial America and, 19, 22, 26, 33–35; space/production of space for, 132; spatio-temporal position and, 129–30, 131, 132; as term of use, 111n11. *See also* blackness; the body, male; criminal confessional literary narratives; feminism, black; heteronormativity, black; homosociality, black; masculinity, black; men, black; preachers, female; preachers, male; uplift (racial uplift ideologies); violence, black; visibility, black; white(s); women, black

Black Women's Manifesto, 237–41, 243–49, 250–55

blaxploitation films, 233, 235–37, 239–40, 255n1

Block, Sharon, 33, 34, 35, 37n5

blogs (weblogs): overview and use of term, 198–99, 212–13, 214n2; as confessional literary narratives, 198, 200; as life narratives, 198–99, 212; as self-publication/production activities, 198. *See also* Internet

the body, female, 196, 233, 234, 236–37, 239

the body, male: and buildings, photographs of, 92; in criminal confessional literary narratives, 19, 20, 21, 23, 25, 32–33, 35, 37; gallows literature on, 20; racial differences and, 95; racial knowledge and, 96; text and visual interactions and, 90, 97; and visibility, black, 95–96; in visual properties of black autobiographies, 92, 97–98, 101–2, 104–5, 107, 108. *See also* the body, female

The Book of Sarahs: A Family in Parts (McKinley): overview of, 9–10, 217, 227–28; African cultural customs in, 227, 229n12; African identifications in, 224; alienation from adoptive families/culture and, 223; biracial women in, 222; blackness in, 222–23, 224, 225, 226–27; black/white binary in, 224–25, 226–27; community and individual's relationship in, 223, 227; cultural imaginaries in, 224–25; hybridity in, 223, 226–27; identity formation in, 223, 227; kinship in, 225; NABSW in, 226; racial differences in, 219, 223–24, 225; racial identity/identities in, 224, 225, 226–27; slave narratives compared with, 223; transnational adoptions and, 223, 226, 229n10; whiteness in, 224–25

Bread & Wine: An Erotic Tale of New York (Delany and Wolff): overview of, 7–8, 146, 161, 170n14; "Brod und Wein" (Hölderlin) in, 161, 162, *163*, 166, 167; density in, 162, *163*, 165, 166; page design in, 150, 161–62, *163*, *164*, *165*, 165–67; Rickett as partner in, 146, 161, 162, *163*, *164*, 165, 166; the self and the other encounters (public contact) in, 162; Wolff's visual artistic collaboration in, 150, 161, 162, *163*, *164*, *165*, 165–67, 170n14. *See also* Delany, Samuel R., and life/life writings

Brockden, Magdalene Beulah, 10–11, 14n8

"Brod und Wein" (Hölderlin), 161, 162, *163*, 166, 167

The Broke Diaries: The Completely True and Hilarious Misadventures of a Good Girl Gone Broke (Nissel), 198, 199–206, 207, 209, 211

Brown, Kathleen, 23

Brown, William J. See *The Life of William J. Brown of Providence, R.I., With Personal Recollections of Incidents in Rhode Island* (Brown)

Bryant, John, 6, 12–13, 15n14, 16n16, 68, 83n13

Buddhist lives/life narratives of women: overview of, 8–9, 174, 176; biracial women and, 177; Buddhist beliefs and practices and, 174–77, 179, 184, 185, 187; collective identity and, 184, 194n7; community and individual's relationship and, 177, 178–79, 180–87, 191, 194nn7–8; differences among women and, 176; fear/fearlessness and, 183–85; gender roles and, 187, 189, 192; geographic locations or changes in settings and, 177–78, 180–81, 186–87; individual vulnerability and, 177, 187–89, 191, 192–93; interiority and, 175, 179; race and, 189; racism and KKK experiences in, 178, 181–83; rape and, 190–91; slaves/slavery and, 189, 191; solitary practices and, 177, 179, 184, 186, 190, 191, 192, 193; spiritual health and, 175, 177, 191; subjectivity and, 176, 184 buildings, photographs of: autobiographies with, 97, 112n14, 112n16; the body as replaced by, 92; interiority and, 101, 104, 105, 106, 109; privacy representation in, 97, *107*, 107–8; race buildings representation in, 97, 101–2, *103*, 105, *106*, *107*, 109; uplift representation in, 101, *103*, 104, 107, *107*; in visual properties of black autobiographies, 92, 97, 101–2, *103*, 104–9, *106*, *107*, 112n15

Burgess, Ernest W., 117, 121, 131

Burrow, Trigant, 119, 136–37

Butler, Robert J., 138n1

Byrd, Rudolph P., 59–60

Byron, Gay L., 43, 59, 60

camps, Red Cross flood victim, 122, 123, 124, 125, 128

Cappetti, Carla, 117, 138n2

Carby, Hazel V., 43

Carretta, Vincent, 69, 78, 84n21

Casper, Monica J., 21, 36

Cayton, Horace R., 119–20

celebrity autobiographies, black, 234–35, 254, 255n3. See also *Foxy: My Life in Three Acts* (Grier)

Chaney, Michael A., and topics: African Americans literature and comics relationship, 147; autobiographical comics narratives, 148–50, 168, 169nn7–8; engraved portrait, 6; "new kinds of seeing," 3–4; visual qualities of narratives, 161

changes in settings (geographic locations). See geographic locations (changes in settings)

Chavis, Reverend Benjamin, 139n18

Chaykin, Howard, 161

Chicago School of Sociology: equilibrium and, 118, 121, 139nn13–14; human ecology and, 117–18, 119–20, 133, 138n2, 138n5, 139n11; spatiotemporal position and, 131, 140nn30–31; urban environment and, 117–18, 121, 138n5, 139n11, 140nn30–31

Christian heteronormativity: Golden Rule in, 44, 48–49, 59; military service intersection with, 43, 44, 45, 56–57; in spiritual autobiographies of men, 41–45, 47–49, 52, 53, 58, 61n15, 61n22; and violence, black, 47, 48–49, 52, 53; white hegemony intersection with, 54. See also under conversion narratives

Chute, Hillary L., 148

circulation of life narratives and writers, 12, 15n13. See also publication/production of life narratives/writings; reception of life narratives and writers

citizenship, black, 90, 96

civil rights movement, 60n5, 174, 196–97, 233

Clasquin-Johnson, Michel, 185

"classic" African American literature, 3, 7

Clements, F. E., 121, 129

clothing. See sartorial self-fashioning

Coffy (film), 233–34, 239, 254, 255n4

collaborative autobiography, 74–75, 84n18

collaborative process between writers and visual artists, 150, 161, 170n15

collective identity, and Buddhist women's lives and life narratives, 184, 194n7

Collins, Lisa Gail, 95, 111n7

Collins, Patricia Hill, 56, 192, 253–54

colonial America: biopolitics during, 21; and the body, black, 20, 23–24; clothing and sumptuary laws in, 24–25, 29–30, 38n8; criminal confessional literary narratives during, 19, 20; dandyism and, 30–31, 36; gallows literature about black criminals from, 19; masculinity in, 20, 23–24; Native American and blacks' relationships in, 26, 27–28, 36; rape in, 33–35; social order in, 35–36, 38n12

color lines, 118, 132, 135, 137, 139n6, 217, 222. See also racism

comedic traditions: comics compared with, 147, 148; description of, 148; digital public sphere life narratives and, 198, 200–201, 205, 206, 211; Prinze and, 244; Pryor and, 147, 148, 251. See also parodies

comics, and superhero parodies, 146, 147, 152, 153, 156, 157. See also comics narratives, autobiographical

comics narratives, autobiographical: overview of, 7–8; the autobiographical self in, 145–46, 147, 148–49, 156, 157, *158*, 159, *160*, 161; collaborative process between writers and visual artists in, 161, 170n15; density in, 148, 149–50, 151, 153, 154, 162, *163*, 165, 166; geographic locations in, 148, 151, 152, 153–54; humor in, 147, 152, 156; and literature, African Americans, 147–48, 159–60, 169nn6–7; page design in, 149–51, 153–54, *155*, 156, 161–62, *163*, *164*, *165*, 165–67; queer communities in, 148; race in, 147, 150–51; readership

Index

and, 147, 149, 161–62; the self and the other encounters (public contact) in, 146, 147, 149, 162; self-publication/production of, 146, 156, 170n13; sense of self in, 149; silences or "space of concentration" in, 162, *163*, *164*, 165–67, 171n17; underground publishers for, 147, 152, 156; urban contacts in, 145, 147, 151, 153, 154, *155*, 156, *157*, 169n5; visual artist's collaboration with writer in, 150, 161, 162, *163*, *164*, *165*, 165–67, 170n14

community and individual's relationship: autobiographies by women and, 180; Buddhist women's lives/life narratives and, 177, 178–79, 180–87, 191, 194nn7–8; digital public sphere life narratives and, 211, 213–14; in transracial adoptees' lives/life narratives, 219, 220, 221, 223, 227

Comte, August, 121

confessional literary narratives, as blogs, 198, 200. *See also* criminal confessional literary narratives

Congress on Racial Equality (CORE), 239

conversion narratives: of black self, 99–100, 101–2, 104–5, 113n17; Christian, 44–45, 47, 50, 53, 55–58, 141n32; transracial adoptees' lives/life narratives as, 220–21

Cooper, Arnold, 113n17

Cooper, Carol, 174–75

counterarchives of blackness, 96, 112n10

Couser, G. Thomas, 80

"crazy" (signs of "crazy"): Angelou on, 242; Grier and, 234, 238–39, 242–43, 247, 248, 253; as term of use, 238; Vanzant on, 242–43, 249

criminal confessional literary narratives: overview and description of, 19–22; antebellum slave narratives compared with, 19; during pre-Revolutionary era, 19, 20; slave narratives compared with, 20, 37n4. *See also* Arthur's criminal confessional literary narrative; gallows literature about black criminals

Crumb, R., 149

cultural imaginaries, in transracial adoptees' lives/life narratives, 217–18, 220, 221–22, 224–25

curriculum, Free School, 66, 68, 71, 75–77, 80–81, 83n11, 84n20

dandyism, 30–31, 36, 38n10. *See also* sartorial self-fashioning

Davis, Charles T., 37n1

decoding skills, 125, 134, 140n25

Delany, Samuel R., and life/life writings: overview and comics of, 167, 168; the autobiographical self in, 146, 147, 161; biographical information about, 146; density in, 148; geographic locations in, 148; as influence on comics artists, 147, 169n5; queer communities in, 148; readership and, 147, 161–62; Rickett's relationship with, 146, *164*, *165*, 166–67; the self and the other encounters (public contact) in, 146, 147, 149; silences or "space of concentration" in, 162, *163*, *164*, 165–67, 171n17; *Times Square Red, Times Square Blue*, 146, 147, 169n2, 169n5; urban contacts in, 147, 153, 169n5; writings of, 161, 169n2. *See also Bread & Wine: An Erotic Tale of New York* (Delany and Wolff)

DeLombard, Jeannine Marie, 5, 19, 20, 37n4

density, in autobiographical comics narratives, 148, 149–50, 151, 153, 154, 162, *163*, 165, 166

depression (mental illness), in digital public sphere life narratives, 205, 209–11

digital platforms, and genealogical and genetic information, 11–12, 15n12

digital public sphere, and life narratives: overview of, 9, 197–98, 205, 212; biracial women in, 198, 206, 207–9, 214n3; blogs in, 198–99, 212; *The Broke Diaries . . .* (Nissel) and, 198, 199–206, 207, 209, 211; comedic tradition and, 198, 200–201, 205, 206, 211; community and individual's relationship and, 211, 213–14; confessional literary narratives and, 200; depression (mental illness) in, 205, 209–11; fictionalized experiences in autobiographies and, 199–200; "getting ovuh" tales and, 200, 205, 213; media expertise and, 205–6, 212; *Mixed: My Life in Black and White* (Nissel), 198, 206–11, 214n3; "neteracy" and, 212; new media and, 198, 202, 204–5; open-mic poetry performances in, 200, 202; poverty theme in, 202–4, 207; public and private spheres divisions in, 198–99; public sphere and, 197–98, 205; racism in, 206–11, 214n3; self-fashioning in, 197, 199, 202, 204; self-help literature and, 200; self-publication/production in, 198, 212; website development in, 198, 205, 212. *See also* Nissel, Angela

dignity (personal dignity), 28, 51, 57, 180

disasters, human-made ecological: equilibrium and, 121–22, 139n14. *See also* flood of 1927 in Mississippi
double-consciousness ("twoness"), 111n3, 151, 217, 219
Douglass, Frederick, and topics: abolitionism, 82n7, 112n9; "classic" African American literature, 3; feminists, black, 59, 62n31; fugitive slave status, 82n7; marriage between blacks, 53; Mott's friendship with, 68, 85n23; violence, black, 46, 61n13
Douglass-Chin, Richard J., 177
Drake, St. Clair, 119
Dreaming Me: An African American Woman's Spiritual Journey (Willis): overview of, 8, 174, 176, 178, 193, 193n2; community and individual's relationship in, 177, 180–83, 191; geographic locations or changes in settings and, 180–81, 187; individual vulnerability in, 177, 187–88, 191, 192; racism and KKK experiences in, 178, 181–83; slaves/slavery in, 191; solitary practices in, 193; spiritual health in, 191
Drexler, Michael J., 4, 10, 13n3
drug culture, celebrity, 248, 249–53
Du Bois, W. E. B., and topics: autobiographies by men, 216; "classic" African American literature, 3; color line, 139n6; double-consciousness ("twoness"), 151, 217; feminists, black, 59, 62n23, 62n31; flood exposé, 128; sociology, science of, 120; the Veil, 149
Dunn, Stephane, 236
Durrell, William, and publication of *The Interesting Narrative* . . . (Equiano), 69–75, 78, 79, 83n12

education: and curriculum, Free School, 66, 68, 71, 75–77, 80–81, 83n11, 84n20; higher, 234, 245–47. *See also* literacy
Edwards, Paul, 69
Edwards, William J.: biographical information about, 100–101; Black Belt life of, 91; conversion narrative of, 99–100, 104–5, 113n17; as New Negro, 89, 100, 108; Snow Hill Institute founded by, 91, 100, 105–6; as Tuskagee Institute graduate, 99–100, 113n17; uplift in life of, 99–100, 113n17. *See also Twenty-Five Years in the Black Belt* (Edwards)
Eisner, Will, 151–52, 156, 167
Ellison, Ralph, 141n33
Emerson, Ralph Waldo, 134–35

England, and Afro-British subjects, 69, 74, 77, 84n21
entertainment industry, 211–12. *See also Foxy: My Life in Three Acts* (Grier)
environment, ecological: environmental justice movement and, 123, 139n18; equilibrium and, 118, 121–22, 128–29, 139nn13–14; risk modeling and, 129, 133
Equiano, Olaudah, life and life narratives of, 69, 73, 74, 76–77, 81n1, 83n16, 84n18. *See also The Interesting Narrative of the Life of Olaudah Equiano, or Gustavus Vassa, the African. Written by Himself* (Equiano); *The Life and Adventures of Olaudah Equiano; or, Gustavus Vassa, the African. From an Account Written by Himself, Abridged by A. Mott. To Which Is Added Some Remarks on the Slave Trade* (Mott ed.)
equilibrium, and environment, 118, 121–22, 128–29, 139nn13–14
escape ("steal themselves") activities, 20, 23–24, 26–27, 31, 32–33
"The Ethics of Living Jim Crow" (Wright), 118, 123, 129–30, 131, 132, 133

Fake, Edie, 169n5
Faulkner, William, 123
Faull, Katherine, 10–11, 13n3, 14n8
fear/fearlessness, 56, 183–85
feminism, black: Grier and, 234, 237–38, 240, 244, 245–47, 248–49, 252–54; Islam and, 245–47, 252; patriarchy's conflict with, 238, 244, 245–47, 248–49, 252–54; power relationship critiques in, 43, 59–60, 60n5, 62n23, 62n31
fictionalized experiences, in autobiographies, 199–200
flood of 1927 in Mississippi: and culture, black, 122, 123, 124, 125, *127*, 128, 139n17; as disaster, 123, 129, 140n21; environmental justice movement and, 123, 139n18; human ecology and, 128–29; and laborers, black, 123; media and, 122, 123–24, 125, *126*, *127*, 128, 140n22, 140n25; racism against black victims in, 122, 123, 124, 125, 128, 129; white culture of, 122, 123–24, 125, *126*, 128; in Wright's life and writings, 122–23, 124, 125, 128, 131, 139n17, 140n24, 140nn27–29
fluid text(s): overview of, 6, 12–13, 15n14, 16n16; Equiano's life narrative as, 68, 79, 80, 83n13; *The Interesting Narrative* . . . (Equiano) as, 80,

83n13; *The Life and Adventures of Olaudah Equiano* (Mott ed.) as, 68, 79, 80, 83n13; life narratives as, 13

Foss, Ronald, 152

Foster, Frances Smith, 13n3, 37n5

Foucault, Michel: biopolitics, 21; criminal confessional literary narratives and blacks/blackness, 19–20, 36; criminal confessional literary narratives and "sainthood," 36; visual practices of discipline, 93

Foxy Brown (film), 233–34, 239, 249, 255n4

Foxy: My Life in Three Acts (Grier): overview of, 10, 234–35, 253–55; Abdul-Jabbar in, 238, 242–43, 244–47, 252; action heroines in, 234, 239, 240, 249, 254, 255n4; biographical and characteristics information in, 232, 235, 240–41, 250, 255n1; *Black Women's Manifesto* in, 237–41, 243–49, 250–55; blaxploitation films in, 233, 235–37, 239, 255n1; and the body, female, 233, 234, 236–37, 239; as celebrity autobiography, black, 234–35, 255n3; cervical cancer diagnosis in, 235, 240; *Coffy* (film), 233–34, 239, 254, 255n4; "crazy" or signs of "crazy" in, 234, 238–39, 242–43, 247, 248, 253; and drug culture, celebrity, 248, 249–53; educational goals in, 234, 245–47; and feminism, black, 234, 237–38, 240, 244, 245–47, 248–49, 252–54; *Foxy Brown* (film), 233–34, 239, 249, 255n4; *Friday Foster* (film), 239, 254, 255n4; Ginger the pony experience in, 253, 256n10; *Greased Lightning* (film), 249–50; interiority in, 243, 254; *Jackie Brown* (film), 232, 235, 254; life/life writings and, 235, 236, 237, 239, 242; *The "L" Word* (television program), 235; patriarchy and black feminism conflict in, 238, 244, 245–47, 248–49, 252–54; physical health in, 235, 240, 252–53; Prinze in, 238, 242–43, 244, 247–49, 253; Pryor in, 238–39, 240–41, 242–43, 244, 249–53, 255n1, 256n10; rape of Grier as child and, 235, 240, 250; romantic relationships in, 238–39, 242–54, 255n1, 256n10; savior/caretaker role in, 244, 249–52, 251; scholarship on, 235–36; self-help culture, 241–43; self-love in, 243–44, 253; sense of self in, 239; *Sheba, Baby* (film), 239, 255n4; slaves/slavery and, 246, 256n9; survival strategies in, 237, 252; uplift in, 239, 252, 255n2

Franklin, Benjamin, 22, 29, 30, 38n8

Free Schools: New York African Free School, 68, 70–71, 75–77, 80, 83n11, 84n20; Philadelphia Free School, 76–77

Friday Foster (film), 239, 254, 255n4

frontispiece portrait of black autobiographers: in antebellum slave narratives, 96, 112n11; blackness representation in, 96; in Durrell's publication of *The Interesting Narrative...* (Equiano), 69, 73; in *The Interesting Narrative...* (Equiano), 69, 73, 83n14, 84n16; in Jim Crow era, 96; in *The Life and Adventures of Olaudah Equiano* (Mott ed.), 73, 74–75, 83n14–16; in postbellum slave narratives, 96, 112n11; self-representation in, 96–97; text and visual interactions in, 90, 97; uplift representation in, 97, 101; and visibility, black, 96–97; in visual properties of black autobiographies, 97, 101. *See also* visual properties of black autobiographies

Fyfe, Christopher, 84n21

gallows literature about black criminals, 19, 20. *See also* Arthur's criminal confessional literary narrative; criminal confessional literary narratives

Ganz, Marshall, 51

Gates, Henry Louis, Jr., 10–12, 15n9, 37n1, 46, 81n4, 238, 255n6

gay (queer) communities, 148. *See also* Delany, Samuel R., and life/life writings

gender roles: in Buddhist women's lives/life narratives, 187, 189, 192; in marriages, Christian, 53, 61n23; and masculinity, black, 42–43, 44; and preachers, black male, 43, 60n7; in spiritual autobiographies of men, 42–43, 44, 58

genealogical research, for African Americans, 11, 15nn9–11

genetic mapping, 11–12, 15n9, 15n12

geographic locations (changes in settings): in autobiographical comics narratives, 148, 151, 152, 153–54; Buddhist women's lives/life narratives and, 177–78, 180–81, 186–87

georgic, the, 135, 141n34

"getting ovuh" tales, 200, 205, 213

Giggie, John M., 61n8

Gill, Joel Christian, 6

Gilroy, Paul, 66, 67, 197, 205

Giordano, Dick, 161

God Struck Me Dead (Watson): overview and description of, 42, 53–54, 57; conversion to Christianity narratives in, 44, 50, 55, 56–57; gender roles in, 42; and heteronormativity, black, 58–59; and homosociality, black, 54–55, 54–56; and masculinity, black, 53–54, 55, 57; military service in, 53–55, 56–57; and violence, black, 58; white hegemony in, 54–55; white violence against slaves, 55–56
Golden Rule, 44, 48–49, 59
Goldstein, Nancy, 147
Grant, Jacqueline, 43, 59, 60, 60n5
graphic novels. See *Bread & Wine: An Erotic Tale of New York* (Delany and Wolff)
Greased Lightning (film), 249–50
Green, James, 73, 75, 84n19
Green, Justin, 152
Green, Kim D., 13n3
Green, Richard "Grass," and life and comics: overview and comics of, 146, 152, 160–61, 167–68, 169n3; the autobiographical self in, 145–46, 156, 157, *158*, 159, *160*; biographical information about, 145, 146, 152–53; density in, 148, 151, 153, 154; geographic locations in, 148, 151, 152, 153–54; humor artistry of, 147, 152, 156; influences on, 151, 153; musician experiences in, 146, 153, 159, 160–61, 169n3; page design in, 149–51, 153–54, *155*, 156; readership and, 147; scholarship on, 147–48; the self and the other encounters (public contact) in, 146, 147; self-publication/production by, 146, 156, 170n13; superhero parodies of, 146, 147, 152, 153, 156, 157; underground publishers, 147, 152, 156; *Un-Fold Funnies*, 7–8, 145, 146, 156, 170n13; urban contacts in, 145, 147, 151, 153, 154, *155*, 156, *157*, 159; *Xal-Kor the Human Cat*, 152, 153, 154, *155*, 156, 157, *157*, 159, 169n3
Grier, Pam. See *Foxy: My Life in Three Acts* (Grier)
Griffin, Junius, 233
Groensteen, Thierry, 148, 149, 150
Groth, Gary, 162
group portraits, and visual properties of black autobiographies, 101, 109
Guerrero, Ed, 233, 236
Guy, Melody, 206, 211, 212

Habermas, Jürgen, 9, 196, 197
Haley, Alex, 224
Hall, Justin, 214n2
Hall, Prince, 45, 51
Hall, Stuart, 42, 219, 221, 223, 228
Harper, Phillip Brian, 58
Harris, Leslie M., 77, 80
Harris, Michael D., 95
Harvey, David, 141n36
Hatfield, Charles, 149, 161
health of individuals: depression or mental illness and, 205, 209–11; physical, 235, 252–53; spiritual, 175, 177, 191
heteronormativity, black: and marriage, Christian, 53, 61nn22–23; in spiritual autobiographies of men, 45, 46, 53, 58–59, 61n22
High John the Conqueror, 59–60
Hinks, Peter P., 60n2, 61n19
Hirsch, Marianne, 148
Hölderlin, Friedrich, 161, 162, *163*, 166, 167
Hollywood entertainment industry, 197–98, 201, 211–12, 232, 250. See also *specific actors/entertainers*
Holmlund, Chris, 236
homosociality, black: homosociality described, 41–42; and marriage, Christian, 45; military service intersection with, 54–55; in protection of black women, 41, 51–53; in spiritual autobiographies of men, 45, 48, 50–56; white hegemony intersection with, 51, 54–55
hooks, bell, 174, 242, 243, 244, 253
Hoover, Herbert, 123, 128, 140n22
Horn, Patrick E., 13n3
Howard, William, 140n24
human alienation, 118–19, 132, 135, 137, 141nn34–35
human ecology: Chicago School of Sociology and, 117–18, 119–20, 133, 138n5, 139n11; flood of 1927 in Mississippi and, 128–29; Wright and, 117, 118, 119, 121, 129, 133, 139n11
humanity affirmation, 21, 23, 37
humor, in autobiographical comics narratives, 147, 152, 156. See also comedic traditions; parodies
Hurston, Zora Neale, 3, 138n4, 147, 180, 244
hybridity, in transracial adoptees' lives/life narratives, 217, 221, 222, 223, 226–27

identity formation, in transracial adoptees' lives/life narratives, 217, 218, 219, 220, 223, 227
ideography, black, 92, 96, 97, 98, 101, 109. See also uplift (racial uplift ideologies)
individuals, vulnerability of, 177, 187–89, 191, 192–93. See also community and individual's relationship; health of individuals

Index

Innis, Roy, 239
The Interesting Narrative of the Life of Olaudah Equiano, or Gustavus Vassa, the African. Written by Himself (Equiano): overview and description of, 5–6, 66–67; African cultural customs in, 66, 71–72; Afro-British connections in, 74; and Atlantic literature, black, 66, 67; authorized/unauthorized editions of, 67, 69, 70, 71, 80, 81, 84n18; autoadaptations and, 71, 83n13; as collaborative autobiography, 74, 84n18; as fluid text, 80, 83n13; frontispiece portrait in, 69, 73, 83n14, 84n16; as life narrative, 66; in New York African Free School curriculum, 66, 68, 71, 83n11; practical knowledge in, 76–77; publication/production of, 67; readership for, 67; reception histories and, 67; resettlement project in, 77–79, 80, 85n22, 85n23; subscribers lists and, 69–70, 72–73; talking book trope and history of the book connections with, 6, 14n5; transatlantic and transnational dimensions of, 66–67, 71–72; transatlantic slave trade dynamics in, 66, 72; U.S. and African American literatures context for, 68, 70. See also *The Life and Adventures of Olaudah Equiano; or, Gustavus Vassa, the African. From an Account Written by Himself, Abridged by A. Mott. To Which Is Added Some Remarks on the Slave Trade* (Mott ed.)
interiority: Buddhist women's lives/life narratives and, 175, 179; and celebrity autobiographies, black, 234–35; Grier and, 243, 254; in visual properties of black autobiographies, 92, 98, 101, 104, 105, 106, 109; in Wright's life and writings, 133, 134, 135
Internet, 197, 204, 213–14. See also blogs (weblogs)
interracial couples, 198, 206, 209, 211. See also biracial (mixed-race) people
Islam, and black feminism, 245–47, 252

Jackie Brown (film), 232, 235, 254
Jackson, Leon, 14n5
Jackson, Reverend Jesse, 233
Jacobs, Jane, 146, 147, 148, 153, 169n5
Jakes, T. D., 43, 60n7
Jarman, Joseph, 175
Jea, John. See *The Life, History, and Unparalleled Sufferings of John Jea, the African Preacher* (Jea)
Jefferson, Thomas, 44, 94–95, 111n6
Jim Crow era: autobiographies of, 90, 91, 92; protests in media against, 122, 124, 128; rural environment during, 130, 137, 138n4; "second nature" and, 137; space/production of space during, 132; spatiotemporal position and, 130, 131, 132, 137; visual properties of black autobiographies during, 89, 91, 96, 97; Wright's life and writings and, 122, 124, 128, 130
John, Jaiya. See *Black Baby White Hands: A View from the Crib* (John)
Johnson, Charles, 175
Johnson, Clifton H., 54, 55, 56, 57
Johnson, James Weldon, 3
Julien, Isaac, 240

Kincaid, Jamaica, 232, 236–37, 240, 255n2
King, Martin Luther, Jr., 60n7, 174–75, 185
kinship, in transracial adoptees' lives/life narratives, 217, 218, 219, 221, 225
Kirby, Jack, 150, 151, 153, 154, 156
Kitchen Sink Enterprises, 147, 152, 156
Knapp, Isaac, 70
Kolb, Leigh, 232
Krauthamer, Barbara, 6
Ku Klux Klan (KKK), 54–55, 178, 181–83
Kurtzman, Harvey, 150, 153, 156

laborers: and alienation, human, 118–19, 137, 141n35; flooding's impact on black, 123; space/production of space for, 132
language, retaliatory, 32, 38n12
Lee, Felicia, 240
Lefebvre, Henri, 119, 131–32, 137, 140n31
Lejeune, Philippe, 16n16, 97
Lemke, Thomas, 21, 36
Lemons, Gary L., 58, 59, 60, 62n23, 62n31
Liazos, Ariane, 51
The Life, History, and Unparalleled Sufferings of John Jea, the African Preacher (Jea): overview and description of, 42, 45, 58; biographical information about, 43, 45–46, 48, 61n17; as black preacher, 43, 47, 48, 61n20; Christian heteronormativity in, 43, 47, 48–49; as conversion to Christianity narrative, 47; gender roles in, 43; and heteronormativity, black, 46; and homosociality, black, 48; and marriages, Christian, 47–48, 52, 53, 61n15; and masculinity, black, 43, 47–49; military service in, 43; nonviolent actions in, 48, 49; and violence, black, 43, 46–49, 61n13; white hegemony in, 46, 47–48, 61n13; white violence against slaves in, 46–47, 61n14

The Life and Adventures of Olaudah Equiano; or, Gustavus Vassa, the African. From an Account Written by Himself, Abridged by A. Mott. To Which Is Added Some Remarks on the Slave Trade (Mott ed.): overview and description of, 6, 68, 73–74, 81; Afro-British connections in, 74; authorized/unauthorized editions as sources for, 69, 71, 72–73, 83n12; as collaborative autobiography, 74–75; editorial decisions in, 69, 71, 72–73, 75, 80, 82n8, 85n23; as fluid text, 68, 79, 80, 83n13; frontispiece portrait in, 73, 74–75, 83n14–16; and life narratives, 80–81; in New York African Free School curriculum, 68, 71, 80–81, 83n11; practical knowledge pedagogy in, 75–77, 80, 84n20; preface to, 70–71; publication/production of, 80, 81; reception histories and, 81; resettlement project support in, 78–80; Samuel Wood and Sons as publishers of, 68, 74, 79; scholarship on, 68; as slave narrative, 84n20; slavery and slave trade textuality of, 74–75, 84n19; student readership's backgrounds and, 69, 82n9; transatlantic and transnational dimensions of, 74, 75, 80–81; Vassa, Gustavus as name, 73, 81n1, 83n16, 84n18. See also *The Interesting Narrative of the Life of Olaudah Equiano, or Gustavus Vassa, the African. Written by Himself* (Equiano); Mott, Abigail Field

life narrative(s): overview and description of, 3–4, 37n6; "age of Obama" assessment of, 3, 10, 13; archival works and research in, 10–11, 147; Arthur's criminal confessional literary narrative as, 20, 37n6; circulation of, 12, 15n13; as fluid texts, 13; genealogical and genetic information dissemination in, 11–12; Grier and, 235, 236, 237, 239, 242; *The Interesting Narrative . . .* (Equiano) as, 66; *The Life and Adventures of Olaudah Equiano* (Mott ed.) as, 80–81; of postbellum era, 4; publication/production of, 12, 15n13; reception of, 12, 15n13, 67, 81; self-representation in, 13n1; transnational, and transatlantic dimensions in, 11, 14n8. See also antebellum slave narratives; Arthur's criminal confessional literary narrative; Equiano, Olaudah, life and life narratives of; *The Interesting Narrative of the Life of Olaudah Equiano, or Gustavus Vassa, the African. Written by Himself* (Equiano); lives/life writers/writings; publication/production of life narratives/writings; spiritual autobiographies of men

The Life of William J. Brown of Providence, R.I., With Personal Recollections of Incidents in Rhode Island (Brown): overview and description of, 42, 49–50, 58; biographical information in, 43, 45, 46, 49–50, 61n18; Christian heteronormativity in, 43, 52, 53; as conversion to Christianity narrative, 50; gender roles and, 42, 43; and heteronormativity, black, 61n22; and homosociality, black, 50–52, 53; and marriage, Christian, 52, 53, 61n22; and masculinity, black, 43; military service in, 43; and preacher, black, 43, 50, 61n22; protection of black women in, 51–52, 53; sense of self in, 54; survival strategies and, 50; and violence, black, 43, 46, 52, 53, 61n13; white hegemony in, 46, 61n13

literacy, 133, 141n32, 246, 252, 256n9. See also education

literature, African American: antebellum, 4, 5, 14n4, 42; and Atlantic literature, black, 66, 67; "classic," 3, 7; comics autobiographical narratives' relationship with, 147–48, 159–60, 169nn6–7; confessional, 19–20, 36; gallows, 19, 20 (*see also* criminal confessional literary narratives); postbellum era, 4, 54–55, 57, 96, 100, 109, 112nn11–12 (*see also* antebellum literature); renaissance for women's, 241, 255n6; in U.S., 68, 70; Washington and, 97, 98, 100, 101, 112n14, 112n16. See also life narrative(s); lives/life writers/writings

lives/life writers/writings: overview and description of, 3–4, 10, 13, 15n1, 37n6; circulation of, 12, 15n13; publication/production of, 12, 15n13; reception of, 12, 15n13, 67, 81. See also Delany, Samuel R., and life/life writings; life narrative(s); publication/production of life narratives/writings; Wright, Richard, and life/life writings; *and specific authors and titles*

Looby, Christopher, 44, 45

Loren, Diana DiPaolo, 24, 25

Lovejoy, Paul E., 83n16

The "L" Word (television program), 235

Lynch, Jay, 152

Maccarty, Thaddeus, 36–37

Man, Paul de, 166, 167

manhood, in criminal confessional literary narratives, 19, 23, 27, 29, 31. See also masculinity, black

Mann, Delbert Martin, 121–22, 125, 129–30, 131

marriages, Christian: gender roles and, 53, 61n23;

and heteronormativity, black, 53, 61nn22–23; and homosociality, black, 45; and masculinity, black, 45, 53, 61n21; in spiritual autobiographies of men, 47–48, 52, 53, 61n15, 61n22

Marx, Karl, 118–19, 131, 137, 141nn35–36

masculine heterosexual activities, 21, 24, 26, 27, 29

masculinity, black: based on violence critique, 43, 47–49; feminists' critique of power relationships and, 59–60; gender roles and, 42–43, 44; heteronormative, 41, 42, 58; and marriage, Christian, 45, 52, 53, 61n21; military service intersection with, 53–54, 55, 57; during postbellum era, 57; and preachers, black male, 43; protection of black women relationship with, 41, 45, 51–52; in spiritual autobiographies of men, 41, 42, 43, 44–45; and violence, black, 62n27; white hegemony intersection with, 58, 62n27

masculinity, colonial white, 20, 23–24. *See also* colonial America; masculinity, black

Mask, Mia, 232, 236

Mason, Regina A., 15n11

McBride, Dwight A., 61n21, 62n30, 111n8

McChesney, Robert W., 213

McCloud, Scott, 171n17

McKay, Nellie Y., 180

McKenzie, Roderick, 117, 121, 131

McKinley, Catherine E. See *The Book of Sarahs: A Family in Parts* (McKinley)

McNinch, Carrie, 146

media: expertise in, 205–6, 212; flood of 1927 in Mississippi and, 122, 123–24, 125, *126*, *127*, 128, 140n22, 140n25; Jim Crow era protests in, 122, 124, 128; minstrelry in, 122; print culture participation by minorities and, 124–25, 128, 133, 140n24, 140n26; satire culture in, 124–25, *126*, *127*, 140n25

Meeting Faith: The Forest Journals of a Black Buddhist Nun (Adiele): overview of, 8, 174, 176, 177–78, 193, 193n2; biracial women in, 177; community and individual's relationship in, 177, 179, 180, 183; gender roles and, 189, 192; geographic locations or changes in settings in, 177–78, 187; individual vulnerability in, 177, 187, 188–89; interiority in, 179; race in, 189; rape in, 190–91; slaves/slavery in, 189; solitary practices in, 190, 191, 192, 193; spiritual health in, 191

men, black: fear/fearlessness of, 56; patriarchy conflict with black feminism and, 238, 244, 245–47, 248–49, 252–54; racist stereotype for, 22, 35, 42, 44, 58, 183, 184, 233, 255n1; rape against black male children, 250; and rapists, racist stereotype of, 22, 35; survival strategies for, 30, 50. *See also* autobiographies, by men; comics narratives, autobiographical; criminal confessional literary narratives; spiritual autobiographies of men; visual properties of black autobiographies; women, black; *and specific authors and titles*

Mencken, H. L., 122, 124, 128, 135, 140n24

mental illness (depression), in digital public sphere life narratives, 205, 209–11

Metcalfe, Deborah, 33–35

Micheaux, Oscar, 60n4, 147, 170n13

military service: Christianity's intersection with, 43, 44, 45, 56–57; dignity of soldiers in, 57; fear/fearlessness in, 56; and homosociality, black, 54–55; and masculinity, black, 53–54, 55, 57; in spiritual autobiographies of men, 43, 44, 45, 53–55, 56–57; white hegemony intersection with, 54–55

Miller, Ann, 148

Miller, Monica L., 30–31, 38n10

minstrelry, 93, 94, 95, 112n9, 122

Mitchell, Gail, 205

Mitchell, Michele, 98, 111n2

Mixed: My Life in Black and White (Nissel), 198, 206–11, 214n3

mixed-race (biracial) people, 177, 198, 206, 207–9, 214n3, 222

Moore, Lisa Jean, 21, 36

Moravian Archives, Bethlehem, Pennsylvania, 10–11, 14n8

Morehouse College, 59

Morrison, Toni, 3, 169n6

Mostern, Kenneth, 184, 194n7

Moton, Robert, 128

Mott, Abigail Field: biographical information about, 68–69, 85n23; *Biographical Sketches and Interesting Anecdotes of Persons of Colour*, 79, 83n11, 85n23; New York African Free School's connections with, 68, 70–71, 83n11. See also *The Life and Adventures of Olaudah Equiano; or, Gustavus Vassa, the African. From an Account Written by Himself, Abridged by A. Mott. To Which Is Added Some Remarks on the Slave Trade* (Mott ed.)

Multiethnic Placement Act of 1994, 216, 229n2

multilingual dimensions in African American life narratives, 11, 14n8

mutuality concept, 44, 48–49, 58–59, 61n8

National Association for the Advancement of Colored People (NAACP), 233, 239
National Association of Black Social Workers (NABSW), 216, 226
Native American women relations with blacks, 26, 27–28, 36
Neal, Mark Anthony, 205
"neteracy," 212
Newman, Richard S., 45
new media, 198, 202, 204–5
New Negro(es), 89, 97, 98, 100, 108–9, 111n11. *See also* uplift (racial uplift ideologies)
New York African Free School, 68, 70–71, 75–77, 80, 83n11, 84n20
New York City Colonization Society, 80
New York Manumission Society, 68, 77, 78
New York State Colonization Society, 80
Nissel, Angela: overview and biographical information about, 197–98, 206–7, 211, 213–14; as biracial woman, 198, 206, 207–9, 214n3; blogs by, 198–99, 212; *The Broke Diaries* . . . , 198, 199–206, 207, 209, 211; comedic tradition and, 198, 200–201, 205, 206, 211; community and individual's relationship and, 211, 213–14; confessional literary narratives and, 200; depression (mental illness) and, 205, 209–11; digital public sphere and, 197–98, 205, 212; fictionalized experiences in autobiographies and, 199–200; "getting ovuh" tales and, 200, 205, 213; Guy's discovery of, 206, 211, 212; as Hollywood screenwriter and producer, 197–98, 201, 211–12; life writing and publishing history of, 197–98, 206–7, 212; media expertise of, 205–6, 212; *Mixed: My Life in Black and White*, 198, 206–11, 214n3; new media and, 198, 202, 204–5; open-mic poetry performances and, 200, 202; poverty theme and, 202–4, 207; public and private spheres divisions and, 198–99; racism and, 206–11, 214n3; *Scrubs* (television program), 198, 201, 212; self-fashioning by, 197, 199, 202, 204; self-help literature and, 200; self-publication/production by, 198, 212; strip club dancing experiences of, 205, 214n3; website development by, 198, 205, 212
nonviolent actions, against white hegemony, 29–30, 49, 51

Obama, Barack, 3, 10, 13
Ofodobendo Wooma (Andrew) memoir, 10–11, 14n8
Okayplayer.com, 205, 212
Olney, James, 6, 22–23, 90, 141n32
O'Neil, Denny, 162
open-mic poetry performances, 200, 202
Ormes, Jackie, 147
the other and the self encounters (public contact), 146, 147, 149, 162

page design, in autobiographical comics narratives, 149–51, 153–54, *155*, 156, 161–62, *163*, *164*, *165*, 165–67
Park, Robert E., 117, 120, 121, 131, 140n30
parodies: of blaxploitation films, 240; comics superhero, 146, 147, 152, 153, 156, 157
Pascal, Michael Henry, 73, 81n1, 83n16
patriarchy, and conflict with black feminism, 238, 244, 245–47, 248–49, 252–54
Patton, Sandra Lee, 216–17, 222, 227–28, 229n4
Peebles, Melvin Van, 249
Pekar, Harvey, 149
People United to Save Humanity (PUSH), 233
personal dignity (dignity), 28, 51, 57, 180
Peterson, Carla L., 75, 82n9, 84n20
Philadelphia Free School, 76–77
photographs: in antebellum slave literature, 91; in autobiographies, 89, 91; the body and text relationship in, 90, 97; counterarchives of blackness, 96, 112n10; group portraits, 101, 109; in postbellum era, 96, 112n12; racial differences and, 95; racial knowledge and, 111n7; technical developments for, 91; text and visual interactions in interpretation of, 108; Tuskegee visual culture in, 99; and visibility, black, 92, 93, 97
physical health, 235, 252–53. *See also* rape (sexual assault); spiritual health
Pomeroy, Jane R., 83n14
Porcellino, John, 146, 149
postbellum era, 4, 54–55, 57, 96, 100, 109, 112n11–12. *See also* antebellum literature
postslavery era, 90, 99, 101, 109, 117–18, 131, 133. *See also Twenty-Five Years in the Black Belt* (Edwards)
poverty theme, in digital public sphere life narratives, 202–4, 207
power relationships, 43, 59–60, 60n5, 62n23, 62n31
practical knowledge pedagogy, 75–77, 80, 84n20
preachers, female, 43, 177
preachers, male: gender roles and, 43, 60n7; masculinity intersection with, 43; mutuality

Index

concept and, 48–49, 61n8; in spiritual autobiographies of men, 42–45, 48–49, 60n4, 60n5, 60n7, 61n8; white hegemony intersection with, 44, 45, 61n8
pre-Revolutionary era. *See* colonial America
Prince, Samuel Henry, 121, 122
Prinze, Freddie, Sr., 238, 242–43, 244, 247–49, 253
privacy: public sphere versus, 198–99; racial privacy, 92, 97, 98, *103*, 104, *107*, 107–8, 109, 111n3
production of space (space), 119, 131–32, 140n31. *See also* spatiotemporal position
production/publication of life narratives and writings. *See* publication/production of life narratives/writings; reception of life narratives and writers
property ownership, and photographs, 97, 101, 104, 106–7, *107*
Prosser, Gabriel, 41
Pryor, Richard: comedic traditions and, 147, 148, 251; Grier's relationship with, 238–39, 240–41, 242–43, 244, 249–53, 255n1, 256n10
publication/production of life narratives/writings: overview of, 12, 15n13; Equiano's life narratives and, 67, 80, 81; self-publication of autobiographical comics and, 146, 156, 170n13; underground publishers for autobiographical comics and, 147, 152, 156. *See also* circulation of life narratives and writers; reception of life narratives and writers
public contact (the self and the other encounters), 146, 147, 149, 162
public sphere, 9, 196, 197–99, 205
PUSH (People United to Save Humanity), 233

Quashie, Kevin Everod, 111n3
Queen, Stuart Alfred, 121–22, 125
queer (gay) communities, 148. *See also* Delany, Samuel R., and life/life writings
Questlove (Ahmir Thompson), 205

race: in autobiographical comics narratives, 147, 150–51; Buddhist women's lives/life narratives and, 189; Race Man or Woman, 109, 111n2; in spiritual autobiographies of men, 42–43, 44, 58
race buildings, 97, 101–2, *103*, 105, *106*, *107*, 109. *See also* buildings, photographs of
racial differences, 94–95, 111nn5–6, 218, 219, 223, 225

racial identity/identities, in transracial adoptees' lives/life narratives, 217, 219, 221–22, 224, 225, 226–27, 226–28
racial knowledge production, 90–91, 92, 94–95, 96, 111n7, 112n10
racial privacy (privacy), 92, 97, 98, *103*, 104, *107*, 107–8, 109, 111n3
racial uplift ideologies (uplift). *See* uplift (racial uplift ideologies)
racism: autobiographies' omission of, 180; in Buddhist lives/life narratives of women, 178, 181–83; color lines and, 118, 132, 135, 137, 139n6, 217, 222; in digital public sphere life narratives, 206–11, 214n3; flood victims and, 122, 123, 124, 125, 128, 129; mental illness and, 209–11; in rural environment, 129–32; sociological experiments as allegory and, 119–21; in spiritual autobiographies of men, 54–55; stereotypes and, 22, 35, 42, 44, 58, 183, 184, 233; in transracial adoptees' lives/life narratives, 219, 221
Rak, Julie, 12, 15n13, 255n3
rape (sexual assault): against black children, 190–91, 235, 240, 250; in colonial America, 19, 22, 26, 33–35; racist stereotype of black men as committing, 22, 35
readership: of autobiographical comics narratives, 147, 149, 161–62; of autobiographies, 90; for *The Interesting Narrative . . .* (Equiano), 67; for *The Life and Adventures of Olaudah Equiano* (Mott ed.), 69, 82n9
reception of life narratives and writers, 12, 15n13, 67, 81
Red Cross camps for flood victims, 122, 123, 124, 125, 128
Redfield, Robert, 139n8
Reid-Pharr, Robert, 44
resettlement projects, 77–80, 84n21, 85nn22–23
Richards, Beah, 239–40
Richards, Phillip M., 61n20
Rickett, Dennis, 146, 161, 162, *163*, *164*, 165, 166–67
risk modeling, 129, 133
Robbins, Trina, 152
Roberts, Keiler, 149
Rock, Chris, 200, 206
Romanticism, 118, 119, 134–35
romantic relationships, and Grier, 238–39, 242–54, 255n1, 256n10
The Roots, 205
Roper, Moses, 93

Ross, Marlon B., 107, 111n2
Rucker, Ursula, 185
rural environment: and alienation, human, 135, 141n34; and georgic, the, 135, 141n34; Jim Crow era, 130, 132, 137, 138n4; racism in, 129–32; Romanticism connections with, 118, 134–35; spatiotemporal position and, 129–30, 131, 132; white(s) and, 130, 132, 134, 137; in Wright's life and writings, 117–18, 132–35, 136–37, 138n1, 138nn3–5, 141n33

Saikku, Mikko, 123, 140n21
Samuel Wood and Sons publishers, 68, 74, 79, 83n14
Santamarina, Xiomara, 4, 13n3
sartorial self-fashioning: in criminal confessional literary narratives, 21, 24–25, 26, 27, 28–30, 31, 38n10; dandyism and, 30–31, 36, 38n10; sumptuary laws in colonial America and, 24–25, 29–30, 38n8
savior/caretaker role, 244, 249–52, 251
Schelly, Bill, 152, 153
scientific inquiry, and racial knowledge, 94–95, 111n7, 112n10
Scrubs (television program), 198, 201, 212
"second nature," 119, 131, 137, 140n31
Sedgwick, Eve Kosofsky, 5, 41–42
Sekula, Allen, 108
the self: the autobiographical self, 145–46, 147, 148–49, 156, 157, *158*, 159, *160*, 161; encounters with the other or public contact with, 146, 147, 149, 162; self-fashioning in blog books, 197, 199, 202, 204 (*see also* sartorial self-fashioning); self-help culture, 200, 241–43, 248, 249, 253, 254, 255n7, 256n8; self-love, 243–44, 253; self-publication/production, 146, 156, 170n13, 198, 212 (*see also* publication/production of life narratives/writings); sense of, 54, 149, 239
self-representation: in autobiographies, 89, 96; conversion narrative and, 101–2, 104–5; in frontispiece portraits, 96–97; of New Negro, 111n2; sartorial, 21, 24–25, 26, 27, 28–30, 31, 38n10; slavery and slave trade connections with, 11, 15n11; visual properties of black autobiographies and, 96. *See also* sartorial self-fashioning; the self
sense of self, 54, 149, 239. *See also* the self
sexual assault (rape). *See* rape (sexual assault)

Sheba, Baby (film), 239, 255n4
signs of "crazy" ("crazy"). *See* "crazy" (signs of "crazy")
silences ("space of concentration"), in autobiographical comics narratives, 162, *163*, *164*, 165–67, 171n17
Sims, Yvonne D., 236, 240
Singer, Marc, 147
Skocpol, Theda, 51
slave narrative(s): antebellum, 4, 13n3, 19, 22, 91, 96, 112n11; as autobiographies by men, 37n1; the body and text relationship in, 90; criminal confessional literary narratives compared with, 20, 37n4; *The Life and Adventures of Olaudah Equiano* (Mott ed.) as, 84n19; literacy in, 133, 141n32; photographs and, 91; of postbellum era, 57, 112n11; transracial adoptees' lives/life narratives compared with, 223. *See also* antebellum slave narratives
slaves/slavery and slave trade: abolitionism and, 93, 95, 112n9; auction block as spectacle and, 93, 94, 95, 111n8, 112n9; Buddhist women's lives/life narratives and, 189, 191; in criminal confessional literary narratives, 21, 23, 26–27; education laws and, 246, 256n9; Grier and, 246, 256n9; in *The Life and Adventures of Olaudah Equiano* (Mott ed.), 74–75, 84n19; literacy and, 246, 256n9; self-representation's connections with, 11, 15n11; surveillance and, 93; transatlantic slave trade dynamics and, 66, 72; and violence, black, 44–45, 46, 61nn9–10; white violence against, 44, 46–48, 55, 61n9, 61n14. *See also* antebellum slave narratives; slave narrative(s)
Smith, Bessie, 122, 139n17
Smith, Shawn Michelle, 6, 112n10
Smith, Sidonie, 12, 13n1, 37n6, 74, 176, 229n9
Smitherman, Geneva, 238
Snow Hill school and community, 100, 101, 102, *103*, 104, 106–7, 113n18
social order, in colonial America, 35–36, 38n12
sociology, science of, 53, 120–21, 135, 138n2. *See also* Chicago School of Sociology
solitary practices: in Buddhism, 175, 179, 184, 185, 187; in Buddhist women's lives and life narratives, 177, 179, 184, 186, 190, 191, 192, 193
Soper, Kate, 28
South Carolina Act of 1740, 246
space (production of space), 119, 131–32, 140n31

Index

"space of concentration" (silences), in autobiographical comics narratives, 162, *163*, *164*, 165–67, 171n17

spatiotemporal position: blacks and, 129–30, 131, 132; Chicago School of Sociology, 131, 140nn30–31; Jim Crow, 130, 131, 132; in Jim Crow era, 130; Marx and, 131, 137, 141n36; rural environment and, 129–30, 131, 132; white(s) and, 129–30; in Wright's life and writings, 117, 118, 119, 129–30, 131, 140n31

spectacle(s), 92–93, 94, 95, 111n8, 112n9

speculation, 92–93, 94

Spencer, Herbert A., 121, 139n13

Spiegelman, Art, 148, 159–60

Spillers, Hortense J., 255n6

spiritual autobiographies of men: overview and description of, 5, 58–59, 60; as antebellum texts, 5, 14n4, 42; Christian heteronormativity in, 41–45, 47–49, 52, 53, 58, 61n15, 61n22; conversion to Christianity narratives in, 44–45, 47, 50, 53, 55–58; feminists' critique of power relationships and, 43, 59–60, 60n5, 62nn30–31; gender roles in, 41, 42–43, 44, 58, 60n7; Golden Rule in, 44, 48–49, 59; and heteronormativity, black, 45, 46, 53, 58–59, 61n22; and homosociality, black, 45, 48, 50–56; homosociality described, 41–42; and marriages, Christian, 47–48, 52, 53, 61n15, 61n22; and masculinity, black, 41–45, 43, 47–49; military service in, 43, 44, 45, 53–55, 56–57; mutuality concept in, 44, 48–49, 58–59, 61n8; nonviolent actions in, 48, 49; of postbellum era, 57; power relationships, 43, 60n5; and preachers, black male, 42–45, 48–49, 50, 60n4, 60n5, 60n7, 61n8, 61n22; protection of black women in, 51–52, 53; race in, 42–43, 44, 58; and violence, black, 41–49, 51–53, 55–56, 58, 61nn9–10, 61n13; white hegemony in, 41–42, 44–48, 51, 54–56, 61n8, 61nn9–10, 61n13

spiritual autobiographies of women, 176–77. *See also* Buddhist lives/life narratives of women; *and specific authors and titles*

spiritual health, 175, 177, 191. *See also* physical health

Spurgeon, Tom, 152, 167

"steal themselves" (escape) activities, 20, 23–24, 26–27, 31, 32–33

Steele, Ralph, 175

Stepto, Robert B., 3, 4, 5

stereotypes, racist, 22, 35, 42, 44, 58, 183, 184, 233, 255n1

Stone, Albert E., 216

Stone, Biz, 199, 212–13

subjectivity: Buddhist women's lives/life narratives and, 176, 184; in criminal confessional literary narratives, 23, 26, 31–32, 37; visual properties of black autobiographies and, 92, 96; in Wright's life and writings, 118, 120–21, 132, 133, 135, 137

subscribers lists, and Equiano's life narratives, 69–70, 72–73

surveillance, 92–94, 93, 95, 96, 106

survival strategies, 30, 50, 222, 237, 252

Sweet, Timothy, 141n34

talking book trope, 6, 14n5, 46

Tarantino, Quentin, 232, 254

Tate, Shirley Anne, 227

Taylor, Whit, 146

temporal position, and space. *See* spatiotemporal position

text and visual interactions, 92, 96, 97, 108. *See also* visual properties of black autobiographies

Thomas, Jesse O., 128

Thomas, Roy, 152, 153

Thomas, W. I., 139n11

Thompson, Ahmir (Questlove), 205

Tiebout, Cornelius, 69, 73

Times Square Red, Times Square Blue (Delany), 146, 147, 169n2, 169n5

Tinney, James S., 44, 48–49, 58–59, 60

Toomer, Jean, 147

transatlantic and transnational dimensions in narratives, 11, 14n8, 66–67, 71–72

transatlantic slave trade dynamics, 66, 72. *See also* slaves/slavery and slave trade

transnational adoptees, 223, 226, 229nn10–11. *See also* transracial adoptees' lives and life narratives

transracial adoptees' lives and life narratives: overview of, 9–10, 216–17, 227–28; adoption-search narratives, 217–18, 221, 229n4; African cultural customs and, 227, 229n12; African identifications and, 217, 224; agency and, 219; alienation from adoptive families/culture and, 218–19, 223; autobiographies and, 217, 219; biracial women and, 222; birth parents' reunions in, 217, 219, 220; blackness transracial ... narratives (*continued*) and, 217, 222–23, 224, 225, 226–27; black power movement and, 226; black/white binary and, 224–25, 226–27; color lines and, 217, 222; community and individual's relationship and, 219, 220, 221, 223, 227; as conversion narrative, 220–21; cultural imaginaries and, 217–18, 220, 221–22, 224–25; double-consciousness ("twoness") and, 217, 219; hybridity and, 217, 221, 222, 223, 226–27; identity formation in, 217, 218, 219, 220, 223, 227; kinship and, 217, 218, 219, 221, 225; Multiethnic Placement Act of 1994 and, 216, 229n2; NABSW and, 226; racial differences and, 219, 223–24, 225; racial identity/identities of, 217, 219, 221–22, 224, 225, 226–27, 226–28; racism and, 219, 221; slave narratives compared with, 223; survival strategies and, 222; transnational adoptees and, 223, 226, 229nn10–11; transracial adoption described and, 216, 229nn1–3; transracial as term of use, 229n1; whiteness and, 217, 224–25

Turner, Nat, 41, 44–45, 50, 60n2

Turner, Terence, 24

Turner, Tina, 185–86

Tuskegee Institute, 91, 97, 98–100

Twenty-Five Years in the Black Belt (Edwards): overview of, 7, 89, 91–92, 100–101, 109, 110; Black Belt life in, 91, 102, *103*, 104, 105, *106*, 107, *107*, 108, 113n18; the body representation and, 92, 97–98, 101–2, 104–5, 107, 108; and buildings, photographs of, 92, 101–2, *103*, 104–9, *106*, *107*; conversion narrative of black self in, 101–2, 104–5; frontispiece portrait in, 97, 101; group portraits in, 101, 109; and ideography, black, 92, 96, 97, 98, 101, 109; interiority in, 92, 98, 101, 104, 105, 106, 109; as Jim Crow era text, 89, 97; New Negro in, 108–9; as postbellum autobiography, 109; postslavery era and, 99, 101, 109; privacy representation in, 92, 97, 98, *103*, 104, *107*, 107–8, 109, 111n3; property ownership and photographs in, 97, 101, 104, 106–7, *107*; race buildings representation in, 101–2, *103*, 105, *106*, *107*; Race Man and, 109, 111n2; racial knowledge production in, 92; self-representation in, 97; Snow Hill life in, 100, 101, 102, *103*, 104, 106–7, 113n18; subjectivity, 92; surveillance, 106; text and visual interactions in, 92, 108; Tuskegee Institute and Washington's influence in, 91, 102; uplift representation in, 91, 97, 101, 102, *103*, 104, 106, *107*, 107–8; and visibility, black, 92, 97, *103*, 104, 106, *106*, 108, 109. *See also* visual properties of black autobiographies

"twoness" (double-consciousness), 111n3, 151, 217, 219

Tyson, Cicely, 239–40

Uncle Tom's Children (Wright), 119, 123, 129

underground publishers, for autobiographical comics narratives, 147, 152, 156

Un-Fold Funnies (Green), 7–8, 145, 146, 156, 170n13

uplift (racial uplift ideologies): overview of, 89–90, 111n2; in autobiographies, 89, 90, 98–99; blaxploitation films critiques and, 233, 239; and buildings, photographs of, 101, *103*, 104, 107, *107*; in frontispiece portrait of black autobiographers, 97, 101; frontispiece portrait representation of, 97; Grier and, 239, 252, 255n2; New Negro as representation of, 89, 97, 98, 100, 108–9, 111n11; and privacy, racial, 97, 107–8; self-representation practices in, 98; visual properties of black autobiographies support for, 90, 91, 97, 101, 102, 104, *107*, 107–8; women's role in, 252. *See also* ideography, black

urban environment: Chicago School and, 117–18, 121, 138n5, 139n11, 140nn30–31; urban contacts in autobiographical comics and, 145, 147, 151, 153, 154, *155*, 156, *157*, 169n5; in Wright's life and writings, 117–18, 128, 133–34, 135, 138n5, 140n28, 140n31

Vanzant, Iyanla, 241, 242–43, 248, 249, 253, 254, 255n7

Vassa, Gustavus, 73, 81n1, 83n16, 84n18. *See also* Equiano, Olaudah, life and life narratives of

Vesey, Denmark, 41, 61n9

violence, black: Christian heteronormativity intersection with, 47, 48–49, 52, 53; masculinity based on violence critique and, 43, 47–49; as racist stereotype, 22, 35, 42, 44, 58; slaves/slavery intersection with, 44–45, 46, 61nn9–10; in spiritual autobiographies of men, 41–49, 51–53, 55–56, 58, 61nn9–10, 61n13; against white hegemony, 41–42, 44–48, 51, 55–56, 61nn9–10, 61n13, 62n27

Virginia Revised Code of 1819, 256n9

Index

visibility, black: in autobiographies, 92; the body and, 95–96; in criminal confessional literary narratives, 19, 22–23, 25, 26, 32; double-consciousness and relationship to, 111n3; frontispiece portrait as, 96–97; photographs and, 92, 93, 97; spectacle, 92–93, 94, 95, 111n8, 112n9; speculation, 92–93, 94, 95, 96; surveillance, 92–94, 95, 96, 106; in visual properties of black autobiographies, 91, 92, 97, *103*, 104, 106, *106*, 108, 109

visual artist's collaboration with autobiographic comics writers, 150, 161, 162, *163*, *164*, *165*, 165–67, 170n14

visual properties of black autobiographies: overview of, 6–7, 91–92, 110; and blackness, meaning of, 90; the body and text relationship and, 90, 97; the body representation and, 92, 97–98, 101–2, 104–5, 107, 108; and buildings, photographs of, 92, 97, 101–2, *103*, 104–9, *106*, *107*, 112n15; conversion narrative of black self and, 101–2, 104–5; frontispiece portrait and, 97, 101; group portraits and, 101, 109; and ideography, black, 92, 96, 97, 98, 101, 109; interiority and, 92, 98, 101, 104, 105, 106, 109; during Jim Crow era, 89, 91, 97; New Negro and, 108–9; in postslavery era, 99, 101, 109; privacy representation and, 92, 97, 98, *103*, 104, *107*, 107–8, 109, 111n3; property ownership and photographs and, 97, 101, 104, 106–7, *107*; race buildings representation and, 101–2, *103*, 105, *106*, *107*; racial knowledge production and, 90–91, 92, 94, 96, 111n7; self-representation and, 96, 97; subjectivity and, 92, 96; surveillance and, 106; text and visual interactions and, 92, 96, 108; uplift representation and, 91, 97, 101, 102, *103*, 104, 106, *107*, 107–8; uplift support from, 90; and visibility, black, 91, 92, 97, *103*, 104, 106, *106*, 108, 109. *See also* comics narratives, autobiographical; frontispiece portrait of black autobiographers

Walker, Alice, 59, 252
Walker, David, *Appeal to the Coloured Citizens of the World*, 5, 14n4, 41, 42, 45, 58
Wallace, Maurice O., 6, 45, 53, 58, 62n27, 92, 96, 122n12
Wallace, Robert K., 68
Wanzo, Rebecca, 147
Ward, Lynd, 162

Ware, Chris, 149, 150
Washington, Booker T., and topics: autobiographies as institutionalized, 98–100; buildings, photographs of, 112n14, 112n16; ideography, black, 7, 101, 111n2; Park as secretary, 120; Tuskegee Institute, 91, 97, 98–100, 102, 113n17; writings and publications, 97, 98, 100, 101, 112n14, 112n16
Watkins, Mel, 148
Watson, Andrew Polk. See *God Struck Me Dead* (Watson)
Watson, Julia, 13n1, 37n6, 74, 176, 229n9
weblogs (blogs). *See* blogs (weblogs)
website development, 198, 205, 212
Weiss, Harry B., 73, 74
Wells, Ida B., 112n13, 128
White, Ed, 4, 10, 13n3
White, Shane, 72, 82n9
White, Walter, 128
white hegemony: Christianity's intersection with, 54; and dignity, loss of, 51; and homosociality, black, 54–55; and masculinity, black, 58, 62n27; military service intersection with, 54–55; nonviolent actions to, 29–30, 48, 49, 51; and preachers, black male, 44, 45, 61n8; in spiritual autobiographies of men, 41, 44, 45, 54–55, 61n8; surveillance and, 93; and violence, black, 41–42, 44–48, 51, 55–56, 61nn9–10, 61n13, 62n27
whiteness, 124, 130, 132, 137, 192, 217, 224–25, 250. *See also* blackness
white(s): black/white binary and, 224–25, 226–27; as dandies, 30–31; flood culture and, 122, 123–24, 125, *126*, 128; and masculinity, colonial, 20, 23–24 (*see also* masculinity, black); rape in colonial America by, 33–35; rural environment and, 130, 132, 134, 137; space/production of space for, 132; spatiotemporal position and, 129–30, 137; as violent against slaves, 44, 46–48, 55, 61n9, 61n14. *See also* black(s); racism; white hegemony; whiteness
Whitlock, Gillian, 12, 15n13
Whitted, Qiana J., 147, 169n7
Wiegman, Robyn, 93
Williams, Angel Kyodo. See *Being Black: Zen and the Art of Living with Fearlessness and Grace* (Williams)
Williams, Daniel E., 22
Williamson, Skip, 145, 146, 152, 153, 156
Willis, Deborah, 6

Willis, Jan. See *Dreaming Me: An African American Woman's Spiritual Journey* (Willis)
Wilson, Flip, 251
Winfrey, Oprah, 241, 256n8
Wirth, Louis, 119, 120
Wolff, Mia, 150, 161, 162, *163*, *164*, *165*, 165–67, 170n14
women, biracial, 177, 198, 206, 207–9, 214n3, 222. *See also* women, black; women, white
women, black: autobiographies by, 179–80; *Black Women's Manifesto* for, 237–41, 243–48, 250–55; and the body, female, 196, 233, 234, 236–37, 239; and education, higher, 234, 245–47; literary renaissance for, 241, 255n6; as preachers, 43, 177; protection of, 41, 45, 51–52; rape against female children or, 190–91, 235, 240, 250; survival strategies for, 222, 237, 252; uplift role for, 252. *See also* Buddhist lives/life narratives of women; *and specific authors and titles*
women, differences among, 176. *See also* women, biracial; women, black
women, white, 27, 29, 32, 33–35. *See also* women, black
"words as weapons," 124, 135, 140n24
Wordsworth, William, 134
Wright, Jeremiah, 43, 60n7
Wright, Richard, and life/life writings: overview of, 7, 117–19, 120, 137–38, 138n3, 139n8, 139n16; and alienation, human, 118–19, 135, 137; and autobiographies by men, 118, 123, 131, 132, 133, 138n3, 138n5, 216; "biological recoil" of humans and, 119, 136–37; Burrow's influence on, 119, 136–37; Chicago School's influence on, 117–18, 119–20, 133, 138n2; childhood experiences in, 117, 118, 130, 136, 137, 138n3; color lines and racism, 118, 132, 135, 137, 139n6; decoding skills in, 125, 134, 140n25; environmental justice movement and, 123, 139n18; equilibrium critique in, 118; "The Ethics of Living Jim Crow," 118, 123, 129–30, 131, 132, 133; flood of 1927 knowledge of/writings by, 122–23, 124, 125, 128, 131, 139n17, 140n24, 140nn27–29; and georgic, the, 135, 141n34; human ecology and, 117, 118, 119, 121, 129, 133, 139n11; "image-production" of humans and, 119, 136; interiority and, 133, 134, 135; Jim Crow era, 122, 124, 128, 130; Lefebvre's influence on, 119; literacy and, 133; Marx's influence on, 118–19, 131, 137; print culture participation by minorities in, 124–25, 128, 133, 140n24, 140n26; Romanticism in, 118, 119, 134–35; rural environment in, 117–18, 132–35, 136–37, 138n1, 138nn3–5, 141n33; "second nature," 119, 131, 137, 140n31; sociological experiments as racial allegory in, 119–21; space/production of space in, 119, 131–32, 140n31; spatiotemporal position in, 117, 118, 119, 129–30, 131, 132, 137, 140n31; subjectivity in, 118, 120–21, 132, 133, 135, 137; *Uncle Tom's Children*, 119, 123, 129; urban environment in, 117–18, 128, 133–34, 135, 138n5, 140n28, 140n31; whiteness in, 124, 130, 132, 137; "words as weapons" in, 124, 135, 140n24. See also *Black Boy* (Wright)
writers/writings. *See* life narrative(s); lives/life writers/writings

Xal-Kor the Human Cat (Green), 152, 153, 154, *155*, 156, 157, *157*, 159, 169n3

Yancy, George, 148, 149–51, 162
Yarborough, Richard, 129
Yngvesson, Barbara, 229n4

Wisconsin Studies in Autobiography

WILLIAM L. ANDREWS
Series Editor

The Examined Self: Benjamin Franklin, Henry Adams, Henry James
Robert F. Sayre

Spiritual Autobiography in Early America
Daniel B. Shea

The Education of a WASP
Lois Mark Stalvey

Forbidden Family: A Wartime Memoir of the Philippines, 1941–1945
Margaret Sams
Edited with an introduction by Lynn Z. Bloom

Journeys in New Worlds: Early American Women's Narratives
Edited by William L. Andrews, Sargent Bush Jr., Annette Kolodny, Amy Schrager Lang, and Daniel B. Shea

The Living of Charlotte Perkins Gilman: An Autobiography
Charlotte Perkins Gilman
Introduction by Ann J. Lane

Mark Twain's Own Autobiography: The Chapters from the "North American Review"
Mark Twain
Edited by Michael J. Kiskis

American Autobiography: Retrospect and Prospect
Edited by Paul John Eakin

The Diary of Caroline Seabury, 1854–1863
Caroline Seabury
Edited with an introduction by Suzanne L. Bunkers

A Woman's Civil War: A Diary with Reminiscences of the War, from March 1862
Cornelia Peake McDonald
Edited with an introduction by Minrose C. Gwin

My Lord, What a Morning
Marian Anderson
Introduction by Nellie Y. McKay

American Women's Autobiography: Fea(s)ts of Memory
Edited with an introduction by Margo Culley

Livin' the Blues: Memoirs of a Black Journalist and Poet
Frank Marshall Davis
Edited with an introduction by John Edgar Tidwell

Authority and Alliance in the Letters of Henry Adams
Joanne Jacobson

The Zea Mexican Diary: 7 September 1926–7 September 1986
Kamau Brathwaite

My History, Not Yours: The Formation of Mexican American Autobiography
Genaro M. Padilla

Witnessing Slavery: The Development of Ante-bellum Slave Narratives
Frances Smith Foster

Native American Autobiography: An Anthology
Edited by Arnold Krupat

American Lives: An Anthology of Autobiographical Writing
Edited by Robert F. Sayre

Intensely Family: The Inheritance of Family Shame and the Autobiographies of Henry James
Carol Holly

People of the Book: Thirty Scholars Reflect on Their Jewish Identity
Edited by Jeffrey Rubin-Dorsky and Shelley Fisher Fishkin

Recovering Bodies: Illness, Disability, and Life Writing
G. Thomas Couser

My Generation: Collective Autobiography and Identity Politics
John Downton Hazlett

Jumping the Line: The Adventures and Misadventures of an American Radical
William Herrick

Women, Autobiography, Theory: A Reader
Edited by Sidonie Smith and Julia Watson

The Making of a Chicano Militant: Lessons from Cristal
José Angel Gutiérrez

Rosa: The Life of an Italian Immigrant
Marie Hall Ets

Illumination and Night Glare: The Unfinished Autobiography of Carson McCullers
Carson McCullers
Edited with an introduction by Carlos L. Dews

Who Am I? An Autobiography of Emotion, Mind, and Spirit
Yi-Fu Tuan

The Life and Adventures of Henry Bibb: An American Slave
Henry Bibb
With a new introduction by Charles J. Heglar

Diaries of Girls and Women: A Midwestern American Sampler
Edited by Suzanne L. Bunkers

The Autobiographical Documentary in America
Jim Lane

Caribbean Autobiography: Cultural Identity and Self-Representation
Sandra Pouchet Paquet

How I Became a Human Being: A Disabled Man's Quest for Independence
Mark O'Brien, with Gillian Kendall

Campaigns of Curiosity: Journalistic Adventures of an American Girl in Late Victorian London
Elizabeth L. Banks
Introduction by Mary Suzanne Schriber and Abbey L. Zink

The Text Is Myself: Women's Life Writing and Catastrophe
Miriam Fuchs

Harriet Tubman: The Life and the Life Stories
Jean M. Humez

Voices Made Flesh: Performing Women's Autobiography
Edited by Lynn C. Miller, Jacqueline Taylor, and M. Heather Carver

The Woman in Battle: The Civil War Narrative of Loreta Janeta Velazquez, Cuban Woman and Confederate Soldier
Loreta Janeta Velazquez
Introduction by Jesse Alemán

Maverick Autobiographies: Women Writers and the American West, 1900–1936
Cathryn Halverson

The Blind African Slave: Or Memoirs of Boyrereau Brinch, Nicknamed Jeffrey Brace
Jeffrey Brace
as told to Benjamin F. Prentiss, Esq.
Edited and with an introduction by Kari J. Winter

The Secret of M. Dulong: A Memoir
Colette Inez

Before They Could Vote: American Women's Autobiographical Writing, 1819–1919
Edited by Sidonie Smith and Julia Watson

Writing Desire: Sixty Years of Gay Autobiography
Bertram J. Cohler

Autobiography and Decolonization: Modernity, Masculinity, and the Nation-State
Philip Holden

When "I" Was Born: Women's Autobiography in Modern China
Jing M. Wang

*Conjoined Twins in Black and White: The Lives of Millie-Christine McKoy and
    Daisy and Violet Hilton*
Edited by Linda Frost

Four Russian Serf Narratives
Translated, edited, and with an introduction by John MacKay

Mark Twain's Own Autobiography: The Chapters from the "North American Review,"
    second edition
Mark Twain
Edited by Michael J. Kiskis

Graphic Subjects: Critical Essays on Autobiography and Graphic Novels
Edited by Michael A. Chaney

A Muslim American Slave: The Life of Omar Ibn Said
Omar Ibn Said
Translated from the Arabic, edited, and with an introduction
    by Ala Alryyes

Sister: An African American Life in Search of Justice
Sylvia Bell White and Jody LePage

Identity Technologies: Constructing the Self Online
Edited by Anna Poletti and Julie Rak

Masked: The Life of Anna Leonowens, Schoolmistress at the Court of Siam
Alfred Habegger

We Shall Bear Witness: Life Narratives and Human Rights
Edited by Meg Jensen and Margaretta Jolly

Dear World: Contemporary Uses of the Diary
Kylie Cardell

Words of Witness: Black Women's Autobiography in the Post-"Brown" Era
Angela A. Ards

A Mysterious Life and Calling: From Slavery to Ministry in South Carolina
Reverend Mrs. Charlotte S. Riley
Edited with an introduction by Crystal J. Lucky

American Autobiography after 9/11
Megan Brown

Reading African American Autobiography: Twenty-First-Century Contexts and Criticism
Edited by Eric D. Lamore